England in the Fifteenth Century

Collected Essays

K. B. McFarlane

Introduction by G. L. Harriss

THE HAMBLEDON PRESS

Published by The Hambledon Press, 1981
35 Gloucester Avenue, London NW1 7AX

British Library Cataloguing in Publication Data

McFarlane, K. B.
    England in the fifteenth century.—(History series; 5)
    1. Great Britain—History—Lancaster and York.
      1399-1485
    2. Great Britain—History—Henry VII,
      1485-1509
    I. Title   II. Series
    942.04   DA245

ISBN 0-9506882-5-8 (cloth)
ISBN 0-907628 01 (paper)

Produced by Chambers Green
Origination by Ashford Composition

Printed by Great Britain by
Biddles Ltd., Guildford, Surrey

CONTENTS

Acknowledgements   vii

Introduction by G. L. Harriss   ix

I   Parliament and 'Bastard Feudalism'   1

II   'Bastard Feudalism'   23

III   An Indenture of Agreement between
Two English Knights for Mutual Aid
and Counsel in Peace and War,
5 December, 1298   45

IV   Loans to the Lancastrian Kings, the
Problem of Inducement   57

V   Henry V, Bishop Beaufort and the Red Hat, 1417-21   79

VI   At the Deathbed of Cardinal Beaufort   115

VII   War, the Economy and Social Change:
England and the Hundred Years War   139

VIII   A Business-Partnership in War and
Administration 1421-1445   151

IX   The Investment of Sir John Fastolf's
Profits of War   175

X   William Worcester: A Preliminary Survey   199

XI   William Worcester and a Present of Lampreys   225

XII   The War of the Roses   231

Index   269

ACKNOWLEDGEMENTS

The articles reprinted here first appeared in the following places and are reproduced by the kind permission of their original publishers.

I   Transactions of the Royal Historical Society, 4th. Series, XXVI (1944), 53-79.

II   Bulletin of the Institute of Historical Research, XX (1945), 161-80.

III   B.I.H.R., XXXVIII (1965), 201-8.

IV   Cambridge Historical Journal, IX (1947), 51-68.

V   English Historical Review, LX (1945), 316-48.

VI   *Studies in History Presented to F. M. Powicke,,* Oxford 1948, 405-28.

VII   World Copyright: The Past and Present Society, Corpus Christi College, Oxford, England. The article is printed with the permission of the Society from *Past and Present: a journal of historical studies*, no. 22 (July 1962), 3-15.

VIII E.H.R., LXXVIII (1963), 290-308.

IX   T.R.H.S., 5th Series, VII (1957), 91-116.

X   *Studies Presented to Sir Hilary Jenkinson*, Oxford 1957, 196-221.

XI   Medium Aevum, 30 (1961), 176-80.

XII   Proceedings of the British Academy, L (1964), 87-119.

INTRODUCTION

McFarlane's lecture of 1945 on 'Bastard Feudalism' introduced problems which he was to continue to explore until his death and which form the themes of half the articles reprinted in this volume. Although primarily an investigation of the nature of the permanent retinue as revealed by surviving indentures for service in peace and war, it raised the wider questions of the role of bastard feudalism in the evolution of political society, its contribution to social mobility, its alleged proclivity for lawlessness, and its particular responsibility for baronial rebellion and civil war. Over the past thirty-five years these and other aspects of the subject have been explored in a large number of studies which attest the seminal quality of his insights. A brief introduction cannot attempt to survey this literature; it can only indicate some areas where a consensus has emerged, others on which historians still disagree, and some of the new themes and problems which research has opened up. Reference will also be made to McFarlane's unpublished lectures of 1966 on 'Lords and Retainers' where these show a divergence from, or development of, his earlier views.

While rejecting the pejorative connotations of the term, McFarlane in 1945 regarded bastard feudalism as 'something essentially different while superficially similar' to the feudalism of the fief held by homage and knight service. Subsequent research has perhaps tended to reverse this judgement, seeing it as an adaptation of the forms of feudalism rather than as the manifestation of a radical change in social organisation. It has become customary to speak of it as 'a refinement, not a degeneration of an earlier feudal custom', as 'not an aberration from, but the logical successor to feudalism'.[1] Indeed while McFarlane originally saw the change to a fiscal and contractual obligation as betokening the emergence of a 'loosely knit and shamelessly competitive society', he and others subsequently interpreted the new forms as attempts to strengthen the bonds of lordship and the ideals of fidelity threatened by the multiplication of tenures: 'it was precisely because the tenurial bond had become weak that a contractual one was needed'. Bastard feudalism sought to preserve, not to undermine, the ideals of 'responsibility,

---

[1] G. A. Holmes, *The Estates of the Higher Nobility in Fourteenth Century England* (1957), p. 83; W. H. Dunham, *Lord Hastings' Indentured Retainers* (1955), p. 7; M. C. Carpenter, 'The Beauchamp affinity, a study of bastard feudalism at work', *EHR*, xcv (1980), p. 514.

loyalty and good faith' which for Helen Cam were characteristic of pure feudalism.[2] W. H. Dunham postulated a tertiary stage in the late fifteenth century, when the money fee was itself replaced by the promise of 'good lordship', but though this occurred in some Tudor affinities, in general it has come to be recognised that elements characteristic of 'pure', 'bastard', and 'neo' feudalism were present at all these stages. Thus in the 1966 lectures McFarlane pointed out that, although the emergence of the contractual retinue was usually placed in the reign of Edward I, livery was known in Norman England, maintenance had its origins in the functions performed by Anglo-Saxon 'oath helpers', and the bribery of royal justices to secure a favourable judgement was well attested in the reign of Henry II. J. M. W. Bean has drawn attention to the existence of the household retinue in the eleventh century and a penetrating examination of the role of the royal *familia* has led J. O. Prestwich to conclude that all the characteristics of the later indenture of retainer were present in the agreements by which Henry I recruited knights for his household.[3] Conversely, recent studies have emphasised that feudal tenure continued to play an important role in the structure of late medieval affinities, which often had a nucleus of hereditary tenants; while the granting of manors as fees to retainers, mostly for life but occasionally in perpetuity, was a common feature in many of the larger retinues. By the sixteenth century these tenurial bonds were indeed losing their effectiveness, even in the north where they endured most strongly; but it still remained customary all over England for the nobility to ride with substantial retinues, to distribute their livery within prescribed limits, and to practice maintenance to a degree which their victims at least found unacceptable.

This recognition that the retinue was a continuing element in the practice of medieval lordship has shifted the emphasis away from its military origins and led to a re-assessment of its reputation for disorder. Writing in 1945 in the wake of N. B. Lewis's study of indentured retinues, and drawing primarily on the evidence of John of Gaunt's indentures, McFarlane connected the emergence of the life indenture with the stimulus given by the wars of the three

---

[2] 'Lords and Retainers', lecture 2. These lectures were a revised version of a course on 'Livery and Maintenance' delivered in 1959.

[3] 'Lords and Retainers', ibid.; J. O. Prestwich, 'The military household of the Norman kings', *EHR* xcvi (1981), pp. 8-12; B. D. Lyon, *From Fief to Indenture* (1957), pp. 32-39; J. M. W. Bean, 'Batchelor and Retainer', *Medievalia et Humanistica* n.s. 3 (1972), pp. 117-131.

Edwards to recruit retainers beyond the needs of the household; a view adhered to by Dunham and Bean. But twenty years later he had, like others, come to view retaining primarily as an expression of the lord's need for service in peace rather than war. The permanent nucleus of the affinity would indeed be mobilised for service in arms or for the recruitment and organisation of the larger company which the lord led on campaign; and until late in the sixteenth century the crown relied on the nobility to raise forces for overseas service in this way. But such service was occasional and of short duration. It is in the peacetime composition and function of the retinue that its character and *raison d'etre* must be sought.

The structure of the late medieval affinity has frequently been described as forming a series of concentric circles. In terms of their relationship to the lord, McFarlane listed his kinsmen, tenants, and neighbours. In terms of the service rendered, the affinity can be categorised as menial servants, councillors, estate officials, and local gentry. Or again, on the basis of contract, it comprised those retained by life indenture, those in receipt of an annual fee, and those who were merely tenants. But in each case these categories are apt to overlap, and an affinity has been most aptly described as 'a sea of varying relationships' having its common focus in the service and loyalty to a lord.[4] This indefinite character makes it difficult to establish the overall size of any particular affinity. However, the documentary evidence relating to particular categories allows us to be more precise about some of these. The core of the affinity — those retained by indenture or in receipt of annuities for life, can often be established with fair completeness from accounts. It is clear that there was a world of difference between the 200 lords, knights and esquires retained by John of Gaunt or something like half that number in the service of Thomas of Lancaster, and the mere handful of retainers which the lesser nobility supported. In the fifteenth century even some of the largest retinues like those of Humphrey, duke of Buckingham, Richard Beauchamp, earl of Warwick and William, Lord Hastings, numbered no more than sixty to eighty, and the Tudor licences to retain which set limits of 200 for an earl and 100 for a baron were probably in excess of the numbers actually retained.[5] In particular circumstances, like the Percy and Neville responsibility for defence of the Border, or in particular periods of tension as in the mid-fifteenth century, the retinue would be larger; moreover most affinities grew naturally throughout the lifetime of a

---

[4] 'Lords and Retainers', lecture 4; Carpenter, *op. cit.*, p. 51; Holmes, *op. cit.*, p. 79.

lord since life indentures were frequently the reward for good service. These formed the stable core of the affinity, for although, as McFarlane showed, it was possible for a life retainer to leave his lord or to be dismissed without penalties, recent studies have tended to stress the fact that few life retainers withdrew from the affinity. McFarlane's suggestion that retaining for life was declining in the fifteenth century as lordship became less attractive is difficult to verify as a general trend.

More fluid in membership and far less exclusive in their loyalty were the numerous groups of those who received a fee from the lord. An habitual element among these were his legal counsel. After 1390 they ceased to be Justices of the central court, but they would certainly include many able serjeants at law who would reach the bench. Officials of the central administration, members of the royal household, and, by the sixteenth century, the servants of the king's principal ministers, all figure in the accounts of the nobility as receiving pensions.[6] Local gentry too frequently took fees from different lords, although in many cases this was consequent on a dynastic or political alliance between their masters. The sums paid were usually twenty pounds or marks for a knight, and ten pounds or marks for an esquire, although individual variants from this might be quite large. Wealthy lords and those of the royal blood might be expected to be more generous — John of Gaunt himself was distinctly so — and it has been suggested that a powerful lord who was excluded from royal patronage, as was Thomas of Lancaster, might need to compensate his followers with extra bounty.[7] Livery, distributed twice a year, accompanied the receipt of a money fee and was intended to advertise the lord's social importance, his worldly 'worship'. At least until restricted by legislation, it might of itself be the expression of a bond of good lordship and service, or even of alliance and friendship, as when Richard II chose to wear Gaunt's livery round his neck. The two surviving livery rolls, of Elizabeth de Burgh, lady of Clare (1343) and of Edward Courtenay, earl of Devon (1384), show a distribution of livery to respectively 272 and

---

5 'Lords and Retainers', lecture 7; J. R. L. Maddicott, *Thomas of Lancaster* (1970), p. 45; T. B. Pugh, 'Magnates, knights and gentry', *Fifteenth Century England* ed. S. B. Chrimes, C. D. Ross, R. A. Griffiths (1972), pp. 101-2, 107; C. Rawcliffe, *The Staffords, Earls of Stafford and Dukes of Buckingham, 1394-1521*, (1978), p. 73; Dunham, *op. cit.*, pp. 148-57.

6 J. R. L. Maddicott, *Law and Lordship: Royal Justices as Retainers*, Past and Present Supplement no. 4 (1978), pp. 78-81; K. B. McFarlane, *The Nobility of Later Medieval England* (1973), p. 108.

7 Maddicott, *Thomas of Lancaster*, p. 47.

135 persons of all ranks. In each of these the local gentry formed a prominent group, but the lady of Clare evidently felt greater need to ensure the goodwill of justices, officials of the exchequer, and esquires of the royal household.[8] In the fifteenth century some lists of resident servants and those receiving wages provide occasional figures for the size of noble households. That accompanying Margaret, duchess of Clarence to France in 1419 and those of the first and third dukes of Buckingham all have totals of between 130 and 150 persons, though there may have been less than a hundred in the household of the Beauchamp earls of Warwick.[9]

As to the cost of the retinue, McFarlane reckoned that fees and annuities did not normally exceed 10% of the lord's total income, a figure confirmed by T. B. Pugh. This could rise dramatically in particular circumstances: to as much as 40% in the case of the Percies at the time of their rivalry with the Nevilles in the mid-fifteenth century and when the fourth earl of Northumberland was trying to buy up Richard III's supporters following the accession of Henry VII.[10] But calculation of such percentages depends much on whether they are restricted to the fees paid by the lord's receiver or include sinecure estate offices like stewardships, annuities charged on manors, and even the rent-free grant of the manor itself. How important were such fees to the retainer? McFarlane revised his early suggestion that retaining impoverished lords while enriching the gentry, and it is doubtful whether fees and annuities formed a significant element in a retainer's income, except perhaps at the more humble level.[11] It was the lord's protection, patronage, and prestige which made his service attractive. Men might seek to enter a lord's service in a variety of ways. In his Ford lectures McFarlane described how Sir William Stonor's direct recommendation of himself to Lord Strange won him only the promise of a year's probation. Introduction to an affinity was perhaps more often effected by patronage than by a direct approach. In 1397, Sir William Baldwin, seeking to attach himself to the rising star of Richard II's court, Thomas Holland earl of Kent, sought the good offices of the earl's

---

8 'Lords and Retainers' lecture 5; McFarlane, *op. cit.*, pp. 110-112; Holmes, *op. cit.*, pp. 58-9; M. Cherry, 'The Courtenay Earls of Devon', *Southern History*, 1 (1979), pp. 72-3.

9 McFarlane, ibid.; Rawcliffe, *op. cit.*, pp. 69, 88-9.

10 'Lords and Retainers', lecture 7; Pugh, *op. cit.*, p. 101; J. M. W. Bean, *The Estates of the Percy Family, 1416-1537* (1958) pp. 94, 130-33; M. A. Hicks, 'Dynastic change and northern society', *Northern History* xiv (1978), p. 98.

11 Pugh, *op. cit.*, pp. 98-105; Carpenter, *op. cit.*, p. 519.

mother, the Countess Alice.[12] Recommendation by a magnate's allies (which could produce an interlocking of affinities) or by his councillors and estate officials was not uncommon. But for the most part the lord's choice was restricted, and even pre-determined, by family tradition and locality. Although a lord would attract men with legal and managerial skills from beyond his territorial influence, the circle of his principal tenants would furnish, from one generation to another, the immediate source of his officials; while if he aspired to the leadership of his 'country', the foremost knightly and gentry families would have to form part of his retinue. Although he might occasionally recruit knights of renown from outside — McFarlane cited one of the earliest examples of life retaining, that of Sir John Seagrave, a Midland landowner, by Roger Bigod, earl of Norfolk in 1297 — it was on his firm control of his 'inheritance' and his 'country' that a lord's worship and political influence rested.

The normal service rendered by a knight or esquire was to attend the lord's household for specific periods (for which he was entitled to 'bouche of court'), to give counsel, and to ride with his own followers in the lord's company whenever summoned, particularly to ceremonial and political assemblies. He might also be required to come, defensibly arrayed, to take the lord's part in quarrels against all save the king; but most of his service was more routine and peaceful. The lord's household was the social centre of the affinity and 'menial' service was personal, intimate, and above all honourable, even for the knightly class. McFarlane cited the pride in service displayed on Sir Sampson Meverell's tomb in Tideswell, and an East-Anglian esquire, writing in his will in 1479, recalled the varied patrons whom 'I sum tyme servid in household and had of theim my living according to the degre that his grace called me to and better thenne I coude deserve'. By the end of the fifteeth century such attitudes were not universally shared: John Paston junior could congratulate himself that he had never served any lord, but even as late as the mid-seventeenth century there was still force in the complaint of an impoverished gentleman that

> to serve noblemen in most unnoble offices, to pull
> off their boots, brush their clothes, wait at table
> with a trencher in their hand, ride with a cloak
> bag behind them, dine and sup with footmen and
> grooms, is the ordinary course of gentlemen in

[12] McFarlane, *op. cit.*, p. 109; 'Lords and Retainers', lecture 4.

England, whilst in other countries they go to wars
and scorn to . . . wait upon anyone.[13]

The lord's council managed the business aspects of the inheritance.
Composed of lawyers, officials, and certain local gentry, it
negotiated purchases and sales of land, advised on marriages and
marriage portions, lawsuits and arbitrations. It could be invaluable
in safeguarding the inheritance through minorities or forfeitures, in
providing executors and feoffees from among its members, and in
mediating between a grasping lord and his tenants.[14]

This pattern of service to a noble family — military, social and
professional — gave a well established affinity a corporate identity,
manifested in the intermarriage of its families, their mutual
assistance as feoffees and executors, and their general social inter-
course. It not merely served the interests of the lord, but fulfilled the
needs of its members for associates whose support was assured and
whose trustworthiness was under-written by the lord. The man who
placed himself outside the affinity by quarrel with, or desertion of, his
lord thus estranged himself from his friends and neighbours. All this
made for stability, and within the area of the lord's influence the
affinity was a powerful regulator of social behaviour. But only
exceptionally was an affinity co-extensive with the county
community. Where it was, as in Devon under Edward Courtenay
earl of Devon in the reign of Richard II, or where it could be
stretched to cover the county by alliances with the lesser nobility, as
in Warwickshire under Richard Beauchamp, then the lord could
bring the administration of the shire under his control. In those
shires where lords' estates were intermingled and their areas of
influence overlapped, they might co-operate without friction, as did
the earls of Arundel and Warenne in Surrey and Sussex in the early
fourteenth century; or they might divide the county territorially into
spheres of influence as did the Nevilles and Percies in Yorkshire. In
counties where there were no dominant magnate estates the lesser
nobility and leading knightly families could form a coherent shire
'establishment', but whether this produced a more or a less stable
society than that dominated by an affinity are matters still under

---

[13] D. A. L. Morgan, 'The King's affinity in the polity of Yorkist England', *T.R.H.S.*,
23 (1973), p. 14. The second quotation was used in 'Lords and Retainers', lecture 2,
and was written by Henry Belasyse in 1657 (Hist. MSS. Comm., 55, *Various
Collections*, II, Wombwell MSS, p. 204).

[14] C. Rawcliffe, 'Baronial councils in the later Middle Ages', *Patronage, Pedigree and
Power*, ed. C. Ross (1979), pp. 87-108.

investigation.[15] But it should not be assumed that even where sheriffs, escheators, justices of the peace and other commissioners were frequently or normally members of an affinity, that they were necessarily the nominees of a lord or wholly served his purposes. It was primarily their own status, abilities and inclinations which recommended them for such service, and a lord setting out to build up an affinity would seek men who had held such offices.[16]

The magnates' influence on the choice of members of parliament must be seen in the same terms. In his article on 'Parliament and Bastard Feudalism' McFarlane adduced the evidence of the Paston Letters to argue that while lords attempted to pre-arrange the election of their chosen candidates, these had to be acceptable to the leading families of the shire. This marked a shift in historical perspective; for it implied that lords sought to influence elections not to secure a subservient house of Commons but to attest their own influence in the shire. Moreover his demonstration that the shire representatives were men of substance and ability, whose election was one step in a career that could end in membership of the royal council and even the peerage, underlined the interdependence of lords and gentry and the fact that the patronage network of Bastard Feudalism served the interests of retainers as much as those of their patrons. McFarlane concluded that familiarity with the lives and achievements of the country gentry was necessary if the main outlines of local and central politics were to be revealed, and J. S. Roskell's studies of the careers of knights of the shire have deepened our knowledge of the undercurrents of political and parliamentary history.[17] J. G. Edwards has further shown that 'arranged' elections greatly outnumbered contested ones and that both the legislation on the qualifications of electors and elected, and the evidence of the numbers attending the county court, reflect strong and articulate local interest in representation.[18] With the prestige of both lords and

15 'Lords and Retainers', lecture 5; Carpenter, *op. cit.*; Cherry, *op. cit.*; A. J. Pollard, 'The Richmondshire Community of the gentry during the Wars of the Roses', *Patronage, Pedigree and Power*, pp. 37-59; Hicks, *op. cit.*; M. J. Bennett, 'A county community: social cohesion among the Cheshire gentry, 1400-25, *Northern History* viii (1973); J. R. L. Maddicott, 'The county community and the making of public opinion in fourteenth century England', *T.R.H.S.*, 28 (1978), pp. 27-43.

16 Dunham, *op. cit.*, pp. 27-47, 141-6.

17 J. S. Roskell, *Parliament and Politics in Late Medieval England* (1981).

18 J. G. Edwards, 'The emergence of the majority rule in English parliamentary elections', *T.R.H.S.* xiv (1964), pp. 175-96; 'The Huntingdonshire parliamentary election of 1450'; *Essays in Medieval History presented to Bertie Wilkinson* (1969), pp. 383-95; A. Rogers, 'The Lincolnshire county court in the fifteenth century', *Lincolnshire History and Archaeology*, 1 (1966), pp. 64-78.

gentry at stake contested elections were almost always the product of struggles between rival affinities.[19] Of course the degree of influence exerted by lords over elections varied between shires and elections. In the north the Neville and Percy affinities enjoyed a virtual monopoly of seats, and nomination by their stewards at the county court was almost normal, while for a decade or two at the end of the fourteenth century a Courtenay follower sat for Devon in every parliament. In the North Midlands members of the Hastings affinity were returned somewhat erratically in Edward IV's reign, and in East Anglia Mowbray, de la Pole and York influence combined with strong local sentiment to produce a chequered pattern of representation.[20] It was plainly useful for a lord to have his retainers with him at parliaments and as members of the Commons, but only for certain politically tense parliaments is there any evidence of a concerted attempt to 'pack' parliament to achieve a political end. In general, the close examination of parliamentary procedure by Roskell and Edwards has confirmed McFarlane's view of a community of interest and outlook between Lords and Commons expressed in the Lords' exercise of leadership but not dominance over the lower house. The tendency in the fifteenth century for borough seats to be taken by 'outsiders' from the court or local affinity, while it bears witness to the increasing competition for a seat in parliament and perhaps to the decline of some boroughs, must also be seen in the context of the boroughs' own search for patronage. But while corporations might value representation by an outsider who had influence with the great, they resisted attempts by patrons to intrude their nominees. Similarly, while civic officials and leading citizens not infrequently received annuities from a local lord, town ordinances repeatedly outlawed the distribution of livery which they saw as an incitement to faction and violence.[21]

The affinity thus appears as the means of organising the social,

[19] R. Virgoe, 'Three Suffolk parliamentary elections of the mid-fifteenth century', *BIHR*, xxxix (1966), pp. 185-96; 'The Cambridgeshire election of 1439', *ibid.*, xlvi (1973), pp. 95-101; J. S. Roskell, *The Commons in the Parliament of 1422*, (1954), ch. 1.

[20] P. Jalland, 'The influence of the aristocracy in shire elections in the North of England, 1450-70', *Speculum*, xlvii (1972), pp. 483-507; Dunham, *op. cit.*, pp. 30-6; Cherry, *op. cit.*, p. 85; Virgoe, *op. cit.*

[21] Roskell, *Commons in the Parliament of 1422*, ch. 7; K. N. Houghton, 'Theory and practice in borough elections to parliament during the latter half of the fifteenth century', *BIHR*, xxxix (1966), pp. 130-40; A. Rogers, 'Parliamentary elections in Grimsby in the fifteenth century', *BIHR*, xlii (1969), pp. 212-20; R. Horrox, 'Urban patronage and patrons in the fifteenth century', *Patronage, the Crown and the Provinces*, ed. R. Griffiths (1981), pp. 145-66.

political, and administrative life of the magnate's 'country' — the area over which his good lordship was paramount — for the mutual advantage of himself and the leading gentry families in his service. But, in McFarlane's words, 'lordship lasted only so long as it was found to be *good* lordship or until it was ousted by a better'. A lord who was incompetent or distrusted would soon lose his followers; even the failure of effective lordship through dotage or a minority could undermine a long and strong tradition of local control, as recent studies of the Courtenay and Beauchamp affinities have shown.[22] This, 'want of settled loyalty' together with the non-tenurial nature of its bonds, inclines some historians to view bastard feudalism as essentially unstable. McFarlane did not accept this even though he did emphasise the political acumen of the gentry in refusing to jeopardise their lives and inheritances by a blind and exclusive loyalty to a lord whose course was set towards ruin. For good lordship reinforced mutual advantage with concepts of honour, derived from a remote and primarily military tradition but still influential in chivalric society. For a retainer, fidelity to his lord's person and honour was the condition of his service and the measure of his own and his public esteem, while the affinity was also knit together by its shared honour and fortune, expressed in the concept of brotherhood in arms.[23] For the lord, fidelity to the traditions of his lineage and kin were paramount, but his 'worship' and 'good lordship' were also measured in maintaining the honour of his followers, in ruling his affinity and his country, and in his own fidelity to (and favour with) the king. Lords who allowed their retinues to plunder or terrorise earned condemnation from the time of Rufus to that of Richard II, and Bishop Russell's draft sermon to the parliament of 1483 declaring that 'the politique rule of every region well ordeigned standeth in the nobles', like Thomas Starkey's observation that 'the office and duty of the nobility and gentry of every shire is to see justice among their servants and subjects and to keep them in unity and concord', voiced not just a convention but the basis of Yorkist and early Tudor governance.[24] But while the affinity had an inbuilt hierarchy and cohesion and could impose this

---

[22] C. A. Carpenter, Political Society in Warwickshire, c. 1401-70 (Cambridge Ph.D. thesis 1976); M. Cherry, 'The struggle for power in mid-fifteenth century Devonshire', *Patronage, the Crown and the Provinces*, pp. 123-44.

[23] M. H. Keen, 'Brotherhood in arms', *History* xlvii (1962), pp. 14-17.

[24] M. E. James, *English Politics and the Concept of Honour, 1485-1642*, Past and Present Supplement (3) (1978); 'The first earl of Cumberland and the decline of Northern feudalism', *Northern History*, 1 (1966), p. 43.

on the area under its control, if faced with disruption from within or challenge from outside it could become a powerful instrument for disorder. Historians have remained divided as to which of its two faces was more characteristic or habitual.

In one sense the evidence for the association of bastard feudalism with the perversion of justice, endemic violence, and even civil war is unequivocal. Lords retained royal justices, packed commissions of oyer and terminer with their retainers to convict or intimidate their enemies, bribed juries and sheriffs, and paraded their retainers in court to maintain their causes.[25] Their retinues, led by their officials if rarely by themselves, plundered the property of rivals and occasionally killed their servants, while feuds between rival retinues could lead to armed skirmishes and ambushes. But was bastard feudalism merely the instrument of such lawlessness or was it the cause? Did it raise the level of lawlessness or had lawlessness merely become better documented and more denounced? Does lawlessness mark the disintegration of the crown's authority under challenge from over-mighty subjects, or did the inadequacy of the crown's resources for peacekeeping throw the responsibility on to local shoulders?

In attacking the prevailing orthodoxy that the late middle ages witnessed the spread of corruption and disorder, McFarlane warned that 'as one pushes back out of the well lit fifteenth century into the dark ages before it, it is important not to mistake the decrease in the amount of evidence (for corruption) as a decrease in the phenomena the evidence illustrates'. With regard to the bribery of judges, sheriffs and jurors he pointed out that as far back as evidence exists which is likely to reveal bribes, it does so; and he cited private accounts of the thirteenth century and the well-known bill of legal expenses incurred by Richard Anstey in 1163 for recovering the lands of his uncle, including a bribe of one hundred marks to the king.[26] Noting that Anstey appeared in court 'with his friends and helpers', McFarlane observed that maintenance had a respectable pedigree from Anglo-Saxon oath helpers to the 'mainpast' of the Angevin kings, and that even in 1259 the reforming barons only promised not to give protection in the courts to men who were not their own. But in the fourteenth century what had been a solemn obligation of lords became an offence against the law. It was the laws that were new, not

---

25 Maddicott, *Law and Lordship*; R. W. Kaeuper, 'Law and order in fifteenth century England: the evidence of special commissions of oyer and terminer', *Speculum*, liv (1979), pp. 734-84.
26 'Lords and Retainers', lecture 3. Anstey's case is cited from F. Palgrave, *The Rise and Progress of the English Commonwealth* (1834), pt. ii, pp. lxxv-lxxxvii.

the offence they condemned, and the laws were the answer to a growing volume of complaint. That itself was not indicative of the growth of malpractices but of the new opportunities to seek redress. McFarlane dismissed attempts to quantify the growth of crime from surviving evidence. Like smuggling and tax evasion, judicial corruption might be most rife when least visible in the records, so that quantitative analysis of, for example, the number of cases of maintenance in the Year Books, is pointless. Private muniments alone give unimpeachable, because unsuspecting, evidence of attempts to corrupt justice, and from their abundance in the sixteenth century McFarlane was able to cite evidence of an attitude to the law little different from that of the Pastons' England.[27]

Many historians now see a qualitative approach to the problem of crime as historically more illuminating, beginning with the question how people regarded the law before asking why they broke it and why they demanded its enforcement. Medieval attitudes were conditioned by two fundamental limitations on law enforcement, the lack of adequate investigative methods to establish the truth, and the limited range of punishment. These were more fundamental than the often cited difficulty of apprehending criminals and bringing men to court. For the fact that actions had to be based on complaint, and the jury had to be 'informed' by the parties, made it often difficult to assign culpability: while the minimal availability of detention as a means of punishment rather than custody, and the decline of mutilation, left only the choice between fiscal and capital punishment, so that juries were reluctant to convict felons even for homicide.[28] Instead of conviction and punishment, emphasis had to be laid on redress for damage and the restoration of the social framework: this was appropriate, since practically all crime had a personal motive and a local setting rather than being professional and indiscriminate. At the gentry level both perversion of the law and violent disorder were related to property claims and family prestige. For the phenomenal growth of litigiousness — and of the legal class — in the later middle ages was the result of the diffusion of property rights

[27] 'Lords and Retainers', lecture 8. McFarlane's examples are taken from the Plumpton Correspondence, the letters of Reginald Bray, the Northumberland Household Book for 1514-26, a rejected petition to parliament in 1589 against the payment of fees by subjects to justices of the peace, and the correspondence of Robert Cecil with his aunt the dowager Lady Russell. See also, A. Harding, *The Law Courts of Medieval England* (1970) p. 94; W. T. MacCaffrey, 'Talbot and Stanhope: an episode in Elizabethan politics', *BIHR*, xxxiii (1960).

[28] T. A. Green, 'The jury and the English law of homicide, 1200-1619', *Michigan Law Review*, lxxiv (1976).

amongst an increasingly wide class of landowners, accentuated by the complexity of land law, the confusion of tenures, and the spread of trusts and uses. Most landowners could expect to face litigation in defence of their property at some point, and since it was the basis of their wealth, their family, and their repute, such disputes were literally matters of life and death. It was here that lordship had a natural and effective role to play. For although only the law could give a secure title, it was not the only or even the primary means to dispute or defend title. Lordship could be invoked to deflect an enemy or intimidate a victim by a show of force, but perhaps more frequently to arbitrate a settlement out of court, which would be guaranteed under fiscal penalties and magnate authority. This quasi-judicial role of lordship was parallel to and not essentially a rival of the royal courts; both tended towards a 'political' solution rather than an impartial verdict and private arbitration may have been, if anything, less open to corruption.[29]

Violence, whether directed towards a limited end or the indiscriminate practice of banditry, was a breach of the King's peace and as such aroused popular and official condemnation. But it cannot be viewed purely as evidence of the weakness of central government. For the maintenance of social peace was closely linked to the preservation of the social hierarchy: 'misrule', or disorder, was largely seen in terms of the failure of particular estates to perform their appointed role and keep within their appointed station. Thus banditry was caused by men of mean estate usurping the rights of magnates to distribute livery for perverted ends; while magnates betrayed their own responsibility to uphold the law when they gave livery to malefactors of practised *unlawful* maintenance. The social ethic laid the responsibility for upholding the law and maintaining the peace in the first instance upon the propertied classes, whose ascending hierarchy of wealth and honour, culminating in the king, was also a hierarchy of natural authority. A magnate who tolerated or incited 'misrule' in his 'country' was damaging his own 'worship' and inviting royal intervention.

The relationship between the crown as head of the judicial system and the landowning classes was indeed highly ambivalent. From the

[29] J. G. Bellamy, *Crime and Public Order in England in the Later Middle Ages* (1973); R. Jeffs, 'The Poynings-Percy dispute', *BIHR* xxxiv (1961), pp. 148-64; J. T. Rosenthal, 'Feuds and private peace making: a fifteenth century example', *Nottingham Med. Studies*, xiv (1970), pp. 84-90; B. A. Hanawalt, 'Fur collar crime; the pattern of crime among the fourteenth century English nobility', *Jnl. of Social Hist.*, viii (1974), pp. 1-17.

perspective of the growth of state power, the decline of the eyre in the thirteenth century and the proliferation of local agencies for keeping the peace — justices of trailbaston, oyer and terminer, and the peace — in the fourteenth, marked the weakening of royal control of justice and its delivery into the hands of local interests; and the evidence for its abuse by the latter is indeed plentiful. But it is also clear that the growth of these local agencies came in response to local demand for more effective peace keeping, and greater local responsibility, fed by resentment against the arbitrary and fiscal character of the eyre. The crown was under pressure to extend its responsibilities for dealing with crime and public order, as the growth of common law actions for trespass, of equitable jurisdiction, and of conciliar action over riot testify. Yet it was this same proliferating class of landowners, seeking peace keeping powers for themselves and complaining in parliament of disorder and corruption, who composed the affinities and exploited the opportunities offered for perverting and breaking the law. The anomaly becomes explicable if we realise that their prime concern was the protection of their property and repute, and that they sought this indifferently and as the occasion warranted, from the local community, lordship, manipulation of the legal system, and appeal to the king's own justice. None of these agencies had, on its own, a sufficiently extensive authority to sustain the explosion of law-seeking and law-keeping that occurred in later medieval England; men used them interchangeably and treated them as part of an integral system of social controls responsive to local and individual needs.

The problem of livery as a contribution to disorder was approached in the same terms. Livery was a symbol of the patriarchal authority which society traditionally respected. Its abuse was therefore associated with those who usurped this authority, such as the robber chief indicted in the Yorkshire eyre of 1218 for giving livery to fifteen followers 'as if he had been a baron or earl' and the 'men of small means' who had been distributing livery in 1377.[30] Conversely, John of Gaunt answered the Commons' complaints against liveries in 1384 with the traditional assertion that lords could well enough control their own retainers. This sequence of parliamentary complaint culminated in the ordinance of 1390 and the statutes of 1399-1401 which restricted the right to give livery to those

[30] 'Lords and Retainers', lecture 2, citing *Rolls of the Justices in Eyre*, ed. D. M. Stenton, Selden Soc. lvi (1937), pp. xxxviii, 424; *Rot. Parl.*, iii, 23.

of the rank of banneret and above and permitted it to be worn only by menial servants residing in the household, estate officials, and councillors, embracing in these categories those retained by life indenture. Livery, (apart from the king's and the Prince of Wales's) could only be worn as part of the lord's household, and not by individuals on their own business. It was McFarlane's view, based on the absence of further complaint and legislation about livery, and on the absence of private livery collars on tombs, or references to them in inventories and private accounts, that this legislation brought to an end the era of unbridled distribution of livery by magnates.[31] Complaint and prosecutions under the statutes in the fifteenth century relate exclusively to livery distributed by men of lesser rank.

No attempt to restrain retaining itself was made until the latter fifteenth century, and then at the initiative of the crown. The first act to limit retaining, in 1468, confined it to menial servants, officers and councillors of the lord and permitted it 'for lawful service done', thereby embracing life retainers. This should certainly have restricted the size of retinues, since no lord was likely to retain for life on a large scale, but here again no peers were prosecuted under it and it is difficult to perceive that it had any effect except perhaps on the wording of indentures. The act of 1504 though omitting the lawful service clause, still did not forbid the retaining of household servants, estate officers and legal counsel, but it began the practice by which the crown licensed retaining as a mark of trust and favour. From the numerous licences issued it is clear that the Tudors used their dispensing power freely to keep illegal retinues in being.[32] Both crown and nobility found them indispensable: the crown because it relied on their military potential for overseas expeditions and the suppression of popular dissent, the nobility because they remained the expression of its repute and local control. Only by the end of the sixteenth century were such considerations ceasing to be of first importance and retaining becoming transformed into a clientage network focussed on court patronage.

If the survival of bastard feudalism under the Tudors shows that it was consistent with strong monarchy can it rightly bear the blame for the Wars of the Roses? It is by now well understood that the nobility did not in general see their relationship to the crown as one

---

31 'Lords and Retainers', lecture 6, and cf. *Nobility*, p. 107; R. L. Storey, 'Liveries and Commissions of the Peace', *The Reign of Richard II*, ed. F. R. H. du Boulay and C. M. Barron, pp. 131-52.
32 Dunham, *op. cit.*, ch. iv, v; M. E. James, *A Tudor Magnate and the Tudor State*, Borthwick Papers, 30 (1966), p. 5.

of opposition, but as providing service and support. Service in arms was traditionally the most fitting for their rank, and a king who could bring his nobility into a companionship of honour and renown in war, as did Edward I, Edward III and Henry V, laid a foundation of political support which was not easily shaken. In peacetime the nobility were expected, as we have seen, to serve the king in their countries and periodically in court and council. Service was personal and honourable, rather than public and political. Only in the great offices of state was a tradition of public service appearing, and these were not often held by the greater nobility. Service brought rewards, either gains of war or grants of land, offices, annuities and feudal profits. But service was more important to the great magnate than the rewards he received, for these were merely the manifestations of the crown's favour and good lordship on which his own repute and influence was based. Crown patronage could on occasion be used to advance a particular noble in rank or bring a family into the peerage, but it would be wrong to see the nobility as continually engaged in a struggle for royal patronage, and the belief that such a struggle (prompted by falling incomes) produced the Wars of the Roses has been decisively discredited by McFarlane and others.[33]

Baronial opposition designed to constrain the king might be prompted by the defects of royal government, but armed revolt against him was usually a last resort reaction to royal discrimination against a member or section of the nobility and in favour of their rivals. Fear that the royal authority might be used to the undoing of themselves, their inheritance, and their local standing, far more often precipitated lords into revolt than any ambition to reduce the power of the crown or manipulate it to their advantage. On the whole, therefore, hierarchical bonds of service and loyalty which bound king, lords, and retainers, made for social and political stability. It was rather the horizontal conflicts within these estates which were difficult to contain and which, it has been claimed, were enhanced by bastard feudalism. Conflicts between members of rival retinues touched the honour and repute of their lords and defeat could destroy their control over their 'country'. Struggles between lords for local control could widen and, coalescing with others, form rival factions at a national level. Such factions could seek to manipulate the crown's authority against their rivals or, failing to do this, seek an alternative source of authority in a pretender to the crown. This sequence has been analysed in studies of the Percy-

[33] J. R. Lander, *Crown and Nobility, 1450-1509*, (1976), Introduction.

Neville conflicts in the north and the Courtenay-Bonville ones in the west country in the mid-fifteenth century which, merging by stages into the York-Beaufort feud, came to involve the crown's authority and then its dynastic title.[34] But McFarlane saw no inexorable logic in this development. Agreeing that the nobility were never a naturally coherent group, and that both the ethic and the organisation of the magnate affinity fashioned it for conflict, he argued that at every stage bastard feudalism provided a check to such rivalries by submitting them to the good lordship of a higher authority. Just as a lord should compose his retainers' quarrels so the king should compose those of his lords; although between kings themselves only God could give a verdict by battle. Such arbitration was common, and followed a similar pattern at all levels of society in balancing considerations of personal and family honour (and all that implied in worldly repute and influence) against obedience to lord or king. In managing his nobility, and particularly in composing their feuds, the qualities required of a king were no different from those required of a great lord: he had to inspire them with confidence, manage them firmly and tactfully, and above all lead them in war. Hence McFarlane ascribed the Wars of the Roses to the inanity of Henry VI, who failed his nobility and accentuated rather than healed their divisions.[35]

What was the effect of the Wars of the Roses on bastard feudalism? At the close of his British Academy lecture, McFarlane proffered the view that the experience of civil war had demoralised the nobility and discredited its traditional role as a bridle on royal mis-government. He voiced his own doubts on this theory for, as he pointed out, the tradition of a united baronage acting as a 'constitutional' opposition belongs only to the thirteenth century. But if the Tudors had little need to fear the emergence of latter day Ordainers, neither 'did they show any sign whatsoever of wishing to oppress, still less to destroy, the ancient nobility as a class'. Their answer was rather to give new emphasis and meaning to the traditional obligations of obedience and service to the crown. Obedience to a godly monarch was represented as a christian and political virtue transcending any individual and autonomous sense of honour. Service and office was not something that the magnate could claim

---

34 R. L. Storey, *The End of the House of Lancaster* (1966); R. A. Griffiths, 'Local rivalries and national politics', *Speculum* xliii (1968), pp. 589-632; M. Cherry, *op. cit.*, *Patronage, the Crown and the Provinces*.
35 McFarlane, *Nobility*, pp. 120-1; *Wars of the Roses*, p. 240 below.

by virtue of his inheritance and estate but was to be performed at the royal pleasure and command. As Edmund Dudley wrote: 'though it be . . . tollerable for them to desier yt (office) when they are mete therefore, yet it is more lawdable to have it of the fre disposicion of ther sovereigne: but in all cases lett them not presume to take it of ther owne auctoritie, for then it will suerly choke them'.[36] The early Tudors' insistence on absolute obedience from their nobility was facilitated by the growing shift of power at local level from the nobility towards the gentry. It is important not to exaggerate this and there was certainly no revolutionary change. McFarlane was firmly of the opinion that 'society was ordered in 1603 very much as it had been in 1509', but he also discerned from the last quarter of the fifteenth century a weakening of the attractions of lordship and by the end of the sixteenth century a slow decline in the ethic of service. To a partnership based on mutual advantage, the penalties suffered by those affinities on the losing side in the civil wars were sufficient to discredit the system; or rather they would have been if the 'ambidexters' had not, with habitual acumen, avoided the disasters which engulfed their masters. Nevertheless many long standing affinities were destroyed, and even those where continuity was maintained, like the Staffords and Percies, fell victim to royal suspicion, the counter attractions of royal service, and the decline of tenurial bonds. The study of both the royal and noble affinities in the Tudor age has scarcely begun, but separate studies are beginning to suggest that the crown was now more able to use the lesser nobility and gentry (often those with court connections) as instruments for direct royal influence within the shire, based upon its control of patronage and office to which the nobility no longer had automatic and unchallenged claim.[37]

To end this survey on such a note would, however, be misleading. Bastard feudalism was for too long seen in terms of the old antithesis between royal authority and magnate power: as the instrument of the overmighty subject and as the enemy of strong kingship. But the history of England cannot be written solely in terms of the evolution of central government; it is also the history of communities and classes. Running through McFarlane's studies, forming now a major now a minor theme, is the story of men from the middling ranks of

[36] James, *A Tudor Magnate and the Tudor State*, p. 16, citing Edmund Dudley, *Tree of Commonwealth*.
[37] M. Condon, 'Ruling elites in the reign of Henry VII', *Patronage, Pedigree and Power*, pp. 109-142; E. W. Ives, 'Court and County Palatine in the reign of Henry VIII: the career of William Brereton', *Trans. Hist. Soc. Lancs & Cheshire*, 123 (1972).

society who used their abilities as stewards, councillors, lawyers, and soldiers, or their position as substantial landowners serving as knights of the shire, justices and commissioners, to rise in wealth and status, even in some cases to the ranks of the peerage. Their common ladder to success was service to the crown and nobility, and for them bastard feudalism provided a network of patronage so well attuned to their ambitions that its very existence attests their rising influence. Even the petty and localised turbulence of late medieval society is better read as evidence of an expanding and assertive class beginning to flex its muscles, than as marking a crisis of kingship, a disintegration of central government, or the feuding of the nobility. Indeed the bastard feudal affinity represents an attempt by the traditional leaders of society — crown and nobility — to contain the increasingly diversifying armigerous class within the old traditions of lordship and chivalry. It was an essentially conservative solution and, having served its purpose, disintegrated not under any attack from the crown but as cumulative wealth and access to political authority gave the broad class of landowners independence from the nobility as mediators of patronage and power. In all its phases the workings of bastard feudal society merits study as much from below as from above: as witness to the need of the retainer for patronage no less than that of the lord for service. Yet the compilation of biographies of the gentry is slow and tedious work, and the evidence for their social attitudes is mostly oblique and cumulative. We are likely to wait some time for a study of the gentry of late medieval England to match that which McFarlane gave us of the nobility.

G. L. Harriss

I. PARLIAMENT AND 'BASTARD FEUDALISM'

'EDWARD I', said Stubbs, 'had made his parliament the concentration of the three estates of his people; under Edward II, Edward III, and Richard II, the third estate claimed and won its place as the foremost of the three.'[1] While the resounding emphasis is Stubbs's own—his common sense was of the kind called robust—the sentiment expressed was then and for long afterwards the traditional one. It is only of late years that opinion has swung to the opposite pole and maintained with an equal want of compromise the absolute insignificance of the commons in the political struggles of the later middle ages. The first open challenge to tradition came, I think, from Professor J. E. Neale in 1924.[2] Mainly concerned to trace the growth of free speech in parliament under the Tudors, he found himself confronted with a medieval background to his subject which seemed to him at variance with the course of its later development. The prologue, as it were, anticipated too much of his play. In a bold attempt to refashion it, he outlined a theory which did not at first attract much attention from medievalists, but which has recently, thanks to Mr. H. G. Richardson, begun to enjoy a considerable vogue among them.

As stated by Mr. Neale, this theory was at least simple. While admitting that attacks on the crown in Henry IV's reign, and to some extent in Richard II's, 'were seemingly launched by the commons', he argued that this had only a formal significance. So long as procedure by petition lasted the commons were bound to be 'the petitioners *par excellence*'; but that did not mean that they spoke only, or even primarily, for themselves. They were inspired and sustained by the lords. They were 'the initiating organ of parliament', they 'were necessarily saddled with the task of petitioning', but when they presumed to oppose the king's will, it was because the magnates were in the saddle and had a firm hold on the reins. As evidence of this there could be adduced the custom, followed repeatedly between 1373 and 1407, of assigning a number of lords to assist the commons in their deliberations. 'True, we do not find the entry in every parliament', but after all the clerks were probably careless and omitted

---

[1] *Constitutional history of England*, ii (1906 edn.), 320.
[2] 'The commons' privilege of free speech in parliament', in *Tudor studies*, ed. R. W. Seton-Watson, pp. 257 *et seq.*

to record every instance upon the rolls.[3] Therefore, 'we need no longer conclude that the real test of strength in parliament was between the king and the commons. In all likelihood it was between the king and the lords.'[4]

In adopting this theory of the relations of the two houses, Mr. Richardson wisely preferred to underline the importance of the territorial and personal ties which attached many members of the commons to the magnates of their shires.[5] There is no question that these ties were often close. 'To suggest', therefore, 'that the knights should have been able to provide an independent opposition to the lords appears, in regard to the circumstances of the time, to be little short of fantastic'; rather 'the strength of the commons in parliament was not their own but the lords.'[6] And this was echoed more recently by Miss Helen Cam, after a re-examination of the poem generally known as *Richard the Redeles*; 'the leadership and direction of policy came from the lords, who, by getting their dependents elected members and by the device of sending members of their own order to discuss plans with the representatives, were able effectively to exploit the economic and political resources of the commons.'[7] This, then, is the conclusion, reached — as we are told[8] — 'by converging lines of investigation', and damaging alike to Stubbs and Tout. But before we set about the task of rewriting the political history of two centuries in

[3] Generous use has to be made of this assumption. There were thirty-four parliaments in the period 1373-1407; in only ten of these do the rolls record that lords were either asked for or assigned to confer with the commons (1373; 1376; January and October 1377; 1378; 1381-2; February 1383; April 1384; 1402 and 1407; *Rotuli Parliamentorum*, ii. 316, 322, 363, and iii. 5, 36, 100, 145, 167, 486 and 610). To presume clerical negligence on this scale is surely a desperate course. It should be noticed that nearly all the recorded conferences of this type belong to the period 1373-84 and the rest to the reign of Henry IV. Nor is it without interest that in 1378 the commons' request for one was refused *by the lords themselves*, a fact which makes it difficult to believe that the procedure was designed to enable the magnates to influence opinion and direct action in the other house. In 1383 the king asserted his right, though he did not exercise it, to choose other lords than those named in the commons' petition. In 1402 Henry IV took much the same line, protesting 'q'il ne le vorroit faire de deuete ne de custume, mais de sa grace especiale a ceste foitz' and not only ordered this protestation to be put on record in the rolls, but sent his secretary and the steward of his household to the commons to make his position clear to them. The signs are that the initiative in this as in other matters came from the commons and that the lords were hardly more enthusiastic than the king in welcoming the novelty. It should also be observed that in January 1404 the commons asked that some of their own body should be allowed to go and confer with the lords and that this was granted (*Rot. Parl.*, iii. 523).

[4] Neale, *op. cit.*, pp 261-3.

[5] *John of Gaunt and the parliamentary representation of Lancashire*, reprinted from the *Bulletin of the John Rylands Library*, xxii (1938).

[6] *Ib.*, pp. 27 and 46.

obedience to the new formula, it would be wise to make sure that it is sound.

It has at least one obvious merit, that it takes account of certain facts which were far too lightly set aside by earlier scholars. Such a fact, for example, as that in the first half of the fifteenth century the attorneys of the great lords of the franchises, to whom suit of the county-court was still, it seems, confined, were primarily, if not solely, responsible for the choice of the knights of the shire for York. This was well known to Stubbs, but he does not appear to have regarded it as a stumbling-block to his reading of the Lancastrian constitution.[9] Again the theory derives strength from the discovery, made by Mr. Richardson, that the representatives for the county of Lancaster were returned to parliament more than once by the order of John of Gaunt alone. It would, nevertheless, be dangerous to generalise upon the basis of evidence from such exceptional counties as those of Lancaster and York without unmistakable confirmation from elsewhere. On the other hand, even when allowance has been made for the special conditions of the palatinate and for the tenacious conservation of the

[7] H. M. Cam, 'The relation of English members of parliament to their constituencies in the fourteenth century: a neglected text' in *L'Organisation corporative du Moyen Age à la fin de l'Ancien Régime. Études présentées à la Commission Internationale pour l'Histoire des Assemblées d'États*, Louvain, iii (1939), 152. I am at a loss to understand how the passage in 'Richard the Redeles' (*Mum and the Sothsegger*, ed. M. Day and R. Steele, Early Eng. Text. Soc., 24-6) helps Dr. Cam's argument. Until I read her article, I had supposed it to give some slight support to the exactly opposite view, and that still seems to me the more satisfactory interpretation. One does not expect a medieval satirist to weaken his case by admitting any merit in his victims; but this one does—by accident. For he attacks those who

> '. . . to þe kyng wente,
> And formed him of foos þat good frendis weren,
> þat bablid for þe best and no blame serued
> Of kynge ne conceyll ne of þe comunes, noþer,
> Ho-so toke good kepe to þe culorum' (iv. ll. 57–61).

So there were good men in the commons! Then first place is given to those who only *pretended* to guard the interests of those they represented (iv. ll. 44-52). If that was the worst they could be accused of, their constituents were not badly served. Medieval satire generally tries to prove too much, and the present example seems no exception. The author should have stopped short after accusing the members of ineffectiveness and pusillanimity. But he goes on to describe (iv. ll. 71-82) some as hotheads whose intemperance has to be restrained by the influence of the lords. What is meant to be a bitterly scornful description of Richard II's 'privy parliament' suggests—to me at any rate—that an apologist for the commons would have had an easy task. And after all what parliament from that day to this has not contained men of the types satirised by our anonymous poet?

[8] H. G. Richardson, reviewing the *Études* cited above: *Eng. Hist. Rev.*, lvi (1941), 125.

[9] Stubbs, *op. cit.*, iii (1903 ed.), 424-5.

'highland zone', the existence of such practices cannot but arouse suspicion about the elections in the less atavistic south and east. For, after all, many of the knights returned were, like Sir Peter de la Mare himself, the tenants, retainers or servants of their baronial neighbours, and it would be in the last degree unrealistic to deny considerable influence at elections to the great ones of the shire. Disagreement is only likely when we attempt to decide how much and to assess its effect upon the independence of the commons. The evidence for elections is admittedly slight, but I doubt whether full use has yet been made of the *Paston Letters.* Certain passages have, it is true, been quoted often enough, some to bolster one thesis, others another. Yet, perhaps there is something to be said for considering together all the references to electioneering scattered through the many pages of this Norfolk family's papers.

In all, the *Paston Letters* make mention of five county elections.[10] These belong exclusively to the third quarter of the fifteenth century, namely, to the most disturbed period in late medieval times in England; and, as it happens, to some of its most disturbed years. Such being the case, it would be unreasonable to assume that their conduct was absolutely typical of the century as a whole. Yet whatever abnormalities the wars may have produced, it is not in the least likely that they had the effect of reducing aristocratic influence; rather then did the overmighty subject enjoy his brief eventful fling. If, therefore, the part played by the great East Anglian houses was not decisive in these years, it is most improbable that it was so in more orderly times.

In September 1450, when writs were issued for a parliament to meet at Westminster on 6 November, the country was already preparing for civil war. Before the ministers could recover from the fall and death of Suffolk, rapidly followed by Cade's rebellion, they were threatened anew by the duke of York's landing in arms from Ireland. Three letters written to John Paston in October were concerned with the election. The first, dated 6 October, was from a friend in London informing him of York's arrival and the panic this had caused in the royal household.[11] It contained a great deal of practical advice about how to obtain the boon of York's 'good lordship' and then continued as follows:

> Sir, labour ye for to be knight of the shire and speak to my master Stapleton also that he be it. Sir, all Swaffham, an they be warned, will give

10 References are to pages in J. Gairdner's library edn. of 1904.
11 *Paston Letters*, ii. 174.

you their voices. . . . Sir, labour ye to the mayor that John Damme or William Jenny be burgess for the city of Norwich. . . . Also, sir, think on Yarmouth that ye ordain that John Jenny, or Limnour, or some good man be burgess for Yarmouth. Ordain ye that Jennys must be in the parliament, for they can say well. Sir, it were wisdom that my lord of Oxford wait on my lord of York. In good faith, good sir, think on all these matters.[12]

It is not known whether Paston heeded this advice; but Sir Miles Stapleton was certainly a candidate, and Oxford, with whom the Pastons seem then to have been acting, was not slow to court the friendship of York, at that time expected in the shire.[13] The removal of Suffolk had released the pent-up discontents of his oppressed East Anglian neighbours and it was said that a strong sheriff would be needed to restore the peace.[14] The new head of the de la Pole family was a minor, the lawless Lord Moleyns was rumoured to be out of grace with the duke of York,[15] and the way was therefore open for the pretensions of the duke of Norfolk. On 16 October, after a meeting with his kinsman York at Bury St. Edmunds, he wrote to Paston to tell him whom they had decided were to be knights of the shire, 'convenient and necessary' for its welfare, and to ask him as he valued their favour to 'make no labour contrary' to their desire.[16] Two days later the earl of Oxford wrote to say that he had received from York 'a token and a schedule of my lord's intent whom he would have knights of the shire' and enclosed the names of Sir William Chamberlain and Henry Grey.[17] In spite of these efforts, only the latter was returned, the other successful candidate being Sir Miles Stapleton. But one of York's council and a future servant of the Mowbrays were elected in Suffolk. John Damme represented Norwich and, though neither of the eloquent Jennys secured a Norfolk seat, William got in for the borough of Dunwich.[18]

Mowbray influence was exercised more effectively in 1455, when a parliament was summoned immediately after the Yorkist victory at St. Albans. As the duchess of Norfolk told Paston, it was 'thought right

[12] *Ib.* ii. 176.
[13] James Gresham to John Paston, *circa* October 1450 (*ib.*, ii. 180-1): 'it was told me that my master Calthorpe had writing from my lord of York to await on him at his coming into Norfolk to be one of his men, and that no gentleman of Norfolk had writing to await on him but he; and some folk ween that it is to the intent that he should be either sheriff or knight of the shire, to the furthering of other folks &c.' William Calthorp was neither sheriff nor M.P. in 1450. But it is interesting to find that the greatest duke in England was believed to be paying compliments to a mere esquire.
[14] *Ib.*, ii. 182.   [15] *Ib.*, ii. 176.   [16] *Ib.*, ii. 184   [17] *Ib.*, ii. 184-5.
[18] *Returns of members of parliament* (Parl. Papers, 1878, vol. lxii), i, p. 345.

necessary for divers causes that my lord have at this time in the parliament such persons as belong unto him and be of his menial servants.'[19] She therefore asked him to give his voice for John Howard and Sir Roger Chamberlain and to exhort others to do the same. It is difficult to judge from the civil tone of this letter whether the duchess expected, or merely hoped, that it would be obeyed, but the civility should be remarked. Its effect upon Paston was not to make him give up all hope of being returned himself. He still pressed his claims cautiously, and for a time it looked as if he might prevail. Two letters written him by John Jenny a fortnight later reveal more of the mind of a fifteenth-century election-agent than any other in this series. 'I told my lord of Norfolk at London', Jenny wrote, 'that I laboured divers men for Sir Roger Chamberlain and they said to me they would have him; but not Howard, inasmuch as he had no livelihood in the shire nor conversement; and I asked them whom they would have and they said they would have you; and thus I told him.'[20] Next day he expanded his first report:

> My servant told me ye desired to know what my lord of Norfolk said when I spake of you. And he said, inasmuch as Howard might not be, he would write a letter to the under-sheriff that the shire should have free election, so that Sir Thomas Tuddenham were not nor none that were toward the duke of Suffolk; he said he knew that ye were never to himward. Ye may send to the under-sheriff and see my lord's letter. Howard was as wood as a wild bullock; God send him such worship as he deserveth. It is an evil precedent for the shire that a strange man should be chosen, and no worship to my lord of York nor to my lord of Norfolk to write for him; for if the gentlemen of the shire will suffer such inconvenience, in good faith the shire shall not be called of such worship as it hath been.[21]

That after this both Chamberlain and Howard were returned says much for the weight of the duke's authority; but it is also obvious from Jenny's comments that there were limits beyond which it was not wise to go.

That Norfolk's men were not altogether approved of became evident at the next election of which we have any knowledge, that held after Edward IV's conquest of the throne in 1461. In the interval John Paston had at length sat for Norfolk in the parliament of 1460, with the good wishes of the common people—or so his wife assured

---

[19] *Paston Letters*, iii. 34. 'Menial' has not here acquired its modern meaning.
[20] *Ib*. iii. 38; 24 June 1455.   [21] *Ib*., iii. 39.

him—and, what was perhaps more useful, the approval of the mayor of Norwich.[22] When he decided to stand again for the first Yorkist parliament, it was in opposition to the Mowbray candidates. His old rival, Sir John Howard, was now Sheriff. The shire met at Norwich on 15 June, William Pryce, the under-sheriff, presiding. According to a return afterwards made to the king by Howard, his deputy was prevented by the threats of John Berney, who was one of the candidates, backed by a crowd of armed men, from holding the election and only escaped unharmed by the help of three of Norfolk's servants.[23] But the exaggeration in Howard's story is proved by a letter from the under-sheriff himself to John Paston, written on 18 June 1461, but wrongly supposed by Gairdner to belong to 1455.[24] In this Pryce says: 'Sir, as for the election of the knights of the shire here in Norfolk, in good faith there hath been much to-do; neverthelatter to let you have knowledge of the demeaning, my master Berney, my master Grey, and ye had greatest voice; and I purpose me, as I will answer God, to return the due election, that is after the sufficiency,[25] you and master Grey. Neverthelatter I have a master.' Shortly afterwards Margaret Paston was sent a letter of advice by her husband's servant, Thomas Dennis: 'it were expedient that the king were informed of the demeaning of the shire.[26] Therefore I send to you a testimonial, which is made by a great assent of great multitude of commons, to send to the king.'[27] He urges her to have it sent posthaste. 'Beside forth, that ye vouchsafe to let diligent labour be made to a sufficient number to seal [the indenture of election] for my master Paston alone; for if both hold not, I would one held. . . . For on the adversary part Judas sleepeth not. Berney promised to have sent, but for our Lord's love trust not that; for I see his sloth and silly labour, which is no labour.'[28] Evidently his fellow candidate was an embarrassment to John Paston, for on 12 July, by which time the meeting of parliament had been put off until 4 November, he instructed his wife to 'tell the said Berney that the sheriff is in a doubt whether he shall

22 *Ib.*, iii. 239-40.
23 'A Norfolk parliamentary election, 1461' by C. H. Williams, *Eng. Hist. Rev.*, xl (1925), 79-86, where the sheriff's return is printed. The opportune presence of Norfolk's servants is significant.
24 *Paston Letters*, iii. 36.
25 i.e. in accordance with the votes of those qualified to take part in the election.
26 i.e. of the shire-court of 15 June.
27 *Ib.*, iii. 284. It is dated Sunday only, but it must have been written after the meeting of the shire on Monday 15 June and before Dennis's murder on 4 July, that is on either 21 or 28 June.
28 *Ib.*   29 *Ib.*, iii. 290.

make a new election of knights of the shire, because of him and Grey; wherein it were better for him to have the sheriff's goodwill. Item me thinketh for quiet of the country it were most worshipful that as well Berney as Grey should get a record of all such that might spend forty shillings a year that were at the day of election, which of them that had the fewest to give it up as reason would.' [29] So far it is clear that Paston had no anxiety about his own return; he confidently assumed that he had been and would remain at the head of the poll.[30] Even later, on 1 August, when he knew that the postponement of parliament might occasion a fresh election and had observed for himself some shiftiness in the under-sheriff's manner, his optimism was unshaken; Pryce had evidently deserted Berney, but then Berney's chances had never been good, since he had not had a majority of the 'sufficienty'; the other seat at least was safely his own. So he wrote to his wife from London: 'I hear say the people is disposed to be at the shire at Norwich on St. Laurence's day [11 August] for the affirming of that they had done afore, whereof I hold me well content, if they do it of their own disposition, but I will not be the cause of the labour of them, nor bear no cost of them at this time, for by the law I am sure before, but I am well a-paid it shall be on a holiday for letting of the people's work.[31] He did not retain this aloofness for long. Unfortunately his arrival in Norfolk soon afterwards meant an end of correspondence and we have only Howard's *ex parte* statement of what happened next;[32] Paston's rejoinder, if he made one, was not enrolled. But we do know that he was arrested on going to London in October and then released; and this was followed by rumours in Norfolk that Howard in his turn had been imprisoned.[33] In his petition, Howard alleged that Paston swamped the shire-meeting with 'insuffient' [i.e. unqualified] persons, heavily armed and intent on violence, who prevented the return of the duly elected candidates, Sir William Chamberlain and Henry Grey the younger, and forced the sheriff in fear of his life to seal the indenture in the names of Paston and Berney. This neither squares with the previous correspondence already quoted nor with what happened in the sequel. Paston was without any doubt capable of chicanery, but

[30] In view of his remarks about a contest and a count, the phrase is not inappropriate.

[31] *Ib.*, iii. 297.

[32] It is necessary to emphasise its *ex parte* character as compared with the familiar letters of the Pastons, since Mr. Williams seems inclined to regard them as of equal value. Howard was making a case against an enemy in the king's court; the Pastons had no motive for deceiving one another and were not writing 'for posterity.'

[33] *Ib.*, iv. 2. He received a pardon on 6 February 1462 (C. L. Scofield, *The life and reign of Edward the Fourth*, ii. 380 h., citing Pardon Roll 1-6 Edw. IV, m. 43).

there was no need to throw dust in the eyes of his own wife. It is more likely that he was led to intervene violently in response to a last-minute attempt by the sheriff to set aside the earlier election and to substitute candidates of his own. But whatever happened at Norwich on 11 August, it was Paston and Berney who were returned and no action was taken by the king's court as a result of Howard's information.[34] According to Margaret Paston, they were acclaimed as popular heroes by their countrymen, and eventually at a shire-court, held under a new sheriff in January 1462, their election seems to have been peacefully confirmed.[35]

The Pastons had by now established themselves as people of consequence in Norfolk. John Paston, it is more than likely, sat again in the parliament of 1463-5;[36] but he died in 1466 and his son, Sir John, who succeeded to his claims and ambitions, represented Norfolk in the next parliament of 1467-8. It is not however until we come to Henry VI's 'readeption parliament' of 1470 that electioneering is once more clearly mentioned in the *Letters*. Sir John was now anxious to be returned again. The restoration of Henry VI had brought the earl of Oxford into power in East Anglia and it was therefore necessary to impress him with the Paston's importance. As Sir John told his younger brother on 15 November, if he and his friends 'hold as one body' at the meeting of the shire, the earl might realise 'that some strength resteth thereby.' He urged him, therefore, to let the earl know 'that the love of the country and city resteth on our side and that other folks be not beloved nor never were.'[37] How the contest went is not definitely known, but what evidence there is indicates that the result was acceptable both to Oxford and the Pastons. For on 22 November, Margaret Paston wrote to her sons in London to warn them that since the shire-day 'the other part' had been trying to get the returns upset: 'there was made labour and like to be concluded that the election of knights of the shire should be changed and new certificate made and John Jenny [no longer a friend evidently] set therein; therefore do your devoir to understand the truth as soon as ye can, for the said Jenny this day rideth up to Londonward and I suppose because of the same.' In a postscript she advised them to get 'my lord'—probably of

---

[34] According to Mr. Williams (*op. cit.*, 86 n.) the case reappears on the Coram Rege Roll of Michaelmas Term, 4 Henry VII.

[35] *Paston Letters*, iv. 25 and 27.

[36] See *ib.*, iv. 66, for evidence that he was being considered as a candidate and *ib.*, pp. 74-6 and 121-8, for evidence that his visits to London coincided with the sessions of parliament.

[37] *Ib.*, v. 89.

Oxford—to send for the sheriff's deputy on the day before parliament met to make quite sure that the certificate had not been tampered with. For on that evening or the following morning 'it shall be put in and if it is put in, there is no remedy. Jenny saith he will attempt the law therein.'[38] And that is all we hear.

By 1472, when the next election was held, Edward IV was king again and his friends had matters all their own way in Norfolk. Mowbray and de la Pole were acting in concert and Sir John Paston failed to secure their nomination. As his brother told him on 21 September: 'your desire as for the knights of the shire was an impossible to be brought about. For my lord of Norfolk and my lord of Suffolk were agreed amore than a fortnight ago to have Sir Robert Wingfield and Sir Richard Harcourt, and that knew I not till it was Friday last past.' A complication was that he had sent to their friends to be at Norwich 'to serve your intent' and he had therefore great difficulty in avoiding loss of face. However, he pretended that his brother after all would not be in England for parliament. 'So they came not at the shire-house; for if they had, it was thought by such as be your friends here that your adversaries would have reported that ye had made labour to have been one and that ye could not bring your purpose about.' He had been too late also for Yarmouth, but he had procured a recommendation to the bailiff of Malden in Essex for his brother's return there.[39] Yet although this letter was in the most fulsome terms and declared Sir John to be one of the duchess of Norfolk's counsel and 'to stand greatly in favour with my lord chamberlain', it produced no effect.[40] The returns for East Anglia and indeed for all England except Cornwall are extant, but Paston's name does not appear in them.[41] The dukes' nominees were duly elected for Norfolk. Nevertheless John Paston the younger wrote to his brother on 26 March 1473: 'I pray God send you the Holy Ghost among you in the parliament house, and rather the Devil, we say, than ye should grant any more taxes.'[42] So he got there somehow in the end.

---

[38] This letter (*ib.*, v. 159-61) is dated 'Thursday next before St. Katherine' and is assigned by Gairdner to 19 November 1472. But the parliament of that year began on 6 October (*Interim report of the Committee on House of Commons personnel and politics, 1264-1832*, 1932, pp. 86-7) and it was obviously written before the opening of the first session. On the other hand a reference to the manor of Gresham connects it with letter no. 792 (v. 126-7) which in view of its mentioning Sir Robert Harcourt's recent murder, can be dated 1 December 1470; for Harcourt was slain 14 November of that year (J. C. Wedgwood, 'Harcourt of Ellenhall' in *Staffordshire Collections*, William Salt Archaeological Soc. (1914), 203).

[39] *Paston Letters*, v. 149-51.   [40] *Ib.*, v. 148-9.
[41] *Returns*, pt. i, pp. 360-2.

Now, many valuable lessons can be drawn from the Paston's electoral adventures, but one so simple as that the great lords *controlled* the suffrage of the country, I dare assert, can not. Even at the height of a civil war in which the landed classes at least were risking their lives and fortunes, when the country swarmed with armed men fresh from victories in the field of battle and when the sheriff was a notorious partisan, the winning side could not be sure of returning its own men. Those to whom the electors 'gave their voices' were not necessarily the candidates for whom a duke had 'written.' On the other hand there were a large number of voters who were willing to follow the lead of those powerful enough to maintain and protect them, and when two such local potentates as the dukes of Norfolk and Suffolk joined forces and had announced their choice, they could carry sufficient numbers with them to decide the election; to pursue the contest against them then was to court a humiliating defeat. These combines were, nevertheless, a confession of weakness, since their object could only be to secure one seat for each partner. Even so, the alliance of York and Norfolk was only half successful in 1450. In 1461 the Mowbray influence, used too high-handedly and without Yorkist backing, overreached itself altogether. The right deduction seems to be that the opinion of the gentlemen of the shire counted for much. These men would take, as they would give, advice; they appreciated the value of 'good lordship'; and they were willing to be guided by those who had claims on their support; but it was foolish to attempt to drive them with too tight a rein. 'Management' was already a necessary art for those who wished to influence elections.

John Jenny's remarks about Howard's candidature in 1455 are particularly interesting. The objection that Howard had no livelihood or conversement in the shire, although he was the duke of Norfolk's cousin and ultimate heir and, what is more, a considerable landowner in the linked county of Suffolk, proves that the statutable property qualification had its roots firmly planted in local sentiment. All the other ducal candidates, and indeed all those elected for Norfolk in these years, were substantial men in the shire.[43] So substantial indeed as to raise an even more interesting question: how far were they at the

---

[42] *Paston Letters*, v. 178. This letter is fully dated.

[43] Sir Richard Harcourt might be counted an exception, since his lands lay for the most part elsewhere; but he had recently married a de la Pole who was the widow of Sir Miles Stapleton (M.P., Suffolk 1439-40, Norfolk 1442, 1449-50 and 1450-1; *Returns*, pt. i, pp. 333, 339 and 345; J. C. Wedgwood, *History of Parliament, Biographies of the Members of the Commons House, 1439-1509*, pp. 804-5) and was in possession of the Stapleton place at Ingham at the time of his election (Wedgwood, *op. cit.*, p. 419).

disposal of their magnate backers when they arrived at Westminster? Is it really justifiable, for example, to speak of them—the phrase is Mr. Richardson's—as 'credulous and willing to be led' once they had met together in the common house? I very much doubt it. It seems to me to assume a degree of subordination and a want of political training which nothing in their careers would lead one to expect. It is true that they were labelled feeble and hesitant by more whole-hogging chroniclers and satirists, but this was because they had the sense to come to terms with the king. Their critics would have been content with nothing less than a refusal to vote taxation altogether. If the knights preferred to bargain for such safeguards as the appropriation of their grants, only a monastic doctrinaire would have ascribed this to weakness. After all, were they not taxpayers themselves?

If there is any tendency to underrate the capacity of these early M.P.s it can be corrected by a study of their lives. Experienced administrators, rising lawyers and prosperous men of business were from at least the reign of Edward III onwards collected in the commons. Some were old parliamentary hands with half a dozen elections and more to their credit.[45] It is difficult to believe that these still felt any great awe in the presence of the king and lords. Though few, they preserved continuity in the frequent and short-lived parliaments of the fourteenth century. But experience gained elsewhere was commoner and could be just as valuable. Sir Peter de la Mare, whose sagacity and eloquence won him the admiration of all, was actually a newcomer to the house when he was chosen to speak for the commons in 1376. Anyone who showed fewer signs of being credulous and willing to be led, it would be difficult to imagine. He had served his apprenticeship at the council-table of the earl of March. There were many such training-grounds, and to others of less repute than de la Mare long lives of service brought opportunities for knowledge and for practice in debate. Few knights were not actively employed most of their lives in local government, and some, especially such early speakers as Sir James Pickering,[46] Sir William Sturmy[47] and Thomas Chaucer,[48] had quite outstanding and varied records in affairs of state. These were professional administrators. But they and their fellow knights were for the most part also well-to-do country-

---

[44] *John of Gaunt*, &c., p. 33.

[45] For example, in the parliament of 1399, four knights were sitting for the 6th time, two for the 7th, three for the 8th, one for the 9th, one for the 10th, two for the 12th (Sir Robert Neville of Hornby and Robert Urswyk) and one for the 19th (Sir William Bonville). These figures are derived from the *Returns*, pt. i, *passim*.

gentlemen, whose social position as much as their width of experience marked them out for leadership in the commons house.

What the position often was is clearly brought home to us by the records of two graduated taxes on incomes from land voted in the parliaments of 1411 and 1435. Each necessitated an *ad hoc* assessment and parts of both sets of returns have survived. Those made in 1436 were analysed a few years ago by Professor H. L. Gray. They reveal the existence of some ten commoners whose landed wealth was not much less than that of the average baron and of many more who were entitled to be classed in this respect with the lesser baronage.[49] The returns made in 1412 tell the same story in rather a different way.[50] It appears, for example, that there were in all fourteen Dorset land-owners—excluding the house of Lancaster, ecclesiastics and religious houses—whose estates in that and one or more of the adjacent counties of Hampshire, Wiltshire, Somerset and Devon were assessed at more than £200 a year (it is advisable to include the adjacent

[46] Speaker in the parliament of 1378 and February 1383, he was M.P. for Westmorland in 1362, 1365, October 1377, 1378, 1379 and October 1382, for Cumberland in 1368 and for Yorkshire in February 1383, November 1384, September 1388, November 1390 and 1397-8 (here and elsewhere, unless otherwise stated, the elections are taken from the Public Record Office copy of the *Returns*). He accompanied William of Windsor to Ireland in 1369 and was, as 'chief justice of the pleas following the lieutenant and the principal person of his secret council' accused by the Irish of corruption, extortion and malversation (M. V. Clarke, *Fourteenth-century studies*, 186, 206, 220-9 and 231-2). Thereafter until the end of the century the Chancery rolls abound with his commissions and appointments. See also the *D.N.B.* and N. B. Lewis, 'Re-election to parliament in the reign of Richard II', *Eng. Hist. Rev.*, xlviii (1933), 394.

[47] Sturmy or Esturmy (J. H. Wylie, *History of England under Henry the Fourth*, ii. 71, n.1) is not in the *D.N.B.* Speaker in the parliament of October 1404, he was M.P. for Hampshire in April 1384 and November 1390, for Wiltshire in January 1390, 1393, 1399, 1401, May 1413, November 1414, 1417 and 1422, and for Devon in November 1391 and October 1404. He was frequently Henry IV's enjoy to the German princes between 1401 and 1407. For information about him and about all others who sat in the parliament of 1422 I am deeply indebted to Mr. J. S. Roskell's Oxford D.Phil. Thesis, 'The Personnel of the House of Commons in 1422.'

[48] Speaker in the parliaments of 1407, 1410, 1411, November 1414 and May 1421, he sat for Oxfordshire in 1401, 1402, 1406, 1407, 1410, 1411, May 1413, November 1414, May 1421, 1422, 1426, 1427, 1429-30 and 1431. He was chief butler to Henry IV, Henry V and Henry VI, and after various employments was appointed a councillor in 1423 (*Rot. Parl.*, iv. 201). He died in 1434 (*D.N.B.;* see also R. Krauss, 'Chaucerian problems: especially the Petherton Forestership and the question of Thomas Chaucer' in *Three Chaucer studies* by R. Krauss, H. Braddy and C. R. Kase).

[49] 'Incomes from land in England in 1436', *Eng. Hist. Rev.*, xlix (1934), 620-1.

[50] *Rot. Parl.*, iii. 648-9; *Inquisitions and assessments relating to feudal aids, 1284-1431*, vi. 391-501 and 503-51. These returns may not give us the real value of a man's lands to him, but so long as they are only made a basis of comparison between one landowner and another, their absolute trustworthiness is immaterial.

districts in the reckoning, since a county boundary was itself no barrier
to the exercise of territorial influence; only great distances were). Of
these fourteen eight were peers and six were commoners. The
comparable figures for Sussex (taking account of lands in Kent, Surrey
and Hampshire) were four in all, two peers and two commoners.[51]

That is to say that there were in Dorset and Sussex together eight
non-baronial landlords entitled to be classed high among the great
ones of their shires. It is interesting, therefore, to find that all eight sat
as knights in parliament. At their head for wealth stood Sir Humphrey
Stafford the elder of Hooke in Dorset.[52] He was a cadet of the family
which was soon to be granted the dukedom of Buckingham and his
connection with the south-west was recent. He had married the widow
of one Sir John Mautravers, who had sat for Dorset in eight
consecutive parliaments at the beginning of Richard II's reign.[53] This
match had brought him the custody of large estates in Somerset and
Dorset, which he further secured to his descendants by marrying his
wife's daughter by Mautravers to his own son and heir. Along with Sir
John's manors, the Staffords can be said to have inherited his seat in
parliament. Sir Humphrey the elder was a knight of the shire at least
fourteen times, mostly for Dorset, between 1383 and 1410, sitting in all
but four of the parliaments for which the returns are known between
1388 and his death in 1413.[54] Thereafter his heir, who had already
represented Staffordshire in the 'long parliament' of 1406, was elected
ten times for Dorset before 1432.[55] The grandson of this Sir Humphrey
the younger was summoned as a baron to Edward VI's first
parliament and eventually created earl of Devon.[56] For more than a
century before this the Staffords had had the means to support at least
the humbler dignity. Exclusive of their lands in the midlands, they
were assessed at close on £600 a year in 1412.[57]

[51] For a list see Appendix, pages 74-9 below.

[52] S. W. Bates Harbin, *M.P.s for the county of Somerset*, 71-2; *Register of Henry
Chichele*, ed. E. F. Jacob, ii. 677.

[53] Bates Harbin, *op. cit.*, pp. 65-6. M.P. for Dorset, 1368, 1381, May 1382 and
October 1382; for Somerset, February 1383; for Dorset, October 1383, April 1384,
November 1384 and 1385. *Ob.* 1385 or '86.

[54] M.P., for Warwickshire, October 1383; for Wiltshire, November 1384; for Dorset,
September 1388, January 1390, 1391 and 1393; for Somerset, 1394; for Dorset, 1395,
January 1397, 1399, 1401, January 1404, 1406, 1407 and 1410.

[55] April 1414, November 1414, 1417, 1419, 1420, May 1421, 1422, 1426, 1427 and
1432. *Ob.* 1442 (*Chichele Reg.*, ii. 620-4 and 677; J. C. Wedgwood, *Staffordshire
parliamentary history*, William Salt Archaeological Soc., i. (1917), 165-6).

[56] G.E.C., *Complete Peerage*, iv. (1916), 327-8.

[57] £596 exclusive of Staffordshire lands made over to Sir Humphrey the younger
(*Feudal Aids*, vi. *passim*).

Erratum:

p. 14, n. 51, 'pages 74-9 below' should read '262-7 below'. The appendix to Chapter I is to be found at the end of the book.

Sir John Pelham, who was treasurer of England at the time, was said to be in possession of even more than £600 a year in 1412, but some of this may not have been his own.[58] An old supporter of the house of Lancaster, he owed his position to the king's favour. As the second largest non-ecclesiastical landowner in Sussex, he represented it in every parliament but one of Henry VI's reign for which returns survive, and at least twice afterwards.[59] Sir Thomas Brooke the elder, whose lands were mainly in Somerset, sat thirteen times or more for that county between 1386 and 1413, in all the most eventful parliaments of Richard II's majority.[60] His son, Sir Thomas the younger, was elected for Dorset in the first parliament of Henry V's reign and four times for Somerset between 1417 and 1427.[61] He had married the Cobham heiress, Sir John Oldcastle's step-daughter, and his son, Edward, after sitting for Somerset in 1442, was summoned to the lords in 1445.[62] Sir John Tiptoft, scarcely if at all less wealthy than Stafford and Pelham, was the heir of Sir Pain Tiptoft, M.P. for Cambridgeshire in 1399 and January 1404. Sir John had been in Bolingbroke's service before Richard's deposition and was one of the many gentlemen who profited largely from the change of dynasty.[63] He sat for the county of Huntingdon in both the parliaments of 1404 and, as speaker, in that of 1406. From 1406 to 1408 he was treasurer of the king's household and from 1408 to 1410 was treasurer of England. He represented Somerset in the Leicester parliament of 1414 and, after serving for most of Henry V's reign in France, returned in 1422 to become a member of the minority council and to sit from 1426 onwards among the lords.

Not all knights of the shire were as rich or as eminent as these. But in every parliament there was a nucleus of such men, often with one, two or even three ex-speakers among them,[64] not only skilled in business and ripe in counsel, but with a backing of landed wealth and

[58] £618-6-8 (*Ib.*).

[59] 1399, 1401, January 1404, October 1404, 1406 and 1407; 1422 and 1427. *Ob.* 1429 (*Cal. Fine Rolls*, xv. 236; *Cal. Inq. post mortem*, iv. 121; *Chichele Reg.*, ii, 408-9 and 669).

[60] Bates Harbin, *op. cit.*, 67-8: 1386, February 1388, 1391, 1393, 1395, January 1397, 1397-8, 1399, 1402, January 1404, 1407, 1410 and May 1413. *Ob.* 1417 (*Cal. Fine Rolls*, xiv. 196).

[61] 1417, May 1421, 1422 and 1427. Bates Harbin, *op. cit.*, pp. 84-5.

[62] G.E.C., *Complete Peerage*, iii (1913), 346; *Hist. of Parl., Biogs.*, pp. 115-116.

[63] *D.N.B.*

[64] The parliament of May 1382 had at least three (de la Mare, Hungerford and Waldegrave); so did those of October 1382 (de la Mare, Pickering and Waldegrave), February 1383 (de la Mare, Gildesborough and Waldegrave) and September 1388 (Hungerford, Pickering and Waldegrave).

influence to give that counsel weight even among the lords. Such
outstanding parliamentarians as Sir Walter Hungerford[65] and William
Burley of Broncroft[66] immediately spring to mind; or such families as
the Bonvilles of Shute,[67] the Montforts of Coleshill,[68] the Arundells of
Lanherne,[69] the Tyrells of Heron,[70] the Stourtons of Stourton,[71] the
Stanleys of Knowsley[72] and the Harringtons of Farleton and Hornby,[73]
to name but a few whose members often sat in the lower house. If
these men were independent and outspoken in criticism. and swayed
their fellow knights and burgesses, it is surely no matter for surprise.
They represented a powerful and respected element in the community
of every shire, and there was no need for them to stand in dread of the
great, for they were not small themselves. Their existence forbids us to
divide that society into powerful barons on the one hand and humble
commoners on the other, into leaders among the peers and led among
the knights. Even the greater magnates were not a class apart; they had
their place, if they could keep it, at the forefront only of a larger body

[65] Son of Sir Thomas Hungerford (speaker, January 1377, M.P. for Wiltshire, 1357),
1360, 1362 and January 1377; for Somerset, 1378; for Wiltshire, 1379; January 1380
and November 1380; for Somerset, May 1382; for Wiltshire, October 1383; for
Somerset and Wiltshire, April 1384; for Wiltshire, 1386; for Somerset, September
1388; for Somerset and Wiltshire, January 1390; for Somerset, November 1390; and
for Wiltshire, 1393. *Ob.* 1397 (*Cal. Fine Rolls*, xi. 268; *Cal. Inq. post mortem*, iii.
217).) M.P. for Wiltshire, 1401, October 1404 and 1407; for Somerset, 1410; for
Wiltshire, May 1413 and April 1414 (speaker). Summoned to the lords, 1426.
Treasurer of England, 1427-32. *Ob.* 1449 (*D.N.B.*).
[66] M.P. for Salop, 1417, 1419, 1420, May 1421, 1422, 1425, 1427-8, 1429-30, 1431,
1432, 1433, 1435, 1437 (speaker), 1439-40, 1442, 1445-6 (speaker), 1449-50, 1450-1 and
1455-6. *Ob.* 1459. His great-uncle was Sir Simon Burley, victim of the Lords Appellant
in 1388. His father, John Burley, was M.P. for Salop, 1399, 1401, January 1404,
October 1404, 1410 and 1411. (W. T. Weyman, 'Shropshire members of parliament
(1325-1584)' in *Trans. Shropshire Archaeol. and Nat. Hist. Soc.*, x and xi, nos. 89 and
98; *Hist. of Parl., Biogs.*, pp. 139-40; *D.N.B.*).
[67] Sir William Bonville (*c.* 1340-1408), M.P. for Somerset, 1366; for Devon, 1371,
1376, 1378, 1379, November 1380, 1381-2, May 1382 and October 1382; for Somerset,
October 1383; for Devon and Somerset, April 1384; for Somerset, November 1384,
1386, February 1388, 1393 and 1395; for Devon, January 1397 and 1397-8; for
Somerset 1399; and for Devon, 1402. (Bates Harbin, *op. cit.*, pp. 54-5).) His grandson
and heir, Sir William, was M.P. for Somerset, May 1421; for Devon, 1422, 1425 and
1427-8. Afterwards Lord Bonville (1449). *Ob.* 1461. (Bates Harbin, *op. cit.*, pp. 87-9).
His brother, Thomas, was M.P. for Cornwall, 1439-40. (*Hist. of Parl. Biogs.*, p. 92.)
[68] Sir John Montfort, M.P. for Warwickshire, 1361. His grandson and heir, Sir
William (1385-1452), M.P. for Warwickshire, 1422, 1423-4, 1427-8, 1429-30, 1437,
1445-6 and 1450-1. He married the daughter of Sir John Pecche, M.P. for Warwickshire, August 1352, 1354, 1358 and 1373. Sir William's younger son, Sir Edmund, was
M.P. for Warwickshire, 1447 and 1459; for Gloucestershire, 1491-2. Sir Simon, son
and heir of Sir William's eldest son, Sir Baldwin, was M.P. for Warwickshire, 1463-5,
1478 and 1491-2. (W. Dugdale, *Antiquities of Warwickshire* (1656), pp. 728-32; *Hist.
of Parl., Biogs.*, pp. 602-4).

of men, landed and gently-born, in the middle ranks of whom peer and commoner jostled together. The recipient of a personal summons to parliament was expected to have the means to support his rank, but the means alone were not sufficient to earn it; that required military and political services. The Staffords and the Stourtons, in spite of their wealth, had to wait, while the Hungerfords and the Tiptofts moved up rapidly; not, however, across some social gulf dividing masters from men; only higher in the same class. It is this community of aim and outlook which made it difficult for lords and commons to disagree violently or for long in parliament; not the ties of service by which some have set so much store. Without such a community, the ties would not have held, for they had very little strength.

Late medieval lordship, indeed, has not much in common with feudal *dominium*.[74] When a man asked another to be his 'good lord', he was not commending himself and his land; nor did he become anything remotely like a vassal. Rather he was acquiring a temporary

[69] Sir John Arundell, M.P. for Cornwall, January 1397, 1397-8, January 1404, October 1404, 1406, 1411, April 1414, March 1416, 1417, May 1421, 1422 and 1423-4. *Ob.* 1435. His son and heir, John (*ob. v. p.* 1423) was M.P. for Devon, November 1414; for Cornwall, 1419, December 1421 and 1422. Sir John's younger son, Sir Remfrey, was M.P. for Cornwall, 1431, 1433 and 1442. (*Hist. of Parl., Biogs.,* pp. 19-20).

[70] Sir Thomas Tyrell, M.P. for Essex, 1365, 1366, 1369, 1372 and 1373. His grandson, Sir John Tyrell, M.P. for Essex, 1411, May 1413, March 1416, 1417, 1419, May 1421, 1422 and 1425; for Hertfordshire, 1427-8; and for Essex, 1429, 1431, 1433 and 1437 (speaker, 1427, 1431 and 1437). (*D.N.B.*) His son and heir, Sir Thomas, M.P. for Essex, 1442, 1447, February 1449 and 1459. Sir John's 2nd son, William, was M.P. for Suffolk, 1447 and 1459 and *his* son and heir, Sir James, was M.P. for Cornwall, 1478. Sir John's fifth son, Sir William, was M.P. for Weymouth, February 1449; for Essex, 1449-50, 1450-1 and 1455-6. (*Hist. of Parl., Biogs.,* pp. 889-94).

[71] See Appendix, Table A.

[72] Sir John Stanley, M.P. for Lancashire, May 1413 and November 1414. *Ob.* 1437. His son and heir, Sir Thomas Stanley, M.P. for Lancashire, 1427-28, 1433, 1439-40, 1442, 1447, February 1449, 1449-50, 1450-1, 1453-4, 1455-6. Lord Stanley 1456. *Ob.* 1459. His grandson, Sir George, was M.P. for Lancashire, 1478. Lord Strange 1482. *Ob.* 1503. (J. S. Roskell, *Knights of the shire for Lancashire*, Chetham Soc., pp. 123-8 and 162-72; *Hist. of Parl., Biogs.,* pp. 796-7 and 800).

[73] Sir Nicholas Harrington of Farleton (second son of Sir John, M.P. for Lancashire, 1343, 1352 and 1357), M.P. for Lancashire, 1372, October, 1377, 1379, 1386 and 1402. *Ob. c.* 1403. His second son, James, M.P. for Lancashire, October 1404, was the father of Sir Richard, M.P. for Lancashire, 1450-1, 1453-4 and 1459. Sir Nicholas's grandson and ultimate heir, Sir Thomas, was M.P. for Lancashire, 1432, 1437, 1442, 1447 and February 1449; and for Yorkshire, 1455-6. His son and heir, Sir James, was M.P. for Lancashire, 1467-8 and 1478. Sir Thomas's second son, Sir Robert, was M.P. for Lancashire, 1472-5. (J. S. Roskell, *op. cit.,* pp. 33-8, 103-6, 179-86 and 195-8; *Hist. of Parl., Biogs.,* pp. 423-7).

[74] On this subject see H. M. Cam, 'The decline and fall of English feudalism' in *History*, xxv (1940), 216-33.

patron. In this loosely-knit and shamelessly competitive society, it was the ambition of every thrusting gentleman—and also of anyone who aspired to gentility—to attach himself for as long as suited him to such as were in a position to further his interests. For those who wished to rise in the world, good lordship was essential. A successful man, therefore, gathered about him what was sometimes called his 'affinity'; those who staked their hopes on a share of his good fortune. And since *his* chances of winning his desires increased as his following grew, he in his turn used all the arts at his command to attract useful men to his service. It was a partnership to their mutual advantage, a contract from which both sides expected to benefit. And so around the hard core of household and estate officials there accumulated a vast but indefinite mass of councillors, retainers and servants, tailing off into those who were believed to be well-wishers. These were the 'bastard feudatories.'

All this is familiar enough. But it is still necessary to emphasise the political consequences which followed from the impermanence of these associations. Lordship lasted only so long as it was found to be *good* lordship or until it was ousted by a better. As John Paston the younger told his brother in 1475, 'I have given my lady [of Norfolk] warning that I will do my lord no more service; but ere we parted she made me to make her promise that I should let her have knowledge ere I fastened myself in any other service; and so I departed.[75] A few years earlier he had given his mother no thanks for obtaining for him Lord Scales's good lordship, 'whereof I am nothing proud.[76] Many instances could be collected from the *Paston Letters* to illustrate the want of settled loyalty which marked these contracts of service. Those changes of allegiance which have been noted by Tout in the careers of Bushy, Bagot and Green, Richard II's notorious agents, do not seem to have been exceptional.[77] There is not even much sign, though it may perhaps be glimpsed in Paston's promise to the duchess, that any sense of the decencies of public life had yet developed to replace the feudal oath. There were few who in that period clung to one family through good and bad fortune. They might fight for their lords in the gamble for power, but desertion often followed defeat. Watching which way to jump, most, like the Pastons themselves, cultivated friends in every camp and turned the least change in the balance of forces to immediate account.[78] It is, therefore, to the last degree unlikely that when they came to parliament, they were more reliable.

[75] *Paston Letters*, v. 240.   [76] *Ib.*, v. 106.
[77] T. F. Tout, *Chapters in the administrative history of medieval England*, iv. 12-14.

Some have jibbed, and, I think, rightly jibbed, at the use of the word 'party' to describe these political groups. The 'affinity' had little in common with the modern party; but it did, it seems to me, in many ways resemble the eighteenth-century 'connection', so fully anatomised by Professor Namier. There was the same element of voluntary interdependence, the same competition for 'place' and the same absence of any separate fund of political principle. Held together by little else than the hope of gain, these affinities swelled with success and dwindled in adversity. Their management must have called for the exercise of considerable art, knowledge and force of character. The tactful handling of many different types of men came easily no doubt to some magnates. But is it likely that the gift of political leadership was possessed by all or even by most? I should be reluctant to go so far with Professor Galbraith as to think that 'the members of the ruling class were *in general* men of arrested intellectual development, who looked to those below them in the social scale for the intelligence necessary to order and govern society.[79] One can exaggerate the political immaturity of this warrior class. As Mr. Galbraith himself reminds us in another connection, a chronicler could say that 'the temporal lords always feared John of Gaunt because of his power, his prudence and his extraordinary ability.[80] Nevertheless I believe it to be true that the directing brain behind the activities of a baronial household and its extensive connections was not always that of its nominal head. As Pecock remarks in his *Repressor*, there were great lords and ladies who 'could not reckon a sum into a hundred shillings, and who for that reason had to find 'officers under them for to attend sufficiently to all the worldly needs of their lands.'[81] Such men were bound to be to some extent in the hands of their councillors and civil servants for more important matters than estates management and some would be so entirely. Edward IV is reported to have said to Sir William Brandon, one of the duke of Norfolk's council: 'Brandon, though thou can beguile the duke of Norfolk and bring him about the

---

[78] *Paston Letters*, ii. 80 contains an amusing account of one Steward's predicament: 'He enquired me', wrote Edmund Paston, 'of the rule of my master Daniel and my lord of Suffolk, and asked which I thought should rule in this shire; and I said, both, as I trow, and he that surviveth to hold by virtue of the survivor, and he to thank his friends and to acquit his enemies. So I feel by him he would forsake his master and get him a new, if he wist he should rule; and so, ween I, much of all the country is so disposed.'

[79] 'A new life of Richard II,' *History*, xxvi (1942), 227. My italics.

[80] *Ib.*, p. 229.

[81] Reginald Pecock's *Repressor of over-much blaming of the clergy*, ed. C. Babington (Rolls Series), ii. 306.

thumb as thou list, I let thee weet thou shalt not do me so, for I understand thy false dealing well enough'; and the account of the interview continues, 'for he told him that he knew well enough that he might rule my lord of Norfolk as he would; and if my lord did anything that were contrary to his laws, the king told him he knew well enough that it was by nobody's means but by his.'[82] Like other members of Norfolk's council, Sir William Brandon sat in the house of commons. The Brandons of that world usually did. Is it therefore certain that the chroniclers were mistaken when they gave the credit for leadership in the 'good parliament' to speaker de la Mare and not to the earl of March, a young and not particularly distinguished soldier, who in the event showed himself something of a coward?[83] Even the sagacious Gaunt is said to have planned his campaign against the commons in 1376 with the advice of his *privati homines;* and when he railed furiously at the presumptuousness of the knights, it was one of his own esquires who is credited with the rebuke which brought him to his senses.[84] To argue in such circumstances that the initiative always came from the lords is surely to enter the world of fantasy indeed.

The interdependence of magnates and gentry meant that the English body politic in the later middle ages was a complex organism and it would be doing no service to truth to emphasise the share of any one part in the working of the whole. Power was not concentrated in the hands of a few. It was distributed among kings, magnates and commons in various and varying degrees, according to each man's wealth, affiliations and political capacity. A baron inherited rank and great possessions to do with what he could. They gave him vast opportunities had he the wits to use them. But he was dependent upon the goodwill, the confidence and the co-operation of his less rich but still substantial neighbours, many of whom were better educated, more experienced and more prudent than he was himself. Politics were a joint-stock enterprise and he and his advisers had got to make them pay. If they failed, there were always keen competitors ready to enlist the services of those who thought themselves ill-rewarded, slighted or badly led. These are the circumstances in the light of which the evidence for the Norfolk elections must be read. The ramifications of that intricate network of personal relationships, constantly changing and forming fresh patterns, will never be fully traced, but as we make ourselves familiar with the lives and achievements of the country

---

82 *Paston Letters*, v. 31.
83 *Chronicon Angliae*, ed. E. M. Thompson (Rolls Series), pp. 107-8.
84 *Ib.*, pp. 74-5.

gentry, and especially of those who sat in the commons, the main outlines of local and central politics may be expected to emerge.

II. 'BASTARD FEUDALISM'[1]

THE name was, I believe, coined by Charles Plummer; and first appeared in print in his introduction to an edition, published in 1885, of Fortescue's overrated and misleading pamphlet on the *Governance of England*.[2] Let me recall the passage to you:

> The reign of Edward III was . . . the period of that pseudo-chivalry, which, under a garb of external splendour and a factitious code of honour, failed to conceal its ingrained lust and cruelty, and its reckless contempt for the rights and feelings of all who were not admitted within the charmed circle; and it saw the beginning of that bastard feudalism, which, in place of the primitive relation of a lord to his tenants, surrounded the great man with a horde of retainers, who wore his livery and fought his battles, and were, in the most literal sense of the words, in the law courts and elsewhere,
>
> 'Addicti jurare in verba magistri';
>
> while he in turn maintained their quarrels and shielded their crimes from punishment. This evil, as we shall see, reached its greatest height during the Lancastrian period.

Now it is all too clear from this that Plummer, surveying the middle ages from the comfortable security of Victorian Oxford, meant 'bastard feudalism' to be a term of abuse. For him 'bastard' means 'misbegotten, debased, corrupted, degenerate.' Without, however, subscribing to his judgement of value, we can still find a use for the phrase if we understand 'bastard' in the sense—authorised by the Oxford English Dictionary—of 'having the appearance of, somewhat resembling.' For we need some such label to describe the society which was emerging from feudalism in the early part of the fourteenth century, when most if not all of its ancient features survived, even though in many cases as weak shadows of themselves, but when the tenurial bond between lord and vassal had been superseded as the primary social tie by the personal contract between master and man. If 'bastard feudalism' is understood not as a kind of feudalism, however

---

[1] This paper was read to a group of French and English historians at the Institute in September, 1945. I have added the necessary minimum of references and a few supplementary illustrations.

[2] p. 15-6.

modified, but as something essentially different while superficially similar, then it aptly describes the social order in England in the two centuries following the death of Edward I.

Feudalism, if it is to have any recognisable meaning, implies the organisation of society upon a basis of tenure. In a feudal society the principal unit is the fief, 'an estate in land (in England always a heritable estate) held on condition of homage and service to a superior lord.' Whether in England service, even military service, was ever wholly or indeed mainly a matter of tenure, I leave to others to decide. But by the fourteenth century it had largely ceased to be so, at any rate for the free man. In every direction the incidents of service were being commuted for money payments or rents. And by the end of the fifteenth century even servile tenures were rapidly disappearing. Feudalism still existed formally intact, but was becoming for all practical purposes a complex network of marketable privileges and duties attached to the ownership of land, with little or no importance as a social force. It was there, and indeed remained so for centuries to come—all-pervasive but inactive—in the background, while the new order of patronage, liveries and affinities occupied the front of the stage, as it was to do in England throughout the fourteenth and fifteenth centuries, with an epilogue which far outran so-called medieval times. It is this new order that we call 'bastard feudalism.' Its quintessence was payment for service. The idea of lordship was retained, but because it was divorced from tenure it was a lordship which had undergone a scarcely visible process of transubstantiation, leaving all but a few of its accidents unchanged.

The origin of the practice of substituting paid for unpaid service still remains untraced in detail. But its most significant stage was reached when the need was felt for an army more efficient and more durable than the feudal host. Already in the eleventh and twelfth centuries it had been found necessary to supplement the native levies with hired foreign mercenaries; and although their employment was contrary to Magna Carta the presence of continental adventurers in the royal pay can be found under both Henry III and Edward I. It was the latter king, however, who seems first to have extended the practice systematically to his English troops.[3] According to J. E. Morris, who was the pioneer in this still neglected field, the earliest cases of the mobilisation of native soldiers for service in return for wages,

---

[3] J. Smyth, *Lives of the Berkeleys* (ed. J. Maclean), i. 92, cites what appears to be an isolated earlier example, 29 June 1213. Robert Berkeley covenanted to furnish John with ten knights in France for a year for 500 marks.

'contract being reasonably inferred from the details, occur in 1277.' These novel arrangements seem to have been settled verbally and 'wages were issued for 40 days at a time, clearly in imitation of the feudal forty.[4] Edward made his contracts with a number of his greater barons, those evidently whose abilities and loyalty he trusted, and left them to make sub-contracts with the members of their respective contingents. The oldest known example of such a sub-contract in writing, one between Edmund Mortimer and Peter Maulay, was sealed at Wigmore in the summer of 1287;[5] and a very few more have survived from the last years of the thirteenth century.[6]

Considering how grudgingly the old military service had been performed, it was not to be expected that much reluctance would be shown at accepting the king's pay and the transformation was rapid and complete. Only a small number of the greater feudatories, most of them earls, seem to have thought it beneath their dignity to receive money for what they owed gratuitously and to have stood out for the scrupulous performance of their tenurial obligations. But this was only a temporary stand, prompted perhaps by the fear of losing their pre-eminence in the common ruck of mercenary captains, and was soon abandoned. Feudal conservatism so disadvantageous to its upholders had no future and already in the Welsh and Scottish campaigns of the 1280's and 1290's we find most of them quite contentedly drawing pay.[7] In little more than a generation they had all succumbed. The summons of the feudal host for the last time in 1327 caused so much irritation and administrative inconvenience that it was generally recognised that this method of raising an army was obsolete. Scutage followed it into disuse; the poor yield from this 'antiquated and detested due', compared with that derived from lavish parliamentary subsidies, made it not worth the trouble of collection.[8]

At first the contracts between the king and the captains of troops were, as I have said, concluded orally. It is not until Edward III's campaign of 1341 that the later practice of embodying the terms of the agreement in an indenture became a general rule. Henceforward these documents were regularly drawn up and are still preserved in large

---

4 *Welsh Wars of Edward I*, pp. 68-9.

5 N. B. Lewis, 'An early indenture of military service, 27 July 1287', *ante*, xiii. 85-9.

6 For example see *Calendar of Documents relating to Scotland*, ed. J. Bain, ii, no. 905 (cf. nos. 981 and 1004), and N. Denholm-Young, *Seignorial Administration in England*, pp. 167-8.

7 Morris, *op. cit.*, pp. 74-80 and 276-9.

8 *English Government at Work, 1327-1336*, ed. J. F. Willard and W. A. Morris, p. 345.

numbers among the records of the medieval Exchequer. They follow a fairly stereotyped pattern and deal with such matters as 'the strength and composition of the contingents to be brought, the period and place of service, the rate of wages and bonus, compensation for lost horses, liability for . . . [the expenses] of transport and division of the "advantages of war", that is the ransom of prisoners and the tenure of captured castles.'[9] You will find them exhaustively discussed in relation to military organisation in two valuable papers by Mr. A. E. Prince.[10] For the social historian they have two features of exceptional importance. In the first place it is clear that they safeguarded the captains against serious loss on campaign and offered them the chance of considerable profit. I shall return to this point later. Secondly they are in almost all cases contracts of service for very brief periods, rarely for more than a year, generally for half a year and often for only a quarter. In this they differ markedly from the indentures of sub-contract which have survived. Here, as might be expected of documents which derive from many different baronial chanceries, there is a great deal of variety both in form and content. But with a few exceptions they have one characteristic in common, that they are contracts for life, appearing in this to give to the new order a stability in which by contrast with a feudal society it was otherwise singularly lacking.

'Bastard feudalism' thus rapidly developed its own diplomatic. Its peculiar instruments were not the charter of enfeoffment but the indenture and the letter patent; these created not hereditary tenants but feed retainers and pensioners for a term of years. The indenture of retainer was a compact between X and Y by which X grants Y an annual fee in return for which Y promises some form of service commonly for as long as both live but not binding upon the heirs of either. Until recently these sub-contracts have not attracted the study they deserve; many of them are not yet in print and have been very

---

[9] N. B. Lewis, *op. cit.*, p. 86.

[10] 'The Indenture System under Edward III', in *Historical Essays in honour of James Tait*, ed. J. G. Edwards, V. H. Galbraith and E. F. Jacob, pp. 283-97, and 'The Army and Navy', in *English Government at Work, 1327-1336*, pp. 332-93. See also his 'The Strength of English Armies in the reign of Edward III', in *English Hist. Review*, xlvi (1931), 353-71.

[11] This is a rough estimate only. There are 95 military indentures (excluding renewals) in the duke's printed *Registers* (vols. i and ii, ed. S. Armitage-Smith; iii and iv, ed. R. Somerville, Camden Soc. 3rd ser. xx, xxi, lvi and lvii). In addition there are 42 confirmations by the king of other indentures of his in the *Calendar of Patent Rolls, 1367-99, passim* (esp. 1396-1399). The latter source also contains most of the indentures made by others, but a certain number will be found in the *Reports of the Commission on Historical MSS*. The *Calendar of Patent Rolls* generally does not give adequate details.

imperfectly calendared. Their haphazard and patchy survival is no doubt in part to blame. If it had not been for the usurpation of 1399 which added the private records of the house of Lancaster to the royal archives and so secured their preservation we should have very little knowledge of the indenture of retainer. As it is, of those which have found their way into print for the period 1327 to 1485—in all less than 200—something like two-thirds are derived from the semi-royal chancery of John of Gaunt.[11] It still remains doubtful therefore how widespread in time and space the practice of retaining for life extended. The owner of a great palatinate, a royal prince and a titular king cannot be lightly accepted as typical. But the other survivals, many of them confirmed in the chancery and so copied on to the patent rolls, follow the same model so closely (except in detail) as to make it highly probable that most at least of the captains contemporary with Gaunt adopted to some degree the same method of recruitment. The Black Prince certainly did though few of his contracts have been found;[12] and a small number of indentures of retainer by such Riccardian magnates as Edmund, duke of York,[13] Richard, earl of Arundel,[14] Edmund, earl of March,[15] Thomas, earl of Warwick[16] and Thomas, earl of Nottingham[17] has been preserved and all approximate to a pattern which had already been fully elaborated at least as early as 1297.[18] But it is more than likely that only the nucleus of the retinue which accompanied each to the king's wars was composed of men who had made a life contract of service; and there is evidence that this was true even of John of Gaunt's retinue itself, for men are found under his command on expeditions who were not in the narrow sense his retainers.[19] The duke of Lancaster could, however, put a large army into the field without going outside those already on his books. We have a list of the men, all of whom were probably

[12] *Register of Edward the Black Prince*, ii. 34 and 45-6; iii. 475-7; and iv. 288 and 311. *Cal. Pat. Rolls, 1374-1377*, p. 298; *1377-1381*, pp. 155, 161, 192, 239, 249 and 345; *1381-1385*, p. 112; *1388-1392*, p. 71; *1391-1396*, pp. 582-3; *1399-1401*, pp. 16, 22 and 75. *Hist. MSS. Com. Rept., Middleton*, p. 98.

[13] *Cal. Pat. Rolls, 1405-1408*, pp. 12 and 16.

[14] *Ibid., 1396-1399*, p. 255.

[15] *Ibid., 1381-1385*, pp. 99, 116 and 119; *1401-1405*, p. 229.

[16] *Ibid., 1381-1385*, pp. 238, and 277-8; *1391-1396*, pp. 465-6.

[17] Ibid., *1399-1401*, pp. 28, 196 and 224-5; *1405-1408*, p. 29. For one by Thomas of Woodstock see *ibid., 1399-1401*, p. 117; and two by John, duke of Exeter, *ibid.*, pp. 244 and 255.

[18] N. Denholm-Young, *op. cit.*, pp. 167-8.

[19] One example must suffice: Sir Baldwin Berford who went abroad with him in 1373 (*Register*, i, no. 50) was retained for life by the Black Prince and subsequently by his son, Richard II (*Cal. Pat. Rolls, 1391-1396*), pp. 582-3). Sir Baldwin 'le filz' was there too and was *later* retained by Gaunt (*Register*, iii, no. 46).

retained for life, in his service between 1379 and 1383,[20] this consists of seven bannerets, 83 knights, and 112 esquires, making a total of 202. If we added to these the esquires, men-at-arms and horse-archers that many of them were expected to bring with them we shall have little difficulty in arriving at the figure of 1,500 which was for example the size of Lancaster's personal contingent to the expedition of 1373.[21] On the other hand it is scarcely credible that the 14 knights, 65 esquires and 120 horse-archers with which the soldier of fortune, Sir Thomas Dagworth, contracted to serve in Brittany in 1346-7, were permanently fed by him in time of peace; his East Anglian estates were too few and too poor to support such a burden.[22]

So far I have been dealing with the fourteenth century. The rarity of life indentures of retainer for the second half of the Hundred Years War may be accidental, but there is other evidence to suggest that under the Lancastrians less permanent forms of contract were coming into favour. With the outbreak of the Wars of the Roses, however, and the competitive recruitment that may be assumed to have been necessary, life indentures again became more numerous. One case may be cited: an interesting document among the Hastings MSS., compiled in 1474-5, gives the names of two barons, nine knights, 58 esquires and 20 gentlemen, being

> such persons as by indenture, of their own free wills and mere motions, covenanted, belast (= bound) and faithfully promised to aid and assist the right honourable William Lord Hastings and his part to take against all persons within this realm of England during their lives as well in peace as wars, their allegiance to the King's majesty, his heirs and successors only reserved and excepted; with so many able persons as every of them might well make to be furnished and arrayed at the costs and charges of the said Lord; for the which the said Lord promised them to be their good and true lord in all things reasonable; and them to aid and succour in all their rightful causes so far forth as law, equity and conscience required.[23]

[20] *Ibid.*, iii. 6-13. This list seems to have been compiled about 1379-80 and then added to from time to time later. It does not represent Gaunt's retinue at any one time therefore, but is slightly on the large side. A good deal of work would be necessary to make it more accurate without making it completely so.

[21] A. E. Prince, *Eng. Hist. Rev.*, xlvi (1931), 370.

[22] *Ibid.*, p. 364.

[23] W. Dugdale, *Baronage of England*, i. 583.

[24] *Register*, i, no. 836; iii, no. 48.

[25] *Ibid.*, i, no. 818. For clerks see *ibid.*, nos. 783 and 828.

[26] *Ibid.*, iii, no. 55.

[27] *Ibid.*, i, nos. 797-8. John Raynald was a master-cook and an esquire.

[28] *Ibid.*, ii, nos. 859-62. Cf. *Cal. Pat. Rolls, 1413-1416*, pp. 132 and 137.

Bastard feudalism was clearly very much alive in the later years of Edward IV's reign.

Although military service or a combination of menial service in peace time with military service in war were among the commonest objects of these agreements, many other kinds are known. Tenure by serjeanty was another feudal institution in decline; household officers, both royal and baronial, and civil servants of all kinds, had now become stipendiaries, and their engagements were often sealed by an indenture. John of Gaunt, for example, entered into indentures of retainer for life with his surgeons,[24] his chaplains,[25] his falconer,[26] his cook[27] and his minstrels,[28] and to this list can be added from other retinues besides the usual domestic and estate officials[29] such people as heralds[30] and counsel learned in the law.[31] The detailed conditions and rates of remuneration could vary enormously. Even the feudal duty which made the greater barons the king's natural councillors was affected by the prevailing influence, and by the fifteenth century there had grown up a regular tariff for the payment of members of the continual council: for a duke £200 a year, for an earl 200 marks, for a baron, banneret or knight £100.[32] Councillors, however, continued to be appointed and sworn, but not indentured. Only the unpaid attendance of the peers in parliament preserved a vestige of feudal service which has lasted down to our own time.

The indenture was not in any case the only means employed to take formal note of these subfeudal relationships. With its clear statement of the *quid pro quo* it is merely the most characteristic. At first sight more one-sided and non-committal were those even commoner letters patent by which X granted Y, perhaps for good service done or to be done, though more often for no stated reason whatsoever, an annuity or an estate for life. These annuities, like the fees promised to retainers, were generally to be paid from the receipts of some particular manor or lordship belonging to the grantor upon which the beneficiary could distrain in the event of non-payment or undue delay. There thus came into existence between a great lord and those who actually cultivated his estates a class of pensioners resembling the mesne tenants of the old feudalism. By this method many who had no

---

[29] Master of the robes: *Hist. MSS. Com. Rept., R. R. Hastings,* i. 198-9; Chamberlain: *Cal. Pat. Rolls, 1399-1401,* p. 234; 'Lardyner, catour and cook': *Ancient Deeds,* iii, no. D 1172; servitor: *Cal. Pat. Rolls, 1461-1467,* p. 136; 'to perform divine service in the new tower of Southampton and to keep the armoury there and control all works within Southampton castle': *ibid., 1422-1429,* p. 48.

[30] *Ibid., 1381-1385,* p. 158.

[31] *Ibid.,* p. 94.

[32] J. F. Baldwin, *King's Council in England during the Middle Ages,* p. 175.

tenurial connection with their patron were at least given a territorial one.[33]

In many cases the annuitants were already the feed retainers of their lord and the patent merely brought them additional reward; but just as often they were not. Over and above his indented retinue (the hard core as it were of his affinity, a great man therefore was the patron and paymaster of a swarm of hangers-on, both men and women, not bound to do him exclusive service but in receipt of his bounty in ways both more and less permanent. For we can trace scores who were the simultaneous pensioners of several lords. As an example let me quote that rising Yorkist esquire William Hastings, whose retinue when he became a magnate was mentioned above. In April 1457 he was granted by Duke Richard 'for good and faithful service done and to be done' an annuity of £10 a year 'to the end he should serve him before all others and attend him at all times required, his allegiance to the kind excepted.' The last proviso is not likely to have caused him much trouble in 1461. We are told that he stood so high in the esteem of Edward IV that in the first year of the new reign 'sundry persons of honour taking notice thereof bestowed their favours on him.' From the duke of Norfolk he received the stewardship of his manors in Leicestershire with a fee of £10 a year for life, from Anne duchess of Buckingham the stewardship of the manor of Oakham with the constablewick of the castle there for life, from John lord Lovel the stewardship of two manors in Leicestershire with a yearly fee of £10 for life, from Sir Henry Stafford an annuity of £20 for life and from the Woodvilles (not yet allied to the house of York) an annuity of 40 marks.[34] Thus were trusted royal servants courted throughout the later middle ages.

And not only royal servants; men of ability of all kinds, soldiers,

---

[33] To give one example: on 9 May 1388 Sir Thomas Gerberge of co. Norfolk was retained for life by Edmund, duke of York, as steward of his household and to 'work' with him in war; he was to receive in peace time 40 marks a year from the manor of Somerford Keynes, co. Wilts. (*Cal. Pat. Rolls, 1405-1408*, p. 12). Some lords must have greatly reduced their net income by this practice; thus on 18 October 1379 the earl of March charged the revenues of Clifford and Glasbury in the March with 100 marks a year for one retainer and about the same time with 50 marks a year for another (*ibid., 1381-1385*, pp. 99 and 119). Similarly on 29 and 31 March 1383 the earl of Warwick granted away £40 p.a. and £20 p.a. from his manor of Chedworth, co. Gloucester (*ibid.*, pp. 238 and 277-8). Sometimes a manor was demised for life, as when Thomas lord Roos retained Sir John Cressy of Dodford, co. Northants, and granted him the manor of Braunston in the county and 20 marks p.a. from the manor of Eakring, co. Notts, 12 November 1429 (*ibid., 1429-1436*, p. 330).

[34] W. Dugdale, *op. cit.*, i. 580.   [35] *Cal. Pat. Rolls, 1396-1399, passim.*
[36] *Ibid., 1413-1422, passim.*

lawyers, clerks and professional administrators had many anxious to be their good lords and to pay for the privilege. It is unreasonable to suppose that their loyalties were either indivisible or deeply engaged. Or had bastard feudalism its own equivalent to liege homage, a primary duty of obedience to the man by whom you were retained? There are signs that patrons hoped so, as in the case of the duke of York and William Hastings. But even the crown seemed doubtful of enforcing it. Between April and June 1399 Richard II confirmed a score of patents and indentures, mostly John of Gaunt's, on the express condition that the recipient was 'retained to stay with the king only.'[35] This was on the eve of the almost completely unopposed seizure of the crown by Henry of Bolingbroke. The latter's son, Henry V, similarly confirmed all royal grants with the proviso 'as long as he be not retained by anyone else.'[36] If so strong a king was thus equally doubtful of making his service exclusive, lesser men can have had slender hopes of success. This absence or at least degeneration of the notion of liege homage is as much a feature of bastard feudalism as is the loss of that stability which the tenurial relation may be presumed to have maintained in earlier times. A man was allowed greater freedom of choice at every stage in the pursuit of his own interests.

That freedom had nevertheless some limits. It might be curtailed in times of civil commotion by the need for the protection of a powerful neighbour. Not to be of the duke of Suffolk's affinity in East Anglia in the 1440's was to ask for trouble. But even then the future was so uncertain: not for nothing was the wheel of fortune one of the most popular symbols of life in those times. So felt a certain man called Steward whose predicament in 1447 is embalmed in one of the *Paston Letters:* 'he enquired me', wrote Edmund Paston, 'of the rule of my master Daniel and my lord of Suffolk, and asked which I thought should rule in this shire; and I said, both, as I trow, and he that surviveth to hold by the virtue of the survivor, and he to thank his friends and to acquit his enemies. So I feel by him he would forsake his master and get him a new, if he wist he should rule; and so, ween I, much of all the country is so disposed.'[37] Once again it is the *Paston Letters* which give us real insight into the minds of that most unfeudal society. Suffolk was in the ascendant and his opponents were afraid; even so there were those farsighted or foolhardy enough to hold aloof, not to mention the cautious 'ambidexters' who sought to keep in with everyone. Nevertheless fear might work where loyalty would not.

Again a man's choice of master was, it is obvious, often powerfully

---

[37] Ed. J. Gairdner (1904 edn.), ii. 80.

influenced by traditional and tenurial association. Many of John of Gaunt's retainers were, as might have been expected, his tenants; but by this date tenurial relations were so interwoven that a man with several manors could scarcely avoid holding them of nearly as many lords. Yet if their ancestors had been bound in feudal times by close ties to a particular family there was a natural presumption that, given favourable circumstances, the tradition would survive. The house of Lancaster could point to not a few examples of several generations of the same family in its service; Dipres, Hungerford, Roos, Bereford and Botiller. It is, however, risky to argue to the general from such an untypical particular; one would scarcely expect the gentlemen of say the county of Lancaster, over which John of Gaunt enjoyed regalian rights, to refuse the chance of a share in so profitable a joint-stock enterprise or to fail to follow their fathers into membership of it if offered the opportunity. Yet there were several landowners in the palatinate who preferred to go their own way, Sir Thomas Lathom, for example, his son-in-law, Sir John Stanley, and Sir Robert Clifton during Richard II's reign. The last named is a particularly interesting case since he was M.P. for the county in the parliaments of May 1382 and February 1383; yet not only was he never in the duke's service but he was arrested in 1388 for his connection with Robert de Vere's Radcot Bridge adventure and as far as his career can be traced was always a malcontent.[38] Gaunt therefore did not have it all his own way even at the very centre of his influence. It is doubtful whether other affinities were as alluring as his—and they were certainly less prosperous.

Mere neighbourhood seems to have been nearly as strong an attraction as tenure and tradition. Fourteenth century society was strongly provincial and men believed that compatriots, those who came from the same 'country' as they called each district, should stand

[38] J. S. Roskell, *Knights of the shire for the County Palatine of Lancaster, 1377-1460*, pp. 51-3. Mr. Roskell is almost certainly mistaken in identifying this Sir Robert Clifton with the man of the same name who was retained for life by John of Gaunt on 9 May 1373 (*Register*, ii, no. 863). The latter was more probably the son and heir of Sir Gervase Clifton of a Nottinghamshire family who was sick and aged in July 1388 and died shortly afterwards (*Cal. Close Rolls, 1369-1374*, p. 567; *ibid.*, *1385-1389*, p. 516; *1389-1392*, p. 224. N. H. Nicolas, *Scrope and Grosvenor Controversy*, ii. 356-7; R. Thoroton, *Nottinghamshire*, i. 104 and 106). Sir Robert, son of Sir Gervase, probably died well before his father. If Mr. Roskell is right, then Clifton must be added to the list of those retainers of John of Gaunt who left his service; see below, pp. 18-9. Mr. H. G. Richardson, in his paper on 'John of Gaunt and the parliamentary representation of Lancashire' in the *Bulletin of John Rylands Library*, xxii (1938), 175-222, seems to have overlooked the difficulties presented by the biography of this Lancashire M.P.

[39] *Op. cit.*, p. 71.

together. But it is often difficult to trace any reason, hereditary or geographical, why a particular indenture of retainer was sealed. The earliest sub-contract known, that between Edmund Mortimer of Wigmore and Peter Maulay in 1287, is between a Welsh marcher and a Yorkshire tenant-in-chief, all the more surprising since the northern counties seem to have retained their attachment to the tenurial relationship longer than the south. J. E. Morris quotes a number of other instances of the same kind from the thirteenth century[39] and J. H. Wylie noted a similar lack of territorial connection in the armies of Henry V.[40] The great self-made captains of the Hundred Years' War with no inherited landed position seem to have drawn men from all parts by their fame. Service under such soldiers of fortune as John Chandos, Thomas Dagworth, James Audley or Hugh Calverley had its own attractions stronger than ties of kinship and locality. An illustration of this willingness to take service anywhere is afforded by an unusual epitaph which still exists in Tideswell church, Derbyshire. We do not often have contemporary biographies of late medieval worthies and this account of the career of a mere knight is particularly precious; it reads to me like autobiography.[41]

Under this stone lieth Sampson Meverell, which was born in Stone in the feast of St. Michael the Archangel and there christened by the prior of the same house and Sampson of Clifton, Esq.[42] and Margaret the daughter of

Philip Stapley[43] in the year of our lord MCCCIIIIVIII and so lived under the service of Nicholas lord Audley and Dame Elizabeth his wife the space of VIII years and more;[44] and after, by the assent of John Meverell, his

[40] *Reign of Henry the Fifth*, i. 462-3. The example Wylie chose is however an unfortunate one. William Bourchier's retinue of Welsh and west-country men-at-arms is less striking when we remember that he was the husband of Anne countess of Stafford, heiress to Thomas of Woodstock's half of the Bohun inheritance.

[41] Printed by J. C. Cox, *Notes on the Churches of Derbyshire*, ii. 301-2, and by J. M. J. Fletcher in 'Sir Sampson Meverill of Tideswell, 1388-1462' in *Journal of Derbyshire Arch. and Nat. Hist. Soc.*, xxx (1908), 1-22. The original inscription was stolen in 1688 and 'exactly renewed' in 1702 by Sir John Statham. Fortunately two transcriptions, by William Wyrley (1565-1618) and Ralph Sheldon (1623-84), were made before the theft. Mr. Fletcher prints the variant readings. Sheldon's transcript (Bodl. MS. Wood C 10) seems to me the most accurate and I have adopted it here, modernising the spelling and introducing some punctuation.

[42] He seems to have been an unimportant person, possibly a member of the Derbyshire knightly family of Clifton. The only time he is mentioned in the chancery records is an mainpernor for the abbot of Notley, Bucks, in 1384 (*Cal. Close Rolls, 1381-1385*, p. 425). He was dead by early 1402 ('Extracts from Plea Rolls, 1387-1405', ed. G. Wrottesley, in *Staffordshire Collections, William Salt. Soc.*, xv. 98).

[43] I have failed to find any trace of her.

father, he was wedded in Belper the king's manor[45] to Isabel the daughter
of the worshipful knight, Sir Roger Leche,[46] the XIIII day of Pasch; and
after he came to the service of the noble lord John Montagu, earl of
Salisbury,[47] the which ordained the said Sampson to be a captain of divers
worshipful places in France; and after the death of the said earl, he came to
the service of John duke of Bedford[48] and so being in his service, he was at
XI great battles in France within the space of two years; and at St. Luce
the said duke gave him the order of knighthood;[49] and after that the said
duke made him knight constable and by his commandment he kept the
constable's court of this land till the death of the said duke;[50] and after that
he abode under the service of John Stafford, archbishop of Canterbury,
and so enduring in great worship, departed from all worldly service unto
the mercy of our lord Jesus Christ, the which divided his soul from his
body in the feast of Macute[51] in the year of our lord MCCCCLXII; and so
his word may be proved that grace passeth cunning, amen. Devoutly of
your charity say a paternoster with an ave for all Christian souls and
especially for the soul whose bones rest under this stone.

Of Sir Sampson's four masters, only the first, Lord Audley, had
any connection with the district in which their worshipful servant had
his lands.

 Political capacity or influence had the same power to attract as
military reputation. When on 29 September 1395 John Willicotes of
Great Tew, Oxfordshire (afterwards the earl of Stafford's steward of
Kirtlington,[52] the pensioner of the earl-marshal[53] and Henry V's
receiver-general of his duchy of Cornwall),[54] was retained for life at
Cardiff by Thomas, lord Despenser,[55] it was not because the latter was
an important landowner in the same county (he was not), but probably

---

44 Sheldon reads 'viii', Wyrley and the Statham brass 'xviii'. As Nicholas Audley died
in 1391 it seems unlikely that Meverell served him very long! Elizabeth Audley died in
1400 a good many years before Meverell was 18 years old (G.E.C., *op. cit.*, i. 340). That
he was eight years a page to Lady Audley it is just possible to believe.
45 The 1702 brass reads 'Belser' (? for Bolsover), but Belper is obviously correct.
46 Of Chatsworth and Belper, a prominent Lancastrian household official and
councillor, lord treasurer 17 April 1416 to following 23 September. He was dead by 30
November 1416 (*Cal. Close Rolls, Henry V*, i. 385-6).
47 'John' is a mistake for Thomas (1388-1428) the famous captain.
48 Sir Sampson's name appears in a list of Bedford's retinue, 1435 (*Letters and Papers
illustrative of the wars of the English in France*, Rolls Ser., ed. J. Stevenson, ii. pt. 2,
436).
49 He was a knight by Trinity 1430 ('Extracts from Plea Rolls of Henry V and VI,' ed.
G. Wrottesley, in *Staffordshire Collections, William Salt Soc.*, xvii. 129).
50 Bedford was appointed Constable of England in 1403 and later for life (G.E.C., *op.
cit.*, ii. 70-1). There is some evidence that Meverell was in England 1431-2 (*Cal. Close
Rolls, Henry VI*, ii. 124, 161 and 183). For 'knight constable' compare the brass of Sir
Henry Vernon in Tong church, Salop, where the dead man (*ob.* 1467) is described as
'*quondam miles constabularius Anglie*'.

because of his growing influence at court. And when after the accession of Henry IV Despenser foolishly rebelled, John Willicotes took good care not to be involved; instead he merely obtained the king's confirmation of his fee from the rebel's forfeited lands. How eagerly the courtiers were themselves courted is illustrated by a letter written by Alice, dowager countess of Kent, to her son the earl in the spring or summer of 1397 in which she tells him that a certain Baldwin is anxious to serve him.[56] Hearing that the earl has been put to such great charges that he cannot afford any more retainers for at least two years, Baldwin offers himself at a discount; if the earl will give him commons for himself and his servant, various other usual pickings and ten marks next Michaelmas 'to refresh him' he will ask for nothing else until the two years are up. It is obvious that Kent was going aloft in the world; before the year was out he had been made duke of Surrey and like Despenser was high in Richard's favour. But his chivalrous repute to which Froissart enthusiastically testifies may also have had something to do with Baldwin's desire for a place in his household.[57] It is difficult to believe that the lords who were appealed of treason in the parliament of that year were being offered such cheap service; or that such a contemporary Lord Quondam[58] as the crazy Fauconberge[59] or the impoverished Lisle of Rougemont[60] was similarly importuned.

But, it might be thought, once the choice had been made and the indenture sealed freedom was at an end until one party or the other

[51] St. Machutus, 15 November.

[52] J. C. Blomfield, *History of Bicester, its town and priory*, p. 166 (quoting accounts of Bicester priory 9-10 Henry IV).

[53] *Cal. Pat. Rolls, 1405-1408*, p. 81.

[54] *Ibid., 1413-1416*, pp. 19 and 140; *Cal. Close Rolls, Henry V*, i. 241.

[55] *Cal. Pat. Rolls, 1399-1401*, p. 189. See also F. N. Macnamara, 'The Wilcotes Family', in *Berks, Bucks and Oxon Arch. Journal*, iii. (1897-8), 101-4, and W. F. Carter, 'The Wilcotes Family', *ibid.*, xii (1906-7), 107-13 and xiii (1907-8), 18-21.

[56] *Anglo-Norman Letters and Petitions* (Anglo-Norman Text Soc., No. 3), ed. M. D. Legge, pp. 260-1. Miss Legge favours late 1399 as the date, after Kent had been deprived of his dukedom by Henry IV's first parliament. But the months between 25 April 1397 when he succeeded his father in his earldom and 29 September 1397 when he was created a duke are much more likely.

[57] *Chroniques*, ed. J. M. B. C. Kervyn de Lettenhove, xvi. 229.

[58] W. Dugdale (*op. cit.*, ii, 216), writing of John, lord Dudley (*c.* 1495-1553), 'a weak man of understanding', says that he 'became exposed to the Charity of his friends for a subsistence; and spending the remainder of his life in visits amongst them, was commonly called the Lord *Quondam*.'

[59] G.E.C., *Complete Peerage* (new edn.), v. 276-80.

[60] *Ibid.*, viii. 76-7. Compare the Damorys (*ibid.*, iv. 46-8), the Herons of Ford (*ibid.*, vi. 484-7), the Husseys of Harting (*ibid.*, vii. 1-8) and the Latimers of Braybrooke (*ibid.*, 450-6), all fourteenth century baronial families going down and parting with their estates.

died. It may be so, and if it is then the indenture system was undoubtedly 'a steadying influence in a society where old institutional loyalties were breaking down.[61] A great deal more work will have to be done before we know how effective that influence was. For it is of the nature of that society, the ties of which were personal and divorced from status, that it should only yield its secrets to the investigator who can base his conclusions upon the study of hundreds of fragmentary biographies, many of the sources being still in manuscript. Nevertheless a first impression is that we must not accept the apparent finality of the phrase 'for life' in the indentures at its face value. In the early days of the system some of the contracts had a sanctions clause for breach of the engagement;[62] but after the middle of the fourteenth century this clause disappears. What is more so far no evidence of any attempt to enforce a contract in the courts has been published. Nothing, however, breeds a more positive scepticism than a study of the careers of one or two well-known retainers. It was, for example, while under indenture to serve John of Gaunt for life in peace and war for 50 marks a year that Sir Henry Green was retained, also for life, to stay with Richard II at an annual fee of 40 marks; and he continued to enjoy both annuities until his execution by Gaunt's son and heir at Bristol in 1399.[63] Green's colleague, Sir William Bagot, had an almost exactly similar fortune, but in addition to being Gaunt's and the king's retainer he was likewise a pensioner of the Mowbray, duke of Norfolk who was banished in 1398.[64] Possibly these are exceptional cases; possibly the king could do what another subject could not, namely seduce a man from his affinity; but there is certainly room for doubts. These doubts are increased when Richard II and even Henry V are remembered to have found it necessary to insist that their instruments of retainer should be exclusive.

Professor Newhall has devoted a recent book to showing how the difficulty of keeping the retinues of the English captains in France intact led to the creation of an elaborate machinery of muster and

[61] N. B. Lewis, 'The organisation of indentured retinues in fourteenth-century England', in *Trans. Royal Hist. Soc.*, 4th ser., xxvii (1945), 39. It is obvious how deeply indebted I am to this most valuable paper.

[62] *Ibid.*, p. 38. A good example of such an indenture is that between Sir Geoffrey Riddell of Whittering and John Lavington on 2 May 1333 (*Hist. MSS. Com. 2nd Rept.*, p. 93).

[63] *Cal. Pat. Rolls, 1396-1399*, pp. 87 and 522; T. F. Tout, *Chapters in the Administrative History of Mediaeval England*, iv. 14.

[64] *John of Gaunt's Register*, iii. 10; *Cal. Pat. Rolls, 1396-1399*, pp. 178, 210, 215, *etc.*; *1401-1405*, p. 96; Tout, *op. cit.*, pp. 12-14; G. Wrottesley, 'History of the Bagot Family', in *Staffordshire Collections of William Salt Soc.*, new ser., xi. 45-54.

review when John, duke of Bedford was regent.[65] It is possible that the defaulters were all those with the limited terms of service which were a feature of this period; or they may have been below the rank of the liveried retainers.[66] But there is no doubt that the trouble was chronic in medieval warfare. If strong action by the crown was necessary to maintain the integrity of baronial contingents it is evident that the magnates could not do it by themselves.

The steadying influence of the indenture may perhaps have been diminishing by the first half of the fifteenth century. Yet even earlier its efficacy was at best only relative. This can, I think, be shown from the evidence provided by no less a retinue than that of the duke of Lancaster himself. For it so happens that we have the names of some sixty-six knights and esquires retained by John of Gaunt for life between 1371 and 1374.[67] If these are compared with a list entitled *'Nomina militum et scutiferorum'* preserved in the duke's register for 1379-83, it will be found that twenty-six have disappeared in the interval.[68] A note against four of the indentures states that they were cancelled *'quod mortuus'* and six others are cancelled without any reason being given.[69] Were all twenty-six dead? No. A majority — fourteen[70] — certainly were and it is sometimes difficult to discover the fate of the remainder. But, whatever may have happened to nine,[71] three were undoubtedly alive and their cases seem to me to show the wisdom of questioning appearances. Sir William Beauchamp, younger son of the earl of Warwick, had already distinguished himself as a soldier when on 27 February 1373 he was retained by Lancaster for

[65] *Muster and Review*: a Problem of English Military Administration, *1420-1440* (Harvard Historical Monographs, No. xiii).

[66] By Statute 3 of 13 Richard II (*Statutes of the Realm*, ii. 74-5) liveries might not be given to anyone below the rank of esquire except to household servants.

[67] *Register*, i and ii, nos. 777-9, 782, 784, 787-8, 791-7, 799-800, 803-8, 810-6, 819-20, 822-3, 825, 829-30, 832-5, 837-8, 841-5, 847-53, 855-8 and 863-70.

[68] *Ibid.*, iii, pp. 6-13.

[69] William Bradshaw (*ibid.*, i, no. 793), Edward Gerberge (*ibid.*, 843), William Haybear (*ibid.*, 812) and Walter Oliver (*ibid.*, 858); *plus* Sir Robert Clifton (*ibid.*, ii, 863), Sir William Cantelupe (*ibid.*, i, 790 and 833), Sir Nicholas Longford (*ibid.*, 803), Sir Thomas Travers (*ibid.*, 834), Thomas Tutbury (*ibid.*, 852), and Richard Wyrley, sergeant-at-arms (*ibid.*, 820).

[70] Messrs. Cantelupe, Clifton, Longford, Bradshaw, Gerberge, Haybear, Oliver and Wyrley *plus* Sir Thomas Banaster (*ibid.*, 849), Sir John Doddingsells (*ibid.*, ii. 869), Sir Edmund Frithby (*ibid.*, i. 822), Sir Roger Trumpington (*ibid.*, 848), Sir Thomas Goys (*ibid.*, 791) and Ellis Thoresby (*ibid.*, ii. 865).

[71] Messrs. Travers and Tutbury *plus* Sir Richard Northland (*ibid.*, i. 806), Sir Walter Penhargard (*ibid.*, 784), Sir Richard Whitefield (*ibid.*., 782), Madoc Fernyll (*ibid.*, 842), Simkin Molyneux (*ibid.*, ii. 864), William Stanes (*ibid.*, i. 799) and John Holm (*ibid.*, 814).

life.[72] In the case of so important a recruit it was natural that the terms should be elaborate and the possibility that Beauchamp might arrive at 'the estate of an earl' had to be considered. The most unusual provision was one which allowed the retainer to fight where and under whom he pleased should Gaunt himself not be disposed on any occasion to take the field.[73] This arrangement cannot however explain Beauchamp's disappearance altogether from the Lancastrian retinue six or seven years later. His subsequent career was long and active. In 1383 he became Captain of Calais and held that office until 1390.[74] His inheritance of the entailed castle and honour of Abergavenny in 1389 led to his summons as a peer to parliament between July 1392 and his death in 1411. The young John, lord Welles, before he came of age sealed a much less elaborate indenture with Gaunt on 12 February 1372.[75] He too became a soldier of repute and did not die until 1421.[76] Sir Thomas Dale, de la Dale or Fulthorpe, was a Bedfordshire landowner of some substance whose death took place in 1396.[77]

Now two or three examples do not make a generalisation, though they do serve to shake one's faith in the irrefragibility of the life indenture and in the absolute effectiveness of the retainer system— even in its narrow sphere—as a solidifying influence in a fluent society. If such things could happen to the retinue of the greatest—though not the most popular—lord in England, whose protection and favour had again and again made the fortunes of his clientèle, then how much more were they likely to happen to those less advantageously placed? The indentures may have been cancelled by mutual consent or by one-sided action, we cannot tell; but whatever may have been their intention we can no longer regard them as unbreakable. The strongest inducement to maintain them in being was the common ambitions of the two parties to them. That was strong enough to attach scores of men all their lives to the Lancastrian interest; and we can be sure that

[72] *Ibid.*, no. 832; G.E.C., *op. cit.*, i. 24-6; Dugdale, *op. cit.*, i. 238-40.

[73] 'Et a quelle heure que le dit nostre seigneur ne se taillera meismes estre armez a travailler de guerre adonqe de sa bone seignurie il suffera le dit monsire William chivacher et travailler la ou ly plerra sanz empeschement de nully.'

[74] *Cal. Close Rolls, 1389-1392*, pp. 32-3.

[75] *Register*, i. no. 788.

[76] G.E.C., *Complete Peerage* (orig. edn.), viii. 76-7.

[77] The Dales of Little Barford, co. Beds, were a succession of Thomases which makes investigation difficult. See *Victoria County Hist., Beds*, ii. 207-8 and 227. That our Sir Thomas was the one that died in 1396 is shown by *Cal. Ancient Deeds*, i, no. A550 (cf. *ibid.*, iii, no. D 1223), and *Register*, ii, no. 1661 (where his wife Sibyl is mentioned). His son Thomas who died before 1408 was retained by Gaunt as an esquire in 1389 (*Cal. Pat. Rolls, 1396-1399*, p. 576).

few of them regretted their consistency, particularly if they lived like
the Tiptofts, the Watertons, and the Erpinghams to enjoy the fruits of
1399. It would not be difficult to find many parallel cases to that of Sir
Richard Hastings who was retained for life by Henry, duke of
Lancaster before 1361[78] and who died in the service of his son-in-law in
1398. He was, however, the grandfather of William Hastings, the
much-favoured Yorkist, who cashed in on the 'revolution' of 1461.
The bond which kept these masters and men together was not a sealed
parchment but a calculation of mutual advantage to which that
document bore witness. How easy it was to have a foot in other camps
is proved by the example of Sir Thomas Hungerford, the famous
Speaker and father of one of the most deserving of the new nobility of
the Lancastrian kings. It is a commonplace of historians, whose
tendency to repeat each other has not passed unnoticed, to explain Sir
Thomas's political actions by a reference to the fact that he was John
of Gaunt's steward. He was indeed his retainer as well.[79] But it is never
mentioned that he was the Black Prince's yeoman,[80] lieutenant to
Bartholomew Burwash in the stewardship of the prince's great honour
of Wallingford,[81] and from 1365 steward for life of all the lands of
William, earl of Salisbury.[82] It would in short be dangerous to jump to
conclusions about his political sympathies. But at least he made the
fortunes of his house, and that was probably his first concern.

It must be obvious to anyone who has attempted to follow the
adventures of a fourteenth century soldier in detail that a retainer did
not confine even his military service to the troop of the captain who
fed him. Going abroad in the 'comitiva' of now this commander and
now that, these knights of a late though not decadent chivalry seemed
more anxious to see service than to care whether it was always under
the same banner. It is not known when Michael de la Pole, the future
earl of Suffolk, became John of Gaunt's retainer, but during the
quarter of a century 1355-79 in which he took part in the wars he is
known to have served under Henry of Lancaster, the Black Prince,
and John of Gaunt indifferently as well as holding an independent
command of his own.[83] The case of Robert FitzRalph is curious
enough to deserve particular mention. Before he was retained by John
of Gaunt in 1373[84] FitzRalph had been the servant and pensioner of
Humphrey, the last Bohun earl of Hereford.[85] His hands lay in Suffolk

---

[78] *Hist. MSS. Com. Rept. Hastings*, i. 191   [79] *Register*, iii. 7
[80] *Register of Edward the Black Prince*, iv. 546.
[81] *Ibid.*, and pp. 434, 447 and 529-30.   [82] *Cal. Pat. Rolls, 1364-1367*, p. 169.
[83] *Dict. Nat. Biog.*, s.n.; Dugdale, *op. cit.*, ii. 183.   [84] *Register*, i, no. 844.
[85] *Cal. Close Rolls, 1374-1377*, pp. 40-1.

and it is easy to follow his local activities during the 1370's and 1380's. In February 1382 he was the duke's agent in removing the heiress of the Le Stranges of Blackmere from the custody of her mother the widowed countess of Suffolk.[86] Four years later he accompanied his employer to Spain,[87] but in the interval he had taken service under his diocesan bishop Henry Despenser of Norwich. As one of the captains in charge of the bishop's filibustering crusade of 1383 he helped to put into action a policy, 'the way of Flanders', which was the popular alternative to 'the way of Spain' advocated by Lancaster. That the expedition was led by one of the latter's retainers is therefore noteworthy. FitzRalph soon found himself in trouble when the crusaders were defeated; and in 1384 he was accused in parliament of having taken a bribe from the French to withdraw them from the continent.[88] But his imprisonment did not prevent him from making his peace with John of Gaunt, in whose service in Spain he probably died.[89]

One of the most obvious characteristics of this late medieval society was the opportunity which it offered to the ambitious with the ability to seize it. In the words of Nicholas Upton, 'in these days we see openly how many poor men through their service in the French wars have become noble, some by their prudence, some by their energy, some by their valour and some by other virtues which . . . ennoble men.'[90] One recalls those companions of the Black Prince, Felton, Kyriel and Mauny, who were enriched by his princely largesse. Edward thought nothing of granting the bastard Audley 'for good service rendered at the battle of Poitiers' £400 a year for life;[91] and was capable of rewarding a mere yeoman with an annuity of 100 marks.[92] No wonder lords were impoverished and the gentry flourished! Edward III set his heir many an extravagant example, by his too liberal endowment of William Montagu, first earl of Salisbury, for instance,[93] or by his purchase of the captured count of Eu from Sir Thomas

[86] *Register*, iii, no. 673.

[87] *Foedera*, ed. T. Rymer, vii (1709), 490.

[88] *Rotuli Parliamentorum*, iii. 156-8; *Cal. Pat. Rolls, 1381-1385*, pp 405-6 and 537; *Cal. Close Rolls, 1381-1385*, pp. 368, 374 and 444.

[89] He seems to be dead by 20 April 1388 (*ibid., 1385-1389*, p. 488).

[90] A. R. Wagner, *Heralds and Heraldry in the Middle Ages*, pp. 73 and 125-6.

[91] *Register of Edward the Black Prince*, iv. 291 and 359. According to the well-known story of Froissart Audley was first granted 500 marks p.a. which he promptly gave to his four esquires. When he heard this the Black Prince, not to be outdone in knightly largesse, granted him another £400 p.a. *Chroniques*, ed. S. Luce, (Soc. de l'Hist. de France), v. 61-3 and 66-8.

[92] *Register of Black Pr.*, iv. 392.

Holland for 80,000 florins.[94] His successors were perhaps from necessity more tight-fisted, but even in the service of the Lancastrian kings fortunes could be made. It was under Henry V and Bedford that Sir John Fastolf though not often paid to his satisfaction accumulated the capital which enabled him to spend £6,000 on his castle at Caistor and to add to his estates until they yielded the baronial income of more than £600 a year.[95] Doubtless others were less fortunate. The Greys of Ruthin, for example, had to pay a ransom of 10,000 marks to Owen Glendower when the head of the family fell into his hands.[96] If the wars went well, they paid handsomely; but with the turning of the tide, they might be a crippling drain on the fortunes of a noble house. A detailed calculation has survived of the expenses incurred by Margaret lady Hungerford and Botreaux in redeeming her son Robert lord Moleyns, taken prisoner in Guyenne in 1453; its various items add up to over £14,000.[97] The Greys and Hungerfords had to sell estates, but those who made money in the wars were there to buy them. It is not surprising that there was a large market in land in these years of almost continuous Anglo-French warfare. But this is too big a subject for the tail-end of this paper; let me refer you to Mr. Postan's recent article, which though it barely scratches the surface of the subject is none the less suggestive.[98]

As for the political consequences of bastard feudalism: it is usual to blame it for the defects of government in the later middle ages and more particularly for the Wars of the Roses which brought that epoch to its bloody close. It is possible, however, to take a different view. The real trouble for a century before Towton, as I see it, was not the inability of the English kingship to handle its problems successfully; that it could do that well enough the short reign of Henry V is fortunately there to prove. The fault lay surely in the personal inadequacies of the kings themselves, in the early dotage of Edward III, in the instability of Richard II's character, and most of all in the bad fortune which cut short the life of Henry V just when the inevitable

---

[93] W. Dugdale, *op. cit.*, i. 645-6. For another example, see *ibid.*, ii, 138 (500 marks p.a. to Thomas Bradeston).

[94] G. Wrottesley, *Crécy and Calais* (reprinted from *Staffordshire Collections, William Salt Soc.*, xviii, 272).

[95] H. L. Gray, 'Incomes from land in 1436', in *Eng. Hist. Rev.*, xlix. (1934), 621; Magdalen Coll. Oxon. MSS., Fastolf Papers.

[96] *Cal. Pat. Rolls, 1401-1405*, pp. 155-6 and 171; Rymer, *op. cit.*, viii. 279; J. E. Lloyd, *Owen Glendower*, p. 57.

[97] W. Dugdale, *op. cit.*, ii. 209-10.

[98] *Econ. Hist. Rev.*, xii (1942), 1-12, 'Some Social Consequences of the Hundred Years' War.'

ill-effects of the Lancastrian usurpation were wearing off and placed the crown for forty years upon the head of a baby who grew up an imbecile. It is doubtful whether a feudal, or any other kind of monarchical, society would have fared better in these circumstances. The results of the short reign of Edward do not suggest that the Tudors had solved the problem of government in a minority any more successfully than the Lancastrians. That great 'modern' statesman the duke of Northumberland looks very much like an over-mighty subject to me.[99] The truth is that England was a monarchy, which is to say that it depended for its healthy functioning upon the exercise of kingship. It was only after a prolonged strain of a quite unusual kind had been placed upon it by the nullity of Henry VI that that polity collapsed in civil war. The fact that the so-called 'New Monarchy' succeeded by employing all the old methods—by wielding them, that is to say, once more effectively—merely emphasises how accidental that collapse was. And yet all kinds of quite irrelevant reasons have been adduced for it. It was not livery and maintenance which brought about the Wars of the Roses. I don't mean to imply that maintenance was not a bad thing nor that livery could not be put to destructive uses. But a strong king could prevent them from getting beyond control just as effectively in the days of Lancaster and York as could Edward I in his time or Henry VII in his. Maintenance was after all no novelty. The novelty lay in its being more talked about, denounced and legislated against. It was in fact being measured by men with a higher conception of public order. Being men of their time they believed that the evils with which they contended showed a contemporary falling-off from a more perfect past. In thinking so they were usually wrong. All medieval moralists, and indeed most modern ones, are what we may call saturnians; the dim past is always golden to them. Though they must be given the credit for their better standards, they are unsound historical critics. On the other hand it was their sense of order which made them welcome the active kingship which the Tudors once more offered them.

Livery and maintenance did not disappear at once. They were gradually reduced to more manageable proportions by the vigilance of the central authority. We shall, I believe, gravely misunderstand the nature of Tudor government if we overlook its personal character and fail to take note of the survival of bastard feudalism far into the

---

[99] For maintenance in Edward VI's minority see *A Discourse of the Common Weal of this Realm of England*, ed. E. Lammond, pp. xxxix-lxvii and esp. p. lix.

sixteenth century. Let me end these highly discursive remarks with a quotation:

> If there be, said he, any noble man dwelling in the country, either a duke, a marquess, an earl or baron, he shall lightly have in his retinue all the cobs in the country, which be the questmongers (as he styled the questmen). And if any matters be touching him, his man or his friend, whether it be a crime capital or *nisi prius* sent down for lands, the case shall weigh as he will. For his detainers (as he called retainers) must needs have an eye to my lord, though they should go to the devil for it. And so be some innocents knit up and some offenders delivered and some titles of inheritance lost, against all justice and right. Another is, if my lord will not offend the Statute of Retinue, then must the high sheriff be his friend and the under-thief (under-sheriff I should say) his man. He empannelleth the quest either such as dare not displease my lord, or for good will will not. And so that way betwixt the high-thief and the under-thief, my lord and the curstmongers, poor men are outweighed. This corruption, if it be not looked to, will make this order (of the jury of twelve) which was the best that could be to be the wickedest that can be.

This *laudator temporis acti* was no contemporary of Brunton or Bromyard but John Aylmer, who died bishop of London in 1594.[100] He was speaking not of the days of Lancaster and York but after something like a century of Tudor rule.

---

[100] J. Strype, *Life and Acts of John Aylmer, Lord Bishop of London* (1701), pp. 290-1. For two late Elizabethan examples of maintenance see 'a lamentable discourse taken out of sundrie examinations concerning the willfull escape of Sir Charles and Sir Henrie Danvers, knights, and theire followers after the murder committed in Wilteshir uppon Henrie Longe gent', Brit. Mus., MSS. Lansd. 827 art. 6 and 830 art. 13; and *Three Bloodie Murders* (c. 1613), reprinted by C. W. Foster, *Aisthorpe and Thorpe in the Fallows*, app. I, pp. 188-93.

III. AN INDENTURE OF AGREEMENT BETWEEN TWO ENGLISH KNIGHTS FOR MUTUAL AID AND COUNSEL IN PEACE AND WAR, 5 DECEMBER 1298

DURING the civil wars of Edward II's reign a number of indentures of confederacy for mutual protection were sealed between various great men of the realm. Agreeing to stand together they embodied their common purpose in a formal document and on occasion also entered into recognisances to indemnify one another in the event of failure. Unusual dangers, it has been assumed, called for unusual remedies; and Edward of Carnarvon has been blamed not only for provoking his subjects' disaffection but also for the kind of covenant in which they set out their aims and bound themselves to ensue them. More, in this sealing of indentures we are told to see 'the germs of that system which did so much to produce and continue the Wars of the Roses.'[1]

Germs and origins are often difficult to trace; hence their perilous fascination to even the soberest of historians. Yet further research usually reveals that bad novelties as well as good, livery and maintenance as much as the new monarchy and the new bureaucracy, are older than their confident discoverers imagined. For we now know that retaining by indenture was not the fatal invention of Edward II but flourished under his masterful parent, if not in still earlier reigns; and many of us would question whether its introduction or later employment can necessarily be regarded as deplorable. After all the act of subinfeudation had long proved itself an imperfect means of securing loyal service by man to lord. An indenture of retainer might well have seemed to offer a better guarantee that what was due—and stated in writing to be due—by both parties would be performed.

Likewise we may doubt whether it set the bad example followed by Edward II's magnates. Agreements such as theirs were at least as old

---

[1] J. Conway Davies, *Baronial Opposition to Edward II* (Cambridge, 1918), pp. 33-8. The quotation comes from p. 38. As so often in works produced in the wake of the political crisis of 1909-11 the tone of this immensely learned book is markedly anti-baronial.

as Stephen's reign and had been then embodied in documents of similar form.[2] If no such *conventio* as those between the earls of the 'Anarchy' seems to be known between the confederates who opposed Edward I in 1297, this is far from certain evidence that none was made. The fact that they are described as *confoederati* may seem to suggest that they did embody their resolution to stand together in some form of bond. All we have are their *monstraunces* which they showed to their lord the king, and their reported acts.[3]

The existence of such a *conventio* between two humbler contemporaries of the earls of Hereford and Norfolk may help to demonstrate that there was nothing extraordinary in a treaty of alliance between subjects in the last years of the thirteenth century. The parties to this indenture were, it is more than probable, not conspiring against the king. But that such a formal çovenant could be entered into for an apparently innocent purpose, or for one which at least did not obviously trespass upon the king's interests, made it all the more suitable for purposes less innocent.

On 5 December 1298, when Edward I was at Newcastle-upon-Tyne directing measures to consolidate the advantage he had gained over the Scots at Falkirk, Sir Nicholas Kingston and Sir William Mansell met at some unnamed place to seal the indenture of which one half is preserved among the Pusey archives in the Berkshire Record Office.[4] The terms of their agreement are disappointingly vague. Sir Nicholas engages himself to furnish Sir William with counsel, to be 'with him' and to help him when called upon in all his affairs. He is to be prompt with him in everything both in peace and war at Sir William's charges as often as the latter shall need his counsel and help and wish to retain him in a manner befitting a

---

2 For the *confederatio amoris* between Robert of Gloucester and Miles of Hereford see *Sir Christopher Hatton's Book of Seals*, ed. L. C. Loyd and D. M. Stenton (Oxford, 1950), no. 212, and for the *conventio* between Ranulf of Chester and Robert of Leicester see F. M. Stenton, *First Century of English Feudalism, 1066-1166* (2nd edn., Oxford, 1961), pp. 286-8.

3 N. Triveti . . . annales sex regum Angliae, ed. T. Hog (Eng. Hist. Soc., 1845), pp. 358-68: *W. Rishanger . . . chronica*, ed. H. T. Riley (Rolls Ser., 1865), pp. 178 and 180-2; *Chronicle of Walter of Guisborough*, ed. H. Rothwell (Camden 3rd Ser., lxxxix, 1957), p. 312. The word used in the letters patent in which the king and his councillors indemnified the remonstrators is 'alliaunces' (*Parliamentary Writs*, ed. F. T. Palgrave (Record Comm.), i, 61-2). I have been greatly helped by J. G. Edwards's lucid study of the documents of this crisis in '*Confirmatio Cartarum* and baronial grievances in 1297', *Eng. Hist. Rev.*, lviii (1943), 147-71 and 273-300.

4 I must thank Mr H. M. Colvin for bringing this document to my attention and for allowing me to publish it. It was only after I had begun work on this article that I discovered that I had long ago noted its contents in my copy of the Hist. MSS. Comm., *7th Report*, app. i, p. 681, and then forgotten it. It is printed below, p. 54.

knight. The most unusual provision is that in which Sir William undertakes to do the same for his ally. It is an indenture of mutual retainer in peace and war. Turn and turn about, as opportunities or needs arise, each shall retain and, it seems, pay the other. In this the parties are distinguishable from brothers-in-arms, partners who agree to share the risks and spoils of war. No clause deals with the division of ransoms and plunder; it may be that there was already a recognised tariff in such matters.

Nor is this the only omission. There is no mention of the duration of the bond, no hint that it was either temporary or to last for their two lives. Nothing again is said about the penalties to which default might render the offending party liable. If, as seems likely, the two knights entered into reciprocal recognisances for the performance of their contract, evidence of the fact is wanting. Finally their specific reasons for desiring each the other's help are not given. Though it may not be difficult to imagine what these may have been so soon after the turmoil of 1297, the indenture itself offers absolutely no guidance. And we know nothing whatsoever about the activities of either Kingston or Mansell, whether political or military, in the closing years of the thirteenth century. Of their personal affiliations during those critical times the evidence is almost equally scanty. Such as it is it needs to be sifted a little further.

It is convenient to begin with Mansell since his background and connexions can be more securely established. That he was a Gloucestershire man is clear, though the historians of that county are deplorably vague about the family which gave its name to the hamlet (and telephone exchange) of Frampton Mansell in the Cotswold parish of Sapperton and owned land thereabouts for something like two centuries.[5] To a quarter of a knight's fee in Frampton, held in 1284-5 by John the son of another William Mansell, Sir William had succeeded before 1303.[6] In addition he possessed a knight's fee in Over Lypiatt and Tunley across the valley from Frampton.[7] Until he exchanged them for lands elsewhere in 1299 or 1300 he had also held the manor and advowson of Tortworth near Berkeley which in 1235-6 had belonged to a namesake, possibly the above-mentioned

---

[5] S. Rudder, *A New History of Gloucestershire* (Circencester, 1779), p. 643, merely repeats R. Atkyns, *The Ancient and Present State of Glocestershire* (2nd edn., 1768), p. 335. Since Sir Robert Atkyns himself possessed the manor of Sapperton, his lack of interest is surprising.

[6] *Feudal Aids*, ii. 236 and 251.

[7] *Ibid.*, p. 251. It is not clear when the Mansells acquired their important holding at Over Lypiatt.

John's father.[8] And there is reason to believe that an estate of a hide in Redland by Bristol, of which one William Mansell was seized in 1208-9 and another in 1284-5, descended to him with Tortworth.[9] In 1300 royal officials reckoned Tortworth and Redland together to be worth £40 a year.[10] The Mansells were therefore well-established in the county and of some modest standing there by the beginning of Edward I's reign. There is no sign that they were as yet holders of land elsewhere.[11] What expansion there was into other shires seems to have begun after 1298. The label on Sir William's seal of arms might suggest a cadet, but no Mansell bearer of the arms undifferenced seems to be known to the heralds.[12]

That the lords of Tortworth should have been drawn into the service of the baronial house to which Berkeley and Wootton-under-Edge belonged was natural. Evidence that at least one of them was prominent in that service comes to us from Smyth's *Lives of the Berkeleys*. When in response to a writ of 5 December 1276 Maurice Berkeley performed the service of three knights owed for his barony, he was accompanied by his son and Sir William Mansell, elsewhere

[8] *Victoria History of the County of Berkshire*, iv. 18 and 473 citing Feet of Fines, Berks., 28 Edw. I, no. 1 (P.R.O., C.P. 25 (1)/9/36); Atkyns, p. 412 followed by Rudder, p. 775; *Book of Fees*, p. 439.

[9] *Book of Fees*, p. 38; *Feudal Aids*, ii. 234. The fine cited in the previous note included Redland as well as Tortworth (see below, p. 53).

[10] *Parl. Writs*, i. 338 shows Nicholas Kingston holding £40 p.a. in Gloucs. on 15 Jan. 1300. As will be shown later this can hardly be other than the estimated yield from Tortworth, Redland and their appurtenances.

[11] The William Mansell who held a fee in Turvey, Beds., in 1278-9 and 1316 as well as an estate in Chicheley, Bucks., in 1284-5 (sold by him on 25 March 1287) was the son of Sampson Mansell (G. Lipscombe, *The History and Antiquities of the County of Buckingham* (4 vols., 1831-47), iv. 112 n.1; *V.C.H. Beds.*, iii. 113; *Feudal Aids*, i. 17, 83). His parentage seems to distinguish him from his Gloucestershire namesake.

[12] The seal is on a notification of the receipt of homage by him, n.d. but *c.* 1300 (Berks. Record Office, E Bp/F2). The arms are a fess with a label of five points. This agrees with the Parliamentary Roll of Arms, *c.* 1312 (*Parl. Writs*, i. 418), where under Gloucs. Sir William Mansell's arms are given as Gu. a fess Arg. a label Arg. In the St. George's Roll of *c.* 1285 (*Three Rolls of Arms*, ed. W. S. Walford and C. S. Perceval (Soc. of Antiqs., 1864), p. 57) 'William Maue . . . l' has these arms but the label is Or. The heraldic evidence does not support the theory. (W. R. Williams, *Parliamentary History of the County of Gloucester, 1213-1898* (Hereford, 1898), p. 6) that the Mansells of Margam, whose arms were Arg. a chevron between three maunches Sa. (J. W. Papworth, *Ordinary of British Armorials*, p. 457) were connected with those of Frampton.

[13] J. Smyth, *Lives of the Berkeleys*, ed. Sir J. Maclean (Gloucester, 3 vols., 1883-5), i. 143 and 169; *Parl. Writs*, i. 204 and 212.

[14] There are two charters, one dated 1246-7 and the other temp. Hen. III, in the muniment-room at Berkeley which were witnessed by a William Mansell (I. H. Jeayes, *Catalogue of the Muniments at Berkeley Castle* (Bristol, 1892), nos. 293 and 370). The second of these is in the hand of Thomas, clerk of Tortworth.

described by Smyth as one of the 'domesticke knights' of the Berkeleys.[13] This is probably the tenant of Redland and less certainly of Tortworth in 1284-5.[14] But although another knightly Mansell, to whom Smyth denies a Christian name, crops up in association with Maurice Berkeley's heir Thomas in 1312 and is without much doubt our man, it is rather as an inhabitant of the same shire than as a dependant.[15] There is no indication that either Mansell or his friend Kingston was attached to the Berkeley or to any other baronial affinity.[16] Their alliance might well have been a substitute for such dependance.

Sir Nicholas Kingston's identity and employments are badly tangled with those of a contemporary of the same name and rank.[17] Only the fact that in 1316 he was described as the elder and of Gloucestershire enables us to distinguish him with reasonable certainty from a younger Sir Nicholas with lands in Wiltshire and beyond Trent.[18] The latter's death shortly before 6 February 1323 antedated his by more than a year. After being described as 'impotens propter etatem' on 9 May 1324 the Gloucestershire Sir Nicholas is heard of no more.[19] He left a daughter Hawise, the widow of Robert Veel, who was his sole heir.[20] The two Sir Nicholases were certainly related.[21] Though complete proof may be

[15] Smyth, i. 181. By that date Mansell's nearest land to Berkeley was either at Frampton or Minchinhampton (*Cal. Close Rolls 1313-18*, p. 158; *Cal. Fine Rolls*, ii. 164).

[16] The only hint of a connexion is Kingston's appearance as the first witness to a grant by Maurice Berkeley of a messuage in Woodford, dated Berkeley 13 July 1304 (Jeayes, no. 470). But by then Kingston was seated at Tortworth (see below, p. 53), a couple of miles from Woodford. An affinity must of course be distinguished from the retinue led by a magnate or captain to the king's wars. The latter usually contained some members of the former but also men-at-arms recruited *ad hoc*. Maurice Berkeley's retinues in Scotland in 1298 (with Aymer de Valence) and in 1301 (with Edward of Carnarvon) contained neither Mansell nor Kingston (P.R.O., E 101/6/39, m. 2 and E 101/9/23).

[17] For the resulting confusion see *Knights of Edward I*, ed. C. Moor (5 vols., Harleian Soc., 1929-32), ii. 286.

[18] *Parl. Writs*, II. ii. 164 and 168; *Cal. Fine Rolls*, iii. 196 and 207; etc.

[19] *Parl. Writs*, II, ii. 655.   [20] Rudder, p. 775.

[21] This is clear from their coats of arms. Our Sir Nicholas's seal bore a lion rampant with a forked tail and a label of three points (Berks. Record Office, E Bp/Fı (the indenture printed below, p. 54); Gloucs. Records Office, D 340a/T 126/2/1-3 (28 Apr. and 6 Oct. 1312). I am indebted to the Records Officer, Mr Irvine E. Gray, for this useful information). In the Parl. Roll of Arms of *c*. 1312 only one Sir Nicholas Kingston is mentioned; his arms are given as Sa. a forked-tailed lion. Or with a label Gu. This would fit the seal of the Gloucs. knight, but the fact that the compiler of the roll lists it under Yorks. (*Parl. Writs*, i. 416) indicates that it is that of the Sir Nicholas with lands N. of Trent, i.e. the Wilts. knight. Presumably their labels were of different colours.

wanting, the records make it highly probable that they were uncle and nephew, being respectively the younger brother and the son of Sir John Kingston, a Berkshire and Wiltshire landowner who was constable of Edinburgh castle from November 1298 until some time after the parliament of September 1305 and who in 1301 sealed the 'Barons' Letter' to the pope.[22]

The Kingstons, who may have taken their name from the nearby Kingston Bagpuize, were descendants of one Roger of that name who bought the manor later known as Mansell's Court in Pusey, Berkshire, before 1221.[23] In the twelve-nineties this belonged to Sir Nicholas the elder; in 1297 he and his wife Margaret are found adding a messuage and four virgates in the village to his holding.[24] Margaret was an heiress, whether a daughter or not we do not know, of William Bagpuize who had alienated his manor of Kingston Bagpuize to Sir John Kingston the elder in 1290. In 1292 after

---

[22] For his coat of arms see *Parl. Writs*, i. 410 and for his seal see Ellis, Thomas Evelyn, Lord Howard de Walden, *Some Feudal Lords and Their Seals, MCCCI* (1904), pp. 159-60 and plate. His arms were those of the two Sir Nicholases but without a label. That Sir John had a brother Nicholas in 1290 is proved by *Cal. Close Rolls 1288-96*, p. 140. The younger Sir Nicholas, who died childless, also had a brother Sir John (who was his heir), a contrariant in 1322 and among those who 'fuyrent outre mier' after Boroughbridge (*Parl. Writs*, ii. ii, App., p. 201; *Cal. Close Rolls 1318-23*, pp. 549 and 611; *Cal. Inquisitiones post mortem*, vi, no. 426; *Abstracts of Wiltshire Inquisitiones post mortem*, ed. G. S. and E. A. Fry (Index Libr.), i. 432-3 and 439-40). This is presumably the Sir John whose arms are given by the Parl. Roll (*Parl. Writs*, i. 420) as those of Sir John the elder with a label Arg. If as seems likely he was the latter's son and heir the label would suggest that these were his arms before he succeeded to the inheritance. Sir John the elder had become possessed of an estate in Kingston Bagpuize, Berks, in 1290. It was held by a John Kingston in 1316 and 1328 (*V.C.H. Berks.*, iv. 350). The later Kingston lords of this estate bore the arms of Sir John the elder without a label (E. A. Greening Lamborn, *Armorial Glass of the Oxford Diocese, 1250-1850* (1949), pp. 22, 157-8 and pl. 56; P. S. Spokes, 'Coats of arms in Berkshire churches', *Berks., Bucks. and Oxon. Archaeol. Jour.*, xxxvi (1932), 41, 131-1). One difficulty about making the younger Sir John the lord of Kingston Bagpuize in either 1316 or 1328 or both and the ancestor of the Kingstons who remained there until the 16th century is that in 1322 his only child seems to have been Joan wife of Andrew son of Nicholas Braunch (*Cal. Close Rolls 1318-23*, p. 611). Another is that the Wiltshire lands of both the younger Sir John and the younger Sir Nicholas do not appear to have descended with Kingston Bagpuize. These objections could be overcome if at Sir John's death Joan Braunch was no longer his only issue and if it is assumed that his forfeiture in 1322 was never reversed. Since Kingston Bagpuize had been entailed on the elder Sir John and his heirs by William Bagpuize in 1290 it may have escaped forfeiture.

[23] *Berks, Bucks. and Oxon. Archaeol. Jour.*, x (1904), 60; *V.C.H. Berks.*, iv. 473.

[24] Berks. Record Office, E Bp/Ti (cartulary roll of deeds relating to Pusey etc., *c.* 1250-1300), m. 3v: a fine of 1 July 1297 between Margaret widow of Richard Pusey and Henry, Richard's son, querents and William son of William Fokeram deforciant in which the latter recognised the right of Nicholas Kingston and Margaret his wife and Nicholas's heirs in his former tenement in return for £20.

William Bagpuize's death Sir Nicholas and his wife surrendered all her right in it to his brother.[25] Their price may have been the manor in Pusey. By 1296 another of William Bagpuize's manors, that of Ashden (or West Compton) in the Berkshire parish of Compton, was also in their possession.[26]

The position on the sealing of the *conventio* of 5 December 1298 appears therefore to have been: (a) Sir William Mansell was the lord of Frampton Mansell, Over Lypiatt and a number of other properties in the Frome valley above Stroud, of Tortworth and of Redland, all in Gloucestershire; (b) Sir Nicholas Kingston held, jointly with his wife and at least partly of her inheritance, manors in Pusey and Compton on either side of Wantage in Berkshire.

It is not at all obvious why these men, whose estates lay in different counties and something like a day's journey apart, should have wished to make a treaty of mutual aid and counsel. Only one possibility seems to account for it; that they were already comrades-in-arms in Edward I's wars. Neither had hitherto been active in the affairs of his county and Kingston for one was no stripling.[27] Yet both had been knighted.[28] However recent their dubbing, the assumption that they were 'fighting' knights would alone seem to

[25] *V.C.H. Berks.*, iv. 350.

[26] *Ibid.*, p. 18. Presumably it had come to Margaret Kingston on Bagpuize's death, *c.* 1291.

[27] The very latest Kingston could have come of age was 1292 when he joined his wife in the surrender of her right to succeed Bagpuize at Kingston. His brother's debt to him in 1290 (*Cal. Close Rolls 1288-96*, p. 140) would tend to put the date still further back; and if, as seems likely, it was he who with Roger Kingston and two Osbert Giffards was in prison for deer-poaching in 1280 (*Cal. Close Rolls 1279-88*, p. 10), he must have been well on in his thirties by 1298. This would have made him about 65 when he was incapacitated by age in 1324, which seems reasonable. His brother John was old enough to have fought in the Welsh wars in 1277 (*Parl. Writs*, i. 205, 211 and 213). On the other hand William Mansell could have come of age recently in 1298. His eldest surviving son was born in or shortly before 1294 (*Abstracts of Gloucestershire Inquisitiones post mortem*, vol. v, ed. E. A. Fry (Index Libr., 1910), p. 190).

[28] They are first so called in their agreement, but since there are few earlier mentions of them this may not be significant.

[29] He was summoned to musters at Carlisle on 24 June 1300 (*Parl. Writs*, i. 338) and at Berwick precisely a year later (*ibid.*, p. 352). Though the distinguishing adjective 'senior' does not appear until 1316 and then often, there is reason for thinking that the Nicholas Kingston summoned to the muster at Carlisle on 15 Aug. 1314 (*ibid.*, ii. ii. 429) was the younger of that name. For on 28 Sept. 1314 Nicholas Kingston was in trouble for exchanging a Scottish prisoner without licence for his own yeoman Thomas Laurence lately captured on service in Scotland (*Cal. Pat. Rolls 1313-17*, p. 181); and Thomas Laurence was going to Wales with John Kingston on 1 Feb 1316 and so was Nicholas Kingston (*ibid.*, p. 383). Since nothing is heard of Sir John the elder after 1308 or at the latest 1311 (*Parl. Writs.* ii ii. 56, 372 and 375), it is likely that we are here dealing with the younger generation. But see p. 54 below.

make sense. For Kingston at least there is some evidence of his being one later.[29]

The difficulty is to find any evidence at all of their military employments in the twelve-nineties. It does not appear that they were with the royal army, as were the Berkeleys and Kingston's brother John, on the Falkirk campaign.[30] It is reasonably certain that, unlike John Kingston, they were not members of the royal household.[31] Nor did they form part of the little garrison in Edinburgh castle under its new constable.[32] Yet it is difficult to avoid seeing some connexion between their agreement to join forces and the royal favour which only ten days before had given the brother of one of them his first independent command. On 25 November 1298 Sir John was ordered to make a raid into Scotland as soon as he was able to raise a sufficient force.[33] Here was an opportunity for a younger brother to improve his fortunes and a reason why a knight from a different part of England should have thought his aid and counsel worth securing. Unfortunately the books and rolls of accounts for the Scottish wars are so far from complete that the names of those men-at-arms who fought in the retinues of others than the king are only rarely to be traced.[34] Our two knights had as yet no local

[30] The horse-rolls, P.R.O., E. 101/6/40 for members of the household retinue and E 101/6/39 for those not of the king's house (printed in *Scotland in 1298*, ed. H. Gough (Paisley, 1888), pp. 161-237) enable members of the retinues to be identified. That of Aymer de Valence, in accordance with the indenture of 2 July 1297 (*Cal. Docs. relating to Scotland*, ed. J. Bain, no. 905, and cf. nos. 981 and 1004), contained in addition to Thomas Berkeley and his two sons, Maurice and Thomas, five knights (*Scotland in 1298*, p. 216). Sir Maurice Berkeley's horse was killed at Falkirk.

[31] Sir John, accompanied by Osbert Kingston and two other valetti, appears in the 1298 household horse-roll (*Scotland in 1298*, p. 185). He is also on the Flanders horse-roll (P.R.O., E 101/6/37) 21 Aug. 1297. E 101/6/29 is an incomplete list of horses used in the Scottish war 1297-8; it contains nothing to our purpose; and no Kingston appears on the household horse-roll of 1300 (E 101/8/23) or on that of 1301 (E 101/9/24). Horse-rolls other than those of the king's household or his eldest son's (E 101/9/23) are extremely rare in this period.

[32] A list is attached to 'le ordenement fet du chastel de Puceles' 22 Nov. 1298 (P.R.O., E 101/7/24, m. 1). Neither of our men is on it nor in John Kingston's 'comitiva' in 1302 (E 101/10/5). The accounts for the Edinburgh garrison, 1298-1300 (E 101/7/28-9) are almost wholly illegible.

[33] *Documents illustrative of the History of Scotland, 1286-1306*, ed. J. Stevenson (2 vols. 1870), ii. 336-49.

[34] For example there are two books of accounts of the expenses of Warenne's army in Scotland in 26 Edw. I, kept by Walter Amersham (P.R.O., E 101/6/35 and 7/2). These do not name many of the knights in the various contingents brought by the principal captains. They contain no reference to either Kingston or Mansell in the sections headed 'Vadia liberata comitibus, baronibus, militibus et aliis hominibus ad arma.' No other accounts of this type survive for the years between Stirling Bridge and the end of the century and not many at any time in Edw. I's Scottish wars.

administrative duties and were to have none for several more years. They solemnly engaged themselves to go to one another's assistance not only in peace but in war, each retaining the other as befits a knight. Yet as warriors they elude us.

'In peace', the words which accompany 'in war' in virtually all indentures by which fighting-men were retained for life in the later middle ages, were for Kingston and Mansell at least no empty formula—though it does not follow that 'in war' therefore was.[35] The most enduring consequence of their alliance was another transaction between them which was given legal sanction before the king's judges at York on 1 May 1300. It had almost certainly taken effect some months earlier. Kingston and his wife agreed to exchange their lands in Pusey and Compton for the manor and rectory of Tortworth, Redland and their appurtenances; the Mansells—for William's wife, another Margaret, was associated with her husband—were in addition to receive £300.[36] By this exchange the Kingstons severed their hereditary connexion with Berkshire and became tenants exclusively in Gloucestershire. The Mansells, on the other hand, retained their more northerly group of estates in the Frome valley and added to them two smallish manors by the Berkshire Downs. They did not transfer themselves outright from one county to another; and Gloucestershire remained their place of residence and the centre of their active lives.[37]

But for Sir Nicholas Kingston the migration was final. He had

[35] 'In peace and war' is an almost invariable feature of such documents until the reign of Edw. IV when, if the indentures of William Lord Hastings are any guide, the words 'within the realm of England' begin to appear instead (W. H. Dunham, Jr., 'Lord Hastings' Indentured Retainers, 1461-83', *Trans. Connecticut Acad. of Arts and Sciences*, xxxix (1955), 123 et seq.).

[36] P.R.O., C.P. 25(1)/9/36. The summary in *V.C.H. Berks.*, iv. 18 and 473 is incomplete. Since Kingston was already known to hold lands worth £40 p.a. in Gloucs. on 15 Jan. 1300 (see p. 48 n. 10 above) the exchange must have occurred before that date.

[37] William Mansell sold Ashden to John de la Beche in 1321 (*V.C.H. Berks.*, iv. 18). In 1298 John's father Philip held an estate in Compton; it, Ashden and Kingston were all held of the honour of Leicester (*ibid.*; *Cal. Inquisitions post mortem*, iii. 307). The de la Beches could therefore have had some acquaintance with any of the Kingstons and the fact that John de la Beche was a fellow mainpernor with the Nicholas Kingston for the Scottish prisoner they exchanged for Kingston's yeoman after Bannockburn (above, p. 51, n. 29) does not help to determine whether it was Nicholas the elder or the younger. The Mansells retained Pusey, but as late as 1395 its lord is referred to as Philip Mansell of Gloucester (*V.C.H. Berks.*, iv. 473). The notion that William Mansell died holding lands in Gloucs., Herefs., Worcs., Salop., Staffs. and the March of Wales (*Knights of Edward I*, iii. 140) is due to a misunderstanding of *Cal. Fine Rolls*, iii. 290. There was a single escheator, John Hampton, for all these counties; it does not mean that Mansell had lands in any but Gloucs.

been provided with his stake in the land of Gloucestershire; and it was as a shire-knight with a modest estate beside the Severn estuary that he spent the remaining years of his life.[38] His lack of surviving male issue meant that the Kingstons of Gloucestershire were extinguished at his death a quarter of a century later. Before that, however, he had played a part the equal or more of Mansell's in the administrative chores that fell to the lot of the members of their class. These begin with his election to represent that shire in the parliament of May 1306. Thenceforward it was as sheriff, tax-collector, commissioner and representative of Gloucestershire in parliament and council that he left his mark on the records of the central government.[39] Even his military duties seem to have become increasingly administrative rather than belligerent.[40] Though he and Mansell were sometimes associated in their work, there is no sign of anything approaching a special relationship between them.[41] Nor can the bare bones of their public careers be filled out with the flesh and sinews of their private lives.[42]

Berkshire Record Office, Pusey Archives, E Bp/fı

Hec est convencio facta die Veneris in vigilia Sancti Nicholai anno domini m°cc° nonogesimo octavo inter dominum Nicholaum de Kyngeston' militem ex parte una & dominum Willelmum Maunsel militem ex altera: videlicet quod dictus dominus Nicholaus prestabit dicto domino Willelmo consilium suum & erit eidem intendens & in negociis suis auxilians quotiens per eundem

[38] On 28 July 1304 he received a grant of the right to hold a weekly market at Tortworth and free warren in his demesnes in Tortworth and Redland (*Cal. Charter Rolls*, iii. 44).

[39] Sheriff, 12 March-2 Dec. 1308 and 28 Oct. 1312-1 Jan. 1313; kt. of shire, 30 May 1306 and 20 Jan. 1315; assessor and collector of taxes, 28 Nov. 1313, 8 June and 5 Aug. 1316 and 30 May 1319; conservator of the peace 13 Apr. 1314 (*Parl. Writs*. i. 688 and ii, ii. 1056-7).

[40] On 20 May 1311 he together with Mansell, Thomas Berkeley and John Wilington was ordered to raise 500 footmen mostly from the forest of Dean; Kingston and Mansell were to lead them north; it does not look as if the king's command was obeyed (*ibid.*, ii ii. 409-10 and 416). A similar order on 26 March 1316 was also subject to delay (*ibid.* pp. 465, 469 and 474-5); William Mansell was once again involved. In 1317 Kingston was no longer required to lead the footmen when they left the county (*ibid.*, pp. 489, 492, 496 and 498).

[41] Mansell was sheriff, 1 Jan. to 2 Apr. 1313; kt. of shire, 8 Aug. 1311 and 23 Sept. 1313; collector of scutage, 28 Nov. 1314; supervisor of the assize of arms, 1 Sept. 1315; commissioner of array, 15 Feb. 1322; summoned to attend Great Council, 9 May 1324, which, unlike Kingston, he seems to have been able to attend (*ibid.*, p. 1158). He was dead by 13 July 1324 (*Cal. Fine Rolls*, iii. 290). Outside Gloucs. he had kept the pesage of Southampton from 30 Sept. 1311 (*ibid.* ii. 164).

dominum Willelmum rationabiliter fuerit premunitus et erit sibi promptus in omnibus tam in tempore pacis quam guerre sumptibus dicti domini Willelmi[43] fide consilio suo vel auxilio indigeat & eundem prout decet militem voluerit retinere. Dictus vero dominus Willelmus obligavit se facturum erga dictum dominum Nicholaum in omnibus premissis[44] fide consolio suo[45] vel auxilio aliquo tempore indiguetur & in singulis quibus ab eodem domino Nicholao auxiliatus existat modo simili sumptibus que dicti domini Nicholai mediantibus eidem promisit fideliter subvenire. In cuius rei testimonium sigilla sua alternatim sunt appensa.[46]

[42] The appearance of both Mansell and Kingston as witnesses to a grant by John Giffard of Brimpsfield to Hugh Despenser, 20 Nov. 1309 (*Catalogue of Ancient Deeds*, i, no. A 931 and cf. iii, no. A 5904 and iv, nos. A 6902 and A 7526) is suggestive but no more.

[43] Some such word as 'quando' or 'quotiens' seems to be needed here.

[44] Again a word is missing; probably 'si'.

[45] This word is interlineated.

[46] Parchment, 120 mm wide and 90 mm high, indented along the top. There are two seal strips cut from the lower edge, one of which has been torn off above the seal: the remaining, upper, one has a small seal of arms without inscription: a forked-tailed lion rampant with a label of three points (Kingston). The capitals and punctuation are mine.

IV. LOANS TO THE LANCASTRIAN KINGS: THE PROBLEM OF INDUCEMENT[1]

THE problem that I am going to discuss this afternoon is one which must surely have exercised the minds of all those who have given a moment's thought to the financing of the Hundred Years' War. What conclusions have been reached it would be hard to say. For apart from two or three illuminating though hardly conclusive pages by Mr A. B. Steel,[2] to whom my indebtedness should soon be obvious, nothing seems to have been printed on this subject in recent times. Yet unless we have some idea why men lent large sums of ready money to the English kings of the later Middle Ages, we must approach the political history of the period at a considerable disadvantage. To an increasing extent as the fourteenth century advanced and preponderantly throughout the course of its successor these lenders were natives and drawn from all sections of the propertied classes. The king's treatment of his creditors was therefore bound to affect his relations with his most powerful subjects. It would be surprising if his success or failure in meeting his obligations did not markedly influence their attitude towards his rule.

It has of course long been known that when the first three Edwards borrowed money from the Italian banking-houses the latter responded generously because in the first place they hoped for gain and later on because they wished to avoid losing what they had

---

[1] Paper read to the Cambridge Historical Society, 5 November 1946.

[2] *English Historical Review,* LI (1936), 45-7.

[3] *Cal. Close Rolls, 1339-41,* p. 176.

[4] 'Extracts from the Liberate Rolls relative to Loans' (ed. E. A. Bond), *Archaeologia,* 1st series, XXVIII, 225-30; W. E. Rhodes, 'The Italian Bankers in England and their loans to Edward I and Edward II', *Historical Essays by Members of Owen's College, Manchester* (ed. T. F. Tout and J. Tait), pp. 140 and 166: E. Russell, 'The Societies of the Bardi and the Peruzzi and their dealings with Edward III, 1327-45', *Finance and Trade under Edward III* (ed. G. Unwin), pp. 101 and 114-17. On 28 June 1339 Edward III granted the Bardi £30,000 and the Peruzzi £20,000 'in remembrance of their timely subsidies for the king's service and their losses, labours and expenses endured for him' (*Cal. Pat. Rolls, 1338-40,* p. 388, and cf. *ibid.* pp. 391 and 392). For his relations with them see A. Sapori, *La Crisi delle Compagnie dei Bardi e dei Peruzzi* and A. Beardwood, *Alien Merchants in England 1350 to 1377,* pp. 4-9 and 122-33; and compare Y. Renouard, *Les Rélations des Papes d'Avignon et des Compagnies commerciales et bancaires de 1316 à 1378,* pp. 512-47.

already invested. Nobody supposes that their services were performed gratuitously. As Edward III could quite frankly admit, he had had 'recourse to usury with sundry creditors.'[3] Whatever other advantages they expected to derive from their willingness to accommodate the king there seems little doubt that there was a prearranged return on all moneys lent, though that return took various forms.[4] Nor was Edward's principal native financier, Sir William de la Pole, treated any less generously.[5] What then are we to think about the loans, amounting to thousands and often tens of thousands of pounds a year, which barons, bishops, merchants, knights, esquires and even civil servants, not to mention towns and other corporations, made to the Crown in the Lancastrian period? Were they usurious? If not usurious, then what inducement or what other motive had these men for putting good money for months and generally years at a time at the disposal of an impoverished and none too scrupulous king?

The answer which used to be favoured was that these loans were made without direct reward by those who were anxious to serve or save their country. In the words of Stubbs, Cardinal Beaufort, who was the greatest of them, was 'ready to sacrifice his wealth . . . for the King.'[6] For this his many defects deserved to be excused. The phrase used by William Hunt in the *Dictionary of National Biography* that 'he at least made his country a gainer by his wealth' is, for all its studied vagueness, obviously intended to convey the same meaning.[7] It is easy to understand why this explanation has struck some recent scholars as inadequate. For it would indeed be odd if in an age when political morality, as we are often reminded,[8] was so low, when corruption and venality flourished in every department of the royal service and when the traditional restraints on acquisitiveness are held to have become ineffective, the propertied

---

[5] Edward III's numerous grants to him are conveniently summarised by H. A. Napier, *Historical Notices of Swyncombe and Ewelme*, pp. 276-80. On 27 November 1338 he was given £4000 'pro dampnis que sustinuit pro diuersis cheuanciis denariorum per ipsum factum' to Edward III abroad, and a few weeks later another 20,000 marks for the same reason (Exchequer, Treasury of Receipt, Misc. Books, E. 36/203, fols. 102 and 102v. This is William Norwell's 'Liber de particulis compoti garderobe regis', 11 July 1338 to 28 May 1340).

[6] *Constitutional History of England*, III (5th ed. 1903), 144.

[7] Ed. 1908, II, 47*b*.

[8] For a recent exposition of these views see J. E. A. Jolliffe, *Constitutional History of Medieval England*, pp. 409 et seq.

[9] W. I. Haward, 'The financial transactions between the Lancastrian government and the merchants of the Staple from 1449 to 1461.' *Studies in English Trade in the Fifteenth Century*, pp. 300-1.

classes in their scores were willing to entrust their capital for long periods without return to a discredited government. Even if one is not prepared to accept current estimates of the public spirit of fifteenth-century Englishmen, the contrast with the practice of Edward III's time would still be too glaring. If William de la Pole and his contemporaries lent for high rewards then it is at least improbable that their grandsons were content with less.

And so the traditional view has been modified. The answer to our problem now preferred—for example by Mr Steel and by at least one contributor to Messrs Power and Postan's volume of *Studies*[9]—is that these native capitalists received their consideration in the form of trading concessions and licences and in the expectation of further benefits to follow.[10] One weakness of this explanation is that it is often impossible to discover those conjunctions of loan and grant which it requires; another that it implies a reliance upon the capricious and ephemeral gratitude of a preoccupied king far more trusting than these same lenders were ever guilty of in their dealings with one another. Such blind confidence in the government's sense of obligation would not be far from the disinterested patriotism with which they were credited by Stubbs. Before we accept either as a sufficient answer, all reasonable alternatives deserve to be ruled out. There seem to be two that are not wildly out of keeping with all that we know of contemporary financial practice. Both were briefly considered by Mr Steel but not pressed. Let me be more rash. Either these loans were unprofitable and compulsory or they were voluntary and carried with them a guaranteed reward. It is by no means impossible that some were of one sort and some of the other; we should hardly expect all creditors to have received the same treatment. But until the evidence has been examined with these points in mind we are not likely to make much progress.

In the first place, is there any support for the theory that they were forced loans? Yes, there is some. But before considering the record

[10] One such case occurred in 1435 when on 2 December three well-connected merchants, William Estfield, Hamon Sutton and Hugh Dyke, in return for a loan of 8000 marks received in addition to repayment a concession that they should 'in selling of their wools at the town of Calais be preferred before all other merchants there to the value of the aforesaid sum [i.e. 8000 marks] and that they . . . should be able freely to sell their wools . . . to the value aforesaid . . . to whatever person and in whatever manner that they wished before the other merchants . . . and to keep the same proceeding therefrom to themselves without any restriction or partition to be made of them in the Staple of Calais between the merchants thereof, any statute or ordinance made to the contrary notwithstanding' (Early Chancery Proceedings, C. 1/11/289). There is no mention of this additional reward in the patent which they had confirmed in parliament (*Rotuli Parliamentorum*, IV, 484-6 and *Cal. Pat. Rolls, 1429-36*, p. 498).

of the house of Lancaster in this matter it would be wise to remind ourselves that according to the St Albans' chronicler, Thomas Walsingham, the forced loan was an innovation of Richard II's 'tyranny.' In a well-known passage in the *Annales* he describes how when news was received that he was about to be elected Emperor, Richard compelled all the rich men in England to lend him money.[11] This action, is is implied, was something altogether different from that of the Great Council in 1379 with which it has lately been compared.[12] Richard's own appeals for loans in the past had almost certainly been more than once rejected, as for instance by the merchants in the parliament of May 1382[13] and in 1392 by the citizens of London.[14] It may have been as a result of past failures that in 1397 he adopted what Walsingham regarded as a novel method of trying to secure compliance with his wishes:

> habentes executores hujus negotii secum litteras regali sigillo signatas, intus quidem continentes summam quam volebant petere sed non indorsatas, donec invenissent tales a quibus petere aliquid voluerunt. Qui, venientes ad urbes et villas, inquisierunt occulte qui praestabant divitiis, et mox accepto cujusque nomine, indorsaverunt litteras, tanquam specialiter talibus destinatas.[15]

It is evident that Walsingham regarded this inquisitorial procedure as even more objectionable than the use of compulsion. Granted that it was less easy for a capitalist to excuse himself when asked for a loan if his financial circumstances had been accurately assessed, there still remains no description of the means by which the compulsion was applied. Nor does Walsingham provide us with any clue to the identity of the 'executores.' It is difficult to avoid the impression that he has exaggerated the amount of force which the king's agents could bring to bear and that what he is really complaining about is the efficiency with which they sought out those who could be persuaded to lend. The records of the Exchequer show

---

11 *J. de Trokelowe et Anon. Chronica et Annales* (ed. H. T. Riley), p. 199. Mr V. H. Galbraith (The St. Albans Chronicle, 1406-1420, pp. xxvii-lxxi) has given convincing reasons for regarding Walsingham as the author of these annals.

12 *Rot. Parl.* III, 55-6. Note particularly: 'touz les Seignurs illoeqes esteantz appresterent *voluntrisment* a nostre Sir le Roi diverses grandes sommes de deniers.' For those lending see *Foedera* (ed. T. Rymer), VII (ed. 1709), 210-3 and *Cal. Pat. Rolls, 1377-81*, pp. 635-8.

13 *Rot. Parl.* III, 123.

14 *Polychronicon Ranulphi Higden* (ed. J. R. Lumby), IX, 270 ('Monk of Westminster').

15 *J. de Trokelowe*, etc., p. 200.

that their labours yielded a slightly higher proportion of loans than usual but not enough to justify our full acceptance of the chronicler's story.[16] The country was humming with rumours of Richard's intentions and a malicious interpretation was put on everything he did. It is therefore noteworthy that the taking of forced loans does not feature among the all-embracing articles of his deposition, though the equally unsubstantiated allegation that he intended to bilk his creditors has a place there.[17] In short, apart from Walsingham's statement, there is really strikingly little evidence that Richard exerted undue pressure to obtain his loans. The most that we can safely conclude is that talk of such practices was in the air. The fact that they were not formally condemned by those who stage-managed the deposition at least left the hands of the usurper unfettered.

The new dynasty made no secret of its wish to stand as free in its prerogatives as any of its predecessors. That being its policy, it would not be remarkable if the practice of taking forced loans, supposing it to have existed in a form however embryonic before 1399, were to have survived into the following period. The evidence, patchy and inconclusive as it is, was extensive enough to disturb Stubbs, though he did his best to clear his favourite Lancastrians from suspicion. His defence cannot be regarded as wholly satisfactory since he failed to make a clear distinction between a forced loan and a benevolence.[18] Contemporaries were unanimously of the opinion that the 'benevolence' of 1473 was a new and unheard-of imposition.[19] But this does not justify us in arguing with Stubbs that the forced loan was therefore also a Yorkist novelty. There is after all sufficient difference between a gift and a loan to account fully for the chroniclers' disgust.

Between 1399 and 1461 many methods of borrowing were

---

[16] Mr Steel's total of 'genuine loans' for the year 1396-7 is £30,355 (*Eng. Hist. Rev.* LI, 49). This is the highest for the reign, but it is less than £2000 more than the next highest, that for the year 1385-6. The totals for 1397-9 are below the average for the reign.

[17] *Rot. Parl.* III, 419 (§ 31).

[18] *Op. cit.* III, 283, n. Stubbs may be right in wishing to date later than 1461 the two sets of Instructions assigned by N. H. Nicolas (*Proceedings and Ordinances of the Privy Council*, IV, 152 b-e and V, 418-21) to 1436 and 1442 respectively. But it is very unusual to find Nicolas out in his dating of these conciliar documents. If he is right then the credit for inventing the benevolence must be awarded to the government of Henry VI.

[19] 'Historiae Croylandensis Continuatio' (ed. W. Fulman in *Rerum Anglicarum Scriptores*, I, 558); *Great Chronicle of London* (ed. A. H. Thomas and I. D. Thornley), p. 223.

employed and it is impossible to state any consistent practice. There were times when it was thought that enough money to tide over a temporary shortage could be raised by negotiating directly with a few likely magnates, merchants or corporations. Those near the seat of government, the holders of the great offices of state, the members of the royal council and the principal London citizens were often willing to come to the king's aid.[20] At other times letters under the privy seal were dispatched to a wide selection of people specifying the amount desired and leaving the recipients in no doubt about the Crown's pressing need. A long list of those applied to in February 1436 has been preserved.[21] Such letters are in fact commonly met with among municipal archives.[22] But the method most usually employed by the Lancastrians was to issue commissions *de mutuo faciendo*, appointing a group of persons in every shire to collect promises of loans from their neighbours and to send to the central government the names of those willing to subscribe together with a note of the amounts promised. A somewhat imperfect list of commissioners for 1402 is preserved among the records of the council;[23] a fuller one is entered on the Fine Roll for 1405.[24] At first copies of these commissions seem to have been rather haphazardly kept, but from 1419 onwards, when the renewal of the French war had made frequent borrowing necessary, it became a fairly general practice to record them on the Patent Rolls.[25] Instructions issued to the commissioners by Henry VI's government have in several cases survived and tell us something of the procedure they were expected to adopt.[26] Here again a certain lack of uniformity in detail suggests the experimental stage. But it appears that as a rule they were provided with letters of credence or 'letters exhortive' from the king, setting

[20] In June 1404 the council told Henry IV that the Treasurer had borrowed 500 marks from Lord Lovell, £100 each from the bishop of Bath and Sir Hugh Waterton (all councillors) and various other sums from individual Londoners (*Proceedings and Ordinances*, I 267-8).

[21] *Ibid.* IV, 316-29.

[22] In 1435, for instance, the men of Beverley were invited, politely enough it is true, to lend 200 marks (*Hist. MSS. Comm. Rep., Corporation of Beverley*, pp. 22-3), while in the following year the citizens of Salisbury were asked for £200 (*ibid. Various Collections*, IV, 198).

[23] *Proceedings and Ordinances*, II, 72-6 (21 October).

[24] *Cal. Fine Rolls*, XII, 317-19; *Foedera*, VIII, 412-14 (4 September 1405).

[25] *Cal. Pat. Rolls, 1416-22*, pp. 249-52; *Foedera*, IX, 814-15 (26 November 1419), etc. In the *Calendar*, although they are generally indexed under 'loans', there are some omissions; for example that of 26 February 1434 (*Cal. Pat. Rolls, 1429-36*, pp. 353-5). There is also an isolated earlier example, 14 June 1410 (*ibid. 1408-13*, pp. 204-5).

[26] *Proceedings and Ordinances*, V, 187-9 (14 May 1442); 414-18 (2 March 1443); VI 322-5 (? late 1444); 46-9 (20 July 1446); 234-44 (14 May 1455).

forth his poverty and urging all loyal men to assist him to the limits of their capacity. In spite of their obvious bearing on our problem these instructions have not, as far as I am aware, been at all thoroughly studied. Those dated 20 July 1446 may be taken as typical. After reciting at tedious length the king's reasons for troubling his subjects, they ordered the commissioners to 'entreat all the good cities, townships, knights, squires and thrifty men dwelling within the abovesaid shires to lend as much money as they shall more goodly get of them.'

> And forasmuch as the king is not fully informed which of his subjects may pay and lend as above, the king sendeth therefore unto his said commissaries letters under his privy seal (after the tenor hereto annexed) with blank tails; the which letters the king will that they direct them to such persons, cities and townships as that them shall seem good and write in the tails of the same letters the names of the persons that they shall be directed unto and so deliver them to the said persons.[27]

The sums raised were to be sent to the Receipt of the Exchequer in all haste and by the following Michaelmas at the very latest. In return those bringing them were promised assignments on the grant made to the king in his last parliament. This would fall due for payment at Martinmas 1447.[28] When it did the lender had only to present his tallies to the tax-collectors against whom they were drawn to recover his money. That at any rate was the theory, though in practice there were often long delays and tallies which had been dishonoured had not infrequently to be exchanged for fresh ones.[29] Only those whose loans took the form of advances on their own taxation were safe against loss. The commissioners *de mutuo faciendo* were in short employed in hawking drafts on the Crown's future revenues in exchange for cash.

The resemblance between their work and that of Walsingham's 'executores' will not have escaped notice. But there was one important difference. None of the specimen letters 'with blank tails' annexed to the instructions contained any note of the sum desired. The total amount hoped for from each shire was sometimes

[27] *Proceedings and Ordinances*, VI, 47-9. The Latin form was 'littere cum albis caudis' (*ibid*. p. 235).

[28] *Rot. Parl.* V, 69.

[29] For the meaning of 'mutuum per talliam' entries on the Receipt Rolls see A. B. Steel, 'Mutua per talliam, 1377-1413', *Bull. Inst. Hist. Res.* XIII (1936), 73-84. A list of worthless tallies to the nominal value of £30,000, cut between 1422 and 1433, is preserved in Exchequer of Receipt Misc., E. 407/6/126.

indicated, but the commissioners were left free to 'commune' with individuals about the size of their contributions.[30] It is obvious, however, that such a system of collection, though harmless enough in appearance, could easily lend itself to abuse. On the other hand, the 'letters exhortive' contain nothing whatever that could be interpreted as a threat. They are eloquent and reasoned requests, never commands. Yet even reassuring phrases about 'affection', 'kindness' and 'goodwill' may be thought to have an ominous ring when we remember what Edward IV meant by 'benevolentia' and what Richard II's subjects learn to call a 'plaisance.' It is more conclusive that the surviving instructions to the commissioners speak the same language. They again and again emphasise the need for entreaty and afford no evidence that force was contemplated.

Against this impression must be set the statements of contemporary writers. There are three relevant passages. One, from a short Latin Chronicle printed by C. L. Kingsford, tells us that in 1416 Henry V's commissioners excited much alarm and resentment by the high-handed fashion in which they pressed the royal demands upon the monasteries.[31] This was not long after Italian merchants had been given a choice between lending and going to prison and had in some cases preferred prison.[32] The description of the same king's 'unbearable exactions' in 1421, with which Adam of Usk ends his lively narrative, is better known.[33] The king himself undertook a recruiting tour of the provinces in order to stimulate his subjects' flagging interest in his war of conquest and summoned them before him to exhort them to aid him with their money as well as their persons.[34] Lastly, we are informed on somewhat doubtful authority that in 1460 the then Treasurer, the much-hated earl of Wiltshire, assessed the amount of each man's contribution and compelled all to pay.[35] Here are three not very precise allegations and there are no more. In 1460 the government was desperate and all pretence of peace and order had been abandoned amid the clash of faction. There remains the evidence against Henry V. Whatever weight we attach to it—and it is difficult to attach much where Adam of Usk is concerned—it applies only to two of Henry's long series of loans.

---

[30] *Proceedings and Ordinances*, I, 343-4.
[31] *Eng. Hist. Rev.* XXIX (1914) 511-12.
[32] *Proceedings and Ordinances*, II, 165-6.
[33] *Chronicon Adae de Usk* (ed. E. M. Thompson). p. 133.
[34] E. de Monstrelet, *Chronique* (ed. L. Douët d'Arcq), IV, 25. On this tour see J. H. Wylie and W. T. Waugh, *Reign of Henry the Fifth*, III, 270-3.
[35] *English Chronicle of the reigns of Richard II, Henry IV, Henry V, and Henry VI* (ed. J. S. Davies). p. 90.

Certainly Henry was an impatient and masterful man. But there were many things which the Lancastrian kings had more will than strength to do: that is indeed the essence of their so-called constitutionalism. At the height of their success during the glorious years between Agincourt and Henry V's early death, they came nearer to being able to satisfy their natures than at any other time in their brief tenure of the kingship. England may then have had a foretaste of compulsion, but defeat and civil war were needed to make her people accept it as an ingredient in their regular diet. There was always a limit to the amount they would stomach.

It was a large part of Stubbs's defence of the Lancastrians against the charge of unconstitutional exactions that their loans were raised 'by authority of parliament.' This refers to a series of enactments from 1416 onwards by which the proceeds of certain taxes were assigned for the repayment of those willing to lend. It was on the strength of the first of these that the commissioners of 1416 did their unpopular work. As the marginal note in the Rolls makes obvious, the intention was to increase the yield by offering better security to subscribers.[36] A similar parliamentary assignment was made in 1419[37] but the failure of the Commons to make a grant in May 1421 necessitated a different form of words. The king's council was given 'full power' to secure repayment 'in such form and manner as seems to the said lords [of the Council] honest and sufficient . . . and that by the authority of the said parliament.'[38] In 1423 a limit of 20,000 marks was set, but in later years this was raised until by 1442 it had reached £200,000, well beyond any sum that the king was ever likely to collect or the assigned tax to produce.[39] After the parliament of February 1449 these enactments either ceased or, it may be, were no longer enrolled. A conditional clause attached to that of 1429 and to most subsequent ones gives us the Commons' view on the subject of forced loans. The council was to exercise the authority committed to it, but

> provided always that no lieges of our lord the king by force of this ordinance shall be induced or compelled against their wills to make loan, chevisance, obligation or other surety whatsoever to the king or to any

---

[36] 'La seurete de la Chevance a faire a Roy' (*Rot. Parl.* IV, 95-6).
[37] *Ibid.* pp. 117-18.   [38] *Ibid.* p. 130.
[39] *Ibid.* pp. 210-11. It was £20,000 in 1425, £40,000 in 1426, £24,000 in 1427, £50,000 in 1429, and 1430-1, 100,000 marks in 1433, £100,000 in 1435, 1437, 1439-40, 1442, 1447 and 1449 (*ibid*, IV, 277, 300, 317-18, 339-40, 374-5, 426-7, 482-3, 504; V, 6-7, 39-40, 135-6 and 143-4).

other person for the chevisance of the sum aforesaid or of any parcel of it.[40]

It would be rash to claim that this proviso settled the question —either way. But it is unlikely that it would have been framed so mildly had there been any danger of forced loans becoming usual. The wording suggests that the need was felt for some safeguard against an occasional abuse, not that the Commons were protesting against a well-entrenched practice. Parliament while authorising the collection of a loan had given the king's subjects a statutory right to refuse the commissioners' entreaties. If it can be shown that they did refuse the case against compulsion becomes overwhelming.

Nor is this difficult. The Receipt Rolls show that a good many appeals for loans met with little response. That, for example, of 1419 hardly produced anything at all, a fact which seems to prove that Henry V's presence was necessary to make his government's pressure effective.[41] Again, in 1434 a great council told ministers that a projected campaign would have to be abandoned as impracticable because 'men will not lend . . . as may also clearly appear by the report of your foresaid commissioners [*de mutuo faciendo*].'[42] This refusal to subscribe was put down to 'vexation' at the government's failure to offer the crown jewels as pledges for repayment. Nothing could be less suggestive of compulsion than this insistence on good security. Another excuse was given when in 1426 a commission headed by the abbot of St. Albans had to inform the council that the men of Hertfordshire were too poor to contribute anything.[43] There

---

[40] *Ibid.* IV, 340, etc.

[41] Exchr. of Receipt, Receipt Rolls, E. 401/690 and 693; R. A. Newhall, 'The War Finances of Henry V and the Duke of Bedford', *Eng. Hist. Rev.* XXXVI (1921), 173 and 175.

[42] *Proceedings and Ordinances*, IV, 214.

[43] *Foedera*, IX, 499-500. Rymer misplaces these documents. The reference to the last parliament at Leicester proves that they belong to 4 Henry VI. In any case Whethamstede did not become abbot of St. Albans until 1419 (W. Dugdale, *Monasticon*, ed. 1846, I, 425).

[44] The commissioners in 1542 were told that 'if anyone shows himself stiff in condescending to the same, upon allegation of poverty or other pretence which seems insufficient, they shall use what persuasion they can, and if all will not draw him to some reason and honest consideration of his duty they shall charge him to keep secret what they have said, note his name and command him to return to his house, and so pass him over in such silence as he be no empeachment or evil example to the rest.' (*Letters and Papers of Henry VIII*, XVII, no. 194, quoted by K. Pickthorn, *Early Tudor Government, Henry VIII*, pp. 390-1). The term 'forced loan' seems to be of nineteenth-century coinage.

[45] *Cal. Pat. Rolls, 1436-41*, p. 249. The example is typical.

is no evidence that any steps were taken to induce them to change
their minds. Neither in the patents by which the commissioners were
appointed nor in their instructions is there any mention of sanctions.
It is even doubtful whether the forced loans of the Tudors deserve
their epithet.[44]

The truth would seem to be that compulsion was impracticable.
The subject's liberty to lend or not as he pleased might have no very
solid foundation in constitutional theory, but, given the way society
was organised, it had little need of protection. Nothing brings this
out more clearly than the fact that those who were given the duty of
negotiating the loans were the most likely contributors to them.
When, for example, in March 1439 the abbot of Darley, Sir Richard
Vernon of Haddon, Sir Thomas Gresley of Drakelow, Sir Thomas
Blount of Barton Blount and John Curzon of Croxall were ordered
to levy loans in Derbyshire, they were obviously chosen for their
wealth and standing in that area.[45] The commissioners were not
subservient officials backed by force, but the local representatives of
the propertied classes upon the willing collaboration of whom the
monarchy depended; and it would be just as reasonable to imagine
them becoming the instruments of royal extortion as to suppose
them capable of overthrowing the social order itself. The central
government for the greater part of the Lancastrian period was in the
hands of an aristocratic council, the members of which, whatever
their sense of the king's needs, had strong local ties. Neither it nor its
provincial agents were the men to carry out a policy of soaking the
rich for the Crown's exclusive benefit.

Those who disagree with Stubbs's reading of the evidence are apt to
rest their case upon a group of royal letters which I have so far
ignored. One, dated 20 July 1453, may be quoted as typical:

> Right trusty and well-beloved. How it be that by our other letters of
> privy seal of the date at Westminster the xiiij day of this present month we
> willed and also charged you either to have sent unto our treasury the cc
> marks like as ye agreed by motion of our right trusty and well-beloved our
> Treasurer of England to lend us for succours of our cousin the earl of
> Shrewsbury . . . in our duchy of Guyenne, or else to have appeared
> personally before us and our council at certain day now passed, as in our
> said letters it was contained more at large. Nevertheless that notwith-
> standing ye neither have sent the said money nor appeared according to
> our said commandment whereof we have great marvel. Forsomuch we
> write to you eftsoons straightly charging you that as ye will eschew to be
> noted and taken for a letter and breaker of the army which is appointed to

be sent unto our said duchy for the said succours, ye without delay or tarrying either send by the bearer hereof the said cc marks unto our said Treasurer or come in all possible haste personally before our said council to have knowledge of such matters as shall be declared unto you.[46]

This, says Plummer, seems too clear to be explained away. 'That the man had promised to lend the money does not affect the constitutional question, if the promise was one which the government had no right to exact.'[47] It is difficult to accept this judgement. There is no evidence that the promise of 200 marks had been exacted by improper methods. The commissioners *de mutuo faciendo* were instructed to enter into indentures with those willing to lend, 'in the which shall be specified the sum that shall be . . . lent and the day when it shall be brought into the king's Receipt'; and they were to forward their halves of the indentures to Westminster.[48] In threatening a contumacious defaulter with penalties, the government could hardly be accused of unconstitutional taxation. It had at least the right to ask men who broke their contracts to explain. As far as I know the only ones to receive such letters were those who without explanation had gone back on their promises.[49]

In what very different terms did the king couch his request for a loan. These begging letters have nothing in common with the *sub poena*.[50] Nor because he sometimes asked for a definite amount does it follow that he was able to obtain it. The city of London, we know, made a practice of consenting to lend less than the sum asked for and no attempt was made to apply further pressure. The citizens were too influential not to be treated with consideration.[51] The same is true of those wealthy individuals upon whose financial help the Crown largely relied. These were men to be courted, not coerced, though doubtless they were expected to honour their bond like any other man of business. Perhaps in the case of the most important of them the disadvantage lay with the Crown. Cardinal Beaufort was prepared to advance large sums, but it was for him to impose conditions. These were clearly set down by him in a series of what he

46 *Proceedings and Ordinances*, VI, 143-4.

47 J. Fortescue, *Governance of England* (ed. C. Plummer), p. 12, n. 6.

48 *Proceedings and Ordinances*, VI, 48.

49 *Ibid*. II, 280-2 and VI, 330-1; *Wars of the English in France* (ed. J. Stevenson), II, ii, 481-2, 486-7, 491-2; and in other collections.

50 *Proceedings and Ordinances*, II, 72-3; VI, 175-6, etc.; *Original Letters illustrative of English History* (ed. H. Ellis, 3rd ser.), I, 75-81; *Foedera*, VIII, 245.

51 E. J. Davis and M. I. Peake, 'Loans from the City of London to Henry VI, 1431-1449', *Bull. Inst. Hist. Res.* IV (1927), 165-72.

styled with characteristic frankness his 'demands', to be granted before a penny was forthcoming.[52] Nothing could be less ambiguous than the following minute of the council for 25 May 1443:

> And at the which day that my said lord cardinal's patent was read in the abovesaid place and before his departing from the same place, he said that he would have his patent after the minute that was made and else he would lend no money; the which minute was afterwards read and passed. And my lord of Gloucester said at the time that it was reading before my said lords: 'What needeth it to be read sith that it is passed my lord? For mine uncle saith plainly that he will lend no money unless that he have it under that form.'[53]

Inappropriate language surely in which to discuss the terms of a forced loan.

On all this varied evidence, only one conclusion seems possible: namely, that in spite of some suspicious circumstances which tend to show that they may have willed otherwise than they could perform, the Lancastrians did not extort their loans by force; and that except in isolated cases some other explanation must be sought to account for men's willingness to lend. As usual, if partly for the wrong reasons, Stubbs's caution appears to be justified. On examination the case for compulsion breaks down. Is there a better case for reward?

In approaching the question of usury it is fortunately no longer necessary for me to waste any time in demonstrating that ecclesiastical prohibitions of that 'horrible and abominable vice' were largely ineffective in medieval England. It flourished under cover of fictions 'originally contrived', as Blackstone put it,[54] 'to evade the absurdity of those monkish constitutions' which restricted its employment.[55] Lawyers seem here for once to have stolen a march upon historians by realising before they did that 'to the devices fallen upon to defeat those laws the greatest part of the deeds in use both in England and Scotland owe their original forms.'[56] Nevertheless it is hard to believe that the ecclesiastical authorities were hoodwinked. That may have been the original purpose of concealment; but what was more important for the moneylender was that his bonds should be enforcible in the lay courts. He was never safe against an outbreak

[52] *Proceedings and Ordinances*, iv, 233-6.
[53] *Ibid.* v, 279-80.
[54] *Commentaries on the Laws of England* (ed. 1844), iii, 433-4.
[54] W. J. Ashley, *Introduction to English Economic History and Theory*, i, ii, § 65.
[56] W. Ross, *Lectures on the Law of Scotland* (1793), i, 4.

of Puritanism even in the city of London.[57] Hence the need for a great variety of fictions which have left a lasting mark upon the forms of action in English law. Some were so successful that they make modern investigation almost impossible. We may often suspect but we are rarely in a position to prove that a particular transaction was usurious. Happily this is not always so; and thank to Mr Postan many of the delusions of earlier economic historians on this point have been dispelled.[58]

This then is the background against which our problem has to be viewed. It prompted Mr Steel to write that 'it is almost certainly untrue that in the fourteenth and fifteenth centuries, when concealed usury was an everyday affair, English kings were really powerful enough to refuse a *quid pro quo* on that special class of loans which happened to be made to the crown.'[59] Such scepticism commands agreement. Even if the most frequent lenders had not been merchants who could ill afford to put their money to unprofitable uses, it would still be a mistake to rely upon the economic innocence of the country gentry. Some of them at any rate were familiar enough with the practices of the counting-house. Take the case of Sir John Fastolf, whose receiver-general's account for 1433-4 has survived among the muniments of an Oxford college.[60] These show that in the seventh year of Henry VI's reign (1428-9), finding himself with 2000 marks in hand, Fastolf advanced them to John Wells, warden of the London Grocers' Company and shortly afterwards mayor of the city.[61] He stipulated that he should receive 100 marks 'employ and gain' *per annum* for seven years and that at the end of that period his capital should be returned to him undiminished. This is but one of a number of investments of money *ad mercandizandum* on which this Norfolk knight was receiving interest at 5% in 1433-4.[62] It was thus that he added to his very considerable landed

[57] *Calendar of Plea and Memoranda Rolls of the City of London, 1413-47* (ed. A. H. Thomas), pp. 95-109 and 285-7.

[58] See below, p. 65, n. 77.

[59] *Eng. Hist. Rev.* LI (1936), 45.

[60] Magdalen College, Oxford, Fastolf Papers, 9 (John Kirtling's Account, Mic. 12 Henry VI to Mic. 13 Henry VI).

[61] *Cal. Pat. Rolls, 1429-36*, pp. 78 and 214; *Calendar of London Letter Book K* (ed. R. R. Sharpe), pp. 123-4.

[62] He had lent £500 to William Cavendish, £100 to William Trumpington, £150 to John Fastolf of Olton and £100 to Richard Ellis. Of these Cavendish and Trumpington were citizens and mercers of London (*Cal. Pat. Rolls, 1422-9*, pp. 305, etc.), Richard Ellis was a burgess of Great Yarmouth, being one of its bailiffs in 1423, 1427, 1430-1 (F. Blomefield, *History of Norfolk*, 8vo ed., XI, 324-5) and Falstolf was Sir John's cousin and man of business.

wealth and accumulated the means to pay for the building of his castle at Caister. Now both Fastolf and Wells made loans to Henry VI, whose record as a debtor was not encouraging.[63] Is it likely that they did so without the prospect of a return at least equivalent to that which they were accustomed to expect in their dealings with one another?

The probability that Cardinal Beaufort was willing to accept less favourable terms is scarcely stronger. Reputed 'the greatest merchant of wools' in England, he had close business relations with a number of prominent London merchants.[64] Between his resignation of the great seal in 1417 and his final withdrawal from active politics in 1443 he is known to have lent the Crown more than £200,000. Except for the two years (1427-8) when he was abroad in the service of the Pope there was no time when the Exchequer was not more or less heavily in his debt. Although he generally obtained ample security and punctual settlement there can be no doubt that for more than a quarter of a century he was prepared to forgo the chance of certain profit elsewhere. If he lent without interest the sacrifice was not a negligible one. Yet when the Duke of Gloucester in 1440 invited Henry VI 'to consier the great lucre of the said cardinal' and catalogued a variety of fraudulent practices usury was not precisely mentioned.[65] We must either believe that it was too well recognised to be regarded as a subject for complaint or else that Beaufort never resorted to it. The Tudor chroniclers on the other hand had no such qualms. For Hall—who may have had it from the cardinal's chaplain—and for Hall's successors, Beaufort was 'a most pernicious usurer';[66] and so he continued to be depicted until the nineteenth century. Much that Lingard and Stubbs had to say in his

---

[63] A list of Fastolf's recent loans was drawn up in 1455. It consists of £1000 in September 1436, 1000 marks in February 1437, £100 in 1449, 400 marks in 1450 and £400 in 1452 (*Paston Letters*, ed. J. Gairdner, 1904 ed., III, 60 and 63-4). Wells made a loan in 1426 (*Cal. Pat. Rolls, 1422-9*, p. 318). It appears that all Fastolf's loans were unpaid in 1455.

[64] For his connection with William Estfield, Hamon Sutton and Hugh Dyke see *Rot. Parl*, IV, 484-6; *Cal. Pat. Rolls, 1429-36*, p. 498 and Earl Chancery Proceedings, C. 1/11/289. The account of this business given by E. Power (*English Trade in the Fifteenth Century*, ed. E. Power and M. M. Postan, pp. 86-7) is in several respects erroneous. On 8 November 1435 Beaufort made over 1000 marks a year from his temporalities to Thomas Walsingham and Hugh Dyke (*Cal. Close Rolls, Henry VI*, III, 38-9 and Exch. Treasury of Receipt, Council and Privy Seal, E.28/57; the *Calendar* obscures the special position of the two London merchants).

[65] *Wars of the English in France*, II, ii, 440-51.

[66] E. Hall, *Chronicle* (ed. H. Ellis), pp. 210-11; W. Shakespeare, *Henry VI*, pt. i, III, i.

defence remains unshaken. But we may share their admiration for his statecraft without admitting that the grounds for his financial rehabilitation were equally substantial. The more they are examined they slenderer they become.

In any case the fact remains that the monarchy had to float its loans in competition with financiers who like John Wells were ready to pay interest. Its creditors were justified by contemporary practice, which they followed in their daily business, in expecting a profit, if a small one, and *prima facie* at least it is improbable that they were likely to lend without. When they were offered royal tallies in their private dealings they took them at a heavy discount.[67] There is therefore every reason why we should look closely for evidence of financial inducement when they bought them from the king. For that is what they did when they made him a loan.

Some scraps are immediately forthcoming. The first is perhaps merely curious though it ought not to be ignored. You will remember that in the parliament of 1376 it was one of the charges against the London merchant, Richard Lyons, that he had asked and received from the royal exchequer a premium of 50% on a loan of 20,000 marks. Indignant members of the impeaching Commons said that they knew of those who would have been prepared to lend without return until John of Gaunt came to Lyons' defence with the thesis that the rate was nothing out of the ordinary for a royal loan.[68] It would be unwise to rely heavily upon an *obiter dictum* of this sort if it stood in isolation. But when ten years later the Commons came to draw up the articles of another impeachment they themselves assumed without any apparent signs of disapproval that a loan of 10,000 marks must have cost the king 3000 marks to raise.[69] If the rate was lower it was still ruinous.

---

[67] For example Robert Worsley, mercer of London, took two royal tallies for a total of £500 in settlement of a debt of £400 owed him by John, Duke of Bedford. The latter's death made them worthless and they were returned to his executors (Exchr. K.R. Accounts E. 101/411/7).

[68] 'Adonqes le seignur de Loncastre dist qe tiel case et tiel necessite purroit avenire qe le roy serroit bien lee de doner la somme de x mille marcz pur chevauns avoir de xx mille marcz' (*Anonimalle Chronicle*, ed. V. H. Galbraith, p. 86). See also *Rot. Parl.* II, 323-4.

[69] 'Item, par la ou ordinance feust faite au darrein parlement pur la ville de Gant, qe dys M marcz deussent estre cheviz, et pur celle chevance deussent estre perduz iii M marcz, la en defaut et negligence du dit nadgairs chancellier [i.e. Michael de la Pole, Earl of Suffolk] la dite ville feust perduz: et nientmeyns les x M marcz paiez, et les ditz iii M marcz pur la chevance perduz, comme desuis est dit' (*Rot. Parl.* III, 216). N. B. Lewis (*Eng. Hist. Rev.* XLII (1927), 402-7) makes unnecessary difficulties about the sense of this passage.

Both these instances come from outside the Lancastrian period, but they help to bridge the gap between William de la Pole and Henry Beaufort. The next witness is the latter's contemporary and fellow-councillor, Sir John Fortescue.[70] In his *Governance of England*, a book evidently more often cited than read, there occurs this passage:

> If a king be poor, he shall by necessity make his expenses and buy all that is necessary to his estate by 'creaunce' and borrowing; wherethrough his 'creauncers' will win upon him the fourth or the fifth penny of all that he dispendeth. And so he shall lose when he payeth the fourth or the fifth penny of his revenues, and thus he thereby be always poorer and poorer as usury and chevisance increaseth the poverty of him that borroweth. His 'creauncers' shall always grudge for lack of their payment and defame his highness of misgovernance and default of keeping of days; which if he keep he must borrow also much at the days as he did first; for he shall be then poorer than he was by the value of the the fourth or fifth part of his first expenses and so be always poorer and poorer unto the time he be the poorest lord of his land.[71]

In spite of some inadequacy of language—their jargon was not our jargon—the meaning of these words is not in doubt. Not only does Fortescue, who was in a better position than most men to know, take it for granted that all royal loans were usurious; but he cites a figure for the consideration, between 25% and 33⅓%, which agrees with the estimate made by the Commons in 1386 and gives us the measure of John of Gaunt's exaggeration. We can scarcely wonder that the Lancastrians were bankrupt. Their attempt to avoid the consequences of an annual deficit by borrowing at this ruinous price could end in no other way. We catch an occasional glimpse of their deepening embarrassment from the estimates which their Treasurer placed before them in parliament and council. Thus when he took office in 1433 Ralph Cromwell, after painstaking inquiry, found that the king's debts amounted to £168,000.[72] Sixteen years later his successor had to tell the Commons that they had risen to £372,000.[73] The first Act of Resumption which followed in 1450 might have given the Exchequer a fresh start had not the mass of exemptions

[70] They were present together in the Star Chamber on 3 May 1443 etc. (*Proceedings and Ordinances*, v, 266, 268 and 269).
[71] *Op. cit.* p. 118.
[72] *Rot. Parl.* IV, 436-8.
[73] *Ibid.* v, 183.

tacked on to it wholly destroyed its effect. Although the *Governance* was written under a Yorkist king, Fortescue was obviously moralising on the fate of the House of Lancaster which he had served to its tragic but hardly unmerited end. There was every reason for calling Henry VI 'the poorest lord of his land.'

In the teeth of Fortescue's unambiguous statement further discussion would be otiose did it not give rise to another and yet tougher problem. Granted that these loans were usurious there is still nothing in the *Governance* to explain how the consideration was paid. It might be assumed that all that was needed for its solution was a search of the Exchequer records. If that were so we should have been saved much tedious speculation. The flank attack was necessary because the direct assault had failed. The Receipt and Issue Rolls of the Lower Exchequer are full and apparently informative; loans and their repayments are regularly entered on them with a businesslike system of cross-references. Yet these detailed records contain practically no evidence to substantiate Fortescue's thesis. What is seemingly perhaps even more conclusive, all the surviving patents, warrants, indentures and receipts make no reference, directly or indirectly, to reward. Hence the reluctance of most students to admit its existence. 'The tallies of assignment which [lenders] usually received in payment', writes Mr Steel, 'seem to have been made out for the precise amount which they had lent, and there was normally no other consideration.'[74] This judgment is, if anything, over-cautious. With very few exceptions indeed loan and repayment exactly balance. In fact I have only noticed one case where the difference was in favour of the creditor. On 18 July 1433 Cardinal Beaufort lent the government 3500 marks; on 14 June 1434 he received assignments to the value of 5000 marks in repayment; and yet on 29 November following he gave the Exchequer an acquittance for the smaller sum.[75] It is difficult to rule out the possibility of a clerical error, the most likely being a failure to record a second loan of £1000 made on the same date as the first.[76] But in any case a single isolated example merely brings into higher relief the

[74] *Eng. Hist. Rev.* LI (1936), 47.

[75] Exchr. of Receipt, Receipt Rolls, E. 401/733 and 737; Issue Roll, E. 403/715; *Antient Kalendars and Inventories of the Treasury of His Majesty's Exchequer* (ed. F. Palgrave), II, 154. The entries are quite specific and there are the usual full cross-references.

[76] It is unfortunate that neither the Patent Roll nor the records of the Council have any reference to this transaction. The warrant to the Treasurer and Chamberlains does not seem to have been preserved.

already painfully obvious fact that the rolls do not help us. As far as can be seen there is nowhere a significant admission to suggest that the Hendes, Whittingtons and Beauforts obtained as a rule any covenanted benefits from their liberality. How then can Fortescue be vindicated?

The solution that I am going to propose is one which would bring the Exchequer into line with contemporary business houses. It is that for the same reason that merchants concealed their usurious transactions under such fictions as 'dry exchange', 'feigned sale' and the like,[77] so the payment of reward by the king was arranged to enable the usurer to take his profit while appearing to receive none. Fortescue uses a technical term which should provide us with a clue to his meaning. In the passage which I quoted just now he talks of usury and 'chevisance.' Similarly John of Gaunt is made by the chronicler to employ the word 'chevance' and this reappears in the article of Suffolk's impeachment. These terms 'chevisance' and 'chevance' occur in many contexts, always with the sense of some disguised form of usury. Thus the Commons on one occasion towards the end of Richard II's reign denounced those who were guilty of 'the horrible and abominable vice of usury and call it chevance.'[78] A dozen years later their successors echo them when they speak of 'the horrible and damnable sin of usury, customarily practised under the name of chevance.'[79] It was against 'damnable bargains founded in usury by name of new chevisance' that the statute of 1487 was directed.[80] Contemporary literature will be found to yield other excellent examples. Wycliffe, for instance, writes of what merchants do 'by usury under colour of truth that they clepen chevisance',[81] and as late as Francis Bacon we hear of 'unlawful chievances and exchanges which is bastard usury.'[82] Such citations could be multiplied indefinitely, but a last one from the *Paston Letters* should suffice. In 1474 Sir John Paston gave his mother an account of a conversation he had had with his inquisitive uncle William:

I told him that I was in hope to find such a friend that would lend me £100. He asked me, who was that? I answered him, an old merchant, a

[77] M. M. Postan, 'Private financial instruments in Medieval England', *Vierteljahrschrift für Social- und Wirtschaftsgeschichte*, XXIII (1930), 26-75; 'Credit in Medieval Trade', *Econ. Hist. Rev.* I (1928), 234-61.
[78] *Rot. Parl.* III, 280 (1390)　　　　　　　　[79] *Ibid.* III, 541 (1404).
[80] 3 Hen. VII, c. 6.
[81] *Selected English Works of John Wyclif* (ed. T. Arnold), III, 88.
[82] *History of the Reign of King Henry VII* (ed. J. R. Lumby), p. 64.

friend of mine, but mine uncle thought that should be by way of
chevisance and to my hurt; wherefore I was plain to him and told him that
ye were surety therefor and purveyed it of such as would do for you.[83]

There can, I think, be no doubt that 'chevisance' and 'chevance'
were, to quote the *New English Dictionary*, 'commonly applied in
the 15th-16th centuries to some device by which the laws against
usury were evaded.[84]

Now there is equally no doubt that both words were repeatedly
used in connection with the loans of the Lancastrian kings. When the
authority of parliament was sought it was generally for a
'chevance.'[85] The clerks of the council, especially if they were writing
English, preferred 'chevisance.' But the terms were obviously
interchangeable. Nor was their use confined to any particular class of
loans. The following minute, dated 24 August 1442, contains
references both to those raised by direct application and by the
mediation of local agents:

> The letter as for chevisance of money shall go to townships and other
> singulars persons for to lend money is read and passed etc. for Guyenne.
> Be there made commissions to the lords, sheriffs and mightiest men in
> every shire of England to lend amongst themselves and also to chevise of
> other for the said necessity of Guyenne.[86]

When the king borrowed a few marks from one of 'the thrifty men
of the shires', it was just as much 'by way of chevisance' as when he
obtained ten thousand pounds and more from Henry Beaufort.

We have, therefore, to look for some fairly simple device which
while leaving no trace whatsoever in the records nevertheless so
committed the king to the payment of reward that his creditors were
insured against default. There does not seem to be a very wide field
of choice. The best, indeed I believe the only possible, answer is that
each lender was as a matter of course credited at the Exchequer with
a larger amount than he was actually prepared to advance. To
'chevise' a thousand pounds meant to borrow a good deal less; the
sum recorded was understood to include both principal and
consideration. Before discovering whether there is any evidence for
the existence of such a practice, it would be wise to face an obvious
difficulty. This can best be illustrated by a concrete example. At a
meeting of the king's council on 18 April 1437 it was minuted that

---

[83] *Op. cit.* v 211.　　　　[84] *S.v.* 'chevisance'.　　　　[85] See above, p. 65.
[86] *Proceedings and Ordinances*, v, 201　　　　[87] *Ibid.* v, 16.

Cardinal Beaufort 'hath lent 10,000 marks.'[87] On 14 May a *mutuum* for that amount was entered on the Receipt Roll.[88] According to my interpretation of 'chevisance', we should probably take this to mean that he had handed over something like £5000. Now if the Roll had been a record of genuine receipts for which the Treasurer were accountable, such a transaction would clearly have reduced the book-keeping system of the Exchequer to a state of intolerable confusion. That it was not such a record has now for some time been realised, but the old prejudice which led Sir James Ramsay into error dies hard. Loans and assignments balance exactly; there was therefore no consideration. That is still felt to be conclusive. A 'mutuum' entry, it is supposed, was the record of a genuine receipt; it is only the 'mutuum per talliam' which was fictitious. In view of past misunderstandings this is a dangerously simple doctrine and takes too little account of the purpose which an entry on the Receipt Rolls was intended to serve. In the case of a 'mutuum' this is defined with reasonable precision in a royal warrant of 11 July 1454.[89] The Staple had made the king a loan of 7000 marks and the Treasurer and Chamberlains were ordered 'to enter a mutuum of the said 7000 marks to remain of record in our Exchequer as reason would.' The object, that is to say, was to entitle the creditor to repayment, not to prove that the amount stated had been received by the Exchequer. Often enough the money was not paid over to the Treasurer; he was merely responsible for seeing that the debt was ultimately discharged.[90] Far from presenting any difficulties, the book-keeping methods of the medieval Receipt actually facilitated the practice of discounting loans in advance. It was doubtless for this very reason that chevisance took the form it did.

For that it did at least once take that form can fortunately be proved. The loan in question is that which was the subject of Richard Lyons' impeachment in the Good Parliament of 1376 and which John of Gaunt defended in the words I have already quoted. Lyons had, it was said, lent 20,000 marks and received back £20,000. How was this transaction recorded in the Lower Exchequer? You will find that he was credited there with a 'mutuum' of £20,000.[91] There is

[88] Receipt Roll, E. 401/752.

[89] *Wars of the English in France*, II, ii, 495; cf. *ibid.* 505-6.

[90] For example, the loans which Cardindal Beaufort had made to the king's government in France were entered on the Receipt Roll on 15 July 1432, some time after his return to England (E. 401/731).

[91] E. 401/514 (23 August 1374). The rumour that John Pyall was associated with Lyons in making this loan, though denied by Pyall (*Anonimalle Chronicle*, pp. 89-90) and disbelieved, is shown by the Roll to be true.

nothing in the enrolment to suggest that the loan was in any way abnormal. It is therefore no longer possible to accept such entries at their face value.

On the other hand, there is no obvious method of discovering how often they were deceptive or to what extent. If the private accounts of those who lent the Crown money had survived, there might be some means of judging. But unfortunately such accounts are extremely rare. The only one known to me which contains the necessary data comes from the archives of the duchy of Lancaster. It proves that the trustees who administered the revenues earmarked by Henry V for the payment of his debts gained nothing from their loans to his son.[92] This is hardly surprising since the lands with which they were enfeoffed were those of Henry VI's ancestral duchy and were meant to revert to him as soon as his father's debts were paid. It is to be hoped that the accounts of some more typical creditors may come to light.

The evidence then is for the moment, and perhaps always will be, too scanty to justify the conclusion that 'bastard usury' was a normal feature of the Crown's loans. Possibly royal boroughs and other corporations were regarded as having a duty to lend without gain.[93] And there is no reason for supposing that all creditors were treated as generously as those who like Lyons and Beaufort had great influence in the courts and councils of the king. But when all allowances have been made there still exists a strong presumption in favour of a high rate of reward. Fortescue's assertion is too definite to be easily set aside.

---

[92] D.L. 28/5/1. This is the 'certificacio compoti Johannis Leuenthorp junioris Receptoris Generalis domini Henrici Cantuariensis Archiepiscopi et aliorum secum coniunctim Feoffatorum Regis Henrici Quinti Ducatus sui Lancastrie de anno regni Regis Henrici sexti decimo' (1431-2). It records two loans, one of £1333. 6s. 8d., the other of £2133. 6s. 8d. These will be found on the corresponding Receipt Rolls, E. 401/725 and 729 (£1000, 16 May 1431; £333. 6s. 8d., 30 May 1431; £333. 6s. 8d., 18 June 1431; £1000, 30 November 1431; and £800, 17 January 1432).

[93] This would seem to be the case with the city of London (E. J. Davis and M. I. Peake, 'Loans from the city of London to Henry VI, 1431-49', *Bull. Inst. Hist. Res.* IV (1927), 165-72), but the evidence is by no means clear.

V. HENRY V, BISHOP BEAUFORT AND THE RED HAT, 1417-1421

To speak of the 'New Monarchy' as if it were almost something different in kind from what it replaced does far less than justice to those who ruled before 1461. The political structure of which Edward of York is the reputed architect discloses on a nearer acquaintance few original features. To recognise the full truth of this it is only necessary to cast the eye back across the short period of abnormal anarchy which was the reason and the excuse for Yorkist usurpation to 'the victorious acts of King Henry the Fifth.' At no time, probably, did the practical authority of the Crown stand higher than it did between 1415 and 1422. Two years had been long enough for Henry of Monmouth to dispose effectively of sedition and rebellion; for the rest of his brief reign the royal will was imposed without challenge. He achieved all this by methods upon which his ablest successors were hardly to improve. There was little indeed that he could have learnt from them—except the meaner vices. Nor was he more enslaved than they by that respect for inconvenient constitutional forms with which, thanks to Stubbs, his dynasty has sometimes been erroneously credited. On the contrary, his inclinations were despotic and his practice not markedly different from that of Edward III on the one hand or that of Edward IV on the other. And like most successful despots he knew when to unbend. In his capable hands at least the medieval kingship betrayed no sign that age had brought fragility.

Nothing better illustrates his grasp and statesmanship than the firm yet moderate fashion in which he dealt with a budding Wolsey. In this he showed Henry VIII's strength without his ingratitude. In December 1417 Bishop Henry Beaufort of Winchester, without first seeking the royal permission, accepted a cardinal's hat at the hands of Pope Martin V. Beaufort was the king's uncle, his oldest and closest councillor; his services before 1413 had alone given him large claims on Henry's indulgence, while those he had performed since had been scarcely less valuable. But the king would not tolerate disobedience, especially when, as then, his vital interests were in jeopardy. The *fait accompli* was not a wise trick to play on him. Without compunction he killed the project; and what is more, killed it with so little fuss that it passed without mention in any contemporary English chronicle. An extract from Martin's bull of creation, a letter of protest from Archbishop Chichele, and a somewhat vague and probably prejudiced reference in the duke of Gloucester's *Complaint*, written nearly a quarter of a century after the event, have for long been the only available sources of light on this interesting episode. From these and from the ensuing silence it has been deduced that Beaufort obediently resigned his new honour, returned a penitent to the English court, and was granted forgiveness by his master. But even this was far from certain, while such important matters as the bishop's subsequent relations with Henry V and his position at the latter's death were subjects for unaided conjecture. This unsatisfactory state of affairs can now to some extent be mended. For there exists, unprinted among the Public Records, part of a memorandum by Thomas Chaucer, the bishop's cousin, which can be used to fill some of the gaps in our knowledge. Its discovery—or, to be more correct, its identification— must serve as an excuse for this attempt to tell once more in detail the story of Beaufort's ambition and its disappointment. The result is, if anything, to magnify still further Henry V's reputation as an exponent of authoritarian kingship. But there is displayed also that quality for which he deserves most credit, namely, the politician's dislike of spoiling a success by vindictiveness. Having gained his point and made a disobedient servant acknowledge his authority, he was ready to be magnanimous. Even his opponents were willing to admit that his prudence and sagacity were equal to his energy and courage.

It was on 18 December 1417, a little over a month after his election to the papacy, that Martin V created Beaufort a cardinal.[1] His action was prompted in part doubtless by gratitude for the influence exerted in his favour by the English bishop in the later stages of the recent conclave. But the wording of the bull makes it quite obvious that it was not past services alone that he was minded to reward. Martin was not the man to overlook the significance of the expanding Lancastrian empire. The new cardinal was appointed *legatus a latere* for life in England, Wales, Ireland, and the other lands in the obedience of Henry V beyond the sea.[2] He had displayed his wisdom and acumen in the matter of ending the schism, thereby hamstringing reform, but

[1] '*xv Kal. Jan.*' and not 'v Kal. Jan.' (28 December), as in H. Wharton, *Anglia Sacra*, i, 800. Wharton states that the bull existed among Bekington's letters, i.e. in B. M. Cotton, Tiberius B VI (fos. 61-61ᵛ). Unfortunately this volume was badly damaged in the Cottonian fire and Martin's bull is no longer wholly legible. I have therefore not ventured to print a transcript. It is headed: 'Copia bulle confecte de assumpcione domini Wintoniensis Episcopi in Cardinalem.' The date is reasonably clear.

[2] I cannot find any mention of the appointment *for life* in Cotton, Tib. B VI, fo. 61ᵛ, but there are several gaps in the manuscript at the point where it might have been expected to come. Alternatively, like the grant of the see of Winchester *in commendam*, it may have been the subject of a separate bull. Chichele's letter to Henry V (see below, n. 4) makes it practically certain that it was an appointment for life.

there was still work to be done: the papacy to be defended from its enemies, peace negotiated between the warring princes of France and England, order and discipline restored within the Church. The bull is in short a manifesto, the outline of a papal programme, the bearing of which was not lost on Henry V when he came to see it. It would be interesting to know exactly what Martin had in prospect for his lieutenant. If he was already thinking of an assault on the obnoxious Statute of Provisors—the condition of the papal finances may have soon suggested it—he showed remarkably little appreciation either of the strength of English prejudice or of the character of Henry V. Yet, in view of his ill-considered handling of this same question from 1426 to 1428, such obtuseness is not improbable.[3] The weakness of this explanation lies rather in his choice of instrument. Beaufort was the last man to risk his credit on a task which he must have recognised as hopeless. Assuming that he was consulted, an assumption which is rendered more than likely by the fact that he was in close touch with the pope at Constance, it is hard to believe that the repeal of the statutes was the only, or even the main, purpose of his appointment. He was ambitious but rarely foolhardy, not given to sacrificing himself in pursuit of the unattainable. It is conceivable that he and Martin had very different ideas about the nature of his duties. Unfortunately the phrasing of his bull is vague and unhelpful here. He was to be legate 'with full power.' It is difficult to define what this would have meant in practice, but that it meant something worth having is certain. One has only to remember to what uses Wolsey was later able to put a similar grant with the connivance of his king; and this would not have been the only respect in which Wolsey was anticipated by Beaufort. As Chichele reminded Henry V, the powers of a legate *a latere* were very wide; 'and over that what he may have in special of the pope's grace no man wot, for it stands in his will to dispose as him good liketh.'[4] That Beaufort's appointment was made 'without prejudice to other *legati nati* in those parts' does not seem to

---

[3] In December 1421 Martin was hoping for Beaufort's assistance 'for the recovery of the pristine liberty of the Church in that most Christian kingdom' (J. Haller, 'England und Rom unter Martin V,' *Quellen und Forschungen aus ital. Archiv.*, Bd. viii, ht. 2, pp. 289-90).

[4] The original of this letter appears to be lost. It was printed by A. Duck in his *Vita Henrici Chichele* (1617), pp. 77-80; English edn. (1699), pp. 125-31. A more accurate copy will be found in B.M. Add. MS. 27,402, fos. 19-20. See also *The Register of Henry Chichele*, ed. E. F. Jacob, I. xli-ii. I must take this opportunity of thanking Professor Jacob for the information that those parts of the Register still to be published contain nothing bearing upon the subject of this article. The fragment of Beaufort's own Register at Winchester stops short at the tenth year of his translation.

have reassured Chichele; nor can it have signified much, since whatever authority the commission conferred must, in the very nature of the case, have been granted at the expense of the metropolitan.[5] No wonder, therefore, that the archbishop was profoundly disturbed.

It was the unprecedented character of the appointment upon which the primate laid the heaviest emphasis in writing to the king from Lambeth on 6 March 1418:

'By inspection of laws and chronicles was there never no legate *a latere* sent into no land and specially into your realm of England without great and notable cause; and they when they came, after they had done their legacy abide but little while not over a year, and some a quarter or two months, as the needs required. And yet over that he was treated with ere he came into the land, when he should have exercise of his power and how much should be put in execution, an adventure,[6] after he had been received, he would have used it too largely, to great oppression of your people. Wherefore, most Christian prince and sovereign lord, as your true priest whom it hath liked you to set in so high estate, the which without your gracious lordship and supportation I know myself insufficient to occupy, beseech you in the most humble wise that I can devise or think that ye will this matter take tenderly at heart and see the state of the church be maintained and sustained, so that everich of the ministers thereof hold them content with their own part—for truly he that hath least hath enow to reckon for—and that your poor people be not piled nor oppressed with divers exactions and unaccustomed, through which they should be the more feeble to refresh you, our liege lord, in time of need and when it liketh you to clepe upon them, and all pleas and slanders ease in your church.'[7]

Chichele evidently interpreted Martin's action as an attempt to impose closer fiscal control upon the English Church and saw Cardinal Beaufort in the rôle of an extraordinary and additional papal tax-gatherer. Or at least he wished Henry to do so. In view of the later activities of John of Obizzi and Simon of Teramo his warning was not misplaced; nor was it one which the king was likely to ignore. But Chichele was also afraid lest his own powers of visitation and

---

[5] For a useful discussion of the status and functions of legates see A. F. Pollard, *Wolsey*, pp. 165-216. The 'scroll . . . containing that [which] is expressed in the pope's law and fully concluded by doctors,' which Chichele said was enclosed in his letter is unfortunately missing.

[6] 'An adventure' = lest (O.E.D. under 'adventure'). The worthy Chichele appears here to have become incoherent with emotion, but a plentiful use of commas may have helped to clarify his meaning.

[7] B.M. Add. MS. 27, 402, fo. 20.

correction should be usurped; for, as he said, 'if any trespasses of man's frailty fall, [they] well may be corrected and punished by the ordinaries there, as the case falleth.'[8] It is impossible to assert that he magnified unduly the dangers to be expected from so unusual a mission.

If Chichele's information is to be trusted, Beaufort had already received another mark of the pope's favour, to wit, the grant of the see of Winchester *in commendam* for life. This does not figure in the bull of 18 December 1417, but there is good reason for believing that it was procured at a slightly later date, probably after the new cardinal had left the Curia. For it is almost certainly referred to in one of the articles of Gloucester's last indictment of Beaufort's career:

'Item, the said Cardinal, then being bishop, was assoiled of his bishopric of Winchester. Whereupon he sued to our holy father the Pope to have a bull declaratory that notwithstanding that he was assumed to the state of cardinal that the see was not void, where in deed it stood void by a certain time ere that bull was granted. And so he was exempt from his ordinary by the taking on him the state of cardinal. And the bishopric of the church of Winchester then standing void, he took it again of the Pope, ye not learned nor knowing wherein he was fallen in the case of provision, whereby all his good was clearly and lawfully forfeited to you, my right doubted lord, with more, as the statute declareth, to your advantage.'[9]

From the reference to Henry VI in the last sentence, it might be supposed that Gloucester was here dealing with the events of 1426-7. But apart from the fact that his remarks follow immediately after a statement of Henry V's attitude towards Beaufort's earlier promotion, this is by no means clearly the case. For when some nine years earlier Gloucester had launched his most successful attack upon the Cardinal, it was upon what had happened at Constance in 1417 and 1418 that he based the same charge as that made in the article quoted above. There is indisputable evidence of this, although its relevance has been generally overlooked. When on 6 November 1431 the King's Serjeants and Attorney claimed before the Council that there was no precedent for the holding of an English see *in commendam* by a cardinal after his elevation to the Sacred College, it was Gloucester himself, presiding as

---

[8] B.M. Add. MS. 27, 402, fo. 19.
[9] *Letters and Papers illustrative of the wars of the English in France*, ed. J. Stevenson (Rolls Series), II, ii. 442; *The Customs of London, otherwise called Arnold's Chronicle*, ed. F. Douce, pp. 279-80.

the king's lieutenant, who succeeded in eliciting some damaging information about Beaufort's original dealings with Martin V. He charged the bishop of Worcester on his faith and allegiance to tell the court whether or not the Cardinal had acquired in the Curia an exemption for himself, his city and diocese from the jurisdiction of the archbishop of Canterbury. Worcester, 'after divers excuses and refusals to speak in this matter, at length said that the late bishop of Lichfield told him that he prosecuted the said exemption in the Curia and paid for them,[10] and that the said Cardinal repaid him.'[11] By translating '*quod nuper Episcopus Lychfeldensis asseruit sibi*' as 'that the Bishop of Lichfield formerly told him', writers from Lingard onwards have obscured the meaning of this passage and created quite unnecessary difficulties of interpretation.[12] It was observed that the bishop of Lichfield was among those present in the Council of 6 November and therefore well able to speak for himself. The fact that he did not and that the lords preferred 'the hearsay testimony of a second person' has been adduced by Nicolas as a reason for doubting the truth of the story and for suggesting that the proceedings were a put-up job.[13] Yet for once this mistrust of Duke Humphrey is unfounded. Had a moment's thought been given to the identity and past history of the bishop of Worcester, the real value of his evidence and the irrelevance of his brother of Lichfield's silence would have become obvious. For Worcester was Mr. Thomas Polton who had been papal notary and king's proctor in the Roman Curia throughout Henry V's reign.[14] There he had had as his colleague John Catterick, from 1 February 1415 until a month before his death at Florence on 28 December 1419, bishop of Coventry and Lichfield.[15] Catterick had formerly been Beaufort's chancellor,[16] and was therefore his obvious choice as agent for business in the Curia. He had been one of Martin's

10 *Sic.*

11 *Proceedings and Ordinances of the Privy Council of England*, ed. N. H. Nicolas, iv. 100.

12 With the solitary exception of W. T. Waugh ('The Great Statute of Praemunire,' *ante*, xxxvii. 200), who was not, however, concerned with the implications of his correction and does not seem to have been aware that he was making one.

13 *Proceedings and Ordinances*, IV, xxxi-iv.

14 Exchequer, Treas. of Rec., Issue Roll, E 403/643, 22 November 7 Henry V: £81 6s. 8d. to Thomas Polton, king's proctor in the court of Rome by the hands of Giovanni Victori for his expenses. The appointment dated from 8 June 1414 (*Deputy Keeper's Report XLIV*, 532). Polton was provided to the see of Hereford in 1420, translated to Chichester in 1422 and to Worcester in 1426. He died at Basel 23 August 1433 (*Chichele's Register*, I, xliii-iv, l, liv, lxxxix, xcii-iv and 69-73; II. 485-95 (will) and 671; H. Wharton, *op. cit.*, i. 537 and 805; *Register of Thomas Poltone* (Worcester *1426-33*), ed. J. H. Parry and W. W. Capes, iii).

electors at Constance and accompanied the new pope into Italy when the council was dissolved.[17] On the other hand, there is no evidence that his successor at Lichfield, William Heyworth (1419-47), whose silence has been such a stumbling-block, was in the Curia either from 1417 to 1420 or from 1426 to 1431, the only years in which Beaufort's suit could have been urged.[18] Everything points, in short, to Catterick as Beaufort's agent and to a date soon after 18 December 1417 as the occasion when the exemption was purchased, at or by which time the Cardinal must have obtained the see of Winchester *in commendam*. In 1431 Polton's evidence, secondhand though it was, was taken because he alone among those present was in a position to have heard the facts from Catterick's mouth. And the cardinal was threatened with the penalties of *praemunire* not on account of a recent lapse, but for what he was believed to have attempted to do during the reign of Henry V.

It remained to be seen how Henry V would receive the news of his uncle's unlicensed self-advancement. According to Duke Humphrey, his attitude was such as might have been expected of him. He 'would have agreed him to have had certain clerks of this land cardinals, they having no bishoprics in England', his object being 'that in general councils and in all matters that might concern the weal of him and of his realm he should have promoters of his nation, as all other Christian kings had, in the Court of Rome.'[19] It is not surprising that he had no use for a resident legate *a latere*, even one like Beaufort on whose counsel and service he had long relied, but whose least activities as legate could scarcely fail to threaten the liberties of the English Church and by extension those of the English state. Had Chichele been a rebellious or even an unsatisfactory primate, it might have been different; but Chichele had never given him an instant's anxiety. And so he did not now appeal to his king in vain. Gloucester reports with malicious relish how Henry exclaimed 'that he had as lief set his crown

[15] *D.N.B.*; his will and a biographical note will be found in *Chichele's Register*, ii. 178-82 and 645. He was appointed king's proctor at the papal court soon after Henry V's accession, 22 May 1413 (*Foedera, Conventiones,* &c. ed. T. Rymer, 1704-35 edn., ix. 12).

[16] Reg. Beaufort, *Bulle,* &c., fo. 32.

[17] See a letter from Catterick to Henry V, written at Mantua '*in comitiva Papae*', 5 February 1419, with its reference to his '*socius*', T. Polton (*Foedera*, ix. 680-1). Polton, on the other hand, was probably on a visit to England in the spring of 1419 (*Deputy Keeper's Report XLIV*, 610).

[18] It is always difficult to prove a negative, but until his provision to the see in 1419, Heyworth was abbot of St. Albans. He was certainly present in person at Lambeth on 28 November 1420 to make his profession of obedience to the archbishop (*Chichele's Register*, i. 73-4).

[19] *Wars of the English in France*, II, ii. 441-2; *Arnold's Chronicle*, p. 279.

beside him as to see him [i.e. Beaufort] wear a cardinal's hat, he being a cardinal.'[20] His notion of an English cardinal, that is to say, differed radically from Martin's; he wanted an English envoy at the papal court, not a papal envoy at the English court. When he uttered these remarks in Gloucester's hearing is not made clear. As far as is known, he and Beaufort did not meet for another year and then, as will be seen presently, the question of the latter's fate had still to be decided.

It is difficult to trace the bishop's itinerary in any detail during these critical months. By the time Chichele's letter was written he was already on pilgrimage again.[21] On Palm Sunday, 20 March 1418, he arrived at Venice from Padua with upwards of sixty horse; in his company being Thomas Spofford, abbot of St. Mary's, York, whom he was to maintain against the king and the English bishops before many years were past.[22] After being honourably entertained by the Doge and Signory, he set sail for the Holy Land on 10 April in the galley *Querina* with about eight attendants and baggage reputed to be worth between forty and forty-five thousand gold ducats.[23] The fact that he had so much of his moveable wealth with him was perhaps not without a bearing upon his subsequent negotiations with his king. He returned to Venice in a galley from Rhodes on 10 September following, having fallen in with the duke of Naxos in the course of his travels,[24] and having sworn a solemn oath which was to play its part in the ensuing trouble.[25] From then until 3 March 1419, when he met Henry V at Rouen on his way to England,[26] he is lost to view. A small coincidence, however, suggests that some part if not the whole of this interval was occupied by a visit to the papal court. This would have involved him in no detour, for Martin was in Lombardy, marking time until he could safely take the road to Rome.[27] In the pope's train as it moved slowly down the valley of the Po was Poggio Bracciolini, the illustrious humanist. Now, early in November, Poggio suddenly quitted the Curia at Mantua in order to proceed to England, where he

[20] *Ibid.*

[21] His safe-conduct from Martin is dated Constance, 19 February 1418 (*Cal. Papal Registers, Papal Letters,* ed. J. A. Twemlow, vii. 6). He had been '*in habitu peregrini cum cruce*' when met at Ulm by John Catterick in October 1417 and brought to Constance (*Acta Concilii Constancienis,* ed. H. Finke, ii. 147).

[22] *The Register of Thomas Spofford (1422-48),* ed. A. T. Bannister, ii-iv, 5-6, 18-9 and 28-9.

[23] *Chronique d'Antonio Morosini, extraits relatifs à l'Histoire de France,* ed. G. Lefèvre-Pontalis, ii. 158-61; J. H. Wylie and W. T. Waugh, *Reign of Henry the Fifth,* iii. 100.

[24] *Morosini,* ii. 164-7.

[25] *See below,* p. 89.

[26] B.M. Add. MS. 38,525, fo. 75.

is later found in Beaufort's *familia*.[28] That this rapid decision was arrived at after a personal interview with his future patron cannot be proved, but all things considered the supposition is not unlikely. Further speculation would be idle; the remaining four months are in any case completely blank; only one thing seems certain, that this time was spent by Beaufort on the continent of Europe.[29]

At the beginning of March 1419 he had made Calais on his way homeward when he turned aside into Normandy in order to pay his respects to the king. This decision to break his journey was governed —or so he was later at pains to emphasise—by the terms of a vow which he had taken while on the Mediterranean during the previous summer. He had then sworn—it is permissible to guess that a storm was raging—that once safely back in England he would cross the seas no more until he went on pilgrimage again, this time to the shrine of St. James at Compostela.[30] As he had no intention apparently of fulfilling his vow at once, he therefore seized his last chance of meeting Henry before the latter's return to England from campaign. It is clear that he wished his promptness in reporting himself to create a good impression. And indeed his reception was outwardly an honourable one. Whatever passed between him and the king in private, he was treated in public as if nothing blameworthy had occurred. Already on 21 January 1419 his name had appeared in a commission to sundry persons, including his critic Chichele, to treat with the Dauphin's party for a final peace,[31] and a number of similar appointments now

---

[27] He left Constance on 16 May and went by Berne (2 June; *Cal. Papal Registers, Letters,* vii, 78 and 81) and Freiburg (4 June; *ibid.,* 66 and 93) to Geneva, where he stayed from 11 June to 3 September. On 6 September he was at Annecy (*ibid.,* 76), on the 18th at Susa (*ibid.,* 91), and on the 21st at Turin (*ibid.,* 65). From 5 to 12 October he halted at Pavia, visited Milan between 12 and 18 October and then moved on by way of Brescia to take up his residence at Mantua on 25 October (M. Creighton, *History of the Papacy during the Reformation,* 1882 edn., ii. 3-4: Morosini, ii. 166-7, n. 4. E. Walser, *Poggius Florentinus, Leben und Werke,* p. 71, gives 24 October as the date, but without citing his authority).

[28] Walser, *op. cit.,* p. 71.

[29] This is implied by him in his letter to Henry V (see below, pp. 89-90) unless he made a second voyage on the Great Sea between September 1418 and June 1420, of which there is no record. It would be convenient to fill these months with a first journey to the Hussite wars for which Wavrin is our only authority (*Chroniques* ed. W. Hardy, ii (1399-1422), 324-6. Dr. L. B. Radford (*Henry Beaufort,* pp. 93-5) places this journey in the summer of 1420. But the siege of 'Souch' (Zacz) to which Wavrin refers took place in September 1421 (*Geschichtschreiber der Husitischen Bewegung in Boehmen,* ed. K. Höfler, Fontes Rerum Austriacarum, Abt. 1, Bd. 2, 60-1, 64 and 494-6; F. Palacký, *Geschichte von Böhmen,* iii. 250-4).

[30] See below, p. 89.

[31] *Foedera,* ix. 670-1. When he did not appear his place was taken by William Allington (*ibid.,* p. 686, &c.).

followed his arrival. On 9 March he and the primate were authorised
to issue safe-conducts to the Dauphin's ambassadors coming to
Dreux.[32] On 30 May he was at the king's side with his peers when
Queen Isabel of France and the duke of Burgundy arrived at parley at
Meulan.[33] Two days later he was chosen along with Chichele, Clarence,
Gloucester and Exeter to represent the English at what proved yet
another abortive conference.[34] Released by the breakdown of these
negotiations, he soon afterwards took his leave of the court and by 23
August 1419, when he attended a council at Coldharbour in London,
he had crossed the Channel.[35]

From this interlude of diplomatic employment, and still more from
the renewed activity in council and parliament which succeeded it,
most previous writers on this subject have drawn a very natural
deduction.[36] It has been assumed that Henry V, having first
extinguished his uncle's Roman ambitions by a blunt negative, chose
to regard them as a temporary aberration and restored him forthwith
to favour; while the bishop, his hopes of preferment shattered,
returned without repining to the loyal service of the Crown. The
printed evidence, although scanty and at best circumstantial, seemed
to allow no other construction. Little or nothing, it is true, was known
of the bishop's personal relations with the king during the three
remaining years of the latter's life. But superficially they seemed as
intimate as ever. If doubts arose these were due to the unusual
spectacle of one who was commonly pertinacious abandoning the
struggle without effort. Was Henry V's notorious ruthlessness a
sufficient answer? Perhaps. Nevertheless the doubts were justified.
Far from being willing to surrender his pretensions, Beaufort in fact
continued for another year at least to work for their attainment. This
is shown by two letters which have been preserved among the Ancient
Correspondence at the Public Record Office. Both are incompletely
addressed, dated and signed, but the problems these omissions set the
reader, though difficult, are not, I think, insoluble. The first and less

---

32 *Ibid.*, p. 704.

33 *Oeuvres de Georges Chastellain*, ed. J. M. B. Kervyn le Lettenhove, i. 194.

34 *Foedera*, ix. 761-2; *the Brut, or the Chronicles of England*, ed. F. W. D. Brie
(E.E.T.S.), ii. 423-4.

35 P.R.O. Chancery Warrants, C 81/1543/14. On 9 September 1419 an order was
given to the customers of London to deliver to him or his deputy certain goods bought
and purveyed in foreign parts to his use; the shippers were Italians (*Cal. Close Rolls,
Henry V*, ii. 29).

36 E.g. Wylie and Waugh, *op. cit.* pp. iii. 99-100; C. L. Kingsford, *Henry V*, 274-6;
J. H. Ramsay, *Lancaster and York*, i. 390; Radford, *op. cit.* pp. 88-90; and the
Dictionary of National Biography, 'Henry Beaufort.'

intrinsically valuable was printed in *Facsimiles of National Manuscripts*. It is from a correspondent signing himself 'your humble subject and true liegeman, H.W.', and is addressed to a king.[37] The writer thanks him for his 'gracious letters of the peace and marriage concluded', which marriage he understands will take place as soon after the feast of Trinity 'as convenable time cometh.' He has been commanded to be present and his main purpose in writing is to make his excuses for his failure to obey. This he does as follows:

'And trwly, my souereyne lord, but if ʒowr hynesse hadde comand-did me the contrarie, if I myht haue be to Goddis wrshyp and ʒowrys at that blessid gladde mariage, I nolde for no thyng be thennys. But Godde, blessid mote he be, wylle not þᵗ I haue in thys worde[38] þᵗ þᵗ I moste desirid, of the whyche to see þᵗ joyfull day of ʒowr mariage haht ben on. Besechyng ʒow, my souereyne lord, to haue in ʒowr noble remembrauncce wyht what conclusion of reste I departid laste owte of ʒowr graciouse presence and aftir þᵗ I haue demenid me syht I kam in to thys ʒowr reaume and wyht Goddis grace shall to my lyuys ende, lyk as I truste to Godde ʒowr humble lyge man, my cousin Chaucer, haht pleinly enformid ʒowr hynesse or thys time. Also, my souereyne lord, whanne I was on the grette see[39] I made a wowe þᵗ aftir time I were onys in ʒowr reaume of Engeland I sholde no see passe saue on pilgrimage vn to I hadde be at Seint Jamys.[40] And for þᵗ cause, whanne I was at ʒowr toun of Calays, for the grete desir I hadde to see the prosperite of ʒowr moste dredde and noble persone, I wentte streht fro thennys to ʒowr moste gracious presence. For if I hadde goone in to ʒowr reaume of Engeland, I myht not haue come in to Normandie to my pilgrimage hadde be doo. And therefore, my souereyne lord, wyht all the humblesse þᵗ any subgit kan þennke or deuise I beseche ʒowr hynesse to take not to displesaunsse my nowht comyng. For Godde knowht I ne feyne not ne no colour seke. Besechyng Godde in all wyse, my souereyne lord, to saue and kepe ʒow body and sowle, and sendde ʒow in thys blissid sacrament of mariage joye, prosperite longe to endur, wyht heyrys of ʒowr body to his blissid wrshyp and ʒowrys, in singuler comfortes of all ʒowr trwe

---

[37] Ancient Correspondence, S.C.I./xliii/192. *Fascimiles*, ed. H. James and W. B. Sanders, I. no. xxxvii; *Deputy Keeper's Report XXVI*, 60.

[38] Evidently 'world' is meant. I have quoted this document in its original spelling partly because of the difficulty of modernising some of its forms, but chiefly because it is, as I hope to show, a holograph. The punctuation is mine, and I have introduced a few capitals.

[39] I.e. the Mediterranean; cf. 'To pass over the grete See, To werre and sle the Sarazin' (J. Gower, *Works*, ed. G. C. Macaulay, ii. 293), and 'in the Grete See, At many a noble aryve hadde he be' (*Works of Geoffrey Chaucer*, ed. W. W. Skeat, iv. 3).

[40] I.e. Santiago de Compostela.

pepyll, of the whyche I am on and ever shall be. Wrytyn at Waltham, the vj day of Jun.'

This was believed by its editors to be a letter from Henry, prince of Wales, to his father Henry IV, and assigned to the year 1402. But as the late J. H. Wylie pointed out,[41] there is strong internal evidence for the view that it was written by Henry Beaufort to Henry V in 1420. As a good deal depends upon the truth of this ascription, it had better be submitted to a closer scrutiny than Wylie seems to have given it. In the first place, the king to whom it was addressed and whose forthcoming marriage was to bring peace to his people of England was evidently in Normandy only a short while before. The only king from Edward III to Henry VII, to go no further afield, of whom this was true was Henry V. From the end of July 1417, when his fleet anchored in the mouth of the Seine, until the beginning of May 1420 he was continuously in the duchy; on 21 May 1420 he sealed his treaty with Charles VI of France at Troyes; and on 2 June, Trinity Sunday, in the same year, his wedding with Catherine of Valois took place in Troyes Cathedral. That he was the king for whom this letter of apology was intended, and that it was written on 6 June 1420 are deductions which therefore seem to be well established. That the writer 'H.W.' was Henry Beaufort is less obvious but scarcely less certain. There is the address from which he wrote; Waltham, or Bishop's Waltham, in Hampshire contained a palace of the bishops of Winchester, and one, moreover, which he is known to have used.[42] There is the reference to his cousin Chaucer, the Thomas Chaucer whom he had acknowledged in a formal document as his 'beloved kinsman';[43] and not even the unsleeping zeal of transatlantic Chaucerians has been able to furnish the poet's putative son with any other relation either by blood or

[41] In a letter to the *Athenaeum*, 14 April 1888, p. 468. See also his *History of England under Henry the Fourth*, iv. 313. His correction has been generally accepted; see, for example, *Life-Records of Chaucer*, pt. iv. (Chaucer Soc., 2nd ser. 32), 334; H. G. Maxwell Lyte, *Catalogue of Manuscripts, &c., in the Museum of the Public Record Office*, 14th edn. (1933), p. 44; R. W. Chambers and B. M. Daunt, *Book of London English, 1384-1425*, pp. 298-9.

[42] For example, see his last will (*Collection of Royal Wills*, ed. J. Nichols, pp. 339-40): 'Item lego Domine mee Regine lectum blodium de panno aureo de damasco que pendebat in camera illa in manerio meo de Waltham in qua eadem Domina mea Regina cubabat illo tempore quo fuit in dicto manerio, unacum tribus tapetis d'arras in eadem camera tunc pendentibus.'

[43] 'Dilecto consanguineo nostro', *Calendar of Patent Rolls, 1405-1408*, p. 406. The fact that the Lancastrian dukes and kings in their many grants to Thomas Chaucer never once acknowledged his kinship suggests that at this date such words as *consanguineus* and cousin were generally, if not invariably, reserved for blood relations.

marriage who could conceivably have signed himself in 1420 with the initials 'H.W.'[44] We may suppose that it was someone well known to the king. Indeed, the only serious objection to the choice of Beaufort is that he is not otherwise known to have used this signature.[45] *H. Wynton*' is the form which almost invariably appears at the foot of the acts of the Council during the minority of Henry VI until after 1427 when it changes to *H. Cardinal.*'[46] No such uniformity of practice is to be found in his private letters, though these are too few to exhaust all the possible variants of spelling and language. Of the many that he must have written to Henry V, no other seems to have survived. *H. Evesq' de Wyncestre* will be found on two letters (in French) to Thomas Langley, his successor as Henry V's chancellor, and both belonging to the year 1417;[47] while, on the other hand, an undated English letter written after 1427 is signed *H. Cardinal of Engeland*.[48] This last is of special interest, since it is the one indubitable holograph from Beaufort's hand known to survive.[49] Less than a hundred words long, it contains two unusual, spellings, "wlle" for 'will' and "haht" for 'hath', and half a dozen others less uncommon, every one of which will also be found in the letter of 6 June 1420.[50] All things

---

[44] Of an extensive literature two works deserve special mention, namely, *Thomas Chaucer*, by M. B. Ruud (University of Minnesota Studies in Language and Literature, no. 9, 1926), and 'Chaucerian Problems: especially the Petherton Forestership and the Question of Thomas Chaucer', by R. Krauss in *Three Chaucer Studies*, by R. Krauss, H. Braddy, and C. R. Kase. Thomas Chaucer's tomb at Ewelme, co. Oxon, is decorated with the coats-of-arms of some twenty of his more important connections. Henry Beaufort appears among them, but no one else whom this cap fits. For a recent examination of this evidence see 'The Arms on the Chaucer Tomb at Ewelme' by E. A. Greening Lamborn, *Oxoniensia*, v (1940), 78-93.

[45] The king may have encouraged his familiar correspondents to use initials when writing to him in France, perhaps for reasons of secrecy. Compare Chichele's letter (see above, p. 81, n. 4) signed 'H.C.' and the duke of Gloucester's (see below, p. 92, n. 55) signed 'H.G.'

[46] *Proceedings and Ordinances*, iii. 152 and 221; iv. 15 ('H. Cardinalis'), 35, 76, &c.; J. F. Baldwin, *King's Council in England during the Middle Ages*, plate x; and the files of Ancient Petitions, Chancery Warrants and Exchequer T.R., Council and Privy Seal, *passim*.

[47] *Proceedings and Ordinances*, ii. 234-5.

[48] *Original Letters*, ed. H. Ellis, 1st series, i. 8.

[49] 'Wrytyn of myn owne hand at London the xij day of Marche.'

[50] H. W.'s spelling was unusually consistent. It is striking to find so many of his orthographical habits appearing in the cardinal's brief note. E.g. 'zow' for 'you', 'goo' and 'goone' for 'go' and 'gone', 'wrytyn' for 'written', 'Engeland' for 'England', 'herttely' and 'hertlyly' for 'heartily', and 'hit' and 'hyt' for 'it.' These coincidences by themselves would prove nothing, but they produce a cumulative effect. 'Wlle' and 'haht' are in a class by themselves, and are not listed by the Oxford Dictionary. I am indebted to my colleague Dr. C. T. Onions for his willing help here and elsewhere.

considered, the evidence for ascribing the latter to the pen of Henry Beaufort seems to me overwhelming.[51]

The bishop was some days late with his excuses. Yet he could not plead either want of information or even short notice. For although he was at his country place and the Treaty of Troyes, registered in the *Parlement* of Paris on 30 May[52] was not proclaimed in London until 14 June,[53] he had in fact received a personal summons from the king at the very latest nearly three months before the event.[54] What is more, elaborate preparations for the ceremony had been going on in England throughout the spring,[55] and he had himself been commanded to supervise musters at Southampton, whence a train of lords and ladies had set sail.[56] There is therefore more than a suspicion of disingenuousness in this dilatory reply. Beaufort's letters are rare enough to be precious; and in spite of an insufferable wordiness which may betray an uneasy conscience, this one at least shows that the man whose name became a byword for arrogance could on occasion be almost grossly humble in the fulsome style of those times. Apart from this, it is chiefly valuable for its help in fixing the date and authorship of a far more important state paper, which must now be considered. This is an unsigned document, the earlier portion of which is lacking, contained on two large sheets of paper and too rambling for adequate summary. When it becomes legible, it runs as follows:[57]

[1].....................my lordes goynge vn to Seynt James, he ys gretele set to go, bot he w[oll] wyst of zowr ententes be fore þat ze w[olle haue] desirede hym for to haue be atte thys blessedfull day of pees, þe wyche ys so d[esir]ede and so y prayed for þat y trowe þe crye of þe pepill perseth þe heuen to haue yt. Y trowe y schult haue stired hym for to haue made hys wey by zowe, bot now he maketh many dowtes and on in especiall ys for drede of countre maundynge,

51 Dr. Wylie seems to have based his case on the close resemblance between H.W.'s handwriting and that of Beaufort's signature reproduced by J. G. Nichols, *Autographs of Royal and Noble Personages in English History*, no. 3 A 9. But a signature is rather little to judge a handwriting by. Owing to the fact that Cotton MS. Vesp. F iii is stored in an underground repository for the duration of the war, it has not been possible for me to see the holograph letter printed by Ellis. When it is visible it should go far to settle the question.

52 *Foedera*, ix. 911.

53 *Ibid.*, pp. 916-20. The date, 14 July, given in the *Calendar of Close Rolls, Henry V*, ii, 118, is an error.

54 See below, pp. 92-3.

55 A letter from the duke of Gloucester to Henry V from Southampton, 14 May 1420, describing these preparations will be found in Ancient Correspondence, S.C. l/xliii/191.

56 *Cal. Patent Rolls, 1416-1422*, p. 319; 13 April 1420.

to þe wyche as y durste y haue ƺeven hym comforte þat he schuld
haue no dreede þerof and made hym þys reson þat y suppose fully
þat he schuld haue more ffauoure of ƺowr grace to goo whither þat
euer hym lyste to departe frome þens when he had seen w^t Goddes
mercy thys blissedfull day of pees þan for to departe frome hens and
[see] noght þerof. F[or] me thoght ƺe [had] suffre [58]þan fo hym to be
oo day atte þe couyone of þe churche and atte a nothir day atte þe
a[lli] e[59] of both þye rea[um]es.

[2]   Souereyn lorde, when þat ƺowr letter come to me, y was yn
dreede of hys goynge of..........for y wyste noght fully hys entente
to which ende he schope thys pilgremage; for y felt by hym þat he
schope hym a nothir [way than the w]ay to seynt James, þe wyche
y drede and thys was my cause: þat for alsmuche as ƺe, my souereyn
lorde, wrote vn to me atte m[y last com]ynge in to Englonde howe
þat my seid lord had made ƺowe be heste þat he nold noght put in
execucion suche powe as ƺe wot of, comaundynge me also þat ƺife y
see any cause þat my seid worde wold doo þe contrarie of ƺowr comaundement þat y schuld let ƺe, als fare as yt sytteth a seruaunt to do vn
to hys lorde and so y haue and euer woll God wote.

[3]   Souereyn lorde, þys was my drede in þe mater: my seid
lorde comoned thys mater vn to a persone of ƺowr londe of gude
astate in easyng of hys herte and told hym whate power he had in
grete partie. And my seid lorde also told hym what lorde he founde
ƺowe in thys mater; to þe whiche he answerede vnto my seid lorde
þat he wondrede gretelee þat ƺe, my souereyn lorde, wold let hym
of þe ceysynge of hys power, seynge also vn to my seid lorde þat,
ƺife ƺe wolde aske hym of thys mater, he wold plenle sey als ffarre
as ƺe wold ƺife hym leue þat yt wer noght aƺeyns ƺowe ne aƺeyns

---

[57] Ancient Correspondence, S.C. l/lx/9. It is impossible to say how much is lost.
These words can be read at the end of the previous paragraphs:

‘..e paiement of þe wyche y
...............................[co]unsell of þe duchye of Launcastre
..........................þe price w^t my seid lorde nor to resceyue
...................................e entente þat shull be don in thys
....rde muche sese þe sub-
....anothyr wey and y tryst to
....................................and after God þe wyche hath
hys chosen man....................cause of all thys grace þat . . .’

I can find nothing in the Register, Chancery Rolls or Receiver-General's Accounts of
the Duchy of Lancaster to throw light on this reference. The Duchy Council seems to
have been occupied at this time with a dispute with the Countess of Stafford over the
Bohun inheritance (D.L. 28/ix/ll, fos. 14-5 and 31-31^v), but there is no reason for
connecting Beaufort with it. He was, however, one of the feoffees of Duchy lands
appointed by Henry V under his first will, that of 24 July 1415 (*Foedera*, ix. 289-93;
Cal. Patent Rolls, 1413-1416, pp. 356-7; *Royal Wills*, pp. 236-43) and their enfeoffment included the king's moiety of the Bohun estates.

[58] This reading is doubtful.   [59] This word is possibly 'amite.'

zowr londe to sese hys [pow]er. Of þe wyche comforte þat my seid
lorde had of thys man trewle he proyesed hym gretele y n so þaty
was aferde of þe [mate]r. And yt happenede þat y was in þe towne
when thys mater was comoned be twen my seid lorde and þat man.
Bot trewle, my souereyn lorde, ne by my trowth þe man þat my
seyd lorde comoned thys mater to zafe my lorde comforte more for
plesaunce and for to ease hys hert wᵗ þan for any othir ende þat he
would þe mater had goon forth. Bot alson as þys mater was comoned,
my seid lorde sent after me and told me þe substaunce of all þer
comonynge. And blessed be God[60] or y departede frome hym hys
hert was eased and zowr comaundment kept. And of thys laste mater
y haue nowe wruten zowe twyes.

[4]   Also souereyn lorde, ze haue a bull of my lordes in zowr
warde as my lorde telleth me, þe wyche hath hevyded hym full sore,
save zowre hyghe reuerence, of zowr mys truste, þe whyche bull he
hath y dowblede and ys yn hys warde. Bot for þe ende of all thys
mater and for to lete zowe haue full knowledge of hys ententes, my
lorde hath desired me to come vn to zowe wᵗ letters of hys owne
honde and credence, also þe wyche he woll euer fully kepe and never
doo þe contrarie; bot y haue made hym no beheste to come vn to
zowe wᵗ hys will yn to þe tyme þat y wote whate ze woll comaunde
me to doo.

[5]   Souereyn lorde, ffor als muche as þe maters aren grete þat
my lorde desireth me to come vn to zowr presence, þar for y wryte
zowe þe substaunce of my lordes ententes:

[a]   ffyrst, my souereyn lorde, y blessed be God, my lorde
ys fully set and agreede neuer to seyse suche power by hys bulles
as ze haue defended hym þat he schuld noght syse nor ryght fewe
othir.

[b]   Also, he ys fully set wᵗ zowr leve to go to Ierusalem
when þat he hath ben atte Seynt James and þer to abyde halfe a
zere and þan to come home a preste and noght a bysshope.

[c]   Also, souereyn lorde, for als muche as y note[61] whome
zowe lyste to set in þe chirche of Wynchester, y dar noght labour
my lorde vn to no man in especiall yn to þe tyme þat y haue
zowr comaundement what þat ze will be doone in þe mater. My
lord hath told me þat he comoned parcell of thys mater vn to
zowe nowe in Normandye and þat ze and he comoned of ij
persones þe wyche on was maister Ric' fflemynge and þe tothir
þe Pryve Seall. Bot my lorde[s e]ntente ys to lab[our] to
zowr grace for a nothir man, þe wyche ys a well favorde man
of hys astate þoroghe owte all zowr lond and a gude person and

---

60 After 'God', 'who' has been written and crossed out.
61 'note' = 'know not', the sense requires.

a trewe; alder corioste⁶² clerke ys he noght; bot my lorde seyth þat suche men as he ys hath profited moste þe chirche of Wynchester befor thys tyme and so, he tresteth to God, schall he. Besechynge ƺowe, my souereyn lorde, þat ƺe woll vouche safe to sende me worde what ƺe woll þat y do yn all thyes maters. ffor and ƺowe lyste to comaunde me to come vn to ƺowe, y have a saffe condit all redy atte Caleys of þe Duke of Burgoyn, bot my safecondit dureth bot vn to þe laste day of Aprill. And howe þat euer ƺowe lyste to comaunde me of my comynge or myn abydynge, y beseche ƺowe of ƺowr grace þat ƺe woll send me hastle worde. And y wold wᵗ all myn hert þat ƺe wer syker of my lordes stuffe as ƺe and he myght acorde. For yt sytteth best for ƺowe or elles y drede me yt woll goo a nothir wey. ffor, y wen, he schapeth hym to dye ryght a poer man, as he seyth. ƺe hau a terme, *operibus credite*.⁶³

[6]   Souereyn lorde, he sendeth ƺowe þys bill þe wyche ƺe may well knowe who yt ys by hys voyde langage. Wrytyn atte Ewelme, þe xj day of Marche.

ƺowr humble liege man þe wyche desirethe to stonde in ƺowr grace as y haue stonde euer þane all erthe.⁶⁴

The relationship between this document, in spite of its many baffling obscurities, and Beaufort's Waltham letter is quite plain, once they are set side by side. We have here beyond any reasonable doubt two chance survivals from a considerable correspondence in which Henry V, Beaufort, and the latter's cousin, Thomas Chaucer, took part.⁶⁵ In one Beaufort explains to the king that he cannot be present at 'that joyful day' of Henry's 'blessed glad marriage' because of his vow to go on pilgrimage to Santiago; in the other an unnamed lord and

---

⁶² This idiomatic phrase may be rendered as 'most curiously of all.'

⁶³ John, x. 38.

⁶⁴ The punctuation and capitals are not those in the manuscript. The words or letters within square brackets are editorial guesses. For convenience of reference I have numbered the paragraphs and the sections of paragraph 5.

⁶⁵ This correspondence seems to have consisted of the following at least.

(a) A summons to the bishop from Henry V to be present at his marriage.

(b) Thomas Chaucer's first report, mentioned at the end of paragraph 3 of (d).

(c) Henry V's letter to Chaucer, mentioned in paragraph 2 of (d).

(d) Thomas Chaucer's second report, 11 March 1420—S.C. 1/lx/9.

(e) A 'bill' from Beaufort enclosed in (d) and mentioned in paragraph 6 of (d).

(f) Henry V's reply to (d), granting Chaucer permission to cross to France and to report in person.

(g) 'Letters of his own hand and credence' from Beaufort carried by Chaucer to the king and mentioned in paragraph 4 of (d).

(h) Possibly a second summons to the bishop from Henry V.

(i) Beaufort's letter of 6 June 140—S.C. 1/xliii/192.

I have failed to trace any of these missing documents. They are not in Ancient Correspondence.

almost certainly a bishop is prevented from being at 'this blessedful day of peace' for the same reason. In the one Beaufort hopes that by the date of his letter his conduct since his return to England will have been fully described to the king by his cousin Chaucer; in the other, dated from Chaucer's Oxfordshire manor, the writer desires leave to cross to Normandy on just such an errand. Closer study, especially of such details as the mention of papal bulls and the reference to a vacancy in the church of Winchester, strengthens the first impression that this second document is part of a detailed memorandum on the bishop's conduct and plans, composed by Thomas Chaucer at Ewelme on 11 March 1420 and intended for the eye of Henry V alone. It is of course possible that the missing portions at the beginning contained the names of the writer and of his lord, but there is at least good ground for believing the contrary. Chaucer's reticence strikes one reader as deliberate, as though he desired to throw unauthorised persons off the scent. He may have thought that if his news leaked out, his kinsman's reputation would suffer damage; and in those troubled days in France letters could easily go astray. The allusions, for example, to 'such power as ye wot of', to a 'person of your land of good estate', otherwise not particularized, from whom Beaufort drew comfort in his tribulation, and to the mysterious lay candidate for the see of Winchester, all betray an over-cautious correspondent. A like secrecy is implied in the remark that the king would recognise the author of the enclosed 'bill' not by his signature or his seal but 'by his void language'; a circumstance which may help to explain why the bishop signed his letter of 6 June with his initials only. Apart from such intentional obscurities as these and others which arise from the intractability of the English of that date as a medium for accurate statement—a void language if ever there were one!—we have also to contend with those due in the main to our own ignorance of what had been said and written by the parties before. Yet an effort must be made to establish the chief outlines of this unsuspected prolongation of the crisis in Beaufort's relations with his royal nephew. But first a little more about Thomas Chaucer and his reliability as a witness.

In 1420 Chaucer was probably rather more than fifty-five years old, having been born, according to an Elizabethan tradition, 'about the 38 or 39 year of Edward III.'[66] Thomas Gascoigne, the author of the *Theological Dictionary*, who may be thought to have known, since he was chancellor of Oxford University when Chaucer was one of the

---

[66] *The Workes of our Antient and lerned Poet, Geffrey Chaucer*, ed. T. Speght, p. 2. 38 Edward III began on 25 January 1364.

chief men in the shire, tells us that he was the son of the poet.[67] That he was the son of the poet's wife, Philippa Roet, is proclaimed by the heraldic decorations of his tomb.[68] Through his aunt, Dame Katherine Swynford, John of Gaunt's mistress and last duchess, he secured a share in the fortunes of the house of Lancaster which was to profit him greatly throughout his career. Its first dividend was paid to him at Bayonne in 1389 when he was retained for life in John of Gaunt's service.[69] In, or a little before, 1395 he married Maud, younger daughter and co-heir of Sir John Burghersh (who had died in 1391) and great-niece and ward of Joan, Lady Mohun of Dunster, a formidable dowager prominent at Richard II's court.[70] By this match

---

[67] *Life Records*, iv. 332.

[68] Krauss, *op. cit.*, chapter ii. In chapter ix Mr. Krauss argues ingeniously, but (to my mind) not quite convincingly, in favour of an old theory that Chaucer's father was none other than John of Gaunt himself. The strongest argument against his legitimacy is surely the absence of any evidence that he inherited a claim to a part of his maternal grandfather's lands in Hainault; but he may have done or he may have disposed of his claims to others. If Sir Thomas Swynford had not been obliged to obtain a notification of his legitimacy under the great seal we should not have known of the existence of this Roet inheritance at all (*Cal. Patent Rolls, 1408-1413*, pp. 323-4). But to disprove Chaucer's legitimacy is a far cry from proving Gaunt his father.

[69] At a fee of £10 a year. This was doubled in 1394, and from time to time confirmed by the duke's successors (*Cal. Patent Rolls, 1396-1399*, p. 490; *Rotuli Parliamentorum*, iv. 39, &c.). Such engagements rarely began an association, but usually followed an apprenticeship. If this was so in Chaucer's case, then the previous service is likely to have been done in Spain, whence Lancaster was returning in 1389. Some time before the duke's death in 1399, Chaucer was appointed to offices in the lordship of Pickering, but he was deprived of these by Richard II on 20 March 1399 in favour of the earl of Wiltshire, and given an annuity of 20 marks from the farm of the town of Wallingford instead (*Cal. Patent Rolls, 1396-1399*, p. 494; *Cal. Close Rolls, 1396-1399*, pp. 467-8; *Cal. Fine Rolls*, xi. 295).

[70] Widow of John, last Lord Mohun (1320-75), and a Burghersh by birth, she succeeded in gaining control of her husband's Somerset estates to the exclusion of her own daughters, sold the reversion of them out of the family for 5,000 marks, and went to live at court on the proceeds (H. C. Maxwell Lyte, *History of Dunster*, i. 44-57). She had been Sir John Burghersh's guardian during his minority.

[71] For Maud Burghersh's inheritance, see Ruud, *op. cit.* p. 61. To her original assignment of 1395 (*Cal. Close Rolls, 1392-1396*, p. 446) were later added other lands on the death of her mother in 1420 and by various arrangements made with her sister (*Cal. Close Rolls, Henry V,* ii. 162-3; *Cal. Fine Rolls*, xiv. 335 and 398). They were derived mainly from Sir John's maternal grandmother, Margaret, daughter and co-heir of Sir Edmund Bacon of Ewelme (*Cal. Close Rolls, 1364-1368*, pp. 259-60; *Cal. Fine Rolls*, vii. 18; H. A. Napier, *Historical Notices of Swyncombe and Ewelme*, p. 21). Burghersh, a cadet member of his family, was the heir of the baronial house of Kerdeston (and according to modern doctrine, Lord Kerdeston), but from want of influence or some lack of pertinacity he allowed himself to be ousted from his inheritance by his grandfather's bastard. Thomas Chaucer took steps for its recovery, and his daughter Alice finally gained possession in 1448 (G. E. C., *Complete Peerage*, vii. 193-9).

[72] See page 98.

72 Apart from Lady Mohun, these can best be shown by a pedigree:

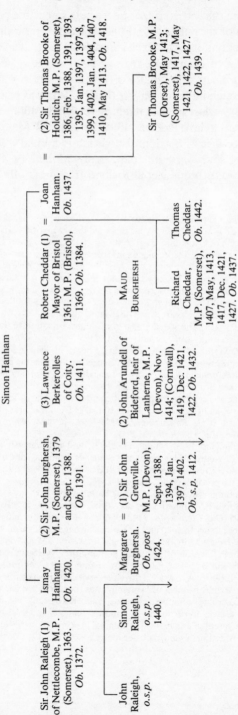

Simon Hanham

Sir John Raleigh (1) of Nettlecombe, M.P. (Somerset), 1363. *Ob.* 1372.

= Ismay Hanham. *Ob.* 1420.

(2) Sir John Burghersh, M.P. (Somerset), 1379 and Sept. 1388. *Ob.* 1391.

(3) Lawrence Berkerolles of Coity. *Ob.* 1411.

Robert Cheddar (1) Mayor of Bristol 1361. M.P. (Bristol), 1369. *Ob.* 1384.

= Joan Hanham. *Ob.* 1437.

(2) Sir Thomas Brooke of Holditch, M.P. (Somerset), 1386, Feb. 1388, 1391, 1393, 1395, Jan. 1397, 1397-8, 1399, 1402, Jan. 1404, 1407, 1410, May 1413. *Ob.* 1418.

John Raleigh, *o.s.p.*

Simon Raleigh, *o.s.p.* 1440.

Margaret Burghersh. *Ob. post* 1424.

= (1) Sir John Grenville. M.P. (Devon), Sept. 1388, Jan. 1394, 1397, 1402. *Ob. s.p.* 1412.

(2) John Arundell of Bideford, heir of Lanherne, M.P. (Devon), Nov. 1414; (Cornwall), 1419, Dec. 1421, 1422. *Ob.* 1432.

MAUD BURGHERSH

Richard Cheddar, M.P. (Somerset), 1407, May, 1413, 1417, Dec. 1421, 1427. *Ob.* 1437.

Thomas Cheddar. *Ob.* 1442.

Sir Thomas Brooke, M.P. (Dorset), May 1413; (Somerset), 1417, May 1421, 1422, 1427. *Ob.* 1439.

For these, see J. W. Bates Harbin, *Members of Parliament for the County of Somerset*, pp. 53, 61, 67-8, 79 and 84-5; H. C. Maxwell Lyte, *Some Somerset Manors*, pp. 79-81, 300-2, 354-6 and 367-72; G.E.C., *Complete Peerage*, iii. 346; and W. H. Hamilton Rogers, 'Brook of Somerset and Devon' in *Proc. Somerset Archaeol. and Nat. Hist. Soc.*, 3rd series, iv (1898), pt. ii. 1-78; v, ii. 1-24; vi, ii. 109-24.

he acquired *iure uxoris* not merely the manor of Ewelme and other properties, mostly in the home counties,[71] but also many useful connexions in the south-west.[72] The Lancastrian usurpation still further brightened his prospects. Less than three weeks after the change of dynasty, on 16 October 1399, he was appointed constable of Wallingford Castle for life;[73] and to this on 26 October he added the stewardship for life of the honours of Wallingford and St. Valery and of the south Chiltern Hundreds;[74] thus greatly increasing his

[73] *Cal. Patent Rolls, 1399-1401*, p. 15.

[74] *Ibid.* p. 34. He was also granted valuable stores of malt, wheat and victuals in Wallingford, belonging to the household of Richard II's child queen (*ibid.* pp. 88 and 93; *1401-1405*, p. 356).

[75] Ruud, *op. cit.*, pp. 32 *et seq.*

[76] In addition to the Burghersh manors of Ewelme ('Wace's Court' and 'Burghersh') and Swyncombe he held the following manors, &c., in this area in 1434: the manors of Hook Norton, Kidlington, Garsington ('Louches' and 'Haviles'), Hanwell, and Thrup, and lands in a number of places, including Woodstock, Begbrook, and Newnham, co. Oxon; and the manors of Buckland and Hatford, co. Berks (*Calendarium Inquisitionum post mortem*, iv. 160 and 177-8). In 1415 he bought from Sir Richard Abberbury and settled on his own daughter Alice at the time of her marriage to Sir John Phelip the castle and manor of Donnington and the manors of Peasemore, Penclose (or 'Pentelow'), and Winterbourne Mayne, co. Berks (*Cal. Close Rolls, Henry V*, i. 234; *Victoria County History of Berkshire*, iv. 56, 65, 82 and 91-3). In 1411 he became the tenant for life at a rent of £127 16s. 6d. of the royal manors of Woodstock, Handborough, Wootton, and Stonesfield, and of the hundred of Wootton, co. Oxon (*Cal. Patent Rolls, 1408-1413*, pp. 283 and 298-9). From 1404 to 1415 he had the custody of the lands of Sir Ralph Stonor during the minority of Thomas, the son and heir, for which he paid £200 (*ibid. 1401-1405*, p. 455); he had already obtained the marriage of the heir (*ibid.* p. 335). These lands included the manors of Stonor, Bix Gibwen, Bix Brand, and Brownesdon, co. Oxon, of Didcot, co. Berks, and others in Gloucestershire, Devon, &c. (*Cal. Inq. p.m.* iv. 11 and 12); *Stonor Letters and Papers*, ed. C. L. Kingsford (Camden Soc.), i. 29-30). From 1431 onwards he had the custody of the lands of Sir William Moleyns during the minority of Eleanor, the daughter and heir, for 500 marks (Nicolas, *Proceedings and Ordinances*, iv. 98-9; *Cal. Patent Rolls, 1429-1436*, p. 156). A third part was set aside for the Moleyns dowagers, Margery and Anne, but Chaucer's two-thirds included the manors of Brill, Beachendon in Waddesdon (both included in his return 1434; see *Cal. Inq. p.m.* iv. 160), Stoke Poges, Ilmer, Aston Mullins, Datchet, and Great Pollicott, co. Bucks, and those of Henley-on-Thames, Broughton Poggs and Aston in Bampton, co. Oxon (*ibid.* iv, 127, 190 and 328-9; G. E. C., *Complete Peerage*, ix. 42-3). Eleanor Moleyns, whose marriage was included in the grant, was Maud Chaucer's third cousin once removed. This wardship is an excellent example of the fifteenth century's keen memory for relationships—when they were profitable ones. It is doubtful whether this list is exhaustive. There is, for example, evidence that in 1415 Chaucer and one Thomas Beeke were farming Rycote manor, co. Oxon (Ruud, *op. cit.*, p. 14 from the Receipt Roll), after the death of Nicholas Englefield on 1 April in that year (brass in Great Haseley Church, co. Oxon. See *Oxford Journal of Monumental Brasses*, i. 170). In 1420 he and John Golofre obtained the custody of the manor of Bradfield, co. Berks, during the minority of Edward, grandson and heir of Sir William Langford (*Cal. Fine Rolls*, xiv. 338); the heir took seisin when he came of age in 1438 (*Cal. Close Rolls, Henry VI*, iii. 155).

importance in Oxfordshire, of which county he was sheriff in 1400 and knight of the shire for the first time in 1401. He was to represent it in at least thirteen other parliaments before his death in 1434.[75] Soon, by purchase, lease and grant, he began to amass land and in various ways to improve his territorial position in the middle Thames valley;[76] nor was Somerset forgotten.[77] At the time of his death, although he had declined knighthood, there can have been few knights in England richer than he.[78] Meanwhile his official career prospered notwithstanding the political dissensions that robbed Henry IV of all pleasure in his crown. It was a situation which called for some adroit trimming on Chaucer's part if he was to remain throughout the reign's difficult closing years the pensioner simultaneously of the king, of the prince of Wales, and of the bishop of Winchester. But he succeeded brilliantly. Only once does he seem to have been blown off his course, and then not for long. Appointed Chief Butler of England for life in 1402, he was superseded on 13 May 1407; and when he recovered his place on 3 December following—the day after the dissolution of the Gloucester Parliament in which he had been Speaker for the first time—his new patent allowed him to hold it only 'during pleasure.'[79] It says much for his political skill that he did not forfeit a single office for his part as

[77] On 23 November 1405 he was made forester of Neroche, Exmoor, and Mendip forests, and keeper of the park at Petherton during the minority of Edmund Mortimer, earl of March, rendering £40 a year to the king (*Cal. Fine Rolls*, xiii. 21-2). The earl obtained livery of his inheritance on 9 June 1413 (*Cal. Patent Rolls, 1413-1416*, p. 45) and on 17 September following regranted these offices to Chaucer for £50 a year. The latter held them for the rest of his life (Krauss, *op. cit.*, pp. 104-5). On 20 June 1406 Henry Beaufort appointed him constable of Taunton Castle and *supervisor* of the very considerable estates of the see of Winchester in Somerset, together with £40 a year and all the usual fees and emoluments (*Cal. Patent Rolls, 1405-1408*, p. 406). All Chaucer's annuities and stipends mounted to a considerable sum.

[78] He paid a fine of £5 in 1430, 'quia non cepit ordinem militarem' (Ruud, *op. cit.* p. 66, from the Receipt Roll). In other districts than those listed above he also had lands and offices: the Burghersh manors of Hatfield Peverell, co. Essex, Stratford, co. Suffolk, East and West Worldham, co. Hants; the keeping of the forests of Wolmer and Aliceholt, co. Hants, granted him by Henry V on 3 September 1413 (*Cal. Patent Rolls, 1413-1416*, p. 102); the office of havener, co. Cornwall and Plymouth, co. Devon, rendering £80 a year to the king but without presenting accounts (*Cal. Fine Rolls*, xiv. 141), granted 4 December 1415; and the keeping of the manor of Drayton, co. Hants, during the nonage of Philip, son and heir of William Pageham (*ibid.*, xv. 47), 3 July 1423; their heir obtained livery in 1438 (*Cal. Close Rolls, Henry VI*, iii. 148; *Victoria C.H. of Hampshire*, iii. 150 and iv. 8, n. 78).

[79] Appointed 5 November 1402 (*Cal. Patent Rolls, 1401-1405*, p. 170); superseded by Sir John Tiptoft 13 May 1407 (*ibid. 1405-1408*, p. 334); reappointed 3 December 1407 (*ibid.* p. 380). In the first parliament of Henry VI, 5 December 1422, he obtained the confirmation of his original life appointment (*ibid. 1422-1429*, p. 7; *Rot. Parl.*, iv. 178).

Speaker in the two succeeding parliaments, at one of which at least demands were voiced for the king's abdication; and that he retained the confidence of both sides in what at one time threatened to become a civil war. The accession of Henry V found him high in favour. How greatly he was trusted is proved by his being sent in the winter of 1413-4 on a secret mission from the king to the duke of Holland and to other foreign princes to prepare the ground for more formal negotiations (in which he was to take a share) during the following summer.[80] This was but the first of a series of varied diplomatic employments. And in spite of his mounting years he played some part, too, in the military conquest of France, accompanying the king at the head of a retinue to Normandy in the summer of 1417, although much of his time was probably occupied in treating with the French ambassadors.[81] He seems to have returned to England at the beginning of 1419 and to have stayed there until the spring of 1420.[82] Although the main purpose of his next visit to the king may have been to report fully on his cousin's 'intents', he was soon engaged on negotiations with Brittany.[83] By the end of the year he was back again in England.[84]

This, then, was the author of our memorandum, a life-long servant of the house of Lancaster, one of the inner circle of its confidential agents, eight times already a member of the house of commons, four times its Speaker, and soon to be Speaker again, one who was thought worthy of a place on the largely aristocratic minority council of Henry

[80] £76 13s. 4d. was paid to Chaucer on 2 March 1414: 'misso in nuncio Regis versus ducem Holandie et alios diversos dominos in partibus exteris existentes in certis negociis et materiis secretis dictum dominum nostrum Regem ad hoc moventibus et commodum regni sui specialiter tangentibus' (Issue Roll, printed by Ruud, *op. cit.* p. 22). On 21 June 1414 he was paid another £60 when about to set out with Lord Scrope, Hugh Mortimer, and Mr. Philip Morgan, 'versus ducem Burgundie et abinde ad ducem Holandie in ambassiata Regis ad tractandum et communicandum cum dictis ducibus de certis articulis et materiis secretis' (*ibid.* 23). See also *Foedera*, ix. 136-8; *Dep. Keeper's Report XLIV*, 554.

[81] Ruud, *op. cit.* pp. 25-7.

[82] There are various traces of his presence in England during this period. He was appointed to several local commissions in Oxfordshire, 5 March, 19 May, and 26 November 1419 (*Cal. Patent Rolls, 1416-1422*, pp. 212, 269 and 251), and 27 January 1420 (*Cal. Fine. Rolls*, xiv, 317). And after being omitted from the commission of the peace on 26 April 1418, he was again included on 12 January 1420 (*Cal. Patent Rolls 1416-1422*, pp. 457-8). His and John Golofre's grant of Bradfield (see above, p. 99, n. 76) was dated 19 May 1420. The municipal records of Oxford refer to his supping in the city on three occasions during the year beginning Michaelmas 1419 (*Munimenta Civitatis Oxonie*, ed. H. E. Salter, pp. 281-2). He was going abroad on 26 June 1420 (Dep. Keeper's Report XLIV, 620).

[83] *Dep. Keeper's Report XLII*, 375 and 379; *Foedera*, x, 5-6 and 15-6.

[84] On 6 December 1420 he was mainpernor for a neighbour (*Cal. Fine Rolls*, xiv. 363) and on 21 December he was granted the marriage of Joan, daughter and heir of Sir Richard Arches, king's ward (*ibid.*, p. 371).

VI,[85] and whose virtues were celebrated in a ballad by one of the better poets of the day;[86] a self-made man of great wealth, acquisitive yet circumspect, politic and *affairé*, well-versed in all branches of administration and diplomacy, a practised chairman and envoy, influential and respected.[87] There could have been no more obvious choice for the post of intermediary between his errant cousin and the angry king; for his ties with both were strong and of long standing. The fact that they were goes far to settle the question of his truthfulness as a reporter. Whose interests, we ask ourselves, was he in the last resort intent on serving, the king's or the bishop's? The right answer is, I think, the king's, but that this did not prevent him from trying to do his utmost for his kinsman. He did not intend to deceive Henry, but he was willing to put the best interpretation possible in the circumstances on Beaufort's conduct. Thus, while he does not attempt to conceal past failings and his own fears of the outcome, he is anxious to accept his cousin's professions at their face value. Yet even here scepticism keeps breaking in. This, he tells Henry, is 'the substance of my lord's intents . . . , a-blessed be God', but '*operibus credite*', deeds speak plainer than words. His very hesitations are reassuring; we can share Henry V's confidence in his trustworthiness.

From what he tells us there emerges in the first place an impressive reflection of Henry V's will to be absolute master in his own house, in church as well as in state. The only mark of consideration which he permitted an old servant was that he did not immediately make his displeasure public; and even this may have sprung less from kindness than from policy. Henry kept the conduct of affairs very closely in his own hands, writing diplomatic instructions personally, and even at the height of the French war maintaining firm control over the acts of the

[85] Appointed in the parliament of 1423 (*Rot. Parl.* iv. 201). He seems only to have served for one year, 25 January 1424 to 24 January 1425. In December 1424 he went to France 'ad communicandum ibidem cum domino Johanne duce Bedfordie, Regente regni Francie ac consiliariis eiusdem regni super certis, materijs specialibus dictum dominum regem et consilium suum predictum ad hoc moventibus' (Ruud, *op. cit.* p. 31, quoting Issue Roll).

[86] 'Balade made by Lydegate at þe Departyng of Thomas Chaucyer on Ambassade in to ffrance' and another 'compleynte' on the same theme, printed by F. J. Furnivall, *Notes and Queries*, 4th series, ix. 381-3, the first of which has been reprinted in *Modern Philology*, i. 333-6 and by Ruud, *op. cit.*, pp. 119-21.

[87] On 14 September 1429 he and his wife were admitted to the confraternity of Christ Church, Canterbury (*Literae Cantuarienses*, ed. J. B. Sheppard, iii. 152). Leland, writing a century after Chaucer's death (*Leland's Itinerary in England*, ed. L. Toulmin Smith, i. 112), reports: 'Sum say that this Chaucer was a marchant man and bout a 1000 li. landes by the yere, and that wollesakkes be yn Ewelm in token of marchaundise.' He was, however, a vintner rather than a wool merchant.

government at home.[88] In view of the new pope's alliance with
Beaufort it behoved him to feel his way cautiously. It is doubtful how
far even Gloucester, head of the English administration, was taken
into his confidence. The duke clearly knew something, for he had
heard at least what were probably the indignant exclamations wrung
from the king when first told of what was afoot. But that he knew the
whole story in detail it is impossible to believe. Had he done so it is
quite certain that he would not have refrained from making political
capital out of it when he had quarrelled with the cardinal later. The
silence of the chroniclers, an absolutely unbroken silence, suggests
that others learnt still less. Yet, while the bishop went about his
diplomatic duties in Normandy, all unknown to the outside world a
sentence of extreme severity was hanging over his head. Not only had
he been forbidden to assume the dignity and responsibilities conferred
upon him by Martin V, his bull having been impounded by the king,
but he was threatened with the loss of his bishopric, degradation to the
rank of priest and, judging from some dark hints in Chaucer's
memorandum, with the forfeiture of all or part of his worldly goods as
well. It will be noticed that these penalties correspond fairly closely
with those imposed under the Statute of Provisors of 1390, and it is
therefore more than likely that it was Henry's intention, if necessary,
to invoke that act as Gloucester was to do against Cardinal Beaufort
when he repeated the offence during the next reign.[89] For the moment
it was a threat and nothing more. Angry though he may have been,
Henry did not act with precipitation. As far as he was concerned,
delay had slight dangers and might, if properly employed, bring
definite gain. During 1419 he was secretly involved in an attempt to
strike a bargain with Martin V, in which papal assistance in some
form against the French was sought, it appears, in return for a mere
half-promise—for it was made dependent upon the concurrence of
Parliament—that the Statute of Provisors would be relaxed.[90]
Unfortunately, Martin asked that his letters should be destroyed as
soon as they had been read, and although it would not have been
surprising had his wishes been quietly ignored, little has been

[88] A highly characteristic product of Henry's pen is printed in *Foedera*, ix. 427-30;
for some of his letters to the English council see *Proceedings and Ordinances*, ii.
passim; Chambers and Daunt, *op. cit.*, pp. 67-84, print those to the citizens of
London.

[89] *Statutes of the Realm* (Record Commission), ii. 69 and 74; W. T. Waugh, *ante*,
xxxvii. 200-2.

[90] *Foedera*, ix. 680-2 and 806-7; T. Haller, *op. cit.* pp. 249-60; J. H. Wylie and W.
T. Waugh, *The Reign of Henry the Fifth*, iii. 171 and 375-6; E. F. Jacob, *Chichele's
Register*, I, xlii.

discovered of these negotiations save that they proved unfruitful. If Beaufort's plight was mentioned, there is no record of it.[91] But in the papal concordat with England, concluded in July 1418 and confirmed by Martin in April 1419, there was vague talk of proportional representation of all Catholic *nationes* in the College of Cardinals,[92] and we have Duke Humphrey's evidence that this proposal was mixed up with the question of Beaufort's disgrace. In any event, the effect of these diplomatic exchanges may well have been to retard the king's decision until the full extent of Martin's gullibility had been tested. As things turned out, the pope revealed himself to be a wary and practised negotiator with no intention of abandoning his neutrality for illusory gains, and by 1420 he had already taken the measure of the English offers. Meanwhile, with the murder of Duke John the Fearless at the Bridge of Montereau on 10 September 1419, Henry's hands were full enough in France. So Beaufort retired to England to cool his heels in uncertainty and to scheme without achieving anything, while Thomas Chaucer was deputed to keep an eye on him and to report all suspicious actions to the king, especially any attempt to put his legatine powers into action.

Henry cannot have found his information altogether reassuring. Chaucer soon discovered that all was not as it should have been. His cousin, he told the king, had procured from the pope a fresh copy of the offending bull, which could only be meant for use. Then again, Beaufort had poured out his troubles to a friend in England, whose identity we have no means of guessing, and although the advice he had received was not intended to be taken seriously but was rather 'for to ease his heart with than for any other end', it had served to rekindle his ambitions. So unsettled had he become that Chaucer had been hard put to it to see that the royal commands were kept. In his opinion, at least, Beaufort had not merely been hoping for a reprieve; he had actually been planning defiance. The paragraphs describing these fears are the least intelligible in Chaucer's report, probably because he had already written thereon to the king in an earlier letter now lost. But he had, it seems, been trying to persuade Beaufort to make the journey to Santiago by way of Troyes, offering the inducement that leave to go on pilgrimage would be more readily conceded if the king's summons were first obeyed.[93] Chaucer, in fact, did not wholly believe in the

[91] Since Haller's conscientious researches in the Vatican archives failed to unearth anything of note on this point, it may be assumed that nothing much to our purpose survives there.

[92] *Sacrorum conciliorum collectio*, ed. J. D. Mansi, xxvii, 1194, ff.; *Foedera*, ix. 730-2.

genuineness of the advertised pilgrimage; he was afraid that it was a blind to cover the maturing of a very different plan. In this he may not have been wrong. Beaufort at times employed the word 'pilgrimage' loosely, not to say euphemistically. It was as a 'pilgrim' that he found himself conveniently near Constance in 1417; in 1426 permission was given him to make a long-deferred 'pilgrimage', and he used it to obtain the coveted red hat after nine years of waiting;[94] while in 1434 he was again 'under certain vows', too secret to be divulged even to his colleagues on the English council, when he desired to re-enter the papal service.[95] If his pilgrimages were indeed undertaken in good faith, it is consoling to find how often they ended in ecclesiastical preferment. Was Santiago, too, only a stage on the road to Rome? So, at least, and not without reason, Chaucer appears to have been hinting. But what precisely he intended to convey by his allusion to 'the covion of the Church', which Beaufort might be proposing to attend, is not clear. It is a more than misleading way to describe the Roman Curia. Yet the Council of Constance had been dissolved nearly two years before, and that of Pavia was not due to begin until 1423. The problem is further aggravated by a number of disputable readings in the same sentence and must be left unsolved.

Notwithstanding these omens of trouble, Chaucer professed himself sanguine about the future. He had succeeded, he thought, in reconciling his kinsman in all essentials to a policy of passive obedience. On the other hand, '*operibus credite.*' The king can scarcely have needed this warning. But on balance Chaucer's optimism may have been justified. There must have been limits even to Beaufort's intransigence, and it is not unreasonable to suppose that these had at last been reached. He was now, we learn, not only fully agreed to renounce for ever the powers to which his bulls entitled him, but desired the royal permission to go on from Santiago to Jerusalem, 'there to abide half a year and then to come home a priest and not a bishop.' These last words are unambiguous though startling. They imply an intention on his part to resign episcopal orders along with his see, a degradation without recent precedent. In several political crises during the previous half century bishops had been removed from their sees. The primates Neville and Arundel, in 1388 and 1397 respectively, had, for example, been translated by the pope at the government's

---

[93] Poggio wrote on 5 March 1420 as if he thought there was some chance of his patron's soon crossing to France to see the king (*Poggii Epistoloe*, ed. T. Tonelli, i. 31).

[94] *Proceedings and Ordinances*, iii. 195-6.

[95] *Ibid.*, iv. 235.

request to St. Andrews, a diocese conveniently within the obedience of the rival pope and therefore merely titular; and translation was accompanied by banishment from England. But the healing of the Schism had put this solution beyond reach in 1420. There was precedents for less drastic action. When, for example, Robert Walden was ejected from the primacy in 1399, he was enthroned as bishop of London after a negligible interval. But he had given slight offence. His fellow-victim of the Lancastrian Revolution and much more zealous partizan of the deposed Richard, Thomas Merke, was translated from the see of Carlisle to that of Salmas (Selma) *in partibus infidelium*.[96] It would be wrong, I fancy, to assume from Chaucer's letter that his proposal that Beaufort should be divested of his pontificals, the spiritual authority, that is to say, which he enjoyed by virtue of his consecration, came in the first place from the victim rather than from the king. What the former did perhaps suggest himself was exactly when and how the operation should be carried out. Be this as it may, it is not difficult to grasp why he wished to extend his pilgrimage to include Jerusalem. After he had spent six months thus devoutly, his abandonment of worldly honours would stand a good chance of being accepted by contemporaries, if not without comment, at least without the need for humiliating explanations. Stranger conversions had been known, and such comment as there would be was bound in the main to be favourable. What in effect Beaufort was asking was that the real facts of his downfall should not be made public and that he should be allowed to choose his own setting for his inevitable retreat, a fairly safe request in as much as Henry had already given proof of a willingness to humour him thus far.[97] To complete the picture, we have Chaucer's reference to 'my lord's stuff.' The sense of this passage is disputable, but the obvious interpretation is that Beaufort had been negotiating with the king for the disposal of his vast moveable property, which he

[96] *Cal. Papal Registers, Letters,* iv. 351, and v. 395, 504 and 619. Merke did not take out the necessary letters of translation within the prescribed period, and a succession of others were provided to the see. As late as 1404, however, the pope addressed him as bishop and he himself signed '*Episcopus Samastanensis*' in June 1401 (*Royal and Historical Letters; Henry IV,* ed. F. C. Hingeston (Rolls Series), i. 66). The name of his see has given trouble, it being variously rendered as Samothrace (J. H. Wylie, *History of England under Henry the Fourth,* i. 109; but see also iii. 350, n. 2), Samos (H. Wallon, *Richard II,* ii. 519-20), and Samaston (W. W. Capes, *The English Church in the Fourteenth and Fifteenth Centuries,* p. 157).

[97] Another instance of Beaufort's determination to save his face may be recalled. In January 1426 the duke of Gloucester was demanding that the bishop should be dismissed from the office of chancellor as a condition of peace between them (*Proceedings and Ordinances,* iii. 186). But it was not until after the pacification that Beaufort resigned the great seal upon his own terms.

was to give up as well as his rank. I am inclined to think that the trouble was that he had left it somewhere out of reach of Henry V. That he was accustomed to take it with him on his travels is known from the fact that Duke Humphrey was able to seize it at Sandwich in February 1432; and we have seen that he was reputed to have a large sum with him when he passed through Venice on pilgrimage in 1418. If this explanation is accepted, we have yet another reason for the king's delays—and for his harshness. But that the prelate who earned notoriety as 'the Rich Cardinal' should have professed, even as a bargaining gesture, that he intended to die a poor man is an exquisite touch and fit introduction to a quarter of a century of successful and unscrupulous money-grubbing. No wonder that Chaucer sounded incredulous and urged Henry to make sure of his share before it was too late; otherwise, as he sensibly remarked, it would 'go another way' —as indeed eventually it did.

Finally, there remained the problem of filling the vacant see of Winchester. On this, Chaucer's memorandum sheds some interesting light. Possible candidates had, it appears, been discussed by the king and Beaufort when the latter was in Normandy, and although nothing was settled the choice had then seemed to lie between Mr. Richard Fleming, whom Martin provided to the see of Lincoln on 20 November 1419,[98] and John Kemp, keeper of the Privy Seal, chancellor of Normandy and, since 26 June 1419, bishop of Rochester.[99] Both were obviously marked out for promotion, the one as a papal chamberlain and nuncio,[100] the other as an ecclesiastical lawyer and rising civil servant. Subsequently, however, Beaufort's interest was enlisted in favour of a layman whom he put forward with the somewhat eccentric recommendation that such men had most profited the church of Winchester in times past. There is little reason why his opinion should have been worth heeding; his advocacy, for example, of his nephew, Robert Nevill, a youth of small parts and less than canonical years, for the bishopric of Sarum in 1427 does not speak well for his sense of propriety.[101] But since he had himself been 'still a boy' at the time of his own consecration,[102] he may perhaps be

---

[98] *Cal. Papal Registers, Letters,* vii. 116 and 134.

[99] *Ibid.*, vii. 133. He had been elected by the chapter in the previous January. For an interesting discussion of episcopal appointments at this time, see *Chichele's Register*, I, xci-iv.

[100] *Cal. Papal Registers, Letters,* vii. 5. For his biography see R. L. Poole's article in the *Dictionary of National Biography;* and *Visitations of Religious Houses in the Diocese of Lincoln, 1420-1449,* ed. A. Hamilton Thompson, I, xiii-vi.

[101] Martin V was very candid on the reasons why he provided Nevill (*Cal. Papal Registers, Letters,* vii. 32-3).

forgiven for thinking such details unimportant. There is no clue to the
identity of his nominee beyond the fact that he was a layman; even his
rank is unspecified; the field of choice is therefore too wide for
profitable speculation. In any case, Beaufort was himself destined to
occupy the see until his death twenty-seven years later, in spite of more
than one new attempt to oust him.

With the despatch of Chaucer's memorandum darkness descends
again. For some reason, unknown but not unimaginable, Henry seems
to have decided at the eleventh hour upon his uncle's reprieve. By midsummer 1420 he had had a chance of cross-examining Chaucer *viva
voce* and of informing himself of details withheld from the earlier
reports.[103] But even if the impression he gained was favourable, the
bishop's reiterated refusal to obey his summons, though servile and
ingratiating in tone, can scarcely have disposed him to believe the
lesson was yet well learnt. More time was needed to test the genuineness of Beaufort's professions of abject self-abasement, since these
were so far belied by his acts. What sort of obedience was to be
expected from one whose heart was still so set on the forbidden fruit
that a few conventional words of comfort from a friend were enough
to reawaken hope? And had not Beaufort procured and was he not
then cherishing a second copy of the offending bull? Remembering
this, we will do well to seek a later date than 1420 for his final pardon
and reinstatement. It may well be that there was none, and that the
threat of deprivation and forfeiture remained as long as Henry lived.
But on the whole this is unlikely. The king found time to visit England
early in 1421, and if his decision about his uncle's fate is assigned to
the May of that year, it falls at once into a suitable context.

Beaufort's whereabouts during the second half of 1420 can be
traced but intermittently. He was, as we have seen, at Waltham on 6
June, and his attendance is recorded at a council held in the house of
the Black Friars, London, on 17 August.[104] Between these dates and for
some time afterwards a pestilence was raging in the capital and public
business there was suspended.[105] Fortunately at this point a few useful
hints are contributed by Poggio Bracciolini. Owing to the plague, he
informed his friend Niccolo Niccoli by letter, he was obliged to take

---

[102] 'Annales Ricardi Secundi', in *Johannis de Trokelowe et Henrici de Blaneforde
Chronica et Annales*, ed. H. T. Riley, pp. 226-7.
[103] Chaucer had letters of attorney on 26 June 1420 as about to go abroad in the
king's service (*Dept. Keeper's Report XLIV*, 620; H. A. Napier, *op. cit.*, p. 29). His
appointment to treat with the Bretons was dated 15 July (*Foedera*, x. 5-6).
[104] Exchequer, Treasury of Receipt, Council and Privy Seal, E 28/33.
[105] *Cal. Close Rolls, 1419-1422*, p. 77.

refuge in the country for the space of two months; these he spent with his patron, visiting Salisbury and many monastic libraries in the provinces.[106] On 24 October Beaufort, he wrote, was expected in London very shortly,[107] and by the end of the month he had arrived.[108] The only other reference to his presence is his appointment as a Trier of Petitions in the Parliament which met at Westminster on 2 December—and sat about a fortnight.[109] He is next heard of in the following February after the arrival of the king and queen in the capital.[110]

The coronation of Queen Catherine, which took place amid elaborate festivities on 23 February, was not the sole nor even the chief purpose of Henry's visit. Supplies were running short and the recent parliament, with a lack of enthusiasm unparalleled since Agincourt, had declined to make any grant. This situation was met by a royal progress which lasted for two months and extended as far afield as Shrewsbury, Beverley, and Norwich.[111] Although officially undertaken for devotional reasons, this journey was employed by the king, who regarded time as a precious gift of God,[112] in spreading assiduous propaganda about his achievements in France and in demanding reinforcements in men and money for the completion of

[106] Poggii Epistolae, i. 40 (24 October 1420). His previous letter is dated 17 July; the probable inference is that Beaufort took him away after the council of 17 August.

[107] *Ibid.*, 41. One statement of Poggio's raises a difficult question. On 17 July he writes: 'nam herus peregre abest in Scytha ego hic [i.e. London] operior quietus et negotiis vacuus' (*ibid.*, p. 39). It would naturally be supposed from this that Beaufort was in Eastern Europe; but such an assumption would be dangerous. As we have seen (above, p. 89, n. 29); Dr. Radford's date for Beaufort's Bohemian journey, October 1419 to December 1420 (L. B. Radford, *op. cit.*, pp. 93-5) is erroneous; that journey took place in the autumn of 1421. Another between June and August 1420 is not merely otherwise unrecorded; it is inconsistent with the Waltham letter and everything else that we know. Perhaps the explanation is to be found in the elegance of Poggio's latinity and in his low estimate of English civilisation. Scytha may after all mean Hampshire. There is some support for this in an earlier letter. On 5 March 1420, a few days before Chaucer penned his memorandum, Poggio wrote: 'Dominus meus quasi continuo abest, vagus ut Scytha' (*Poggii Ep.*, i. 31); the rest of the letter makes it fairly clear that Beaufort's Scythian wanderings were in England. And this is again and again implied in Chaucer's memorandum.

[108] *Ibid.*, p. 42. There was an important meeting of the council on 27 October (Chancery Warrants, C. 81/1543; the names of those present are not given in full) for which he may have come.

[109] *Rot. Parl.*, iv. 123.

[110] *The Brut*, ii. 445. I have failed to find any contemporary authority for Sir James Ramsay's statement (*Lancaster and York*, i. 289), repeated by C. L. Kingsford (*Henry V*, 322) and Radford (*op. cit.*, 95) that Beaufort was in the royal train which landed at Dover on 2 February 1421. But a midwinter pilgrimage to Santiago and a return journey by Rouen would then have to be supposed.

[111] Wylie and Waugh, *op. cit.*, iii. 270-2.

[112] *Vita et Gesta Henrici Quinti*, ed. T. Hearne, p. 296.

his work.[113] It was this practical object which called forth the famous wail with which Adam of Usk breaks off his chronicle: 'our lord the king, rending every man throughout the realm who had money, be he rich or poor, designs to return again into France in full strength.'[114] The royal methods were typically high-handed and there is more than a slight suspicion that force was used to extort some of the many loans then promised.[115] Not even the story of Clarence's rout and death at Beaugé was allowed to hurry or curtail these essential preparations. But on coming to London for parliament, Henry received a sharp reminder of the precarious basis of his empire when on 6 May the Treasurer submitted his 'budget' to a council of ministers and others at Lambeth. Kynwolmerssh had small hope of balancing his account for the year, still less of being able to pay off the vast accumulation of debt.[116] Since it was thought inexpedient and probably futile to ask parliament for a subsidy, loans had perforce to form the mainstay of his calculations.[117] These, thanks to the king's personal efforts, were forthcoming in fairly large quantities.[118] But without one in particular, the result would have been disappointing. Exactly a week after the Treasurer's gloomy forecast, Henry Beaufort advanced the enormous sum of £17,666 13s 4d.[119] This was, as the Commons through their Speaker, Chaucer, reminded Henry, 'for the exploit of your present voyage to the parts of France and Normandy, for your very great need and necessity and for the easing of your poor commonalty of England.'[120] At this time over £8,300 of the bishop's last loan, that of 1417, was still outstanding, although repayment had gone on without interruption right through the crisis in his relations with the king.[121] By a carefully drafted patent, confirmed in parliament, the customs of Southampton were assigned to the bishop for the repayment of both loans, while as security against default the 'Great Crown of England' was to remain in his hands.[122]

By the generous scale of his financial assistance, Beaufort put Henry

---

113 E. de Monstrelet, *Chronique*, ed. L. Douët d'Arcq, iv. 25.
114 *Chronicon Adae de Usk, 1377-1421*, ed. E. Maunde Thompson, 2nd edn., pp. 133 and 320.
115 *Foedera*, x. 96-8; *Proceedings and Ordinances*, ii. 280-2. This was not the first occasion on which Henry was accused of extorting loans. The charge was made in 1416 ('An Historical Collection of the Fifteenth Century', ed. C. L. Kingsford, *ante*, xxix. 511-2).
116 *Proceedings and Ordinances*, ii. 312-5.
117 *Historical Collections of a Citizen of London*, ed. T. Gairdner ('Gregory's Chronicle'), p. 142.
118 Exch., Treas. of Receipt, Receipt Roll, Easter 9 Henry V, E. 401/696, 10-13 May.
119 *Ibid*. 13 May.
120 *Rotuli Parliamentorum*, iv. 132.

under an obligation to which neither was likely to be blind. Without it, the success gained at Troyes could not have been followed up as effectively as it now soon was. It enabled Henry to lead a well-equipped army to Calais on 10 June and so to prevent the Dauphin from taking decisive advantage of his unexpected success at Beaugé. For all his lack of haste and panic while in England, the king could not but be thankful for the money which thus soon allowed him to rally the Anglo-Burgundian forces and to relieve the pressure upon Chartres. It is therefore pardonable to connect this timely service with his settlement of accounts with Beaufort. To do this is not to assert the crudely simple thesis that the bishop merely bought himself off. A business arrangement it may well have been, for both men were hardened politicians, used to driving keen bargains. Neither uncalculating generosity nor the obstinate pursuit of the impracticable were lines of action at all likely to appeal to them. But this was no agreement between two free and well-matched adversaries. The sacrifices were all on Beaufort's side. It is true that greater ones had earlier been asked of him, that now he was neither required to forego the see of Winchester nor to forfeit his goods, that he was permitted to return to the *status quo* of 1417. But it may be doubted whether the king had ever really meant to exact the savage penalties which he had named while there was still danger that he would be defied. Henry was often implacable, but never, except in hot blood, without an object. It is significant that he had threatened in the first place when he could have acted. If he had really wished to make a public example of Beaufort's disobedience he would not have hesitated. When harshness seemed to him necessary, he could be harsh. The forfeit he had demanded from his uncle—a man, after all, from whom, whatever his failings, he had had much good service, who, if tradition be believed, had been the guardian and mentor of his youth—would only be exacted if the victim proved unexpectedly obstinate. It all depended upon Beaufort, whose resolution was already weakening in March 1420. It is possible to believe that by May 1421 it had crumbled entirely away. In other words, fabian tactics were victorious. Beaufort abandoned—for the reign of that king at least—his most cherished ambition after having tasted its heady flavours; made, indeed, an almost intolerable surrender. He remained a bishop, but he ceased to be a cardinal and a legate; there was not much comfort for him in the

---

121 Rec. Roll, Easter 5 Henry V, E. 401/677, 12 June: loans of 8000 and 13,000 marks. The exact amount owing on 13 May 1421 was £8,306 18s. 7½d.

122 *Cal. Patent Rolls, 1416-1422*, p. 372; *Rot. Parl.*, iv. 132-5; Repayment began on 2 August 1421.

king's permission to continue in the humbler station. For months at least he had schemed and wriggled, though helpless in Henry's grasp, but all to no purpose. No wonder that this reversal of fortune, involving the extinction for ever of all hopes of a Roman future, for a time almost inclined him to embrace a life of apostolic poverty. It is at such crises as this in the careers of worldly men that sleeping consciences are apt to stir. That beneath the hard integument of Beaufort's arrogance and self-seeking was a moist core of fear was to be revealed at his deathbed. In 1421, however, he rejected the temptation to edify an impressionable world, and after oscillating between moods of defiance and dejection, came to terms. No one can say that he was unnecessarily craven. In the fifteenth century, as in the sixteenth, the popular ruler of a nation state was more than a match for all the forces at the disposal of the universal church. Martin V, even had he been unwise enough to raise a finger in his cardinal's defence, could not have saved him. These things being so, there is no difficulty in explaining why eventually Beaufort decided to play Henry's game.

The magnitude and frequency of his loans to the Crown have for long excited a very natural wonder. He owes to them his modern reputation as a public benefactor; and, indeed, they are often held to have more than outweighed his vices of arrogance and ambition.[123] If this is a simple explanation it is also a very simple-minded one. Ancient writers, with more justice and greater knowledge, thought differently. If as much attention had been devoted to the timing of these loans in relation to Beaufort's career as to their indispensability to an impoverished government, their disinterestedness might have appeared less conclusive. Apart from minor exceptions, there is a striking coincidence between their dates and those of their maker's political ups-and-downs. The fact seems to be that although the Cardinal lent freely and often, he did so when it best suited his book or when he had hardly any choice. To achieve power, to avoid impending disaster, to confound his critics and to maintain his hard-won ascendancy when it was in peril, these are the most obvious uses to which he devoted his wealth. The early death of Henry V, his junior by some years, was a chance of which he was quick to snatch unscrupulous advantage. The confused politics of Henry VI's long minority and feeble manhood offered great scope for Beaufort's

---

123 'If he loved it too well he at least made his country a gainer by his wealth' (W. Hunter, *Dict. Nat. Biog.*, 'Henry Beaufort'). Compare W. Stubbs, *Constitutional History of England*, iii. (5th edn.), 144.

talents.[124] But the policy which he pursued with such skill and ultimate success after 1422 was not necessarily a new one; the opportunities were merely greater and the prizes more desirable. Henry V also had needed money, and twice the bishop seems to have been obliged to disgorge his assistance on a princely scale, in 1417 and in 1421. On the first of these occasions a loan of £14,000 bought him permission to retire from the royal service and to go on 'pilgrimage.' It was the prelude to his momentous visit to the Council of Constance. From his misuse of the freedom then allowed him came all his sorrows. It was only after he had deposited in the king's hands what seems to have been almost the whole balance of his fortune, enormous though that was,[125] that he obtained release from the lesser consequences of his transgression. The greater consequences he could not escape—while Henry lived.

Such is all that is known of this curious and impressive episode. If, as some may think, it is rather more than all, that is the fault of the evidence. In some places the path is dimly lit, in others it is totally dark. But there are patches of daylight, and if anything at all is to be discovered it is necessary to grope forward from one to another of these using what illumination there is to the full. An affair which exposes Henry V and his uncle in attitudes so characteristic of them cannot be left unexplored. More, doubtless, is known to the angels in Heaven, but except by another fortunate accident little enough more is likely to be revealed to us.

---

[124] See below, pp. 121-137.
[125] Henry had £26,000 of his in the summer of 1421. That was a considerably larger sum than he ever lent the king at one time either before or after. If he had left his 'stuff' abroad in 1419, he may have brought it home with him in 1421.

VI. AT THE DEATHBED OF
CARDINAL BEAUFORT[1]

THE two very different accounts of the last hours of Cardinal Beaufort
which have come down to us have one feature at least in common:
each claims an eye-witness's authority. Thanks to the melodramatic
crudities with which it was embellished by the youthful Shakespeare,
the version preserved for us by Edward Hall for long enjoyed the
wider vogue. Recent historians, however, following Stubbs, have
preferred the more sober account given by the last of the anonymous
continuators of the *Croyland Chronicle*, in which Beaufort is
described as dying 'with the same business-like dignity in which for so
long he had lived and ruled.'[2]

Though it must be admitted that Hall himself was a deeply
prejudiced witness and one besides who was not over-critical of the
materials at his command, it would, nevertheless, be unwise to dismiss
his story as a deliberate fabrication. The temptation to do so would be
less were it not for the nonsense in which he has embedded it. For
throughout his treatment of Beaufort's policy and character Hall's
judgement was disturbed by two powerful influences, his faith in the
goodness of Humphrey, duke of Gloucester, and his hatred of Wolsey
and the Roman Church. The first led him to accept as truth the whole
mass of misrepresentation and abuse with which Gloucester hoped to
overwhelm the most successful of his political opponents. The second
so violently distorted his vision that he was incapable of keeping the
images of the two cardinals for long distinct. As if they had not
already enough points of resemblance, Hall frequently transfers to
Beaufort the less attractive qualities with which as a strong partisan of
the English Reformation he had already endowed Wolsey. As a result
the passage in which he sums up Beaufort's life is an indiscriminate
medley of phrases drawn some from Gloucester's 'Complaint' and
others from his own far from objective 'discripcion' of Henry VIII's
minister.[3] But the speech which he puts into the mouth of the dying

[1] Thanks are due to Dr. C. T. Onions, Prof. M. D. Knowles, and Mr. L. H. Butler for
help on various points in this paper.
[2] W. Stubbs, *Constitutional History of England*, iii (5th ed., 1903), 143.
[3] Compare, for example, the passages on pp. 210-11 and 773-4 of the 1809 edition (by
Sir Henry Ellis) of *Hall's Chronicle*.

Beaufort is derived from neither of these sources. Nor is it one of those set orations which he was fond of composing for his principal actors. It is given on the specific authority of 'doctor Ihon Baker his [i.e. Beaufort's] pryuie counsailer, and his chappelleyn.' It would be rash to assume that Hall was content to quote Baker's text verbatim; and, indeed, part at least of the speech is obviously apocryphal. But it would be rasher still to argue that Baker was a mere figment and that Hall had no better evidence than his own imagination. When Hall invents he does not trouble to shed his responsibility on to another.

Who then was John Baker? As an author he was, it seems, unknown to Bale since he does not feature in the *Index Britanniae Scriptorum*.[4] As a chaplain and councillor he is not mentioned in the scattered and incomplete references to Beaufort's presumably large *familia*;[5] he will not be found, for example, among the executors of the cardinal's will;[6] nor by name at least as one of its beneficiaries, though he may have received his share of the 100 marks which were to be divided between the clerks of the testator's chapel.[7] Finally, while it is known that Beaufort, like most of his class, possessed a council, no list of its members has so far come to light.[8] It is impossible therefore at present to connect Hall's informant with the cardinal's service.

To identify anyone with both a surname and Christian name as common as those of John Baker is at first sight to attempt an almost hopeless task. A dozen John Bakers flourished in England about the middle of the fifteenth century, most of them obscurely. Only the fact that our man was a doctor as well as a clerk makes the problem manageable, for it would seem to reduce the possible field of choice to one. This John Baker, who supplicated for the degree of Doctor of Divinity at Oxford on 3 July 1454, was a native of Aldermaston, Berkshire.[9] Since he was admitted a scholar of Winchester in 1431 he

---

[4] Ed. R. L. Poole and M. Bateson in *Anecdota Oxoniensia*, Medieval and Modern Series, part ix.

[5] The disappearance of all but the first quarter of Beaufort's register as bishop of Winchester is only one of the obstacles to a complete list of his servants. The Winchester Pipe Rolls, deposited by the Ecclesiastical Commissioners in the Public Record Office, are of little use except for his estate-officials.

[6] *A Collection of Royal Wills*, ed. J. Nichols, p. 331. These include the master of his household, the steward of his temporalities, and his treasurer of Wolvesey.

[7] *Ibid*, p. 329.

[8] 'The Book of Declaration' of Sir Robert Whittingham as an executor of John, duke of Bedford (Exchequer K.R. Accounts, Wardrobe and Household, E 101/411/7).

[9] T. F. Kirby, *Annals of Winchester College*, p. 210 seq.; *Register of the University of Oxford*, ed. C. W. Boase (Oxford Historical Society), i. 20; M. E. C. Walcott, *William of Wykeham and his Colleges*, p. 352; A. F. Leach, *A History of Winchester College*, p. 218.

was probably born about 1420. Proceeding to New College, of which he was elected a fellow on 23 October 1438, he was senior proctor for the year 1448-9.[10] On 2 July 1454 he succeeded his friend and slightly older school-fellow, Thomas Chaundler, as warden of Winchester College. There he remained until his death in February 1487, having added considerably to the lands and buildings of his house. His other preferments seem to have been few, but on 24 March 1481 he was installed as prebendary of All Saints in Lincoln Cathedral.[11] The most interesting thing about him is his membership of that distinguished band of Wykehamist friends commemorated by Chaundler, who as warden of New College was the first serious Oxford humanist, in the *Collocutiones* which between 1463 and 1465 he presented to his patron, Bishop Beckington of Bath and Wells.[12]

It should now be clear that if Hall owed his information to some lost writing of Warden Baker's he was fully justified in making use of it. There is, moreover, nothing improbable in his statement that Baker was the cardinal's privy councillor and chaplain, though the second term is perhaps more credible than the first. Beaufort was after all intimately connected with the two foundations in which almost the whole of Baker's life was spent. In January 1434, not for the first time, he formally visited Winchester College while Baker and his friend Chaundler were among its scholars.[13] Thanks to his many benefactions and watchful interest his anniversary was kept by the grateful society after his death.[14] When that event occurred Baker was a fellow of New College to which the cardinal was perhaps, though not certainly, less attached.[15] But even if he was not one of those present in Wolvesey, he was bound to be informed of the circumstances of the Visitor's last illness; all the more so if they were in any way unusual. Could we be sure that it was his report that Hall garbled, we should have the strongest possible ground for believing that the Rich Cardinal spoilt a good death by cries of thwarted ambition and despair.

---

[10] C. W. Boase, *op. cit.*, p. 287.

[11] Le Neve's *Fasti Ecclesiae Anglicanae*, ed. T. D. Hardy, ii. 100. To this should be added the prebend of Wedmore IV in Wells Cathedral which he may have owed to Bishop Beckington (*Cal. MSS. of Dean and Chapter of Wells*, Hist. MSS. Com. ii. 110).

[12] *The Chaundler MSS.*, ed. M. R. James (Roxburghe Club, 1916), p. 55. For Chaundler see *Official Correspondence of Thomas Bekynton*, ed. G. Williams (Rolls Series), i, pp. xlviii-liv, &c.; the article in the first Supplement to the *Dict. of Nat. Biog.*, by A. F. Pollard; and R. Weiss, *Humanism in England*, pp. 133-6.

[13] Walcott, *op. cit.*, pp. 343-4.

[14] *Ibid.*, pp. 206 and 251; Kirby, *op. cit.*, pp. 171-82.

[15] The archives of the college have been even less carefully searched than those of Winchester.

This might hardly seem to be borne out, though it is not specifically excluded, by the terms in which the scene is described for us by the writer whom it will be convenient to label *Anonymus Croylandensis*.[16] His Chronicle, of which only the first few paragraphs have survived, begins with some refreshingly unorthodox remarks about the *de facto* title of Henry VII. These and the evidence it provides of discontent with the usurper's policy in his first parliament are all the more memorable for not having received the attention they merit from recent writers. It next records the death of Thomas Bourchier and after recalling that of Henry Beaufort takes a perfunctory glance at national affairs before launching out on a detailed description of a local event to which the greater part of what we have is devoted. This was the visit of the diocesan, John Russell, to the monastery in April 1486 to arrange for the appropriation of the church of Bringhurst, co. Leicester, to the abbey of Peterborough. In the middle of this well-documented but somewhat tedious business the narrative breaks off. Apart therefore from the passage which is our present concern its subject-matter is confined to the first year of Henry VII's reign. It is impossible to decide precisely how long after 1486 the chronicler began to write, though his opening sentences imply that the interval was a short one. And unless he incorporated his account of Beaufort's death from an earlier source he can scarcely have been born much later than 1430; for that accounts ends with the definite statement that 'he who wrote this was present, and both saw and heard these things, "and we know that his testimony is true".'[17]

His recollections are sufficiently extraordinary to deserve full quotation:[18]

'There occurs to my memory as I write this a notable action, and one worthy of imitation by others, of that glorious and catholic man, the said Cardinal of Winchester. When he was languishing at the point of death in his palace of Wolvesey beside his cathedral church of St. Swithun in the said year 1447, on the Saturday before the Sunday of the passion of our Lord, on which day the office *Sitientes* is sung,[19] he caused all the ecclesiastics of the parts adjacent, both regular and secular, to be collected in the great

---

[16] Printed by W. Fulman in his also anonymous *Rerum Anglicarum Scriptorum Veterum*, tomus i, Oxford, 1684. This is often said to be the work of John Gale, but although Fulman acknowledges Gale's help there is no reason for believing that this was considerable enough to justify our calling him an editor. Most of the copy from which Fulman's edition was printed survives as Corpus Christi College, Oxford, MS. 208.

[17] John xxi. 24.   [18] Fulman, p. 582.

[19] Saturday, 25 Mar. The Introit for that day was 'Sitientes venite ad aquas, dixit Dominus'.

chamber of the same palace. Here he had his solemn exequies with the mass of *Requiem* chanted in his presence as he lay in bed. On the fifth day thereafter[20] the prior of his cathedral church as executor of the whole office celebrated mass in full pontificals.[21] In the evening after the exequies had been performed the testament of his last will was read aloud before all; and early on the morrow of the mass, when he had added certain corrections and codicils, all these testamentary matters were once more recited, and publicly and in an audible voice he confirmed them.[22] And thus he bade farewell to all and died at the time above-mentioned.'[23]

It would be foolhardy for anyone but a liturgiologist to venture to comment on the significance of these unusual ceremonies.[24] That they were remembered and set down in such detail at a distant fenland monastery some forty years later is itself remarkable. It is the greater misfortune that the chronicler has done so little to reveal his identity. The deduction that he was a monk of Croyland, though reasonable, is by no means certain. The space which he devotes to Russell's visit to the abbey on business of purely local interest would suggest it. But if he was, it is curious that he should not know who was the author of the previous Continuation of the Chronicle, especially when it is noted that that extremely valuable section was composed at Croyland during April 1486.[25] It is perhaps easier to account for his presence at Winchester in 1447. For the family of Beaufort had connexions with Croyland Abbey. On the death of Edmund Holland, earl of Kent, in 1408 the neighbouring Wake manor of West Deeping had been brought by his sister and co-heir Margaret to her husband John Beaufort, the cardinal's elder brother.[26] The relations of the abbey with the lords of Deeping were rarely cordial and never worse than in the 1430s.[27] But with the death of John, the first duke of Somerset, in 1444 they entered on a peaceful and happy period. The duke's widow

---

[20] Wednesday, 29 Mar.; and presumably the evening before.

[21] For *executor officii* see W. H. Frere, *The Use of Sarum*, i. 60-1, &c.

[22] I take this to mean that the first reading occurred on Saturday, 25 Mar., and the second on Thursday, 30 Mar.

[23] 11 Apr. (Fulman, p. 581).

[24] For an earlier parallel see the case of Thurston of York (D. Knowles, *Monastic Order in England*, p. 478). Philip Repingdon, bishop of Lincoln (*ob.* 1424), in his will gave orders that his funeral mass should be celebrated in the parish church of St. Margaret in the close at Lincoln if possible while he was dying. See *Register of Henry Chichele*, ed. E. F. Jacob, ii. 285.

[25] Fulman, p. 578. C. L. Kingsford (*English Historical Literature in the Fifteenth Century*, p. 181, n. 7) suggests that Peter Curteys may have been the author of the second Continuation, but there are serious objections to this proposal. Kingsford was himself aware of them. The plan of his book precluded him from dealing with the third Continuation.

Margaret, as the prior gratefully records, 'had always shown herself gracious and well-disposed towards our monastery' and in 1465 she and her daughter, a more famous Lady Margaret, were together admitted to the confraternity.[28] Apart from this, Cardinal Beaufort was the son of Croyland's most powerful protector in Richard II's reign[29] and had himself in his youth been bishop of Lincoln.[30] His death is recorded in the 'First Continuation' with many laudatory epithets and it would not therefore be altogether surprising if the abbey had sent one of its monks to visit him in his last illness.[31] It may even have been the conversation of John Russell, in 1447 a scholar of Winchester, which during April 1486 recalled to the ageing chronicler this impressive memory of his youth.[32]

Time had certainly dimmed the accuracy of his recollections in spite of their apparent precision. This is shown by the dating of Beaufort's extant will and its codicils.[33] According to the chronicler the will was read first on 25 March 1447 and then again, after the codicils had been added, on 30 March. Since the body of the will is dated Wolvesey, 20 January 1447 there is nothing improbable about the earlier of these ceremonies. But the codicils (there are two of them) are dated 7 and 9 April respectively. As will be seen presently the second modifies the first in an important respect and therefore it is unlikely that drafts of both were read on 30 March. We are forced to conclude that at least as far as the chronology goes our eye-witness is in error, though this need not detract from the general truth of his account. It would after all have been much more extraordinary if he had remembered exactly what happened without mistake after so long an interval. But the result of his proved inaccuracy is to leave us at liberty to believe as much or as little as we please. Perhaps it was an intuitive realisation of this which caused Stubbs to telescope events that are said to have occupied eighteen days into the final two.[34] All that we can conclude is that to one observer, though not necessarily a very close one,

26 G. E. C., *Complete Peerage*, vii. 159-63; Fulman, p. 499.

27 *Ibid.*, pp. 518-19.   28 *Ibid.*, pp. 539-40.   29 *Ibid.*

30 The abbey had also suffered from the ascendancy of Beaufort's opponent Gloucester in 1432-3 (*ibid.*, p. 517). It received no bequest under the cardinal's will.

31 The fact that the steward of Beaufort's temporalities, William Whaplode, bore the name of a village near Croyland, strengthens the possibility of the connexion. Whaplode seems to have settled at Chalfont St. Peter, Bucks. (*V.C.H. Bucks.* iii. 187 and 196-7).

32 For Russell see Kirby, *op. cit.*, p. 195 and *Dict. Nat. Biog.*, *s.n.*

33 Printed from the Canterbury Registers in Nichols, *op. cit.*, p. 321 seq. There is a summary in N. H. Nicolas, *Testamenta Vetusta*, i. 249-55.

34 *Op. cit.* iii. 143. He is faithfully followed by L. B. Radford, *Henry Beaufort*, pp. 289-90. W. Hunt (*Dist. Nat. Biog.*, *s.n.*) tells much the same story.

Beaufort's last weeks were nicely divided between concern for the repose of his soul and the disposition of his worldly goods. The business-like element in his last public appearance has at least that much support; the dignity can only be inferred.

The truth is that we can never hope to see into the mind of the dying cardinal through the eyes of such doubtful and conflicting witnesses as Dr. John Baker and *Anonymus Croylandensis*. Whether we prefer one to the other will depend upon our previous reading of that dark problem, Henry Beaufort's character. Upon the solution of that problem much hangs and it is only just that every clue should be considered, even the denunciations of his most implacable critic, Gloucester.[35] 'For fifty years', wrote Stubbs with but slight exaggeration, 'he had held the strings of English policy.'[36] An understanding of his aims and motives is quite essential to our reading of the political history of at least half that period, the quarter-century since Henry VI's accession. In any state in which kingship implies personal rule, a long minority must always put a heavy strain both on the institutions themselves and still more on those who have a duty to make them work. Henry VI's ministers had the added burden of conducting a great half-finished war of conquest in France. Prolonged almost indefinitely by the king's lack of will, his nonage was a challenge to the statesmanship and self-restraint of the governing classes as testing as it was abnormal. Even had Beaufort wished it, his birth, prestige, wealth, and experience would have made it impossible for him to avoid a large share of responsibility. And yet his contribution to the outcome, which was defeat in France and ruinous civil war at home, is hidden from us in the dust of controversies not yet entirely dead. How far did he subordinate the good of the realm, as his enemies alleged, to the satisfaction of his own greed and ambition? The answer is still doubtful. In spite of the evidence, plentifully scattered throughout the records, of his all-pervasive influence in these years, it is, nevertheless, far from clear what manner of man he was. His few surviving letters offer the barest of hints and are usually on purpose non-committal. He so rarely speaks to us with his own voice that when he does his words deserve the closest scrutiny. It is, therefore, strange that one such utterance has not received more minute attention: that will which he was so anxiously ruminating as he lay *in extremis* and to which he added several fresh paragraphs on the two days, Good Friday and Easter Sunday, when he might

---

[35] The duke has received even less attention than Beaufort.
[36] *Op. cit.* iii. 143.

pardonably have been thinking of other things. In view of the charges with which he stands accused it is pertinent to ask whether the two codicils and the will itself contain any evidence of uneasiness or remorse.

Among the provisions for masses, the numerous charitable bequests and the legacies to kin and servants with which all three documents abound, one theme recurs, namely, the disposal of certain jewels formerly the property of the king.[37] These, the testator twice affirms, had been pledged to him 'by my lord the king and his officials acting in this matter by his authority and that of his parliament' in the year 2 Henry VI in return for a loan and had been lawfully retained by him when the treasurer had failed to content him on the dates agreed. It may be worth seeing whither this scent leads us. The loan can easily be identified as that of 1 March 1424, the first of the new reign. But before its details are investigated something needs to be said about Beaufort's previous financial dealings with the government during the early years of Gloucester's nominal Protectorate.

When Henry V died he owed his uncle the balance of the two great loans of 12 June 1417 and 13 May 1421.[38] This amounted on 31 August 1422 to £20,149. 0s. 5d.[39] By the settlement of 19 May 1421, which merely expanded the provisions of that of 18 July 1417 to cover the recent new loan, the bishop held what was usually described as a 'long commission' of the port of Southampton and its subsidiary havens.[40] The terms of this grant were the model for many of his later concessions and are therefore important. They empowered him to appoint one of the two customers and to enjoy all the profits of the port from customs, subsidies, and tonnage and poundage, exclusive of any assignments made, and annuities granted, from them before 18 July 1417, until such time as he should be fully repaid. Meanwhile, the great crown of England was to remain in his hands as security. Neither the king's death nor the bishop's was to impair the validity of this grant. Finally, as an additional safeguard, it was provided that

[37] Nichols, *op. cit.*, pp. 329, 334-5, and 338.

[38] For these see above, pp. 110-13.

[39] Of the £25,973. 11s. 8d. owed on 13 May 1421, £1,058. 19s. 4½d. had been cancelled against the arrears of the bishop's clerical tenths, £1,666. 13s. 4d. had been repaid from the customs of London, and £3,098. 18s. 10½d. from the receipts of Southampton (Exchr. of Receipt, Receipt Rolls, E 401/696, 699, and 702; Issue Rolls, E 403/652 and 655).

[40] *Calendar of Patent Rolls, 1416-1422*, and *372*; *Rotuli Parliamentorum*, iv. 111-13 and 132-5; Exchr. K. R. Memoranda Roll I Henry VI, E 159/199, Commissiones, Mich., Ebor, m. I. His customer was John Foxholes (Exchr. K. R. Customs Accounts, E 122/140/15).

'if it should happen that by reason of war, or ordinance or any other contingent cause whatsoever, the course or exercise of merchandise in the aforesaid port should have ceased, or that merchants seeking access to the aforesaid port should have been hindered or disturbed to the detriment of the customs and subsidies in the same port',

then the bishop should have the right to make good his losses by taking over, on the same terms as he had been granted Southampton, the port of London 'or any other port or ports whatsoever.' Although apparently he or his nominees were to be sole judges of the necessity for putting the dormant provisions of this clause into effect, there can be little doubt that it was never intended to receive the wide interpretation which he was to place on it soon after Henry V's death.

The occasion arose in the first parliament of the new reign. On 9 November 1422 the Commons, while subjecting alien merchants to taxation at the old rates, considerably lightened the burden for natives; these were to pay customs and subsidy on wool at the reduced rate of 40s. the sack (instead of 50s.) and were exempted from tonnage and poundage altogether. These grants were made on condition that no part of their yield should be spent on any 'other use but only in and for the defence of the . . . realm.'[41] It therefore became necessary for the law officers of the Crown to declare in council that, since Beaufort's loans had been made to help finance the war, this act of parliament did not invalidate his patent.[42] It had, however, unquestionably retarded the speed at which he could hope to obtain repayment. Taking advantage of this, he immediately invoked his right to assume control of other ports and on 17 November began to nominate his own customers.[43] Although the Exchequer acquiesced, the legality of his action may have been challenged; for on 15 February 1423, a week after a further list of nominations, his claim to appoint one customer in every English port was formally recognised by the king's council, of which he was the second most important member.[44] Thenceforward the whole of the government's steadiest source of revenue was diverted to his use. Before the end of the year he had received more than £11,000,[45] though it was not until 21 May 1425 that

41 *Rot. Parl.* iv. 173-4. The new rates dated from 1 Sept. 1422.

42 *Proceedings and Ordinances of the Privy Council*, ed. N. H. Nicolas, iii. 34-5.

43 *Calendar of Fine Rolls*, xv. 18-19 and 22-3. He seems to have indented with his nominees for their services. Richard Ulverston, his collector at Hull, appointed on 17 Nov., on 18 Dec. exhibited his indenture, dated 8 Dec., to the barons of the Exchequer (Exchr. K.R. Mem. Roll 1 Henry VI, E 159/199 Commissiones, Mich., Ebor., m. 1). He had already on 8 Dec. paid over £200 to Beaufort's representative (E 401/703; E 403/658 under 21 Dec.).

the whole of Henry V's debt was paid off.[46]

The inevitable result was to force the council to resort to fresh borrowing. Parliament had granted no direct taxation since December 1421; the clergy refused to be more generous until in the summer of 1425 they reluctantly consented to vote half a tenth;[47] the hereditary revenues of the Crown produced a negligible fraction of its expenditure;[48] and the one really valuable group of indirect taxes upon the yield of which the government was normally dependent was pledged indefinitely to a single creditor. He, it is true, was willing to make new loans as the old were repaid, but only on terms that would extend still further the period during which he was virtually farming the customs. The patent of May 1421, as it was interpreted after Henry V's death, had in short given Beaufort the beginnings of a stranglehold over the royal finances which might easily have become permanent. It was only broken by the settlement which followed his armed conflict with Gloucester in October 1425 and which involved his withdrawal from England for service at the Roman Curia. Between 1 March 1424 and 21 May in the next year he lent the Exchequer rather more than £18,000.[49] By this means he retained his 'long commission' of all ports until, having ceased to lend, he allowed it to expire when repayment was completed on 18 April 1426.[50] If, as seems more than likely, he enjoyed a concealed reward from these loans, there is no need to look for reasons other than financial for his willingness to lend.[51] Starting with little beyond the temporalities of his see, he had by 1424 made his name a byword for great wealth.[52] In

---

[44] *Proceedings*, iii. 35. On the following day, Beaufort being present, the council reduced the subsidy and customs on wool for aliens from 63s. 4d. to 53s. 4d. notwithstanding the decision of parliament. A year later on 28 Feb. 1424 the Commons, when renewing their earlier grant, accepted the council's amendment (*Rot. Parl.* iv. 200-1).

[45] By 15 Dec. 1423 he had received £11,302. 9s. 2d. (E 401/696; E 403/658, 660, and 663).

[46] *Ibid.* and also E 401/677 and 711; E 403/666, 669 and 671. The delay shows the extent to which this form of revenue had been previously assigned in advance to other creditors and annuitants.

[47] *Reg. Chichele*, iii. 91-8 and 103-17.

[48] How little can be seen from Treasurer Cromwell's 'budget' of 1433 (*Rot. Parl.* iv. 433-5).

[49] £9,333. 6s. 8d. on 1 Mar. 1424; £1,000 in obligations on 13 Dec.; £4,000 on 22 Mar.; £3,933. 6s. 8d. on 21 May; total: £18,266. 13s. 4d. (E 401/707, 710, 711, 712 and 713).

[50] *Cal. Pat. Rolls, 1422-1429*, pp. 293-4, where the total was wrongly given as £11,032. 16s. 1d. instead of £9,933. 6s. 8d.; the mistake was afterwards corrected in the Exchequer; *Rot. Parl.* iv. 278-80; Exch. Issue Rolls, E 403-671, 673, and 675. Beaufort did not return the great crown until 26 Feb. 1427 (*Proceedings*, iii. 250). For details of the security offered see ibid., pp. 199-200 and *Rot. Parl.* iv. 275.

[51] For a discussion of this problem see above, pp. 57-78.

the 'long commission' which enabled him to lend the king the proceeds of the one regular national tax as it was collected, he had found a method of multiplying his capital at compound interest as safe for him as it was ruinous for his debtor. On the other hand, he cannot have been blind to the advantage his financial hold gave him in the councils of the minority. His loans reinforced his political influence and this in its turn improved his position as a creditor. Only an appeal to force could shake his ascendancy.

The one loan in these years which was not repaid, though all the others were to the last penny, was that of £4,000 advanced on 1 March 1424.[53] It is the one to which his will refers. Preparations were being pushed forward that spring for an early offensive in France, and in June Lords Willoughby and Poynings were sent across the Channel with a small force in time to take part in the campaign of Verneuil.[54] During February, in anticipation of this, the council was empowered by parliament to negotiate a loan of 20,000 marks on the security of 'the customs and subsidies and all other profits, commodities and revenues of the king . . . and of the goods, jewels, and chattels of the crown', between then and the following Michaelmas. Beaufort had probably already consented to subscribe, for his name alone was mentioned among those with whom the council were to treat.[55] By 26 February, at any rate, his contribution had been fixed at 14,000 marks, and in return the council had agreed to repay 8,000 by immediate assignment on the customs and to hand over crown jewels as security for the remainder. If the latter were not forthcoming, half at Christmas 1424, half at Easter 1425, the pledges were to be forfeit. At the same time the treasurer was commanded to indent with the bishop about the jewels, allowing him a right of sale if the terms of repayment fell through in any particular, and the chancery was instructed to prepare the necessary letters patent.[56] On 28 February a privy-seal warrant read to the council substituted midsummer 1425 for Easter as the final date of settlement.[57] On 1 March the loan was entered on the Receipt Roll,[58] and it appears that parliament that day ratified the whole agreement.[59]

[52] In this year Sir John Mortimer was hanged as a traitor after being accused, among other things, of wishing to strike off Beaufort's head for he 'would play with his money' (*Chronicles of London*, ed. C. L. Kingsford, p. 283).

[53] On the same day he also lent 8,000 marks, making a total of £9,333. 6s. 8d. or 14,000 marks.

[54] *Proceedings*, iii. 135; J. de Waurin, *Recueil des croniques et anchiennes istories de la Grant Bretaigne, 1422-1431*, ed. W. Hardy (Rolls Series), p. 94; E 403/666; *Issues of the Exchequer*, ed. F. Devon, 387, &c.   [55] *Rot. Parl.* iv. 210-11.

[56] *Proceedings*, iii. 144.   [57] *Ibid.*, iii. 146.

The most unusual feature of this transaction was the council's order to the treasurer to agree with Beaufort on the value of the jewels to be pledged, 'notwithstanding that the said jewels have formerly been priced at a greater price than that at which our said cousin shall perhaps wish to receive them.'[60] If this was not intended as a direct encouragement to Beaufort to place the lowest possible valuation on them that the treasurer would accept, the wording was unfortunate. But that does not prove that he took full advantage of the permission given him. One observer with a long memory and an accumulated sense of grievance was perhaps going beyond the evidence when sixteen years later he raked up everything he could remember about the cardinal's past in order to discredit him. According to Gloucester's Complaint, presented to Henry VI in 1440:

'in the tender age of you, my right doubted lord, for the necessity of an army the said Cardinal lent you four thousand pounds upon certain jewels priced till two and twenty thousand marks, with a letter of sale an they were not quit at a certain day ye should lose them. The said Cardinal, seeing your said money ready to have quit with the said jewels, caused the Treasurer of England that time being to pay the same money for part of another army, in defrauding you, my right doubted lord, of your said jewels, keeping them yet still to his own use, to your great loss and his singular profit and avail.'[61]

It is not usual to attach much importance to the duke's rancorous diatribe, but to dismiss it as 'sufficient by itself to establish the writer's incapacity for government.'[62] Yet here for once is a specific point on which its accuracy can be tested.

To do this it is first necessary to examine Beaufort's detailed agreement with Treasurer Stafford. That half of the indenture which formerly bore his seal is still preserved among the archives of the Exchequer, presumably because it was never cancelled.[63] This document, which is partly in English and partly in French, is by ill fortune badly perished, but although a satisfactory transcript is impossible, its more important contents can even now be deciphered.

---

58 E 401/707.
59 The patent (*Cal. Patent Rolls, 1422-1429*, p. 214) is warranted 'by King and Council in Parliament' but it does not appear on the Parliament Roll. See also *infra*, p. 127.
60 *Proceedings*, iii. 146.
61 *Wars of the English in France*, ed. J. Stevenson (Rolls Series), II. ii. 443.
62 Stubbs, *op. cit.* iii. 129.
63 Exchr. K.R. Treasury of the Exchr., E 101/335/15/1.

It is dated 6 March 1424 and states that the treasurer and chamberlains,

> 'by authority of parliament as well as by special warrant sent unto them by the advice and assent of the council of our said sovereign lord, have engaged the jewels and goods underwritten parcelly to the value and price as it sueth after in money.'

The list is headed by a gold collar of which 'the half is engaged to the said bishop . . . in parcel of the said bishop's agreement to the value of £1,000 and that other half left with him of trust', and contains a number of other easily identifiable jewels, described in attractive detail.[64] It can be supplemented by a memorandum kept in the Exchequer of a portion of the total which was actually handed over to the bishop three days earlier.[65]

That Beaufort should have been allowed to hold a jewel which even he admitted was worth at least £2,000 as cover for only half that sum is perhaps the first obviously suspicious feature of this transaction. If the whole collar had been pledged to him it would have been only necessary to give him jewels worth another £2,000 to have made up the full security for his loan. As it was the estimated total value of his pledges was by this arrangement raised to £5,000. But there is good reason for believing that the collar was worth much more than he was prepared to admit. For in the very parliament in which the terms of his loan were ratified it was officially priced by the treasurer at £5,162. 13s. 4d.[66] What is more, half of it had recently been pawned to a group of London merchants, headed by the alderman and skinner Henry Barton, for £2,581. 6s. 8d. and redeemed at that price in order that Beaufort might have it.[67] Finally it and a number of the other jewels were accepted by Beaufort himself on other occasions at a considerably higher valuation than he consented to in 1424.[68] Gloucester may have exaggerated the size of his enemy's profit, but even that is questionable on the surviving evidence. There can be

---

64 The following are the most valuable: the Tablet of Lancaster (1,000 marks), the Tablet of Bourbon (£280), the Tablet of the Salutation (£210), the Sword of Spain (£200), a gold ouch of the Garter (£160), a Tablet of St. George and the Dragon and an Image of St. Michael (together £120). The amounts in brackets are those for which they were pledged.

65 *The Antient Kalendars and Inventories of the Treasury of His Majesty's Exchequer*, ed. F. Palgrave, ii. 117-20.

66 *Rot. Parl.* iv. 214.   67 E 403/666, 8 June 1424

68 The collar for £2,800, the ouch of the Garter for £200, and the Sword of Spain for 500 marks (*Ancient Kalendars*, ii. 142-3 and 182-3, and an indenture of 7 June 1434 in B.M. Cotton, Cleop. F. vi, ff. 336-7).

scarcely any doubt that Beaufort stood to gain very considerably indeed by the failure of the government to honour its bond within the time allowed. And it is difficult to acquit him of intentionally under-estimating his pledges with this in mind.

The question how far he contrived to arrange that the Exchequer should default is not answerable with the same degree of certainty. But the circumstantial evidence against him is black. This is the one loan in all his long career as the crown's financier that was not repaid. Most of the others were accepted as a first charge on the revenues and as promptly dealt with as the stringency of his conditions required. When there was any danger of his foreclosing or of taking advantage of a letter of sale, he was persuaded to agree to a postponement.[69] He did not make any such concession in 1424-5. Yet he was in a position to know how difficult it was for the government to pay, for he was at that time its head. He had returned to the Chancery on 16 July 1424[70] and during Gloucester's absence from England (16 October 1424 to 12 April 1425[71]) he was granted a substantial increase of salary as chief councillor.[72] When, therefore, the first half of his loan fell due for repayment at Christmas 1424, he was by virtue of his offices in the strongest possible position to make his wishes felt at the Exchequer. On the other hand there is no explicit statement anywhere in the surviving minutes of the council to bear out Gloucester's assertion that he persuaded the treasurer to spend the money intended for his satisfaction on another army.[73] In any case it is hardly likely that there would be. A decision, however, was taken at a meeting at which Beaufort was present on 28 November for the payment of the troops in the East March against the Scots that could be made to answer Gloucester's vague description.[74] It involved Beaufort's surrender to the treasurer on 13 December of an obligation for £1,000 which he held against the earl of Northumberland and an assignment of just over £3,000 to the latter on 17 February 1425.[75] Since this assignment was on the customs it was contrary to the terms of Beaufort's long commission and could only have been made with his consent and to

---

69 *Proceedings*, v. 16 and 115. It is fair to add that these concessions were almost certainly at a price.

70 *Cal. Close Rolls, Henry VI*, i. 154.

71 *Wars of the English in France*, II. ii. 397. He was officially absent from Michaelmas 1424 to 12 Apr. 1425, during which period he received no salary as Protector (E 403/707, 17 Feb. 1433).

72 At the rate of 2,000 marks per annum (*Proceedings*, iii. 165).

73 *Ibid*. iii. 160-5. Exchr., Treasury of Receipt, Council and Privy Seal, E 28/46.

74 *Proceedings*, iii. 162-3.

75 E 401/710; E 403/669.

his disadvantage. Such a decision, taken under his presidency though with the connivance of the rest of the councillors, may well have prevented the redemption of the crown jewels at Christmas.

If the king's chief minister and uncle took advantage of the minority to rob him, it is understandable that the integrity of others was not proof against temptation. But few had Beaufort's opportunities and none his tight grip upon the royal finances. Even so the most effective checks upon such conscienceless self-seeking were the mutual jealousies of those in power. Beaufort's own immunity from criticism did not survive the return of Gloucester. He was driven from office on 14 March 1426,[76] and with him went his colleague, John Stafford, the treasurer,[77] as part of the compromise negotiated by Bedford and the other lords in the Parliament of Bats. His past conduct was to escape scrutiny and his Roman ambitions were to be encouraged in return for his disappearance from English politics, presumably for ever.

But for one small piece of evidence it would be reasonable to suppose that the matter of the crown jewels was overlooked by Gloucester in this crisis. Unlike the complaint of 1440, the duke's charges against Beaufort in 1426 do not refer to finance.[78] According, however, to an entry on the Issue Roll, dated 10 May 1430, a *breve generale de magno sigillo* ordering the tardy return of the loan of £4,000 was then found filed among the warrants of Easter term 1426.[79] This suggests that at the time of the Parliament of Bats an attempt was made to undo the damage of the period of Gloucester's absence. If so it was at least for the moment ineffective. The position had greatly changed in the spring of 1430. Beaufort was now on the defensive. His Roman plans had gone awry and though he had succeeded in repulsing several attacks by Gloucester he was still exposed to a charge under the Statute of Praemunire. When, therefore, the boy king was being fitted out for his journey to be crowned in Paris, the cardinal was persuaded to disgorge the finest of his spoils, the Rich Collar itself, for less even than he had given for it. On 10 May 1430 his treasurer, John Burton, clerk, received £908. 2*s.* 1½*d.* for its return.[80] It was probably at about this time that the Sword of Spain and the ouch of the Garter were also surrendered. The former

---

[76] *Cal. Close Rolls, Henry VI*, i. 269. 14 May in *Cambridge Medieval History*, viii. 391, is a misprint.

[77] Walter Hungerford was already treasurer on 16 Mar. 1426 (*ibid.*); the date given by the *Handbook of British Chronology*, ed. F. M. Powicke, p. 84, is wrong.

[78] The best text of these charges and of Beaufort's replies is printed by C. L. Kingsford in his *Chronicles of London*, pp 76-94.

[79] E 403/694.   [80] *Ibid.*

seems to have been in the king's possession at the date of his French coronation,[81] and both, together with the Rich Collar, were pledged to Beaufort as security for a new loan on 20 June 1434.[82] On the other hand there is no evidence of any payment for their return.[83] It is likely that they, and perhaps some of the much less valuable pieces, were exchanged for a Tablet of St. George, bought by Henry VI for 2,000 marks from Sir William Estfield, which was later counted as part of the 1424 deposit.[84] It is otherwise difficult to explain how this tablet found its way into the cardinal's hands. It was to stay there, along with the remainder of the crown jewels, until his death.

Meanwhile Henry VI was growing up and beginning to take a personal share in the government of the kingdom. He had a right, if he was so inclined, to call upon those responsible for the administration during his minority to render an account of their stewardship. It was probably the thought of this which inspired Beaufort in 1437 to obtain a general pardon from the consequences of all his past transgressions and offences. Nothing was more likely than that Gloucester would become a tale-bearer. Now there was no necessary common form for general pardon, and that granted to the cardinal on 26 June 1437,[85] though following the customary lines, had one unusual clause tacked on at the end. The king was made to pardon and quitclaim to his uncle

'also all our jewels and those of our said father which have been delivered to the same bishop as security for wages of war or otherwise in our name or in that of our same father, and also all our right which we have in the same or in any parcel of them.'[86]

Beaufort's legal position, already strong, was thereby rendered impregnable. There remained his conscience.

This showed no signs of premature activity. When he made his will on 20 January 1447 he contented himself with bequeathing to Henry VI the Tablet of Bourbon and a goblet with a ewer 'from which goblet,

---

[81] Exchr. K.R. Treasury of the Exchr., E 101/15/2. It and other jewels were Beaufort's security for a loan of £593. 6s. 8d. made to Sir John Tyrell, the king's treasurer of war, in France between 21 May 1431 and 1 Mar. 1432 (E 403/703, 19 July 1432; *Foedera*, x. 502)

[82] *Antient Kalendars*, ii. 142-6.

[83] If this took place in France it might not be recorded on the Issue Rolls of the English Exchequer. A marginal note in *Antient Kalendars*, ii. 117, suggests that only the Rich Collar was paid for.

[84] See *infra*, p. 137. For Sir William Estfield (*ob.* 1446) see J. C. Wedgwood, *History of Parliament, Biographies of the Members of the Commons House, 1439-1509*, p. 304.

[85] *Foedera*, &c., ed. T. Rymer, x. 670-1. Compare that of 2 Mar. 1443 (*ibid*. xi. 20-1).

made from the gold offered by him on Good Friday, the illustrious prince of worshipful memory his [Henry VI's] father was commonly wont to drink.' This legacy was accompanied by a humble request that the king would assist the testator's executors in everything tending to his salvation, 'as I was, God knows, ever faithful to him, desirous for the prosperity of his estate and wishfully eager for whatever could concern his safety in soul and body.'[87] The Tablet of Bourbon, it will be remembered, was in the 1424 indenture priced at £280; Henry V's goblet and ewer seem to have been there too but cannot now be identified.[88] Nothing was said at this time about the rest of the crown jewels.

Eleven weeks of further thought went to produce the first codicil sealed with Beaufort's signet on Good Friday. In this Henry VI received a fresh bequest: 'I leave to my lord the king my gold dish or plate for spices and my gold goblet enamelled all over with figures (*cum ymaginibus*) together with a ewer of the same work belonging to the said goblet.' This is immediately followed by an order to his executors to offer to the king at the price he had given for them all the jewels and plate pledged in 1424, 'notwithstanding that by the non-observance of the said condition on the part of the lord king and by the non-payment of the said sums they are mine by the best right.' A year was to be allowed for this offer to be taken up; if it was declined the jewels were then to be sold along with the cardinal's other chattels and the proceeds spent for the good of his soul.[89]

Even this did not satisfy him, for two days later in the second codicil he returned once more to the subject. Not only was the time-limit now omitted, but the executors were to apply the greater part of the money repaid by the king to pious uses likely to be particularly pleasing to Henry VI. Eton and King's College were to receive £1,000 each. And once more the dying Beaufort insisted that the jewels were his to do with what he willed.[90]

Henry was slow to exercise his option. It was not until 22 August 1449 that the more interesting and costly of the jewels were deposited with the treasurer in return for a payment of £2,043. 8s. 9d.[91] Nothing

---

[86] *Ibid*. x. 671. This clause was discussed in the council ten days before (*Proceedings*, v. 33-4). The proviso then introduced I take to refer to the jewels pledged for a loan of 4,000 marks made on 15 Feb. 1436 (E 401/744; Exchr. Treasury of Receipt, Council and Privy Seal, E 28/56, 20 Feb. 1436), the settlement of which Beaufort had consented to postpone on 18 Apr. 1437 (*Proceedings*, v. 16). There was an obvious danger that otherwise the pardon might release him from the obligation to return these jewels too.

[87] *Royal Wills*, p. 329.

[88] This appears from a statement in the codicil of 7 Apr. (*ibid*., p. 335).

[89] *Ibid*., pp. 334-5.　　　　　　　　　　　　　　　　[90] *Ibid*., pp. 338-9

was done about the unimportant residue, mostly silver-gilt; if it had not already been dispersed, the task of disentangling it from the cardinal's own immense collection of plate[92] may well have been found too troublesome. One contemporary, the unreliable hagiographer John Blackman, has preserved for us what must be a badly distorted account of Henry VI's dealings with the executors.[93] In this the king is made to refuse their offer of £2,000 for the relief of the kingdom's burdens with the words: 'He was a very dear uncle to me and most liberal in his lifetime; the Lord reward him. Do ye with his goods as ye are bound: we will have none of them.' He then at the entreaty of the executors consented to accept the money on behalf of his two colleges. The will itself disproves this story. Few would in any case attach much value to Henry's judgement of character;[94] but in this instance there is no reason for believing that it was ever uttered.[95]

This minute examination of the history of but one of the many matters which are known to have been occupying the thoughts of Cardinal Beaufort on his deathbed will, it is hoped, have shown that he had grounds for uneasiness. The will itself bears witness to the extent to which it preyed on his mind with increasing force as his end approached. Even the repeated emphasis with which he alludes to his lawful title to the jewels betrays his consciousness of the need for self-justification. He maintained this firm attitude as far as we know to the last. If, after a struggle, he brought himself to make amends it was done in the clearest possible terms as an act of grace; it had not been in the bond.

It is not so very surprising that this exigent moneylender was believed to have tried to drive a hard bargain with death. When, however, he came to part with his money for the last time, the investment was made on poor security. It is unfortunately impossible to make an accurate estimate of his total wealth, but a rough idea of its magnitude may be guessed at from various hints. Thus in February 1433 when he obtained a licence to export £20,000 in money, jewels, and plate to the Council of Basle,[96] he departed leaving rather more

[91] For the indenture of receipt see *infra.* pp. 136-7. See also *Antient Kalendars*, 11. 201-2 and *Proceedings*, vi. 86-7.

[92] Some notion of what this amounted to in Feb. 1432 can be derived from Exchr. K.R. Memoranda Roll, E 159/208 (10 Henry VI), Communia Recorda, Easter Term, m. 2 seq.

[93] *John Blacman's Henry the Sixth*, ed. M. R. James, pp. 10 and 32.

[94] But see Stubbs, *op. cit.* iii. 143.

[95] Henry did not refuse a *loan* of £2,000 in 1452 from the executors (*Cal. Patent Rolls, 1446-1452*, p. 561).

than that sum in the king's hands.[97] The total certainly did not decrease with time.

For some years before his death he had become a landowner apart from his temporalities. His most important land purchase was made on 25 May 1439, when a bargain was struck with the king in the presence of the latter's councillors at Cold Kennington in Middlesex.[98] In return for the sum of £8,900 Henry VI 'of his own motion' and without the council's advice being formally tendered granted to his uncle, his heirs and assigns the castle, lordship, and manors of Chirk and Chirklands in North Wales, together with a number of other manors (mostly in reversion) in Somerset, Dorset and Wiltshire.[99] For this 'delapidation of his crown' Henry was much blamed by Sir John Fortescue, 'whereof never man see a precedent, and God defend that any man see more such hereafter';[100] a view shared, one need hardly add, by Duke Humphrey.[101] If we may judge from the fact that on the very same day, this time with the council's approval, Beaufort was allowed to buy the reversion of an estate worth at least £40 a year for 350 marks,[102] these lands were cheap at the price. They were, moreover, conveniently situated, being near to the centres of his nephew Somerset's territorial power at Corfe, Glyn Dyfrdwy, and Cynllaith Owain.[103] By February 1442 he had further bought out,

[96] *Foedera*, x. 538-9. From this he lent the king's French government 10,000 marks at Calais in May 1433 (*Proceedings*, iv. 162-3, 202-3, and 242-3).

[97] £6,000 deposited for the return of his jewels seized at Sandwich in Feb. 1432 (*Rot. Parl.* iv. 391-2), not repaid until May 1434 (*Proceedings*, iv. 238-9); £14,473. 6s. 8d. in loans made on or before 19 July 1432, on which date assignments were granted to him on the lay subsidy payable at Martinmas 1433 (*Rot. Parl.* iv. 389 and 391-2; E 401/731 and E 403/703).

[98] Exchr. T.R. Council and Privy Seal, E 28/60; *Cal. Patent Rolls, 1436-1441*, pp. 276 and 311. The place is now Kempton.

[99] These were: the manors of Henstridge and Charlton Camville, Somerset, of Canford with Poole, Dorset (already granted him for life, 28 July 1436: *ibid., 1429-1436*, p. 601), and of Amesbury, Winterborne Earls, and Wilton, Wiltshire.

[100] *Governance of England*, ed. C. Plummer, p. 134. This was no doubt why the council refused to endorse it. Compare *Proceedings*, v. 253, where councillors 'abstained them in all wise to speak nor durst not advise the king to depart from such livelode nor to open their mouths in such matters' when the earldom of Kendal was granted to Beaufort's nephew, Somerset.

[101] *Wars of the English in France*, ʼI. ii. 448-9.

[102] E 28/60 (25 May 1439); *Cal. Patent Rolls, 1436-1441*, p. 260; E 401/762 (24 July 1439).

[103] Corfe was granted by Henry IV to his half-brother John Beaufort and his heirs male (it went to Edmund his youngest son when John, duke of Somerset, died leaving a daughter Margaret, in 1444) but I cannot find the grant (*Inquisitiones post mortem*, Rec. Com. iii. 330 and iv. 83 and 268). The inheritance of Owen Glendower was granted to Somerset and his heirs male on 8 Nov. 1400 (*Foedera,* viii. 163-4; J. E. Lloyd, *Owen Glendower*, pp. 14-15 and 141).

possibly with financial aid from the king,[104] the occupants of those manors in which he had been sold the reversionary interest;[105] while a year later, if not before, he had acquired a Dorset manor formerly the property of the abbey of Holy Trinity, Caen.[106] Yet in spite of all this expenditure, which can hardly have amounted to less than £10,000, he was still able to lend money on his old lavish scale to the government. For when on 25 May 1443 he agreed to advance £11,000,[107] he was already owed at least another £14,000 by the Crown.[108] To a minimum of £35,000 in lands and money must be added his jewels, plate, furniture, and other gear. If we assume that he had the disposal of a fortune in all of more than £50,000 when, having made his last small loan to the king in August 1445,[109] he began to set his affairs in order and to prepare for death, we shall not be guilty of exaggeration. The Rich Cardinal indeed deserved his epithet.

The distribution of this huge property as he finally decided it followed conventional lines. To his only surviving Beaufort nephew, Edmund, marquis of Dorset, he left the castle and lordship of Chirk and the manor of Canford with Poole in Dorset.[110] His other kinsfolk, William the younger son of his half-brother Sir Thomas Swinford,[111] an unidentified John 'bastard of Somerset',[112] his own natural daughter Joan and her husband, Sir Edward Stradling,[113] all received small legacies. More interesting perhaps are the omissions. Nowhere in his will does the cardinal mention his former political associate, Wil-

---

[104] It was part of the original agreement that the king should grant to Beaufort and his feoffees to his use lands elsewhere of equivalent value until the reversions fell in (*Cal. Patent Rolls, 1436-1441*, p. 311). Gloucester says that the cardinal was given the promise of lands of the Duchy of Lancaster in Norfolk worth 700-800 marks a year if the king had not made him 'as sure of all the lands toforsaid by Easter now next coming (1441) as can be devised by any learned counsel' (*Wars of the English in France*, II. ii. 448).

[105] *Cal. Patent Rolls, 1441-1446*, pp. 46-7, 129, and 133.

[106] *Ibid.*, p. 174 (2 Mar. 1443): the manor of Tarrant Launceston.

[107] *Ibid.*, p. 182; E 401/781 (6 June and 6 July 1443)); Exchr. T.R. Council and Privy Seal, E 28/71 (25 May 1443); *Proceedings*, v 279-80.

[108] £10,000 lent on 6 Apr. 1443 [E 401/780; *Cal. Patent Rolls, 1441-1446*, 160; Exchr. T.R. Council and Privy Seal, E 28/71 (16 Mar. 1443]; £4,066. 13*s*. 4*d*., part of loans made on 19 Mar. and 7 May 1442, had to be reassigned on Southampton on 29 Nov. 1442 and does not seem to have been repaid until later (*Cal. Patent Rolls, 1441-1446*, p. 76; E 401/780).

[109] E 401/790; E 403/757 (18 and 19 Aug. 1445).

[110] His directions to his feoffees for the disposal of his lands have not survived, but in 1450 Edmund Beaufort, then duke of Somerset, was in possession (*Rot. Parl.* v. 187).

[111] For the Swinford family see *Excerpta Historica* (by S. Bentley), pp. 152-9.

[112] His name suggests that he was the illegitimate son either of John, earl of Somerset, the cardinal's brother, or of John, duke of Somerset, the cardinal's nephew. It is tempting to identify him with Dr. John Somerset, Henry VI's physician (*ob. c.* 1455) who had certainly some connexion with the Beaufort family (*Dict. Nat. Biog.*, s.*n.*).

liam de la Pole, marquess of Suffolk, who until recently had been one of his principal feoffees;[114] it looks as if a coolness had arisen between them. Nor is Suffolk's wife Alice, the daughter of Thomas Chaucer, Beaufort's cousin and close ally many years before, to be found beside Margaret of Anjou among his beneficiaries. It is more difficult to explain the absence of Richard II from those whose souls are to be prayed for in the Beaufort chantry at Winchester; for to that king he owed his early advancement, his first bishopric, and his legitimation. Though he had been one of the last to desert Richard in 1399, neither gratitude nor remorse caused him to share Henry V's devotion to his memory. It is somewhat curious to find that after almost half a century he still preferred to remember the usurper Bolingbroke.

His will also made suitable, even handsome, provision for his tenants, his household, his officials, his executors, the monks of his cathedral church, and those of St. Augustine's, Canterbury.[115] And a few noble debtors were forgiven their borrowings.[116] But the bulk of his wealth was dedicated to masses and works of charity for the repose of his soul. Prayers were to rise for ever not only in his two cathedrals of Lincoln and Winchester and in the two great monasteries at Canterbury but in the houses of the mendicants in London and in his diocese, in Hyde Abbey, in Eton and King's, Cambridge, in the house of the Bonhommes at Ashridge,[117] and wherever else his executors

---

113 Joan Stradling is said to have been Beaufort's child by Alice, daughter of Richard, earl of Arundel. The Earl Richard who died in 1375 had a daughter Alice, from 1364 to 1397 the wife of Thomas Holland, earl of Kent; she died in 1416 (G.E.C., *Complete Peerage*, new ed. vii. 156; M. R. James, *Catalogue of MSS. of St. John's College, Cambridge*, pp. 269-70). She is a less likely candidate than her niece, Alice, daughter of the Earl Richard who died in 1397. This Alice is generally described but without evidence as the earl's youngest daughter (*Royal Wills*, pp. 128 and 144; M. A. Tierney, *History of Arundel*, pp. 192-3; *Dict. Nat. Biog., s.n.* Richard Fitzalan III): if so she must have been born between 1383 and 1385). Before Mar. 1393 she had married John Charleton of Powys who died in 1401 (*ibid.* iii. 161). Her liaison with Beaufort therefore probably took place in her widowhood, i.e. when he was already a bishop. This is borne out by the date of their daughter's marriage with Sir Edward Stradling (*c.* 1389-1453) of St. Donat's, Glamorgan and Halsway, Somerset, in or before 1423 (*Cal. Papal Registers, Letters*, vii. 300; *Cartae et Munimenta de Glamorgan*, ed G. T. Clark, 1910 ed., iv. 1580-5). Sir Henry Stradling, the eldest son of this marriage, was thirty years old when he succeeded his father in 1453 (*Stradling Correspondence*, ed. J. M. Traherne, pp. xviii-xx).

114 *Cal. Patent Rolls, 1436-1441*, pp. 276 and 311; *ibid., 1452-1461*, pp. 233-4; *Monasticon Anglicanum*, ed. W. Dugdale, vi. pt. ii (1830 ed.), pp. 722-4.

115 St. Augustine's was forgiven a debt of £366. 13s. 4d. in return for masses. He also left £1,000 to Christ Church, Canterbury, which house had admitted him to its confraternity (*Hist. MSS. Com. Report*, ix. 113-114).

116 £333. 6s. 8d. owed by John lord Tiptoft; £200 by William Stafford.

117 For this see *Visitations in the Diocese of Lincoln, 1517-1531*, ed. A. Hamilton Thompson (Lincoln Record Soc.), i. p. lxxii, n. 2.

might decide. Even before his death he had transferred to the Hospital of St. Cross by Winchester six manors and a like number of advowsons, extended at £144. 14s. 6d. per annum, to provide a new foundation there of 'noble poverty'; or, as we should say, for indigent gentlefolk.[118] Compared with the colleges endowed by both his predecessor and successor in his see, this was a very modest establishment; and thanks to his failure to see it firmly started in good time before he died, it was ill equipped to withstand the hazards of the civil war that followed. But with the Lancastrian restoration of 1485 his wishes were at length carried out by William of Waynflete.[119] Finally, in addition to all this, the cardinal left the whole residue of his property to be laid out at the discretion of his executors on pious uses 'as they should believe to be of the greatest possible advantage to the safety of my soul.' There is evidence that they carried out their trust.[120] By whatever methods his wealth was accumulated there can be no doubt that its dispersal was exemplary.

About Beaufort the statesman—and few would be rash enough to deny him that title—it has not been the concern of this paper to speak. His aims as a financier were often hard to reconcile with his duties as his great-nephew's most influential and experienced adviser. It is this conflict between self-interest and loyalty which makes his career so difficult to assess fairly. But it is no use trying, as some have done, to dispose of his activities as a moneylender by emphasising his statecraft. The measure of his influence on events can only be taken when each is understood. As he lay dying it was natural that the faults into which he had been tempted by avarice should have been uppermost in his mind. It is therefore not easy to accept Stubbs's far-fetched interpretation of the words which he caused to be inscribed on his tomb: 'I should tremble did I not know Thy mercies.' The obvious meaning is the likelier one.

APPENDIX

The indenture for the return of the crown jewels, 22 August 1449
(Exchr. K. R. Accounts, E010/335/15/3)

Thys edenture,[121] maad the xxij[ti] day of August the yer of the regne of oure souuerayn lord kynge Henry the vj[te] xxvij[ti], wytnesseth that the worshipful fader in God Marmaduk Lomley, bisshop of Karlille,

---

[118] *Cal. Patent Rolls, 1441-1446*, p. 174; *1452-1461*, pp. 233-4; *Rot. Parl.* v. 184-5; *Monasticon*, vi, pt. ii, pp. 722-4.
[119] R. Chandler, *Life of William Waynflete*, pp. 223-6.

tresourer of England, and þᵉ chamberleins of the Eschequier haue receiued of William Port, oon of þᵉ executours of the testament of Henry late Cardinal of England, bisshop of Winchestre, in the name of alle the executours of the sam testament thees jewells vnderwriten layde to þᵉ sayd late Cardinal in hys lyf for seurte of repaiement of mˡmˡxliij li. viij s. ixd. lent vn to oure seide souuerayn lord in hys greet necessite,[122] the same tresorer & chamberleyns yeuing suffisant assignementes to the seyd executours atte receyuyng of þᵉ same jewells for the seyd somme of mˡmˡ xliij li. viijs. ixd.

Furst, j tablet of golde called the Tablet of Lancastre, garnisshed wyth xvj balaiz, iij rubiz, liiij perles & ij saphires, weying al togeders lxij marc' iiij vnces of troys.

Item, ij basins of gold, weying xliij marc.

Item, j cuppe of gold couuered of kerimery werk,[123] wyth iij scuchons of the kynges armes in top, weying iiij marc ij vnces di.

Item, j tablet of gold called the Tablet of Bourgoygne, garnisshed with xxvjᵗⁱ balaiz, xxij, saphires, cxlij perles, weying alltogeders lxx marc.

Item, j ymage of Saint George, garnisshed wᵗ viij balaiz, clxxviij perles, weying altogeders viij lb. x vnces.

Item, j tablet of Saynt George bought by þᵉ kyng of Estfeld for mˡmˡ marc, garnisshed wyth xxx diamantes, cxxxij balaiz, xxxij saphires, xxxvj rubiz, vᶜlxij perles & iij emeraudes, weying al togeders lij marc iij vnces.

Item, j ymage of Seint Michel, garnisshed wyth clij perles, iiij saphires, xxiij baleiz, weying altogeders xj lb. v vnces.

In witnesse of which to þat oo partie of this endenture remaining wᵗ the seyd tresourer & chamberleyns William Port abouesaid in þᵉ name of þᵉ seyd executours hath put to his seel.[124] And to the tother party of this edenture remaynyng wᵗ the same executours the seel of the office of the receyte is put to. Writon the day and yeer abouesaide.

[Endorsed:] Indentura Willelmi Port vnius executorum testamenti Henrici nuper Cardinalis Anglie.

---

120 L. B. Radford, *Henry Beaufort*, pp. 294-5. 121 *sic.*

122 Several works have here been erased.

123 The meaning of this word is doubtful. The *Oxford English Dictionary* (*s.v.*) suggests '? Filigree work'. See *Ancient Kalendars*, ii. 117, 166 and 202.

124 The seal has disappeared.

VII. WAR, THE ECONOMY AND SOCIAL CHANGE

ENGLAND AND THE HUNDRED YEARS WAR

A COUNTRY'S economy and its social organisation can be affected by war in various ways. Its need for men may starve its agriculture and other industries, either temporarily or, if the casualties be high, for long, of the labour-force on which they depend. Its need for money may impose unusual and even ruinous burdens upon its propertied citizens and exact contributions from those far less able to afford them. It may suffer devastation or occupation by the enemy. Should it win the war it may be compensated for these and other losses by the defeated; should it be beaten it may have to indemnify the victors. It may gain or lose territory. It may gain or lose markets. The increased spending-power of the combatants and of those who profit by supplying their needs, armourers, caterers, clothiers and the like, may stimulate and cherish its economic growth. And whether war expands or contracts a country's wealth it can hardly fail to bring about some redistribution of it.

There were many wars in Europe during the three centuries we are here to discuss. All I can do by way of introduction is to consider in what respects the Hundred Years War left its mark on English society in the first half of our period. If, as seems likely, England's experience was not typical, the points of difference will, I hope, be brought out by the contributions of other speakers. Two related causes have, I believe, hitherto obscured the degree of its abnormality: the dogmatic belief, inherited from the nineteenth century, that wars can never be anything but damaging to every society involved in them, and a preference, inspired in part at least by the intractability of the financial evidence, for the oracular phrase, the foggier and shoddier the better. The assertion, for example, that England had been "bled white" by 1340 is no substitute for a balance-sheet, however rough, and to judge from what happened in the next two decades seems exaggerated. Precision may be difficult to attain, but we ought to be able to do better than that.

There are, of course, many important things we cannot discover. For instance how much smuggling there was, for smuggling if successful leaves no trace. To assume for the sake of greater

---

* Paper originally given at *Past and Present* Conference: '*War and Society 1300-1600*,' 1961.

apparent precision, that the amount of smuggling was constant, despite great variation in the rate of duty charged and despite great variation in the efficiency of the central government, would be rash. Yet that assumption is generally made. Or take the amount of cloth consumed by the home market in England during the Hundred Years War. Was it the same throughout, or did it decline with the population, or increase with the growing prosperity of the smaller freeholder, the leaseholder and their fellows? Here as elsewhere it is only possible to guess, though some guesses are likelier to be right than others.

But before guessing need begin there are some things that can be worked out with reasonable certainty from the records and some for which the evidence affords at least the basis for an estimate less precise but still not too rickety to be unserviceable. The size of armies, for example. In terms of available man-power the English war-effort cannot be regarded as large, though modern historians still often prefer the chronicler's inflated figures to the evidence of the records. The largest English army in the Hundred Years War was that collected by Edward III for the siege of Calais in 1346-7: 32,000. He had had less than half that number at Crécy.[1] In 1359 on his winter excursion to Rheims and around Paris he was accompanied by something like 12,000 men. Two thousand fewer enabled Henry V to undertake the conquest of Normandy with success in 1417.[2] But armies of more than 10,000 were very rarely put into the field. The Black Prince's overwhelming victory at Poitiers was won with about 7,000 including Gascons;[3] Edward III had had as many with him in Flanders in 1338-9; and John of Gaunt set out across north-eastern and central France from Calais to Bordeaux in August 1373 with little more than 4,000.[4] In the light of these and other precedents

[1] J. E. Morris, 'Mounted Infantry in Medieval Warfare', *Trans. Roy. Hist. Soc.*, 3rd ser., viii (1914), pp. 97-8. A. E. Prince, 'The Strength of English Armies in the Reign of Edward III', *Eng. Hist. Rev.*, xlvi (1931), pp. 353-71, remains the best extended discussion of the problem.

[2] This is Professor R. A. Newhall's calculation summarised from his unpublished thesis in J. A. Wylie and W. T. Waugh, *The Reign of Henry the Fifth*, (Cambridge, 1914-29), vol. iii. p. 51, n. 13.

[3] A. E. Prince, *op. cit.*, pp. 366-7; H. J. Hewitt, *The Black Prince's Expedition of 1355-1357*, (Manchester, 1958), p. 102. But two other armies of fair size were also in France that summer.

[4] A. E. Prince, *op. cit.*, p. 370. In spite of this Professor E. Perroy (*The Hundred Years War*, trans. W. B. Wells, London, 1951, p. 164) favours 'more than ten thousand' and decimates them *en route*; while A. H. Burne (*The Agincourt War*, London, 1956, p. 23) plumps for 15,000 and thinks that nearly half 'perished by the wayside.' There is little record (and no other precise) evidence of casualties.

Henry V's dash from Harfleur to Calais by way of Agincourt was perhaps not quite so extraordinary or so hazardous as tradition has made it. For the happy few were probably between five and six thousand strong and had nothing like as far to go as Lancaster's men in 1373-4.[5]

This is as much as to say that only once—at Calais in 1347—did the number of soldiers taking part in a campaign reach something like one *per cent* of the population of England and Wales. Most of the pitched battles of the war, in which English arms were rarely beaten, were fought by as little as a half or a third of one *per cent*. Since a great many of the actual combatants were gentlemen by birth and their servants, men who had no other 'gainful employment' than war and the collection of rent, and since the campaigning season, at any rate before 1417, was customarily short and did not begin until the harvest was in, it is unlikely that the raising of armies caused any great dislocation of the labour-market. Their transhipment overseas, on the other hand, made frequent though rarely prolonged calls upon the services of an expanding native-owned merchant marine; and may have contributed to its expansion.[6] But there were many years between 1337 and 1453 when no expeditionary force sailed, considerable intervals of formal peace and frequent truces, both general and local, as well as long stretches of suspended activity of the kind we have learnt to call 'phoney war.' When these occurred there were sideshows in Brittany, Gascony, Flanders, Spain and even Italy in addition to crusading ventures in Prussia and Barbary to provide exercise for those free-lancers, noble and otherwise, who chose to take part in them. It was very far indeed from being total or continuous war. Until Henry V decided upon piecemeal conquest it was a war of raids in which the English chose the time and place of their descent upon France. If sufficient troops or transport were not available, the raid could be called off; in fact it often was. Even after

[5] It is usual to accept 'the Chaplain's' statement (*Gesta Henrici V*, ed. B. Williams, Eng. Hist. Soc., 1850, pp. 36 and 57) that there were 900 men-at-arms and 5,000 archers at Agincourt, but the evidence printed by N. H. Nicolas (*The History of the Battle of Agincourt*, 2nd edn., London, 1832) bears out Sir James Ramsay's contention that only 8000 fighting-men landed at Harfleur and that only two-thirds of these set out overland for Calais. Ramsay's further deduction that the army at Agincourt scarcely reached 4000 rests on less satisfactory evidence and does not seem to have convinced its author (*Lancaster and York*, Oxford, 1892, vol. i, pp. 199-200 and 205-6).

[6] But not so much as the heavier subsidy on wool etc. payable by alien exporters. The naval side of the war is here omitted. Like the war on land and for similar geographical reasons its course was favourable to the English. Those who write of it in terms of winning and losing 'command of the sea' are guilty of anachronism.

1417 the numbers engaged were no greater; they were merely more continuously employed. Nonetheless it is easy to overestimate the amount of military activity between the Treaty of Troyes and the sack of Fougères. For the English it was still largely a war of raids, based on Normandy rather than on England. Henry V's death had put an end to the likelihood that Englishmen would cross the Channel in significantly larger numbers.

Since anything up to a half of the soldiers' wages were payable in advance, the size and timing of these raids depended upon the amount of money the English government could raise from taxation. Not all taxes levied during the years 1336-1453 were spent on war, not even the whole of those specifically voted for that purpose. But although they tended to become part of the king's normal revenues, war or no war, they had been called forth in the first instance by his military needs and only gradually ceased to be justified by them. Great gaps in the records, particularly in those of the royal household, make it impossible to discover, even in the sketchiest fashion, what proportion of their yield went directly or indirectly to pay for the war. But the amount of revenue they put at the crown's disposal should be calculable with some degree of accuracy if also with much labour. Down that road are scattered the bones of many scholars and I am not yet ready to contribute mine. Meanwhile can we not attempt a series of rough estimates, at least of the order of magnitude of the sums involved, so as to obtain some idea of the additional burdens borne by various classes of taxpayers during our period? I think we can. At least it may provoke somebody to correct them!

With minor exceptions direct taxation was raised from laity and clergy separately. Between the Nottingham parliament of September 1336 which preceded the start of hostilities with France and the Reading session of March 1453 which helped to finance Shrewsbury's vain attempt to save Guyenne, the laity voted subsidies which, by my reckoning, produced rather more than two million pounds. What in Edward III's time was still reserved for occasions of

[7] My procedure here has been simply to multiply the number of parliamentary subsidies voted by an estimate of their probable yield. I have assumed, for example, that the average yield of a tenth and fifteenth under Edward III was 50,000 marks and that in the first 31 years of Henry VI's reign it fell from £30,000 to £24,000. These are likely if anything to be under-estimates. In most cases they are less than the amounts arrived at by Sir James Ramsay, whose tables derived from the Enrolled Accounts (*History of the Revenues of the Kings of England*, Oxford 1925, vol. ii, pp. 295 and 433) are less open to objection than his additions of the entries on the Receipt Rolls. I have taken account of poll-taxes and taxes on incomes from land.

special military effort, and might then be high, tended between 1371 and 1422 to become an almost regular levy. But after 1422 the pace slackened.[7] During the same period 1336-1453 a little over one million pounds were raised by the convocations of Canterbury and York. But the clerk's willingness to tax themselves did not persist as long as the laity's. Edward III seems to have been much more successful than the other kings in inducing the church to disgorge.[8]

To this total of something like three and a quarter million pounds produced by direct taxation must be added nearly five millions from indirect taxation, of which the export duties on raw wool, woolfells and hides seem to have accounted for at least four-fifths. The yield of these imports naturally fluctuated with the amount of traffic and the rate of duty, declining slowly under the first of these influences after 1390 and markedly under both after 1422. Edward III and Richard II together received well over three million pounds from this source, Henry VI perhaps as little as £750,000 between 1422 and 1453, an annual average of less than half that of his fourteenth-century predecessors.[9]

Who paid these taxes? Was the result of their collection and subsequent expenditure on the wages and equipment of war a mere 'circular tour of rural wealth?' Can the whole financial history of the Hundred Years War be summed up as far as England was concerned in the verdict that 'wealth, wrung from the land in imposts and taxes, was not returning, much shrunk and depleted, to the place from which it came?'[10]

As far as the million or so pounds received from the clergy were involved, this picture may not have been without truth, at least in one respect. It is unlikely that anything like a million pounds went to the church in new endowments from those on whose behalf clerical

[8] If Ramsey's figures (*op. cit.*, vol. ii, p. 294) are correct, I have seriously underestimated the amount produced by a clerical tenth in Edward III's reign; but it is difficult to believe that a single tenth from the two provinces can ever have produced over £48,000. In addition to taxation there should be some reference to the English revenues of French monasteries ('alien priories'), seized by the king at the beginning of the war and retained in lay hands for long periods and sometimes for ever.

[9] Exports of wool etc. for parts of the period are listed in A. Beardwood, *Alien Merchants in England, 1350 to 1377*, (Cambridge, Mass., 1931), pp. 136-80 and *English Trade in the Fifteenth Century*, ed. E. Power and M. Postan, (London, 1933), pp. 321-60. The chart facing p. xviii in E. Carus-Wilson, *Medieval Merchant Venturers*, (London, 1954), provides a convenient basis for a rough calculation of yield. Detailed figures from the Enrolled Accounts are given by Ramsay, *op. cit.*, vol. ii, pp. 292 and 431. The same source has been used in his *Lancaster and York*, vol. i, pp. 150-1 and 313; vol. ii, pp. 254-6.

[10] M. M. Postan, 'Some Social Consequences of the Hundred Years War', *Econ. Hist. Rev.*, xii (1942), p. 10.

tenths had been converted into soldier's pay. But whatever amount returned—and it was considerable—it by no means returned uniformly to the place from which it came. For a majority of the founders and benefactors among the warriors patronised neither the beneficed clergy nor the regulars from whom most of the taxation was derived. The war-churches—much more easily identifiable than the so-called wool-churches—were colleges, hospitals, schools, and chantries ambitiously endowed and humble. If monastic they rarely belonged to the old possessioner orders. We should be reminded of the Hundred Years War at St. George's, Windsor, at the Newerke in Leicester, at Cobham, Fotheringhay and Ewelme, at the Charter-houses of London and Hull, at Sheen and Sion. The circulation of wealth here meant also a displacement, the taxing of the established in favour of the novel.

That the collection of parliamentary subsidies had a comparable result is a much more doubtful proposition. Assuming that the phrase 'wrung from the land' means wrung from the landowner and or his tenants, a good deal turns upon the method of assessment by which the burden was distributed. To what extent were the soldiers also the taxpayers? There is not much evidence for a straight answer to that question because individual assessments were not recorded after 1334, but a likely one may be inferred from the procedure followed before that date. In the period 1290 to 1334 the tenants of most manors contributed a sum greatly in excess of that due from their lord; the bulk of the tax, that is to say, was levied on the movables of the villagers of England. The country's wealth was predominantly rural. Although man for man the townsman paid at a rate half as high again as the countryman, a tenth as against a fifteenth, townsmen were by comparison scarce.[11] There is no reason to think that the assessment of 1334 altered this distribution in any significant way. The practical consequences are not so easily measured. Frequent parliamentary subsidies may, indeed to some extent must, have made the collection of the lord's rent more difficult and so in effect have increased the contribution of the nobility and gentry—and likewise of many ecclesiastical land-owners—towards the cost of the war. At the same time the lay lords of manors were the very people who stood to gain most financially from the wages which taxation enabled the king to offer. The knightly class received less in rent and more in wages, but the

[11] J. F. Willard, *Parliamentary Taxes on Personal Property, 1290 to 1334*, (Cambridge, Mass., 1934), pp. 162-70.

cultivators of the soil did most of the paying. Only those landowners who were unwilling or unable to fight need have been the losers by this arrangement. The theory that the wealth thus returned was 'much shrunk and depleted' can best be left until after other aspects of the war and its financing have been taken into account.

Of these the *maltote* and its more legitimately voted successors are clearly the most important. The customs and subsidy on English wool shipped abroad produced something like one half of the revenue raised by taxation during the war. Were they paid by the foreign consumer (as Thorold Rogers believed), partly by the foreign consumer and partly—'a good deal'—by the home producer (as Eileen Power argued), or wholly by the home producer (as Professor Postan tacitly assumed)?[12] Apart from one or two small pieces of evidence which Thorold Rogers did not consider, the first of these explanations is credible. So too is the second, although it leaves the proportions uselessly vague. The last seems on the face of it the least probable. Were those who exported English wool or those who bought it in so strong a bargaining position that they could force the graziers to accept £2 or £3 less on every sack? By the second half of the fourteenth century at any rate they had to buy in competition with native clothiers who, when they sold their goods abroad, had no heavy duty to pay and therefore to unload. When raw wool from England cost more in Flanders than the English finished product it is fairly obvious that the consumers rather than the producers were footing most of the bill.[13] The only matter for debate would seem to be how much.

In reaching an answer it is as well to remember that the element of competition was not first introduced by the activities of native clothiers though they may have made it more fierce. For most of the war period the exporters of wool, denizen as well as alien, were competing among themselves to sell in markets which had no other adequate source of supply. Export had only to be interrupted to produce an industrial and political crisis in the Flemish towns. The king's attempts to secure the advantages of monopoly for himself and groups of favoured merchants soon ran into difficulties and were in fact abandoned early in the war. The merchants of the Staple

[12] J. E. Thorold Rogers, *Six Centuries of Work and Wages*, (London, 1884), vol. i, p. 79; E. Power, *The Wool Trade in English Medieval History*, (Oxford, 1941), p. 71; M. M. Postan, *op. cit.*, p. 10.

[13] H. Pirenne, *Histoire de Belgique*, vol. ii (1947) edn.), p. 421. The first steps taken to prevent the importation of English cloth to Bruges were earlier than 1346 (*ibid.*, p. 195).

were not partners; they bought against one another and against the Italians where they could. What evidence is there that they were able to use their position as middlemen to induce the graziers to accept lower prices? In fact there seems none save the protest of the earls in 1297 and an *obiter dictum* of a later abbot of Meaux. It would be reasonable to deduce from these that Edward I's sudden imposition of the *maltote* depressed prices in the home market; but that is very different from holding that this effect lasted beyond 1337, even in Yorkshire.[14] I take leave to doubt whether much or indeed any of it did. As soon as the constitutional struggle over the right to vote the tax had been settled in favour of parliament, it was granted regularly, for longer periods and, until Henry V's death, at increasing rates. Tenths and fifteenths were never voted to a king for life; from 1397 onwards the customs and subsidy on wool often were. Yet it cannot be claimed that the grazier interest was not well represented in parliament; it was, both in lords and commons. In 1336 at Nottingham on the eve of the war its importance was recognised. Minimum prices for wool had to be fixed before Edward III could exercise the royal right of pre-emption on a large scale the following year. Even so the producers' reluctance to sell was one factor in the scheme's failure. The weight of the evidence, circumstantial though most of it is, is heavily in favour of the rightness of Thorold Rogers' diagnosis. Unless something a great deal more solid can be put up against it we shall be justified in concluding that it still holds the field, in believing, that is to say, that about half the proceeds of taxation came not from the English land but from the Flemings and the Italians and their customers, including the French.

That leaves one further item of importance for the balance-sheet: the yield of the war itself. This was derived from many sources: (a) plunder, (b) prisoners' ransoms, (c) the revenues derived from French fiefs in English hands, including royal demesne, (d) the profits of office in occupied territory, (e) the taxation raised from the inhabitants of such territory, (f) indemnities for resisting invasion, (g) the price of capitulation and (h) bribes paid to induce the aggressor to go or stay away. Under most of these heads the French gained nothing, for the simple reason that the war was fought almost exclusively on their soil. England experienced the horrors of war scarcely at all. The efforts of the Scots to open up a second front in the north met with disaster. Only indirectly and for comparatively

---

14 The wool of which was not rated most highly.

short periods were Englishmen injured through their Gascon trade by war's devastation. Though a French invasion of England was planned more than once, it never happened. Against a few coastal raids, in which a town or two was burnt, must be set army after army transported and put ashore on the European mainland without disaster, to be brought off later laden with booty and captives. More damage, it is probable, was inflicted on England by the rising of Owen Glendower than by all the efforts of the French and their other allies in a hundred years. From the war that was fought in their midst the subjects of the Valois kings gained some plunder and some ransoms. But one has only to begin looking into the periods of English retreat after 1369 to 1429 to realise how overwhelmingly French gains then were outweighed by French losses earlier in terms of financial advantage. As for the pitched battles, the English did not lose at Beaugé what they had won at Agincourt, nor at Jargeau, Patay and Castillon the rich harvest of Verneuil. For the French the reconquest was itself expensive; witness the 100,000 francs they paid for the surrender of St. Sauveur-le-Vicomte in 1375.[15] Even as late as 1449 the Bretons had to give 10,000 *écus* for the possession of Fougères. It is not surprising that the invader was bought off with 'danegeld', as Clarence was at Buzançais in 1412 (210,000 *écus*).[16] The precedent for Edward IV's and Henry VII's practice of turning their nuisance-value into cash had been set in 1387-8 when Lancaster abandoned his attempt on the Castilian throne for £100,000 down and a pension for life of 10,000 marks.

But the greatest profit to the English arose from their systematic exploitation of the occupied provinces of France, of Brittany and Gascony in the fourteenth century and of Normandy, Maine, Anjou and the other northern lands in the fifteenth. They lost them in the end, but they enjoyed them first. For thirty years after the fall of Rouen in 1419 (when it was condemned to pay an indemnity of 300,000 *écus* for resisting its lawful duke), many Norman fiefs had English lords and supported English garrisons; the *domaine* of the French kings was administered and squeezed for the benefit of Henry V and his family; the *gabelle*, the *quatrièmes*, the profits of the mint and other customary revenues were collected; and the provincial estates were summoned frequently to grant their

---

15 C. C. Bayley, 'the Campaign of 1375 and the Good Parliament', *Eng. Hist. Rev.*, lv (1940), pp. 376 and 382-3. At that date 6 francs were probably equivalent to £1.

16 J. H. Wylie, *History of England under Henry the Fourth*, (London, 1884-98), vol. iv. pp. 81-4. This was worth £35,000.

conqueror *aides*. Between 1419 and 1435, it has been calculated, the
Norman estates voted 3,154,000 *livres tournois* or £350,000;[17] but
perhaps only two-thirds of this large sum was actually raised. From
these and other sources the English ruler of Normandy received
about £625,000 in those sixteen years alone.[18] These exactions were
far from ceasing with Bedford's death; nor were they confined to the
Norman duchy in his lifetime. In addition much was received by
local commanders and did not appear in the accounts of the central
government. Parliamentary grants fell off in England after 1421; it
was the French taxpayer's turn. This was no circular tour of English
rural wealth. What captains like Sir John Fastolf and their humbler
followers remitted home was sheer profit. This early essay in
'colonialism' increased the wealth of England, which was swollen
still further by tribute from the European mainland in the form of
taxation on exported wool. 'Shrunk and depleted' (I am not sure that
I understand the shade of difference implied by these two terms) it
was not.

What happened to all this money? Most of it passed through the
hands of the landed aristocracy which provided the leadership and
drew most of the wages and prizes of war. According to Professor
Postan, Crécy and Poitiers were won by amateurs; after that
splendid beginning 'professional military contractors' took over and
set about losing what the feudal amateurs had gained.[19] The trouble
about this explanation is that the most usual of all 'professional
military contractors' were the dukes, marquesses and earls. The
players were gentlemen, the amateurs professionals. At every stage
of the war, after as well as before 1356, earls were prominent among
the commanders and were accompanied on campaign by contingents
raised and led by members of the lesser baronage. Military skill and
opportunity enabled some men of mere gentry stock to rise to

[17] R. Doucet, 'Les finances anglaises en France à la fin de la guerre de Cent Ans
(1413-1435)', *Le Moyen Age*, xxxvi (1926), p. 288. Miss B. J. H. Rowe, 'The Estates of
Normandy under the Duke of Bedford 1422-1435', *Eng. Hist. Rev.*, xlvi (1931), pp.
556-9, gives only a slightly different estimate.

[18] This would seem a reasonable deduction from M. Doucet's evidence. Professor
Waugh (J. A. Wylie and W. T. Waugh, *The Reign of Henry the Fifth*, vol. iii, p. 392)
assumes that the *livre tournois* was worth three English shillings. But William
Worcester reckoned nine *livres tournois* to the pound sterling (*Letters and Papers
illustrative of the Wars of the English in France*, ed. J. Stevenson, Rolls series, vol. ii,
pt. ii, p. 534 etc.) and I have converted at that rate.

[19] *Op. cit.*, p. 7. It would be idle to speculate where Agincourt and Verneuil should
be placed in this curious scheme. The whole paragraph is suffused with the purest
moonshine.

prominence and riches, but they were rarely able to outshine, let alone replace, their social betters. The nobility had by far the largest stake in the Hundred Years War which fittingly ended with the slaying of two members of the ancient house of Talbot. If one of the consequences of the war was a direct impulse towards greater social mobility (which I doubt), it was almost wholly confined to movements within the class traditionally associated with martial prowess. The de la Poles and a handful of less spectacularly ennobled families were the exceptions.

But the ways in which the noble captains spent their winnings set up eddies in other parts of the economy. Generally speaking those who had the least land to start with were its principal buyers. They desired the rank, political influence and the security it promised; and the expenditure of capital in the land market was one of their few certain ways of obtaining it. The chief trouble for them was that the best was rarely, if indeed ever, for sale. Those who had much already could find cheaper methods of acquiring more, marriage being undoubtedly the commonest. At least their gains of war cushioned them against the ill-effects of falling agricultural profits and made it unnecessary to sell. The war enhanced their stability. Their stores of cash were used to raise their standard of living, on more personal services, more building, more ostentation, an increased expenditure on luxuries of all sorts, mostly imported. However good for trade, this may not have been the surest way to stimulate economic growth. But it would have been rather odd if they had cared about that.

VIII. A BUSINESS-PARTNERSHIP IN WAR AND ADMINISTRATION 1421-1445

On 12 July 1421 two English esquires met in the church of St. Martin at Harfleur to put their signatures to what for us at least is a somewhat unusual contract. Wishing to augment the love and fraternity already growing between them, Nicholas Molyneux and John Winter engaged themselves to become sworn brothers-in-arms, 'loyal one to the other without any dissimulation or fraud.' They then set out what this was to mean in practice. If either were taken prisoner by the king's enemies—'which God forbid'—the other was bound to do all that was possible to secure his liberation provided that the ransom demanded for him did not exceed £1000 sterling; if it did then the free brother-in-arms was to become a hostage for eight or nine months in order to allow the captive to go home to raise the larger sum. The arrangements thus made were to be at the common expense of the two parties. Should both be taken prisoner at the same time one was to remain as hostage while the other went to procure the ransom-money for both.

Capture was the disaster they most feared and the clauses in which they sought to protect themselves against its damaging consequences were given first place in their agreement. But they also dreamed of fortune, laying down the terms on which it too should be shared. All the gains of war that each could save were to be pooled and sent home to await their return from the wars in a coffer deposited in the church of St. Thomas Acon in the city of London. Whichever reached England first was to invest their accumulated winnings in heritages as judiciously as he could to their joint advantage. When they married and came to live once more on this side of the Channel, whatever they had purchased or put by was to be divided equally between them. One might have contributed far less than the other, but even if he had gained nothing, he was still to have half of what there was. If one alone survived he was to take all, allowing a sixth part for her life as dower to the dead man's widow if there were one. The survivor was also to 'nourish' his comrade's children, pay for their schooling and protect them from complete destitution by sharing among them, but for their lives only, a rent of £20 a year. If both parties to the bargain perished without issue all was to be sold by their executors to endow masses for their two souls and for those of their parents.[1]

Brotherhood-in-arms, as defined in this contract, was thus a business-partnership, an insurance against the heaviest financial loss that could befall a soldier—to be taken alive—and a gamble on survivorship, a kind of rudimentary tontine. The risk of loss was spread and a chance—not a very outside chance—was offered of double gain. If there is nothing here about a retainer's duty to his lord, it may be because the two esquires had not yet attained to indentured service. But the absence of any reference to a subject's loyalty to his king can only be explained on the assumption that it was too obvious to need mentioning. After all there was nothing in the terms of the contract which could be interpreted as an encroachment upon Henry V's rights as king or interests as commander. It should be noticed that in the clauses dealing with ransom only capture by the king's enemies is envisaged as possible; Molyneux and Winter were taking service in the royal army, not in some free company. Yet they make no pretence of fighting for a cause, still less for chivalrous renown. Their concern was with loss and gain reckoned without affectation in terms of cash and heritages, and despite a reference to fraternal love the sort of disloyalty one brother-in-arms desired to guard himself against in another was financial fraud. Hence the need to embody the heads of their agreement in a signed contract which could if necessary be enforced in the courts of chivalry. Here was more professed love than trust. The result is a document rarely evocative of the spirit in which Henry V's men-at-arms set out to conquer a kingdom.

The institution of brotherhood-in-arms had by 1421 a respectable antiquity. The highly successful partnership of the young William Marshal with Roger de Gaugi between 1177 and 1179 shows how it was taken for granted among the aristocratic if frequently landless prize-fighters of the Angevin world.[2] It is less easy to determine how widely it was practised by the English participants in the Hundred Years War. For us the most outstanding pair of brothers-in-arms in Edward III's time were Robert Hawley and John Shakel, the two esquires whose attempt to safeguard their joint rights in the ransom of the count of Denia taken at Najera in 1367, led to the violent death of one before the high altar of Westminster abbey eleven years later and brought little advantage to the survivor.[3] But unless the

---

[1] An unsigned copy of this agreement was preserved among the muniments of a successor in title to one of their heritages and is printed in full below pp. 172-4. I am much indebted to Dr. Pierre Chaplais for his help in producing an accurate text.

[2] *L'Histoire de Guillaume le Maréchal*, ed. P. Mayer (Soc. de l'Hist. de France), i. 123-5.

[3] I hope to tell this story in detail another day.

terms of partnership led to litigation it is unlikely that clear evidence
of the existence of such a bond will be found. And since, as far as
England is concerned, the record of this kind of litigation rarely
survives, it is impossible to say how common brotherhood-in-arms
was. Sometimes, however, its presence may be reasonably inferred.
When, for example, two or more names are bracketed together in the
indenture, the pay-roll or the muster of a captain's retinue,
brotherhood-in-arms is the likeliest explanation. Thus in April 1415
Henry V retained four esquires, apparently in pairs, to serve him for
one year on the expedition to Gascony which he was planning for the
following month.[4] Similarly the six esquires retained on 15 May 1399
by the chamberlain of Chester to accompany Richard II to Ireland
may, since their wages were lumped together for payment, have also
been brothers-in-arms.[5] Then again under the heading '*Vadia guerre*'
in an account of 1422-3 belonging to John Mowbray, earl Marshal,
three pairs of esquires are jointly paid wages for half a year for
themselves and the few archers they brought with them.[6] Such
another pair will be found in the account of Thomas of Woodstock's
treasurer of war for an Irish expedition in the summer of 1391.[7] But
an even clearer example is provided by the musters taken of Thomas
lord Scales's men-at-arms at Verneuil on 14 October 1430. Here the
names of the lances are grouped together as 'of the company' of such
well-known soldiers of fortune as Matthew Gough and Thomas
Gower. Two of the seven companies were commanded not by one
man but by two. Almost certainly these latters were brothers-in-
arms.[8] Nevertheless such cases are rarely found and where they are it
is noticeable that the men involved were as a rule humble in birth and
military rank. They were esquires or gentlemen and the period for
which they were retained, when it is known, was short. Among the
hundreds of indentures of life retainer that survive there is, I believe,
no example of two men taking service together. English brothers-in-
arms may have been altogether commoner than these varied records
suggest. But if they are any sort of guide then it would seem that such

4 Bodleian Lib., MS. Dugdale 2, p. 262. In the spring of 1415 a good many
contracts of service mentioned Gascony as the king's destination: J. H. Wylie, *Reign
of Henry the Fifth*, ii. 6. n. 4.

5 Bodl. Lib., MS. Dodsworth 82, fo. 91.

6 Brit. Mus., Add. roll 17,209, m. 3.

7 *Ibid.* Add. roll. 40,859 A. In fact the voyage never took place, but before it was
cancelled the duke had managed to spend the sum of £6,333 6s. 8d. which he had
received for it from the exchequer and not entirely upon his military preparations.

8 *Ibid.* Add. ch. 7967 (Henry Showe and Robert of Borough, Markyn and Ellis
Longworth).

partnerships were unusual. For of some sixty knights and esquires on Thomas of Woodstock's pay-roll, only two, John Owen and William Sutton, were paired. In John Mowbray's retinue the proportion was higher, but even then there were only three pairs of esquires in a company of forty named men-at-arms.[9]

This evidence also suggests that brotherhood-in-arms had little attraction for those with an already established place in society. Its practitioners were the comparatively obscure, the free-lance adventurers who looked to war as a short-cut to fortune and took temporary service where they could, mercenaries whose gentility, if they lived to achieve it, was won by the sword alone.[10] But it may be doubted whether those members of the nobility who led them had very different objectives in France from theirs. To judge from the language of most military contracts of the period, whatever the social position of the man retained the mercenary considerations so frankly expressed in the agreement between Molyneux and Winter prevailed everywhere. When these formal documents pass silently over the knightly virtues it would be possible to argue that this was merely because the division of the spoils and the payment of reward for so much service were their *raisons-d'être*. But some very informal words used by Thomas Montagu earl of Salisbury suggest that the material gains of war occupied first place in all men's minds. If a commander of Salisbury's breeding and chivalric reputation could write to Henry V himself in such terms as those of his letter of 21 June 1421, it would be rash to try to draw any real distinction between the outlook of the higher nobility and that of the swash-bucklers who were their companions-in-arms if not their brothers. For this is what he said:

> And liketh your highness to write that the Saturday [14 June] afore the date of this I, your humble liege man, come home from a journey which I had made into Anjou and Maine whereat I had assembled with me great part of the captains of your land; and blessed be God we sped right well. For your people is greatly refreshed with this road, for as they sayen in common they were never more in no such road. And we broughten home the fairest and greatest prey of beasts as all those saiden that saw them that ever they saw.[11]

Though they were to serve in Anjou and Maine before they returned to England, Molyneux and Winter are hardly likely to have been

---

[9] John and Thomas Boterell, Thomas Sampson and John Lindsay, Nicholas Hardman and Stephen Fitzwilliam.

with Salisbury on that vaunted foray.[12] But its objects were their objects when that same summer they met to sign their compact in the church at Harfleur. They had joined forces to seize and share whatever prey they could find.

The auspices in July 1421 seemed to favour their venture. France, its piecemeal conquest by battle and siege, its vacant fiefs, its garrisoning, its government, its exploitation in every possible way offered more lucrative openings than had existed since 1204 for those thrusting adventurers who were able and willing to turn their hand both to war and administration. The pitched battles and numerous *chevauchées* of Edward III, his sons and his other captains had been as profitable as they had been spectacular. But in four years Henry V's strategy and economy of effort had put a larger area of France than they had ever controlled at the disposal of his followers. The management and consequent spoiliation of the occupied provinces, enlivened by occasional raids further afield, were for the next quarter of a century tasks to stretch the capacities and fill the pockets of those who had followed Henry into Touques on 1 August 1417 and survived to form the backbone of his brother's government. Molyneux and Winter were soon to add the fruits of office to those of war itself.

Were their dreams of wealth realised? We know something of the fortunes stored and brought home by the captains of retinues;[13] Salisbury's will, like that of his rival for first place among Henry V's lieutenants, Richard of Warwick, bears witness to his affluence, little of which had been inherited.[14] But we are more in the dark about the subordinate men-at-arms who never achieved the position of captain, though it might be guessed that on the average their gains

[10] That a brother-in-arms could mean something rather different in diplomatic usage is shown by the very curious wording of the treaty of alliance between Thomas duke of Clarence and Charles duke of Orleans, 14 November 1412: *Choix de pièces inédites relatives au règne de Charles VI*, ed. L. Douët-d'Arcq (Soc. de l'Hist. de France), i. 359.

[11] Argentan, 21 June 1421: Foedera etc., ed. T. Rymer, vol. x (1710), p. 131. Some earlier examples of this attitude towards war are cited by D. Hay, 'The Division of the Spoils of War in Fourteenth-century England' in *Trans. Royal Hist. Soc.*, 5th ser. iv (1954), 91-92.

[12] I have no evidence for this assumption apart from the obvious deduction from the scene of their alliance on 12 July that they had then just landed in Normandy. They could almost (but not quite) equally well have been on their way home. The king had landed at Calais with reinforcements a month before.

[13] See below, p. 175 ff.

[14] *Register of Henry Chichele, archibishop of Canterbury*, ed. E. F. Jacob, ii. 390-400. His father, like Warwick's, had fared ill in the closing years of the fourteenth century.

were proportionate to their rank and opportunities. And these last must have been fewer after 1429. Death had removed Salisbury before the turning of the tide in favour of the French could begin to erode his accumulated profits. Charles VII may have been slow to take advantage of English weakness in the twenty years that followed the raising of the siege of Orleans, but at least the halted invaders were in no condition to resume the offensive. How did members of the occupying army fare during this period of stalemate ending in collapse? The usual answer is that since their wages were badly in arrears they were ruined. Historians have long made play with the theory that the disorders of the last years of Henry VI's reign were intensified if not actually caused by the presence in England of large numbers of unpaid and mutinous fighting-men recently expelled from France. The fate of Adam Moleyns, of Suffolk and Aiscough would seem to bear this theory out. The captains may have saved something from their years of garrison-duty, but the rank-and-file were a demoralized and penniless rabble. It is therefore worth attempting to trace how the chances of war affected the fortunes of our two esquires. Although there are many gaps in the story, enough can be found to supply the hard outlines of an answer. They may have been more or less lucky than the average of their fellows, but reliable generalisation is unlikely to be forthcoming in the absence of any particular instances.

Their lives are blank up to the day on which they decided to make common cause. But from the terms of their contract they may reasonably be assumed to have then been young, unmarried, nearly if not absolutely landless, comparative newcomers to the profession of arms. That their social origins cannot be traced when so much else is known about them is itself significant. They already called themselves 'esquires' at what was probably the outset of their military service and others, in time at least, were willing to accept them as such. But war, as contemporaries admitted without obvious rancour, ennobled the low-born too easily and quickly for this to tell us anything of real value about their parentage. On the other hand the equipment and training of a fifteenth-century warrior pre-supposed the existence of some modest fortune, the help of a discriminating patron or very uncommon luck; while Molyneux and to a lesser degree Winter were to undertake administrative tasks only suitable for a literate layman passably familiar with at least the three R's. Their agreement was signed by them but does not appear to have been sealed, perhaps because at that date they had acquired no seal of arms. If so this was a disability each surmounted later.

And should thereby have revealed his descent were this from an armigerous family known to our heraldic sources. The survival from the 1440's and later of documents authenticated by their seals of arms at least serves to establish the probability that neither was closely related to the well-known landed family whose name he bore: Molyneux of Sefton, Lancashire, and Winter of Barningham Winter, Norfolk. Of the two, on the heraldic evidence, Molyneux has the better claim to be recognized as a cadet of an armigerous stock. His more elaborate quarterly coat with its marks of difference is almost too complicated to be the adoption of a pretender to gentility and makes his distant kinship with the Molyneux clan from the north-west an outside possibility.[15] If he were a poor relation of Sir Richard Molyneux of Sefton who fought at Agincourt and died in 1439 it is a little unusual not to be able to find a scrap of evidence

[15] There are three examples of the Molyneux seal among the deeds of Magdalen College, Oxford: Titchwell 74 (29 Apr. 1449), Southwark 57 and C 68 (both 1 Dec. 1471). The two latter belonged to Nicholas's eldest son and heir William and seem to be from the same matrix as the first, though on Titchwell 74 the impression of the seal (on which the coat is circular) is almost certainly upside down. I read the arms to be: quarterly 1 and 4 three fleurs-de-lis with an ermine spot in the centre, 2 and 3 a cross moline within a plain bordure. I must thank Mr Michael Maclagan for allowing me to discuss the heraldic evidence with him.

[16] The thread connecting them is insubstantial. On 21 Mar. 1441 Thomas Molyneux was joined with John Stanley and others in a grant of lands in Wandsworth and Battersea to Nicholas Carew, Adam Levelord and others; John Winter was a witness (*Cal. Close Rolls VI*, iii. 460 and 462). On 10 May 1447 after Winter's death, Nicholas Molyneux's co-feoffees in a group of properties in Lambeth, Camberwell, Streatham and Dulwich included John Stanley and Adam Levelord (*ibid.* v. 130-2). Thomas Molyneux and Adam Levelord were feoffees together on at least one other occasion (*ibid.* iv. 462) and Thomas Molyneux was Sir John Fastolf's feoffee in a draft conveyance of Winter's tenement in Southwark 15 July 1446 (Magd. Coll., Oxf., Southwark 166). If we were to believe J. C. Wedgwood (*Hist. of Parliament, Biographies, 1439-1509*, p. 599), he was later, 1473-80, sheriff of Lancashire and hence 'perhaps second son of Sir Richard Molyneux of Sefton.' But the sheriff is more likely to have been Sir Richard's grandson who ultimately succeeded him. Wedgwood also suggests that he was elected at Midhurst 'probably through his uncle the bishop's interest.' Adam Moleyns was bishop of Chichester 1446-50. Though he is described by the *Dict. Nat. Biog.* (s.n.) as the second son of Sir [*sic*] Richard Molyneux of Sefton, no evidence has been produced for this relationship other than family tradition and the occurrence of other Adams in the Molyneux pedigree. If Thomas were a son of that house (for which there is no evidence) and if the bishop were his uncle (for which there is no evidence), then it is not improbable that Nicholas was a member of the same family. The John Stanley of Battersea and the king's house with whom they had the business relations came from the Wirral and may have owed his official advancement in the first instance to his cousin John Stanley steward of the royal household (ob. 1437) and grandfather of the first earl of Derby. But as association based on residence in the hundred of Brixton is just as likely an explanation of these dealings as a common link with north-west England.

for their association in family settlements, mainprises and the like. The only person of the name of Molyneux with whom Nicholas can be shown to have had any dealings—apart from his own son and heir William—was Thomas Molyneux whose interests seem to have been confined to Essex and Surrey and who represented Midhurst in the parliament of 1447.[16] His membership of the Lancashire family is equally unproven.

John Winter can at least be supplied with a more certain kinsman who if not of a landed family himself was the ancestor of one prominent in the Tudor period. This was Roger Winter, sometimes gentleman, sometimes esquire, of Worcestershire, whose son or grandson became by marriage the lord of Huddington in that county and established a family there which lasted in the male line until 1658.[17] The sixteenth-century Winters were armigerous, but there does not seem to be any evidence that John Winter's contemporary Roger was. Since their coat of arms resembled that of the Norfolk Winters, they were either of the same stock or, much more probably, wished to be thought so.[18] It bore no relation to that used by our John Winter.[19] Nevertheless, according to the Elizabethan pedigree-

[17] The pedigree of the Winters of Huddington has been much obscured by the activities of later heralds whose concoctions were swallowed by Thomas Habington, Treadway Nash and the contributors to the *Victoria County History*. It is generally said that Thomas Huddington of Huddington, dying about 1422, left two daughters and coheirs, Agnes the wife of William Russell of Strensham and Joan the wife of our Roger Winter [*Visitation of the County of Worcester, 1569*, ed. W. P. W. Phillimore (Harl. Soc., vol. xxvii), pp. 117-18 and 147-8; T. Habington, *Survey of Worcestershire*, ed. J. Amphlett (Worc. Hist. Soc.), i. 288-92 and 300-1; ii. 117-18; T. R. Nash, *Collections for a History of Worcestershire*, i. 590-1; *Victoria County Hist. Worcs.*, iii. 409. Amphlett in his edn. of Habington (*op. cit.* i., I n. 3) gives strong reasons for thinking that the *Visitation of 1569* was in fact compiled more than a generation later]. But *Cal. Pat. Rolls, 1494-1509*, p. 192 makes it quite clear that it was Joan Huddington's grand-daughter who married a Winter and likely that this marriage took place a good deal later than 1422. In 1500 she was represented by her son Robert. This suggests that she was the wife of the Robert Winter described as of Huddington in 6 Edward IV, 1466-7 (Habington, *op. cit.* i. 171; Nash *op. cit.* i. 258). Whether Robert the elder was the son or grandson of Roger remains doubtful. Most of the Winters in the *Dict. Nat. Biog.*, including those involved in the Gunpowder Plot, were descended from Robert Winter of Huddington.

[18] Winter of Huddington: Sable a fess ermine [J. W. Papworth, *Ordinary of British Armorials*, p. 709; the 1569 *Visitation* (p. 147) adds: in chief a crescent; Habington (*op. cit.* ii. 118) agrees with the *Visitation*, but gives (p. 116): Gules a fess and crescent ermine for Roger Winter temp. Henry VIII and says that Roger's father bore the coat of Huddington as his 'principal' coat; the evidence he cites suggests that Robert used no Winter arms at all and this in its turn suggests that those borne by his descendants were assumed in the sixteenth century]. Winter of Barningham Winter: chequy or and sable a fess argent [F. Blomefield and C. Parkin, *Topographical History of the County of Norfolk*, viii (1808), 99.]

mongers, John was Roger's father and was himself fourth in descent from a castellan of Carnarvon castle in the reign of Edward I.[20] As we shall see a Welsh origin for the family has something to be said for it, but John and Roger seem too nearly contemporary for one to have been the other's son. If the absence of Roger's name from John's will lessens the chance that they were brothers, it does not rule it out.[21] Yet some more distant kinship suits the known facts better and in the absence of definite evidence must be preferred.

Their names first appear together in the records in 1430 when Roger was mainpernor for John and two other men to whom the king was leasing a mill in New Carmarthen for twelve years from Michaelmas 1433.[22] A handful of conveyances and quitclaims shows that Roger acted as John's feoffee and survived him by a few years.[23] Family tradition and, according to Habington, family evidences testified that the Winters 'were of Wich [*i.e.* Droitwich] before they came to Huddington', but about the nature and extent of their property there the sources are vague.[24] The estate of 'Phates' in Droitwich that Nash credits them with seems to be a corruption of the vats used in the extraction of salt. It is therefore probable that Roger Winter obtained his livelihood in part at any rate from the industry upon which Droitwich depended.[25] But wherever John Winter was born and reared, it was not to Worcestershire that he was to look when it came to buying heritages.

His earliest acquisitions seem to have been the result of marriage. In his last will he was to settle the descent of certain lands that had formerly belonged to Thomas Walter of Carmarthen. The terms of his settlement imply that his wife Agnes and her sister were Thomas

[19] The only impression of his seal (Magd. Coll., Oxf., Southwark 171) is small and indistinct. It appears to be: Per pale, barry of six. It has a nearly illegible inscription apparently in English: d. . . . troᵽe.

[20] *Visitation, 1569*, pp. 147-8 (which preserves another family tradition not wholly implausible: 'John Winter Captaine of the Castell of Mayett in France under John Duke of Bedford'); Habington, *op. cit.* i. 292; Nash, *op. cit.* i. 590.

[21] For the will see below, p. 168. John floruit 1421-45 and Roger 1420-49.

[22] *Cal. Fine Rolls*, xv. 319. Roger Winter was old enough to have acted as mainpernor for the heretic Richard Wyche alias Godwote, 15 July 1420: *Cal. Close Rolls, Henry V*, ii. 82.

[23] *Ibid. Henry VI*, ii. 291-2; iv. 473; and v. 130-1 and 132. The last three of these references in which Roger Winter acts with John Cotford belong to the years 1431 and 1449 and thus help to rule out the possibility that the Roger of 1449 was the son of him of 1430-3. But 10 May 1449 is the latest date at which he is known to have been alive.

[24] Habington, *op. cit.* i. 292.

[25] Nash, *op. cit.* i. 591. Habington (*op. cit.* ii. 306-8) seems regularly to have spelt vats 'phates.' The Lollard's association with Roger Winter (n. 22 above) would seem to indicate the possibility that he took his name from Droitwich.

Walter's heirs.[26] When therefore in February 1430 he was joined with Walter in the renewal of a lease previously enjoyed by Walter alone it is reasonable to infer that his marriage had already taken place.[27] As the servant of Henry of Monmouth since at least 1408 Thomas Walter was a person of some consequence in and around Carmarthen.[28] That John Winter should have found a wife in that area lends some needed support to the tradition, current among the Worcestershire Winters a century and a half later, that the family came from Wales.[29] But if Thomas Walter had amassed a little property in the course of a life spent in the royal service in the principality, this search for John Winter's kinsmen and connections reinforces the first impression that his beginnings were small. Were Molyneux's gentility older—a fact far from proved—his resources and prospects cannot have been so superior to Winter's as to render their partnership an obviously unequal one. At Harfleur they agreed to share their fortunes, a clear sign that their stakes were roughly even. In the event Molyneux had far the longer and more remunerative service. It seems possible that Winter's health wore less

[26] Somerset House, Prerog. Court of Canterbury, Reg. Luffenham. fo. 252^v-253^r: 'Also y bequeth to John myn eldest son after the dethe of his moder Anneys all the londes and tenementes the whiche yat y haue or hadde by true and iuste title that was Thomas Walters of Carmarthyn. And hereof y pray yow, John Fountayns and Mathew Fouchere, godfaders to my said son and feoffees in the saide londe by fyne of recorde, that yu make astate to the saide Anneys terme of her lyue and the reuersion to the said John Wynter my son and to the heyres of his body becommyng. And in defaute of heyres of his body becommyng to remayne to John Wynter my yongest son and to the heires of his body begeten. And in defaute of heires of his body begeten to remayne to Jenet the wife of Thomas Wyryot syster to the saide Anneys and to her heires of her body begeten. And in defaute of heires of her body lawfully begeten remayne to the right heires of Thomas Walter.'

[27] *Cal. Fine Rolls*, xv. 319. With Walter and Winter was associated a third man, William Hill, possibly Jenet's husband before Thomas Wyryot.

[28] He was appointed to a commission of array in Carmarthenshire 16 June 1403 on information from Prince Henry's council that a raid by Owen Glendower was expected (*Cal. Patent Rolls, 1401-1405*, p. 280). On 1 Oct. 1408 the prince granted his servant Thomas Walter a vacant plot in the new town of Carmarthen for 24 years at a rent of 6s. 8d. on which to construct a mill (*ibid. 1413-1416*, p. 323). It was this mill that was regranted at the same rent to Walter, Winter and Hill for 12 more years from Michaelmas 1433 in 1430. On 26 Aug. 1411 Walter was appointed the prince's attorney in cos. Carmarthen and Cardigan and steward of Newcastle Emlyn for life [confirmed by Henry VI's government, 17 Dec. 1422 (*ibid. 1422-1429*, p. 15)]. On 25 Mar. 1420 Thomas Walter 'donzel' of the diocese of St. David's obtained an indult for a portable altar (*Cal. Papal Regs., Letters*, vii. 336).

[29] It is just worth noting that there were Winters in Carmarthenshire before our John Winter's marriage, one of whom was also the tenant of a mill. On 25 Jan. 1393 William Fort granted a water-mill in the lordship of Penrhyn Deuddoe in Llanstephan, Carmarthenshire, to John son of Walter Winter for the grantor's life (*Catalogue of Ancient Deeds*, iii. no. D 652).

well than his companion's.

What part the two esquires played during the half-dozen years of military successes and territorial consolidation that followed Henry V's return to France in June 1421 does not appear. Nor is it possible to date exactly the moment at which they entered the service of Sir John Fastolf, though to judge from the very incomplete musters of that captain's retinue in the fourteen-twenties this did not happen for some time.[30] Molyneux is the first to emerge from this obscurity when he is found from 1427 onwards acting fairly often as Fastolf's proctor for the receipt of the wages of various retinues and garrisons in Normandy and elsewhere in the English provinces.[31] By 10 December 1433 he was Fastolf's receiver-general in France.[32] However belligerent his services may have been at first there can be little doubt that by then he had ceased to be an active fighting-man. For at the same time he was employed as the duke of Bedford's receiver of the profits of the seal and signet in Maine and Anjou.[33] It is uncertain when he obtained an official place in the financial administration of Henry VI's French kingdom, but at some date before 22 January 1437 he had become master in the chamber of accounts at Rouen and a titular royal councillor.[34] He was still occupying these offices at late as 1 November 1447 when he headed a commission sent to discuss with the representatives of Charles VII at

---

[30] There are a number of Fastolf's musters in Bibl. Nat., MS. fr. 25,767 (which covers the years 1422-7), but in none do the names of Molyneux and Winter appear. It is unfortunate that B.N. MS. fr. 25,767, no 93 (the muster of those who in Fastolf's company were to advance with Bedford into Maine, 6 Sept. 1424) is incomplete, but at least our men are not among the first forty-five names. Nor are they among the fifty men-at-arms going with Fastolf to the siege of Pontorson, 13 Mar. 1427 (*ibid.* no. 216). It seems likely that they graduated to Fastolf's service after an apprenticeship elsewhere. All references here and below to manuscripts and records in Paris I owe to the very great kindness of Dr J. R. L. Highfield. None of the Fastolf musters in the British Museum belongs to this early date.

[31] The earliest evidence of Molyneux's proctorship is a receipt by him, 1 Oct. 1427, of the wages of Fastolf's men-at-arms at Melun (B.N., MS. Fr., Nouvelles Acquisitions, 4,488, fo. 604). Other receipts will be found *ibid.* fo. 605 (17 Nov. and 29 Dec. 1427); *ibid.* MS. Fr., 26,050, no. 922 (23 July 1428); *ibid.* MS. Fr., Nou. Acq. 4,488 fo. 605 (Rouen, 4 Oct. 1428); *ibid.* fo. 448 (Honfleur for men going to the siege of Orleans, 16 Nov. 1428); *ibid.* fo. 316 (27 Jan. 1429 for the town and castle of Alençon); *ibid.* fo. 269 (28 Jan. 1429); *ibid.* fo. 266 (2 Feb. 1429 for Honfleur); *ibid.* fo. 515 (25 Aug. 1429 for men sent to St. Germain-en-Laye and Possy); *ibid.* MS. Fr. 26,047, no. 1148 (Rouen, 3 Oct. 1429); Magd. Coll., Oxf., Fastolf Paper 7 (6 Dec. 1429 for Bernay); *ibid.* (Caen, 6 Apr. 1430 for Verneuil); B.N. MS. Fr., Nou. Acq. 4,488, fo. 594 (Mantes, 15 and 17 Sept. 1432); *ibid.* MS. Fr. 26,053, no. 1482 (Rouen, 10 Dec. 1433).

[32] *Ibid.* no 1482. The quittance was signed by Fastolf and Molyneux at Rouen on the same day.   [33] Paris, Archives Nat., Reg. KK 324, fo. I.

[34] Magd. Coll., Oxf., Southwark A39.

Le Mans what arrangements could be made to compensate those deprived of their property by Henry VI's hurried surrender of Maine.[35] The importance of his contribution to the policies of the English king's French government is shown by his attendance at a meeting in the autumn of 1444 to discuss with the duke of York and others the steps to be taken after the ratification of the truce of Tours;[36] and by his despatch at York's instance from Rouen to Paris in March 1445 to confer with Suffolk at the time of Margaret of Anjou's wedding-journey to England.[37] By 29 January 1447 he had become receiver-general of the revenues which the duke of York and his son Edmund earl of Rutland derived from the counties of Evreux and Beaumont-le-Roger and the viscounties, castellanries and lands of Orbec, Conches and Breteuil.[38] One would gladly know how much was being collected from these lordships so near the end of the English occupation. Like so many of Bedford's followers who were still in France during the fourteen-forties Molyneux had contracted ties of service with the house of York.

His employment by Fastolf, himself a Yorkist pensioner after 1441, was not confined to France. Nor were its rewards, for on 21 February 1437 'for his laudable service rendered and to be rendered' he was granted an annuity for life of £10 from Fastolf's Essex manor of Dedham.[39] In 1433-4 when the old knight like his master Bedford spent some months in England, Molyneux was there also in his company and taking a share in his private financial business;[40] and on 10 July 1434 the two men together received letters of protection as they returned in Bedford's retinue to France.[41] To judge from letters written many years later Molyneux, though unlike Fastolf he was not specially named an executor, was involved in the protracted

[35] *Letters and Papers illustrative of the Wars of the English in France*, ed. J. Stevenson (Rolls Ser.), ii. pt. ii. 634-92. The deliberations had begun the previous day.

[36] Arch. Nat., Reg. K 68113 (Letters ordering payment of Sir John Cressy and Nicholas Molyneux 'on the relation of the duke of York', Rouen, 14 Oct. 1444).

[37] Brit. Mus., Add. Ch. 8017 (Letters ordering payment at the rate of 4 l.t. a day, Rouen, 23 Mar. 1445).

[38] Bibl. Nat., MS. Fr., Nou. Acq. 3624, no. 367, Rouen.

[39] Magd. Coll., Oxf., Southwark A 19. The grant was by Fastolf and his feoffees in Dedham and on its surrender, either at Molyneux's death or, more probably, at the re-enfeoffment of the manor in 1450 (*Cal. Patent Rolls, 1446-1452*, p. 314), it was cancelled by being cut through.

[40] He received on Fastolf's behalf a hundred marks, part of a larger sum owed by Robert lord Willoughby and he was present when John Wells, Fastolf's merchant banker [for him see below, pp. 179-83], paid a number of their master's creditors (Magd. Coll., Oxf., Fastolf Paper, 9, mm. 3 and 6).

[41] *Forty-eighth Report of the Deputy Keeper of the Public Records*, p. 300.

administration of the Regent's will, a subject over which Sir John uneasily fretted at the tail-end of his own life.[42] These letters indicate by their tone and substance how far the obscure adventurer of 1421 had established himself as the peer, indeed the 'ryght wel belovyd brothyr', of one of the richest knights in England.

When Fastolf addressed him thus fraternally, Molyneux had long been deprived of the companion to whom he had united himself in love and brotherhood at Harfleur in 1421. John Winter added a codicil to his last will and testament on 30 May 1445 and probate was granted to his executors in the prerogative court of Canterbury at London on the 10 July following.[43] He must have died between these dates.[44] When Fastolf came to draw up his own will, signed and sealed on 14 June 1459, he referred to 'one John Winter esquire late my servant' as having had and supposedly lost 'a blank letter in parchment ensealed under my seal.'[45] The service, like Monyneux's, was done on both sides of the Channel and that in France, again like Molyneux's, became in due course administrative rather than military. By October 1437 he had returned home and when in that month he kept Fastolf's court at Castle Combe as steward his colleague the surveyor noted that 'ista curia fuit per Johannem Wynter armigerum, soldarium de Francia olim, tenta . . . adtunc senescallum de Castelcombe.'[46] But the soldier had turned bureaucrat long before that. In a settlement between Fastolf and Thomas Coburley, Winter's principal executor, it was agreed that the latter should deliver to the former 'alle bokes of accomptes, couterollementes & evidences of the duchie of Angeu & counte of Mayn and in semblable wise of any othir garysoun & fortresse & alle othir evidences of the said John Fastolf' still in Coburley's

---

[42] *Paston Letters*, ed. J. Gairdner (Lib. edn., 1904) iii. 50 and 70-71. The earlier of the two letters is only summarised by Gairdner; the original is now Brit. Mus., Add. MS. 39,848, no. 32. Gairdner's ascription of these letters to 30 Oct. 1455 and 26 Jan. 1456 seems justified.

[43] Somerset House, P.C.C., Reg. Luffenham, fo. 253. The last will and testament combined, as so often happened, in a single document was dated 20 May 1445.

[44] In a note written about 1473 by Fastolf's secretary William Worcester, Winter is said to have died in 25 Henry VI, *i.e.* the year ending 31 Aug. 1447 (Magd. Coll., Oxf., Southwark 168). This recollection was more than a year out.

[45] *Paston Letters* (*ed. cit.*), iii. 156.

[46] Brit. Mus., Add. MS. 28,208, fo. 15ᵛ. A year later he was actively pursuing his employer's interests at Castle Combe by extracting a heavy penalty from the rector for cutting down an ash and some thorn bushes in the park there (G. Poulett Scrope, *History of Castle Combe*, p. 226 and n.). The Roger Winter who is mentioned by Worcester in some notes about Oxenton, a Worcestershire manor dependant upon Castle Combe, may well have been John's kinsman (*ibid.* p. 257).

possession.[47] It is not surprising therefore to learn that Winter kept the counter-roll for the year ending at Michaelmas 1434 when Molyneux was the duke of Bedford's receiver in those two provinces.[48] It may be wondered whether one brother-in-arms afforded the best protection against the dishonesty of his fellow, but that they were thus conjoined is some evidence that they had earned the trust both of the Regent and of the grand master of his household. Winter was also employed as Fastolf's agent for the collection of debts in France and was harried, it was said, on his death-bed for his unaccounted-for arrears. As Worcester tells us, 'Sir John Fastolf demaunded m^l salux of goolde that John Wynter should owe hym that he resseyved of his debt of one John Gwyllim, hys conestable of All^{a}unson and sent to Wynter yn hys dede bedd for hys money.'[49] Fastolf also successfully dunned Winter's executors for 160 marks which he claimed the esquire had received on his behalf from Lewis of Luxemburg and for 10 marks Winter himself had borrowed from him at Honfleur.[50] At some date before 1442, but whether in France or England is not clear, Winter had been resident in Fastolf's household;[51] and among the legacies bequeathed by him was 'a lyned gowne of russet of my maistre Fastolf liuery.'[52]

As Fastolf bought estates in England both Molyneux and Winter were called upon, along with his other friends and servants, to act as feoffees in some of the many conveyances by which he endeavoured to protect and reinforce his title.[53] And at least once, with unfortunate consequences for the surviving brother-in-arms, the rôles were reversed.[54] For they too were investing in heritages and needed the same safeguards. The result of their efforts was demonstrated by the number of tenements in Winter's possession at his death, of which in his last will he assumed the right to dispose

---

[47] Magd. Coll., Oxf., Southwark 170.   [48] Arch. Nat., Reg. KK 324, fo. 1.

[49] Magd. Coll., Oxf., Southwark 168. After Winter's death it was made a condition of his executors' settlement of accounts with Fastolf that they should 'stand discharged of the forseyd m^l salux that makyth ij^{c}l m^{a}rc Englysh money, whych appoyntment ys endented vndre Thomas Coburley sele' (*ibid.*). Thomas Gwilym was Fastolf's constable of Alençon on 12 June 1427 when musters were taken there (Bibl. Nat., MS. Fr. 25,768, no. 239).

[50] Magd. Coll., Oxf., Southwark 170 (signed and sealed by Thomas Coburley, 1 Oct. 1450). A similar acknowledgement was sealed by all the executors the same day (*ibid.* Southwark 180); only Coburley's seal remains.

[50] The testament of Edward Tyrell esquire the elder, 1 Oct. 1442, mentions 'vj pleyn cuppes of sylver of the best þat I bought of John Wynter duellyng with Sir John Fastolf' (*Register of . . . Chichele*, ed. Jacob, ii. 634).

[52] P.C.C., Luffenham, fo. 253. The legatee was Harry Perrour, one of Winter's executors.

freely: the manors of Stockwell and Levehurst in Lambeth, Knollys's manor in Camberwell and various lands and messuages held by various tenures in Southwark, Clapham, Streatham and Kennington, all within the Surrey hundred of Brixton.[55] Since he is described as 'John Winter of Stockwell' it is probable that the capital messuage in which Isabel countess of Devon and Aumâle died in 1293 was his usual place of residence.[56] It is a little difficult to obtain an accurate estimate of the size of these manors but an inquisition of 1523 gives the manor of Stockwell 400 acres of arable, 9 of meadow, 58 of pasture and 40 of wood and the manor of Levehurst 100 acres of arable, 8 of meadow, 56 of pasture and 30 of wood.[57] In addition to his freehold tenements Winter held lands at will of the archibishop of Canterbury and the abbot of Bermondsey in both Lambeth and Camberwell parishes.[58] In Southwark his chief property was the Boar's Head which was afterwards disposed of disadvantageously by Thomas Coburley for £213 6s. 8d.[59] The extent, exact whereabouts

[53] On 1 Dec. 1439 Winter was Fastolf's feoffee for all lands in Southwark formerly owned by Henry Yeaveley, mason (*Cal. Close Rolls, Henry VI,* iv. 480-2; Magd. Coll., Oxf., Southwark 2, &c.). On 20 Apr. 1440 he was feoffee for Fastolf's newly-acquired property in Southwark called 'le Herteshorne' (*ibid.* Southwark C 6). On 9 Nov. 1440 he and Molyneux were Fastolf's feoffees for the manor of Drayton, Norfolk (*ibid.* Norfolk and Suffolk 82). On 29 July 1441 they were feoffees for his manor of Caldecott, Suffolk (*ibid.* Caldecotes 27). On 27 Sept. 1445 Molyneux was feoffee for his manor of Titchwell, Norfolk (*ibid.* Titchwell 81) and continued to be until 21 Feb. 1456 (*ibid.* 77 and 157). At some date Winter had become feoffee for Caister and Fastolf's other lands in cos. Norfolk, Suffolk and Essex; he made release of them on 20 May 1444 (*ibid.* Southwark 171).

[54] Fastolf was Winter's feoffee for the Boar's Head, Southwark, 10 Nov. 1439 (*ibid.* 174, 175 and 195).

[55] Apart from being mentioned in his will these are listed in detail in an agreement made between Molyneux and Coburley after Winter's death (Early Chanc. Procs., C 1/21/72, calendared in *Cal. Pat. Rolls, 1452-1461*, pp. 71-72).

[56] He is so called in Magd. Coll. Oxf., Southwark 214, where the evidences for the Boar's Head are also said to be kept in the manor of Stockwell. The codicil of his last will is dated from the house of the Carmelites in Fleet Street to which he left a reversionary interest in his Southwark properties.

[57] O. Mannering and W. Bray, *History and Antiquities of the County of Surrey,* iii. 497. A map of Levehurst, redrawn from a map of 1563, is given in *Survey of London* (gen. ed. F. H. W. Sheppard), Parish of St. Mary Lambeth, pt. ii. Southern Area, p. 168. This shows it to have been on both sides of Knight's Hill between what is now West Norwood and Streatham Common. In 1326 the Stockwell manor later acquired by Winter was said to have had 287 acres of arable, two gardens, a dove-cote and 19 bondmen with 84½ acres between them (*Victoria County Hist. Surrey,* iv. 56-57). It is difficult to reconcile this statement with that of the 1523 inquisition.

[58] *Cal. Pat. Rolls, 1452-1461,* pp. 71-72.

[59] Magd. Coll., Oxf., Southwark 170. Only £100 was actually paid over by Fastolf; the balance was set off against Winter's alleged debts. Since Fastolf as one of Winter's feoffees had already taken possession the price was not arrived at in the open market.

and value of the rest of his holdings cannot be determined with any certainty;[60] nor is it possible to trace the steps by which many of them were acquired. But there is evidence that Knollys's manor had passed into his and Molyneux's possession by November 1433;[61] and that the Boar's Head was bought up by stages between 1439 and 1441.[62] Later events revealed the probability that several of those from whom Winter made his purchases had no certain title to sell.[63]

By 1445, when Molyneux was still active in Normandy, the partners had therefore invested their gains in quite a valuable collection of heritages across the Thames from the city of London. Although their employments in France, whether military or administrative, never brought them any great prominence or rewards beyond the ordinary, they had achieved at least a modest competence for themselves and their families. As the area occupied by the English shrank the prizes no doubt grew scarcer and less valuable, but for the well-dug-in veterans of Henry V's armies they still existed down to the fatal breach of the truce in the spring of 1449. If one of the very last went to an Arragonese mercenary for surrendering

[60] There is reason for thinking that Knollys's manor in Camberwell corresponded with or was part of the manor of Dulwich acquired in 1605 by Edward Alleyn (including the manor house or capital messuage 'called Hall Place *alias* Knowles') and later given by him towards the endowment of his College of God's Gift (Manning and Bray, *op. cit.* iii. 438; *Vict. County Hist. Surrey*, iv. 33). To judge from *Cal. Close Rolls, Henry VI*, ii. 291, it had appurtenances in Streatham. It derived its name from its having once belonged to Sir Robert Knollys, the fourteenth-century solider of fortune.

[61] *Ibid.*

[62] On 10 Nov. 1439 the first step in its acquisition was taken when John Stradling esquire and Maud his wife granted it for their two lives to Sir John Fastolf, Sir Henry Inglose and John Winter (Magd. Coll., Oxf., Southwark 174) and on 14 Dec. that year they further conveyed all their standing and title in the property (*ibid.* 195). Various reversioners released what right they had in it to the same trio in 1440 and 1441 (*ibid.* 157, 191-2, C 67 and C 73). When Fastolf obtained it from Winter's executors he had to deal with a number of rival claimants (*ibid.* 179 and 199) and Bishop Wainfleet as Fastolf's successor found himself confronted by others (*ibid.* 206). Henry Perrour (or Perre as he once called himself), one of Winter's executors, and William Worcester each provided the bishop with slightly different narratives of Winter's proceedings (*ibid.* 214 and 168). According to Worcester, Stradling was 'a sowdeour yn kyng Herry the vj ys dayes' and his stepson Robert William, whose inheritance it was, 'duelled wyth sir John Fastolf for a seson.'

[63] For the Boar's Head see the last note. The manor of Stockwell had been settled in 1419-20 and the remainderman under this settlement made his appearance from Calais in the later 1450's to make a nuisance of himself 'with an hundred menne arraied for werre with the badge of ragged staves vpon them' (it was alleged), he being a servant of the Captain of Calais, Richard Nevill, earl of Warwick (Early Chanc. Proc., C 1/20/30 and C 1/32/329). He was bought out in 1471 (*Cal. Close Rolls, Edward IV*, ii. no. 761). Molyneux had wisely disposed of his interest in the manor before these troubles arose.

Fougères later that year, those Englishmen who clung to their remaining footholds in Normandy were mostly a good deal less fortunate.[64] By then the more prudent had betaken themselves home to dispose of their winnings in England.

When the English sack of Fougères on 24 March 1449 precipitated the final catastrophe, Molyneux may still have held his offices in Normandy, but private business had recalled him to England. His presence there had become necessary on account of the terms of Winter's last will. These were in sharp conflict with the provisions of their original agreement of 1421 and that agreement was still in force. Their mutual obligations, it made clear, were to continue to bind them until either one brother-in-arms died or both had finally returned from the war; and in the event of the first of these alternatives happening the one to die had no power to devise any of their joint property, either heritages or money or goods, away from the surviving partner. Nowhere was there any mention of the possibility that the agreement might be cancelled earlier by consent. That no such cancellation had in fact occurred is reasonably certain from the course of the subsequent litigation. What is more, there is clear evidence that the partnership was recognised to be still in being—and working to Winter's advantage—after he had deserted France for England. For on 22 January 1437 Molyneux handed over to Sir John Fastolf the sum of two thousand *saluts d'or*, the equivalent of five hundred English marks, and received in exchange an obligation by which Fastolf bound himself

la quelle somme . . . de bailler, poier et deliurer pour et on nom dudit Molyneux a Jehan Wynter escuier, frere darmes dudit Molyneux, pour estre employe en achat de heritaiges pour et au proffit dudit Molyneux.[65]

The fact that this obligation, cancelled by being cut through, remains among the title-deeds of Fastolf's own Southwark tenements is proof that the remittance, in coin and by hand to save the high cost of exchange, arrived at its proper destination.[66] It is not without value

[64] Surienne's reward for giving the Bretons possession of Fougères was 10,000 *écus* (A. Bossuat, *Perrinet Gressart et François de Surienne*, p. 345). If Thomas Gower received anything for Cherbourg which capitulated on 12 Aug. 1450 after a month's stiff resistance, it was not recorded in the articles of surrender: *Chronique des Mont-Saint-Michel*, ed. S. Luce (Soc. des anciens Textes Français), p. 238. Somerset's cession of Caen was much less glorious and correspondingly more expensive.

[65] Magd. Coll., Oxf., Southwark A 39. It bears a fine example of Sir John's signature and a poor one of his signet.

for an assessment of what happened after Winter's death to have this unmistakable evidence that Fastolf knew that his two esquires were brothers-in-arms and had agreed to invest their gains of war in heritages. He conveniently forgot these facts when he saw the chance of adding the Boar's Head to his own acquisition in Southwark.

John Winter's memory seems to have been equally faulty when he made his will. In it he left to John his elder son the manors of Stockwell and Levehurst

> and al other londes and tenementz of charter londe that y haue withinne Southwerk and in shire of Sotheray, except the manor of Knolles, and all copie londe and charter londe that was sumtyme William Weston in the parissh of Camerwell and Stretham.

The executors and feoffees were to make estate to him and the lawful heirs of his body 'when he is at full age of xxj wynter.' All his other copyholds the testator bequeathed to his younger son, also called John, together with a reversionary interest in the elder's share.[67] If both sons died without issue, the manor of Stockwell was to go to Nicholas Molyneux for life and then to be sold to provide the endowment for a chantry in Lambeth parish church for a priest and two poor men; his Southwark lands were to be given to the 'craft' of goldsmiths or mercers who in return were to pay £10 or 10 marks a year to the Carmelite friars of London 'to a relefe to her bredewarde'; and all his other lands were to be sold and the proceeds spent 'in charitable dedes as in mendyng of weys and in othir wise' at his executors' discretion. By the codicil of 30 May Winter ordered that Knollys's manor, two messuages in Southwark and another in Clapham should be sold to pay his debts. This was, it seems likely, after he had been badgered on his deathbed by his master. So much did the thought of his debts worry him that he gave orders that Stockwell itself should also be sold if there were not enough without it. It is difficult to avoid the impression that while his brother-in-arms had been hard at work for their common profit in France, Winter had been living beyond his means in England on the proceeds

[66] It was 'tant en nobles, demy nobles que salus dor' (*ibid*.). The cost of exchange between France and England in the fourteen-fifties could be as much as 'viii d. by the noble' or 10 per cent. (W. Dugdale, *Baronage of England*, ii. 209).

[67] John the elder brother was also given the reversion of the younger's copyholds. Meanwhile until they came of age, continued the testator, 'y will that myn executoᵣs gedre vp the reueneues of the saide londe duryng the noun age of my childre and the monneye therof to been imploied to the fyndyng of the said children, byldyng and reparacions makyng sweche as hem semeth nedefull by her discrecions.'

of Molyneux's labour. The executors of the will were Nicholas Molyneux himself, Matthew Philip, Matthew Fowcher, Thomas Coburley and Henry Perrour, while the overseer was Thomas Gower esquire, an experienced and still active soldier who at some date before 1454 bought the neighbouring manor of Clapham.[68]

Winter's state of mind when he made such a will cannot easily be understood. He can hardly have supposed that the partnership with Molyneux had been terminated by his own withdrawal from France. For he had received at least one considerable remittance of money from his brother-in-arms since his return. But if his intentions were fraudulent—and this is the obvious deduction not only from the main provisions of his will but also from his action in transferring some if not all of the purchased heritages to feoffees for its performance—why should he have named Molyneux an executor and a residuary legatee? And why should he have imagined that Molyneux, whom it would have ruined, would not contest it? Altogether it looks like the foolish act of a dying man, influenced by his household and his creditors to try to cheat the associate to whom he owed at least half of what he enjoyed. Unless Molyneux died soon, childless and intestate, the scheme was almost bound to fail.

At first, thanks to Molyneux's absence, it scored an appearance of success. When probate was granted on 10 July 1445 the execution of the will was committed to Philip, Fowcher, Coburley and Perrour, their colleague's power to act being held in suspense.[69] No reference was made to the supervisor who, like Molyneux, had other things to occupy his attention as well as less concern in the result. But, probably in accordance with the wishes of the testator, Coburley who was to receive a legacy double that of his fellow-executors took the initiative in carrying out the provisions of the will.[70] Little seems to be known about Coburley except that he was usually described as 'gentleman', was almost certainly a lawyer by profession and is generally found engaged in business in and around London.[71] Before

---

[68] *Cal. Close Rolls, Henry VI*, v. 510-11; *Vict. County Hist. Surrey*, iv. 39. Gower took part in Bedford's expedition into Anjou in 1425 (*Wars of the English in France*, ii. 412), was lieutenant of Falaise on 1 Sept. 1429 (*ibid.* pp. 118-119), bailli of Le Mans 1433 (*ibid.* p. 552) and captain of Cherbourg during its siege in the summer of 1450 (*ibid.* p. 634; E. Cosneau, *Le Connétable de Richemont*, pp. 420-1 and 640-2). For the presence of his 'company' in the retinue of Lord Scales 14 Oct. 1430, at Verneuil, see above p. 153. His connection with Winter and Molyneux went back at least to 14 Nov. 1433 when as 'esquire of Yorkshire' he was a witness to the quitclaim to them of Knollys's manor (*Cal. Close Rolls, Henry VI*, ii. 291).

[69] 'Reseruata potestate committenda Nicholao Molenes.'

[70] Coburley was left £20 in the codicil of 30 May 1445, the others £10 each.

Molyneux could stop him he had sold Knollys's manor to William
Fitzwalter, gentleman and citizen of London;[72] allowed one Thomas
Parkhouse to enter upon a copyhold tenement in Kennington;[73] and
failed to prevent Sir John Fastolf from converting his enfeofment in
the Boar's Head in Southwark to his own use.[74] Meanwhile
Molyneux, although much occupied in Normandy, had obtained
letters of protection from the king in November 1445; it looks as if he
knew by then that his interests were in jeopardy.[75] He may have paid
a visit to England at that time or soon afterwards, but, as we have
seen, he was carrying out his duties as York's receiver-general in
Normandy and negotiating with the French envoys at Le Mans in
1447. When he did finally return, it was not long before he had
challenged the legality of Coburley's actions and brought a suit
against two of Winter's feoffees, Roger Winter and John Cotford in
the King's Bench 'of forgyng of false dedes.'[76] Then 'be mediacion
of ther frendes' the parties were prevailed upon to submit their
debates to the arbitrament of William Laken, a rising lawyer who
was later to be promoted to the bench by Edward IV.[77] This was
pronounced on 5 May 1449 and confirmed the substantial justice of
Molyneux's case. He was to discontinue his action against the

[71] That he was a lawyer seems to be indicated by *Cal. Pat. Rolls. 1441-1446*, p. 98.
He may have been the M.P. for Hindon, Wilts, in the parliament of 1449-50 (J. C.
Wedgwood, *History of Parliament, Biographies*, p. 200). But he did not sue Molyneux
for £40 in 1455; he sued Agnes Cavendish (*Cal. Pat. Rolls, 1452-1461*, p. 264). Nor
was Molyneux suing him in 1453; that was merely the date at which the arbitration of
1449 was exemplified in Chancery (*ibid*. pp. 71-72).

[72] *Cal. Pat. Rolls, 1452-1461*, p. 264. References to him will be found in *Cal. Close
Rolls, Henry VI*, iv. 62 and 449; v. 39, 93 and 132; and vi. 81 and 207. The 64 marks
Fitzwalter had paid down for possession of Knollys's manor is hardly likely to have
been more than a first instalment.

[73] The only Thomas Parkhouse in the records seems to have been an inhabitant of
Bristol (*Cal. Close Rolls, Henry VI,* iv. 37 and 115). He or another of the same name
was active towards the borders of Wales (*Cal. Pat. Rolls, 1436-1441*, pp. 201, 268 and
518).

[74] Fastolf and Sir Henry Inglose, one of Fastolf's closest friends, held the tenement
with John Winter to Winter's use. On 15 July 1446 the two survivors were planning to
convey it to others (draft grant: Magd. Coll., Oxf., Southwark 166) and on 20 May
1447 Inglose granted three members of his family power of attorney to take seisin of it,
presumably in order to alienate it in his name (*ibid*. Southwark 172). According to
Worcester the story was that Winter had bought it not for himself but on Fastolf's
behalf (*ibid*. Southwark 168). The surviving title-deeds do not bear it out.

[75] *Forty-eighth Report of the Deputy Keeper of the Public Records*, p. 367.

[76] These facts and those that follow were set out in the document which records the
arbitration of 5 May 1449 (Early Chanc. Proc., C 1/21/72, summarised in *Cal. Pat.
Rolls, 1452-1461*, pp. 71-72).

[77] There is a useful and generally accurate biography of him in Wedgwood, *op. cit.*
pp. 522-3.

feoffees and he was to reimburse Fitzwalter. But they were to release all the disputed lands to him and Coburley was to

> do his labo^r and deuoir that Sir John Fastolf knyght shulde make a sufficant estate in fee simple to the seide Nicholas, his heires and his assignes for euer of and in the seide tenement called the Bores Hede w^t the app^rtenances.

Molyneux agreed to give Laken himself 100 marks to be spent on prayers for Winter's soul at Whitefriars in Fleet Street and to employ Coburley on his council for life at an annual fee of 20s. It was as a result of Coburley's intercession on his behalf that Fastolf was induced on 1 October 1450 to buy the Boar's Head for £100 down and the cancellation of Winter's alleged debts to the sum of £113 6s. 8d.[78] With this Molyneux was content. Apart from that one Southwark tenement, all the heritages the brothers-in-arms had amassed were now his alone. Agnes Winter and her two sons were the principal losers by this settlement, though of what they had no right to keep. They disappear forthwith from history.

There are signs that with the end of the war Molyneux too fell on comparatively evil days. The expense of litigation, the discharge of his duty towards his late partner's widow and children, the collapse of English fortunes beyond the seas, may all have contributed something to his embarrassment; for this there is no evidence. But it was not very long after his victory over Coburley in 1449 that he parted with the manor of Stockwell to Ralph Legh of the king's house.[79] The exemplification of the 1449 award in 1453 may have been preparatory to the sale.[80] With Stockwell Legh seems to have agreed to take over an obligation, the fulfilment of which suggests that Molyneux regarded the duties of a brother-in-law rather more seriously than Winter. For on 24 May 1457, when Molyneux may have been dead, Legh and the bishop of Winchester his master obtained a royal licence to found 'Wynters of Stokwell Chauntre' in the church of St. Mary, Lambeth, for a chaplain and two poor men.[81] So was a provision of

---

[78] Since these debts were supposed to have been contracted in France, they could with justice be deducted from the joint possessions of the brothers-in-arms (Magd. Coll., Oxf., Southwark 170).

[79] Legh was in possession by 5 Nov. 1453 (*Cal. Close Rolls, Henry VI,* v. 511).

[80] It is dated 6 May 1453 (*Cal. Pat. Rolls, 1452-1461*, pp. 71-72).

[81] *Ibid.* p. 343. Legh presented a chaplain for institution on 31 Jan. 1461 (Manning and Bray, *op. cit.* iii. 520). In a letter of 3 July 1459 Sir John Fastolf refers to the fee he was paying 'Rauff Alygh squyer w^t my lord Ch^aunceller (William Wainfleet, bishop of Winchester) to be of my councell and supporter of my ten^antes yn Southwork' (Brit. Mus., Add. MS. 39,848, no. 49, summarized in *Paston Letters,* iii, 142).

Winter's fraudulent will carried out. It is difficult to avoid the conclusion that Molyneux was responsible for this service to the soul's health of the man with whom he had sworn faith nearly a lifetime before and who had died trying to cheat him of his due.

The compact of 1421 had ended with Winter's deathbed betrayal of his trust. That had been followed by—and perhaps had helped to cause—a marked contraction in the fortunes of the survivor. The heritages put together by 1445 were soon dispersed. But as long as the brothers-in-arms remained 'loyal one to the other without any dissimulation or fraud' they prospered. Their partnership of just twenty-four years had yielded a good return as the lands in Winter's custody when he made his will prove. Like their masters the little men could do well out of the war even in its later, less glorious, stages.

Magdalen College, Oxford, Southwark 213 (*paper; contemporary copy in a French hand*).

Apointement fait entre Nicholas Molyneux & Jehan Wynter esquiers de entretenir & garder de point en point les articles en la fourme et maniere qui ensuit:

[1]   Premierement pour acroistre et augmenter lamour et fraternite qui est piera en commencee entre ledit Molyneux & Wynter & a celle fin quelle soit plus ferme & estable des oremais lesdictes parties sont presentement jures chascun lun a laultre freres darmes. Cest assauoir que chascun sera loyal lun a laultre sans aucune dissimulacion ou fraude. Et que sil aduenoit, que dieu ne veulle, que lun deux feut prins prisonnier des aduersaires du Roy celluy non prins acquiteroit hors laultre franc & quite pouruer que la finance ne exedat la somme de vj m^1 saluz dor en toutes chosez. Et sil aduenoit que ladicte finance feust a plus grant somme que vj m^1 saluz dor cellui frere darmes non prins tendra & demourra en hostage pour laultre se mestier est viij ou ix moys en tant que ledit frere darmes prisonnier peult trouuer moyen deuers ses amis de recouurer le demourant de sadicte finance.

[2]   Item il est apointe entre ledit Molyneux & Wynter que tout ce que montera ladicte finance pardessus ladicte somme de vj m^1 saluz sera paie aux despens et propre biens dudit prisonnier & de ces autres amis.

[3]   Item toute la despens qui sera faicte tant en hostage que pour faire la poursuite pour ladicte totale finance sera a commun despence tant sur ledit Molyneux que sur ledit Wynter jusques a la plaine deliuerance dudit prisonnier.

[4]   Item sil aduenoit que lesdiz Molyneux & Wynter feussent prins prisonniers ensemble, que dieu ne veuille, lun demourast en hostage pour les deux se le cas requiert & que fere se peult. Si non vng homme seur sera esleu par eux deux pour receuoir & besongnier pour leur plaine deliuerance ainsi que sera aduise & ordonne entre eux.

[5]   Item sil ny auoit asses de biens pour paier leur dice plaine finance le moien sera trouue que lun sera deliure pour pourchasser la deliuerance de eux deux & par lui sera vendicion faicte tant des biens meubles que de leur heritages tant aux despens de lun que de laultre iusques a la deliuerance plennier de eux deulx.

[6]   Item il est apointe entre ledit Molyneux & Wynter que tout les biens que sera par la grace de dieu gaigne par eulx & entre eulx que peust estre espargne sera enuoye en despost & garde en la ville de Londres en vng coffre mis a Saint Thomas Dacres, le quel aura ij clefs lune pour Molyneux & lautre pour Wynter, au quel coffre sera mis autant dor ou dargent ou vesselle quilz ou chascun deux vouldront emploier pour achater des heritages au royaume Dangleterre.

[7][1] Item 1 & 2 le plus tost que faire ce pourra ledit Molyneux ou Wynter sera enuoye audit royaume Dangleterre pour illec demourer & seiourner pour enquerir & achater heritages le plus profitablement que fere ce pourra pour le proffit deulx & le surviuant deulx & pour leur heires.

[8]   Item sil aduenoit que ledit Molineux & Wynter seroient mariez & que ilz demourassent tous deux au royaume Dangleterre lesdiz heritages seroient departis en deux, lune moitie pour Molyneux & lautre pour Wynter.

[9]   Item il est apointe que le surviuant soit ledit Molyneux ou Wynter auroit pour luy & ciens toutes lesdiz heritages generalment qui sera par eulx ou lun deux pourchasse, poureu touteffois que la fame du trespasse auroit la tierce partie des heritages pour sa douere sa vie durant dont son mary sera possessour.

[10]   Item & la surviuant sera tenu de nourrir lez enfans du trespasse sil en auoit & les tenir aux escolles tant quilz soient en age & donques leur sera baille pour viure xxli. desterlynges de rente pour departir entre eux; & apres la mort de ladicte fame & desdiz enfans & leur heires la dicte douere & les xxli. desterlinges sera & retournera au surviuant dudit Molyneux & Wynter & aux heirs de leur corps pour tousiours & jamais.

[11]   Item & sil aduenoit que ledit Molyneux & Wynter trespassent

---

[1] In the margin against this paragraph a later, perhaps late fifteenth-century, hand has written: nota.

sans heirs de leur corps le surviuant ou ses excutours pourroit vendre toutes lesdiz heritages pour faire chanter & prier pour leur ames & pour les ames de leurs peres & meres.

Le tout sans fraude, barat ou mal engin fait en leglise de Saint Martin de Harefleu. En tesmoing desquelles chosez nous auons mis a ces presentes nos signez manuelz cy mis le xij⁰ jour de Juillett lan de grace mil cccc vingt & vng. Ainsi signe: Molyneux & Wynter.

IX. THE INVESTMENT OF
SIR JOHN FASTOLF'S PROFITS OF WAR

IF we may believe John Leyland, a tradition widely current throughout England in the 1530's attributed some of the costliest building of the later middle ages to warriors who had returned home laden with the spoils of France. Everywhere that the antiquary travelled, from Ampthill in Bedfordshire to Hampton Court near the Welsh border, from Streatlam in county Durham to Farleigh, Somerset, he was told of castles raised in stone and brick '*ex spoliis nobilium bello Gallico captorum*', sometimes of a whole mansion paid for from the proceeds of a single battle; and that not merely in the great days of Edward III and Henry V, but also when John of Bedford was 'governor and regent' of his dead brother's hard-pressed conquest.[1] So Henry VIII's subjects, not least those descended from the military captains of the Hundred Years War, were firmly convinced. Members of the Tudor nobility were willing, nay anxious, to swallow some very improbable stories about their family-origins and in a good many cases their faith in a particular forebear's achievement, indeed his very existence, may be open to question. But the fact remains that within a century of Bedford's death the spoils of France were generally regarded as at least a plausible explanation of a family's sudden wealth and of its capacity to embark upon a large-scale building project. There are signs that it had already won acceptance in the lifetime of Leyland's precursor, William Worcester, whose birth in the year of Agincourt and long residence in the household of Sir John Fastolf, the Regent's major-domo from 1422 to 1435, entitle him to speak with more authority.[2] Worcester's memoranda about the builders of Hunsdon and the Rye, houses of which the remains still face each other across the water-meadows of the Lea valley, and his full list of works put in hand by Richard Beauchamp, earl of Warwick, were based upon hearsay, but his informants came by their knowledge at first hand.[3] His concurrence makes it hard to reject as wholly fictitious Leyland's tales of this or that mercenary adventurer who like Sir William

[1] *The Itinerary of John Leland . . . 1535-1543*, ed. L. Toulmin Smith, i. 102-3. (Ampthill), 137-9 (Farleigh Hungerford), ii. 9 (Streatlam), 72 (Hampton Court), etc.

[2] I have dealt with Worcester's uses of his master's recollections and evidences in Chapter X below.

Bowes was reputed to have 'waxid riche and comming home augmentid his lande and fame.'[4] Before they can be treated as myths they at least require the courtesy of investigation.

That may seem a poor reason for taking the case of Sir John Fastolf for extended study since he is not even referred to by Leyland. But it is necessary to look for evidence where it survives and the private papers of those captains whom the *Itinerary* acclaimed as war-profiteers have either been lost or provide no adequate answer. As there no longer exists any satisfactory method of finding out what men like Sir Walter Hungerford of Farleigh or Sir Ralph Boteler of Sudeley brought back from France, the fuller-documented example of their perhaps not quite so prosperous contemporary needs must serve as the rod by which we measure the successes of a fairly numerous class.[5] Had Leyland devoted as much space to East Anglia as he did to the midlands and the west, it is very unlikely that the builder of Caister would have been overlooked. Of Fastolf's papers as of Fastolf's castle only fragments remain, but enough, I think, to prove that he did do moderately well for himself and so, in one case at least, to vindicate the accuracy of sixteenth-century tradition.

By the time we make Sir John's acquaintance in the *Paston Letters* he had become a close-fisted, litigious and irascible old man. With one or two trifling exceptions the letters from, to and about him begin in 1450 when he was already seventy years of age; his active military career had ended a full decade before. Thenceforward until his death after a long illness in December 1459 the material consequences of the English defeat in France and the steady collapse of public order at home combined with the evidence of his own declining physical powers to reduce him to a state of querulous and

---

3 *Itinerarium Symonis Simeonis et Wilhelmi de Worcestre*, ed. J. Nasmith, pp. 86-9 and 352-3. From the measurements he gives it is clear that Worcester personally visited Hunsdon; that he failed to make the short journey thence to the Rye is unlikely. The builders of both houses were old friends and companions-in-arms of Sir John Fastolf. Worcester obtained a note of the cost of Hunsdon from a wardrobe officer of its builder, Sir William Oldhall. He claims to have heard about Warwick's numerous works from the earl's receiver-general.

4 *Itinerary*, ii. 9.

5 Hungerford was assessed at £911 p.a. for the income-tax of 1436 as against Fastolf's £600 [H. L. Gray, 'Incomes from Land in England in 1436', *Eng. Hist. Rev.*, xlix (1934), 615 and 621]. His accounts, surviving among the public records [for which see J. L. Kirby, 'The Hungerford Family in the Later Middle Ages' (unpublished University of London M.A. thesis, 1939)], throw scarcely any light upon his gains of war. Boteler's assessment for tax in 1436 has not been preserved, but his castle at Sudeley, according to Leyland (*Itinerary*, ii. 54-6), 'had the price [i.e. prize] of all the buyldings in those days.'

unmanageable senility. Though he owed much to the Lancastrian dynasty all he cared to remember as he and it sank together into the grave were the debts it had not paid him. Various drafts of a bill of claims against the government compiled by his servants after 1450 later passed into the hands of John Paston and so came to be printed in turn by Fenn and Gairdner.[6] Separated from his other papers they are apt to convey an impression of unrelieved disaster, suggesting that the Hundred Years War brought financial ruin not only to the crown but also to its captains. It remains to be seen whether Henry VI's bankruptcy, if such it was, had such far-reaching results for those who failed to preserve his Valois inheritance. But about one thing these documents leave no doubt: John Fastolf's own sense of ill-usage, though whether his sufferings were as obvious to others as they felt to him is another matter. Creditors of forty years' standing are hardly likely to underestimate the value of services rendered, old soldiers least of all. The figures in this bill of claims may be safely taken as maxima which were intended to leave plenty of room for negotiation, the utmost that a long memory, refreshed by the carefully-hoarded evidence of debentures and accounts, could rake up against an ungrateful but not indifferent administration. Fastolf's demands totalled a little over £11,000.[7] This was indeed a princely fortune and give him every right to sound aggrieved. But before his insolvency is taken for granted, his gains should be set beside these unpaid debts. Unfortunately, he had not the same motive to compel him to draw up a list of what he had received.

Nor will his surviving archives enable us to do it for ourselves. Apart from the state-papers preserved in Worcester's collections, these derive almost exclusively from his English administration. His prolonged residence overseas as well as his acquisition of French castles and lordships made it necessary for him to maintain two households and to employ two sets of estate officials. It was no concern of his ministers at Caister and London how much was received or spent in France. They did not need to know, still less to record, what were their absent master's wages of war, his earnings as

---

[6] *Original Letters Written during the Reigns of Henry VI, Edward IV and Richard III*, ed. J. Fenn, iii (1789), 260-75; *Paston Letters A.D. 1422-1509*, ed. J. Gairdner (Library edn., 1904), iii. 55-65.

[7] This figure may be considerably in excess of the amount actually due to the knight himself since one of the largest items (5,082 marks 13*s.* 3½*d.*) was 'for prests and wagys of hym *and his retenues*'. It is improbable that he had already discharged the king's debts to his men out of his own pocket. Certainly his friend and companion-in-arms Sir Andrew Ogard in his testament (Prerog. Court of Cant., Reg. Stokton, fos. 13v.-15r.) made a solemn disclaimer of any such liability except by way of charity.

a councillor and administrator of the conquered territories, the
ransoms he levied, the plunder gained—or lost—on many a
battlefield and *chevauchée*, nor the revenues gathered from his fiefs
across the water. What little their papers tell us of such matters were
owed to Worcester's later annotation. On one roll the antiquary has
jotted down a rough list of the offices Fastolf held between 1412,
when he was deputy-constable of the castle and city of Bordeaux,[8]
and his retirement from the wars in 1439 as governor of the Channel
Islands.[9] This is embellished with pieces of miscellaneous
information which Worcester may have been storing up for use when
he came to write his lord's biography, the *Acta Johannis Fastolf*,
now long missing;[10] some of them came from the horse's mouth. The
item most valuable for our purpose follows the statement that
Fastolf was promoted banneret at the battle of Verneuil: 'he says',
wrote Worcester, 'that on the said day [17 August 1424] . . . he won
by the fortune of war about 20,000 marks.'[11] And Verneuil, though
an outstanding victory, was far from being the only action between
Harfleur and the Herrings in which he distinguished, and so
enriched, himself. The gigantic prize he claimed to have drawn from
a single throw offers us some idea of the magnitude of the rewards a
successful captain might hope to earn; but it leaves Fastolf's own
total as incalculable as ever. We have not the means to discover what
his gross annual takings may have been nor what proportion of them
he gave or paid away in France. For some notion of his clear profit
we must rely upon the evidence of the surpluses he was able to remit
to his ministers at home for safe keeping and investment.

A few of his original bonds and receipts suggest that such
remittances were frequent and by no means negligible in size. On 23

8 Worcester says that he was constable 'ad terminum vite Willelmi Faryngdon
militis anno xijº regni regis Henrici quarti' (Magdalen College, Oxford, Muniment-
room, Fastolf Papers, no. 69, m. 4. These will be cited hereafter as FP 69, etc. Other
documents concerned with Sir John's affairs are to be found in the boxes labelled
'Norfolk and Suffolk' and 'Miscellanea' as well as dispersed among the title-deeds of
those of his manors which passed into the college's possession. All references in these
notes to a place-name followed by a number are to these last; e.g. Caldecott 22 or
Briggs and Beyton 24. The make-up of FP 69 is discussed more fully below, p. 184, no. 41);
but on 23 March 1413 William Clifford was appointed to succeed Farington (J. H.
Wylie, *History of England under Henry the Fourth*, iv. 86; *Reign of Henry the Fifth*, i.
122-3), so that at most Fastolf's tenure of the office was only temporary.

9 FP 69, m. 5. This was 'sub Humfrido duce Gloucestrie' who had been granted the
islands on 9 April 1437 (*Dep. Keeper's Reports*, xlviii. 317). Worcester adds: 'Et ad
festum Michaelis anno xviijº regis predicti vltimo venit in Angliam de predictis jnsulis.'
There is a reference to this 'viagium domini vsque Jernesey et Garnesey' in FP 26, m.
6.

January 1426, for example, he entrusted 8000 gold crowns, the equivalent of 2000 marks sterling, to Sir William Breton the *bailli* of Caen and Jean Roussel for them to forward on his behalf to England.[12] The money was to be paid to John Wells, alderman and grocer of London, and John Kirtling, clerk, Fastolf's receiver-general on this side of the Channel. A reference to 'some other sums' which Breton at the same time acknowledged to be in his keeping makes it probable that he at one time acted as a regular intermediary.[13] But he was not the only channel Fastolf used. It was from Bartolomeo Spinola the Genoese that Wells and Kirtling took delivery in London on 26 April 1430 of a sum of 500 marks which their master had deposited with another Italian merchant at Paris nearly nine months before.[14] Even after his own return to England about Michaelmas 1439 Fastolf was still engaged in realising the proceeds of his long service abroad. Between 6 December 1439 and 23 November 1441 he collected from Lewis of Luxemburg's English agents an outstanding debt of 900 marks.[15]

The impression created by these haphazard survivals is borne out by the only two account-rolls belonging to Kirtling's tenure of the office of receiver-general that now remain among the Fastolf Papers. Kirtling's responsibility for more than the yield of his employer's English lands is clearly indicated in the heading to the earlier of the rolls, that for the year ending at Michaelmas 1434. Here he is described as

10 T. Tanner, *Bibliotheca Britannico-Hibernica sive de Scriptoribus*, 115.

11 'Item creatus fuit apud bellum de Vernoyle in Perche per Johannem Regentem regni Francie miles banerettus et dicto die belli victoria habita contra Francos dicit se lucrari ex fortuna prelij circa viginti milia marcarum sterlingorum . . .' (FP 69, m. 4). It seems that he never received 4000 of the 5000 marks he was promised by Bedford as his reward for the capture of the duke of Alençon at Verneuil [*Paston Letts.* (1904 edn.), iii. 58-9, 64 and 73-4]. Even if they were included in the total of 20,000 marks, which is by no means certain, the amount he actually enjoyed would still remain considerable.

12 Caldecott 22. This indenture of receipt is now missing. I owe my knowledge of its contents to a summary in W. D. Macray's unprinted calendar of Caldecott deeds.

13 Sometime before the autumn of 1431 he paid £1000 to Wells on Fastolf's account and this money reached Kirtling's hands at intervals during the next five years, £119 11s. 0d. in the year ending at Michaelmas 1431, £58 in 1431-2 and £542 in 1433-4. When Kirtling ceased to be receiver-general on 7 July 1436 he was charged with the residue: £280 9s. 0d. (FP 9, m. 3; FP 14, m. 2 and schedule). This £1000 could, but need not, have been part of the 1426 remittance.

14 FP 6. For 'Johannes d'Franchis Sachus', the Paris banker responsible for this transfer (he received 2000 *saluts* from Fastolf on 3 August 1429), see below, p. 183;

15 A file of six acquittances was returned to him on 7 June 1442 endorsed by Richard Waller, the archbishop's steward, in exchange for two bonds; it is now FP 19.

16 FP 9, m. 1. The manors that follow are exclusively English.

'generalis receptor . . . tam de denariis dicti Johannis Fastolf prouenientibus de partibus Francie quam de exitibus vniuersorum maneriorum dicti Johannis subscriptorum . . .'[16]

But the interposition of John Wells, who often kept the lord's money in his own hands for several years, rules out any attempt to estimate how much of it in fact reached England from France during the period covered by the account. Thus in addition to the residue of the £1000 received from Sir William Breton some years before, Wells had retained possession of another 2000 marks since Michaelmas 1427.[17] The section of the roll entitled '*Forinsece Recepte*' contains two further amounts of £74 and 350 marks which had earlier come to him from Italians '*ad opus domini*' and were only now handed over to his colleague.[18] In any case Fastolf's arrival in England not long after the beginning of the financial year made it unnecessary to transfer money by the indirect and expensive method of exchange.[19] Instead, Kirtling's foreign receipts included 1000 marks in cash and plate to the value of £271 deposited by the lord himself;[20] while a number of other entries would suggest that these by no means exhausted the list of earnings derived from France during the year.[21]

The roll of 1435-6 tells much the same story though Kirtling was succeeded as receiver-general by Walter Shipdam on 7 July and the lord was continuously absent. There are similar references to capital held on Fastolf's account by Wells and his fellow-merchants;[22] and the receiver-general is likewise charged with sums derived in the past from Lombard changers.[23] More important, there continues to be

---

[17] For the £1000, see above, p. 179, n. 13; for the 2000 marks, see FP 9, mm. 1 and 9, and below, p. 182. It is nowhere stated from whom Wells received the second sum.

[18] From 'Johannes Walence' and 'Amfryan Spynolf' respectively (m. 3). The former is elsewhere described as 'Johannes Valence lumbard' (FP 14, m. 2); I have failed to identify him. Aumfry or Amphrion Spinola, a Genoese dwelling in London, appears frequently in the records, on one occasion as the factor of his namesake Bartolomeo (*Calendar of Plea and Memoranda Rolls of . . . London, 1413-1437*, ed. A. H. Thomas, p. 272).

[19] Fastolf was in London in November, February, April and June; he visited Hellesdon in Norfolk and made oblations at two Norwich churches, probably at Easter (28 March); he seems to have left for France soon after 22 June (mm. 5-7).

[20] m. 3. The cash was received 'per manus Rogeri Frost camerarij domini.'

[21] £466 13*s*. 4*d*. was received from Richard Buckland, treasurer of Calais, and £60 from 'Johannes Lukes lumbard' (m. 3). But £200 was returned to Buckland and £10 to 'Luke' later in the year, perhaps at the time of Fastolf's departure (m. 7).

[22] The most notable addition is the sum of £448 13*s*. 4*d*. in the hands of Sir Henry Inglose (FP 14, m. 1).

[23] He is credited (m. 2) with the receipt of £1000 from this source; the only new name is that of 'Benedictus Burneys lumbard' who had paid him 250 marks. I cannot identify this banker.

evidence of new foreign remittances. The thousand pounds which reached Kirtling '*de partibus Francie* on 10 March 1436 by the hand of William Eastfield, like Wells a London alderman, is a pointed reminder that long after the English advance to the Loire had been stayed and when Henry VI's French crown, it is easy to assume, was as good as lost, his captain could still draw profit from his service overseas.[24]

A petition which Fastolf addressed to the archbishop of Canterbury some considerable time after John Wells's death in 1442 reveals clearly the part played by this London grocer in the soldier's affairs.[25] Wells, wrote Fastolf,

'by appoinctement and orden*a*nce of the said besecher at his goyng ouere the see wyth the kyng was one of the resceyvours of the same besecher as one of thaym that he moost trusted too. Which John Welles resseyvyd dyuers tymys certeyn sommez of goold by the handys of Lombardys and dyuers othyr str*a*unge personys and also by the handz of dyuers seru*a*ntz of your said besecher to the vse of þe same beseecher as by letters of acquict*a*uncez of the same John Welles and othyr evydencez autentyk therof had is redy to shew opynlye may appere. Which acquict*a*uncez and evidencez whereby the said John Welles shuld been charged with and accompted for were sent vnto your said besecher from by yond the see be the Lombardz that made the esch*a*unge (& be othir)[26] long tyme after the decesse of the said John Welles, the which sommes your said besecher trustyth that the said John Wellys had treuly kept to his vse and avayle and that he shuld dispose and delyuere after the wylle and intent of the same besecher. And forasmoch as som of the resseyvours and seru*a*ntes of the said besecher been decesed and that it apperyth not cleerly by the accomptes of theym and of othir of his officers and seru*a*ntes now beyng on lyve how your said besecher of dyuers sommys of the sommys forsaid drawyng to grete gode ys aunsuerd, the which myght be to the said besecher grete losse and hynderyng wytout remedye be had to hym by your gode grace in this mater as ryght and consciens requireth. Wherfore . . . .'

[24] *Ibid*. Eastfield is called John, but the alderman's name was William (A. B. Beavan, *Aldermen of the City of London*, ii. 6, etc.) and no John Eastfield is recorded in the city's printed records. Kirtling's foreign receipts also included £135 6s. 8d. 'oneratis super diuersos debitos domini de partibus Francie hoc anno' in the hands of Richard Woodville (£72), William earl of Suffolk (£60) and John FitzRauf (66s. 8d.) by obligation (m. 2).

[25] FP 60. On parchment and carefully written in a formal hand, this can scarcely be a copy or a draft. It is not endorsed and perhaps may never have been presented. The punctuation and capitals are mine. For the date, see below, p. 182, n. 28.

[26] The words in brackets are interlineated. There are no other interlineations or corrections.

A clause in the will which Fastolf sealed on 14 June 1459 shows that he had not then received full satisfaction.[27] Nowhere is Wells's honesty impugned, but without an examination of his books the accounts of Fastolf's other officials could not be properly discharged. On the other hand, in a private letter the old knight shows that he had persuaded himself that Wells died owing him 'grete good.'[28] His want of urgency in seeking redress belies his suspicion.

Several times master of the Grocers' Company and often M.P. for London and Southwark, Wells was elected mayor of the city in 1431;[29] and when in 1437 Norwich's charter was suspended by Henry VI's council he became the royal warden of that borough.[30] His testament reveals not only his wealth and civic pride but also his Norfolk origins and at least distant kinship with the Fastolfs.[31] He acted both as Sir John's English receiver and as his broker, handling much of his financial business for him; he 'had', as Fastolf put it, 'grete godes of myne in his governaunce whyl I was in the partyes of Fraunce and Normandie.'[32] As we have already seen, monies remitted to him were often allowed to stay in his hands 'to merchandise with' for long periods until the lord needed them at Caister. On such occasions they bore interest, variously described as '*relucrum et incrementum*' or '*employ et gayn*' at the rate of 5% *per annum*. He was not the only merchant with whom Fastolf invested his capital. In 1433-4, for example, William Cavendish, another London citizen with roots in East Anglia, repaid £350 of the £500 he

---

[27] The orginal of this will is now FP 65 and the clause comes on m. 2. For an inaccurate text see *Paston Letts.*, iii 155; what Gairdner there calls the 'first draft' of the will dated 3 November 1459 is a copy of the earlier will made in the course of drafting the nuncupative version put forward as genuine by John Paston and his supporters.

[28] Brit. Mus., Add. MS. 39848, no. 42 (abstracted *Paston Letts.*, iii. 109). The postscript reads: 'Item, cosyn, I pray yow þat ye will comon with William Worcestre to see by þe meane of my lord of Caunterbury or oþerwise þᵗ maister William Clyf and oþer of þexecutoʳs of John Wellys may be spoken wᵗ for þe recouere of grete good þat, as Worcestre knowᵗ weel, it may be prouid þat þe seid Wellys ought me in his lyve &c. þat I myght knowe sum answere þerof in my daies and þᵗ my lord of Caunterbury may knowe & be prevy þerto.' This letter obviously precedes the petition in date, but the arguments used by Gairdner for assigning it to 1456 are far from conclusive. There is, for example, no reason to suppose that Fastolf was never at Caister before 1454.

[29] Beaven, *op. cit.*, ii. 6.

[30] *Proceedings and Ordinances of the Privy Council*, ed. N. H. Nicolas, v. 45; *Hist. Collections of a Citizen of London*, ed. J. Gairdner (Camden Soc.), p. 180. Gregory calls him 'The nobylle Aldyrman' (*ibid.*, p. 184).

[31] *Register of Henry Chichele*, ed. E. F. Jacob and H. C. Johnson (Cant. and York

had borrowed for a like purpose and consideration,[33] while a number of lesser sums had been ventured with William Trumpington cordwainer of London,[34] Richard Ellis of Great Yarmouth[35] and John Fastolf of Oulton.[36]

To what extent Sir John derived similar benefit from his association with the Genoese financial houses is less clear, though a nine-months' delay in remittance between Paris and London renders some kind of advantage possible.[37] That he set a high value on the services of the Lombard opposite-number to Wells in France is shown by the direction in his will that the soul of 'John Sak, marchaunt of Parys, my trusty frend & seruaunt' should be prayed for along with 'the soule of John Kertlyng, parson of Arkesey, my right trusty chapeleyn & seruaunt domestycall xxx wynter & more' and of his 'other lordes, frendes and kynnesmen' after his death.[38] John 'Sak' may be identified as the John 'de Franchis Sachus' who

Soc.), ii. 615-20. This mentions (p. 618) that he was baptized in the church of St. George in Colegate, Norwich. Sir Henry Inglose of Dilham, Norfolk, whom he claims as kinsman (p. 617), died 1 July 1451 (*Paston Letts.*, ii. 251; his will, dated 20 July and proved 4 July 1451, is in the District Probate Registry, Norwich, Reg. Betyns, fos. 62r.-63v.); he is described by Sir John Fastolf as 'of my consanguiniti' (FP 65, m. 2). The Thomas Fastolf whom Wells also calls kinsman (*Reg. Chichele*, ii. 617) was either the merchant of Ipswich who was an executor to John Fastolf of Oulton (see below, n. 36) or the boy over whose wardship Sir John Fastolf of Caister had so much trouble (*Paston Letts.*, *Passim; Rotuli Parliamentorum*, v. 371-2). The former's relationship with the knight is uncertain. The latter was the son and heir of John Fastolf esquire of Cowhaugh in Nacton, Suffolk, and was said to be eight years old at his father's death on 9 November 1447 (Briggs and Beyton, 24). He was the great-great-grandson of our Sir John's uncle, Hugh Fastolf the under-admiral (Spitlings 95; Hobland Hall 3; Norfolk and Suffolk 53; Beighton 3, 6, 10, 99 and 101; the descent in W. A. Copinger, *Manors of Suffolk*, iii. 68, requires correction); he too was later of Ipswich (Beighton 6, 6 March 1479; the two Thomas Fastolfs are hopeless confused in J. C. Wedgwood, *History of Parliament, Biographies. 1439-1509*, p. 313).

[32] FP 65, m. 2.

[33] FP 9, mm. 1 and 9. Cavendish was a mercer (*Cal. Plea and Mem. Rolls, London, 1413-1437*, 35 etc.).

[34] *Ibid.*, 180, etc.

[35] He was bailiff of that town in 1423, 1427, 1430 and 1431 [F. Blomefield and C. Parkin, *Topographical History of Norfolk*, xi. (1810), pp. 324-5].

[36] A cousin, servant and feoffee of his Caister namesake, he died, according to his brass formerly in Oulton church (A. Suckling, *Hist. and Antiqs. of Suffolk*, ii, pl. facing p. 40) on 31 January 1445/6. His will, dated 12 January 1444/5 is in the District Probate Registry, Norwich, Reg. Wilbye, fos. 64v.-65r.

[37] On the other hand, the delay may have allowed the bankers to recover the cost of the exchange.

[38] FP 65, m. 2; *Paston Letts.*, iii. 157, where, by the way, William 'Gunnour' is a mistake for William 'Gravere.' William Graver was 'magister noui operis domini apud Castre' (FP 9, m. 8); his accounts have been printed in translation by H. D. Barnes and W. D. Simpson in *Norfolk Archaeology*, xxx (1952), pp. 178-88; see also the same authors' 'Caister Castle' in *Antiquaries' Journal*, xxxii (1952), pp. 35-51.

was Bartolomeo Spinola's colleage in 1429-30.[39] He was one of the Genoese ambassadors employed in the negotiation of peace between his city and Henry V a decade earlier.[40] His name is an interesting addition to the group of tradesmen and financiers who were also Fastolf's servants.

These shreds and patches of evidence make several things clear: that even as late as 1436—and possibly for some time longer—war could be made to pay, that one captain at least had a fairly elaborate organisation for the despatch of his profits to England and for ensuring that once there they were not suffered to lie idle, and that both English and Italian financiers had a share in this type of exchange business. Further, it seems probable that Fastolf's big interest-bearing deposits with men like Wells and Cavendish were never intended to be anything but temporary. His long-term investments were those of most of his fellow-captains: land, building, furniture, plate and jewellery, but above all land. Here at last we reach firm ground.

This is provided by a valor of Fastolf's estates founded upon their receipts in the year ending at Michaelmas 1445.[41] It contains no gross

[39] Above, p. 179.

[40] *Cal. Pat. Rolls, 1416-1422*, p. 276, which has the spelling 'de Francis Sachiis.'

[41] FP 69, a roll of 8 membranes. The heading reads: 'Incipit declaracio empcionum & perquisicionum omnium dominiorum, maneriorum, messuagiorum, terrarum, tenementorum & reddituum per Johannem Fastolf militem in comitatibus Norff', Souff', Essex' & Surr' existencium cum custibus edificiorum in diuersis manerijs cum annua valore de claro pro anno xxiijⁿ [followed by an erasure; it is clear from other entries that the year beginning Michaelmas 1444 is intended] regni regis Henrici sexti; fuit appruatum [*sic*] tempore . . . [*blank*] supervisoris dictorum maneriorum ac prout in compotis Johannis Kyrtelyng clerici, Thome Howys clerici, Walteri Schipdam et Lodowici Pole receptorum dicti militis specificantur.' But Kirtling ceased to be receiver-general on 7 July 1436 (above, p. 180) and thereafter disappears from Fastolf's deeds and papers; he was certainly dead by 9 November 1440 (Norfolk and Suffolk 82). Again the section (m. 4) entitled 'Ista maneria fuerunt vendita' contains properties sold both before [e.g. Davington, Kent, sold before Michaelmas 1433 to buy Hellesdon and Drayton, Norfolk (FP 9, m. 2)] and after [e.g. Blickling, Norfolk, which was still Fastolf's in 1451 (*Cal. Close Rolls, Henry VI*, v. 228-9)] 1444-5; nor is this section a later insertion. The obvious explanation is that the roll was compiled in the 1450's on the basis of old accounts to show the knight's estate at its greatest extent, i.e. before the agreement to surrender Maine. Later still Worcester added (on mm. 5-6) the list of offices and dignities (above, p. 178), a few other notes and the following new heading: 'Status annui valoris omnium dominiorum Johannis Fastolf militis baronis de Cyllyeguillem tam jn Anglia quam in Francia necnon perquisiciones & empciones dictorum dominiorum terrarum & tenementorum jn isto rotulo compilato per W. Wyrcestre seruientem suum subcompendio extra compota & registra dicti militis jn anno quo ipse obijt.' I propose to assume that the original caption was the more accurate one and to include in my totals for 1444-5 the 'values' of any manors listed as sold which I know to have been still in Fastolf's possession.

yields, only the clear values after the subtraction of all reprises;[42] but this disadvantage is more than offset by the addition in the case of each manor or tenement of the price at which it was acquired. Both English and French holdings are included as well as those of the lord's wife, Dame Milicent Tiptoft, in which he had obtained a life-interest. And there are also notes of what had been spent upon major building-works. From these invaluable data and with the help of another, though incomplete, valor for 1446,[43] an early will for lands drawn up on 22 February 1420,[44] various accounts and memoranda as well as the title-deeds of a handful of manors, it is possible to plot with fair accuracy the stages by which a military adventurer of modest fortune and family rose to be a great landowner.

At Michaelmas 1445 the clear annual value of Fastolf's estates in England was rather more than £1,061.[45] Of this his inheritance from his father, made over to him by his mother on 1 October 1404,[46] accounted for almost exactly £46.[47] This modest patrimony consisted of two small manors in Caister by Yarmouth and a third at Repps in Bastwick about six miles to the north-west. To these he had added by his marriage on 13 January 1409 a life-tenancy in his wife's share, namely a third part, of the Tiptoft lands, valued in 1445 at £240 per annum, an acquisition which first lifted him out of the ranks of the smaller gentry.[48] The rest of his manors, worth £775 a year—or

---

[42] For a brief discussion of the meaning of 'reprises' in a medieval valor, see *Eng. Hist. Rev.*, lxix (1955), pp. 110-11. They may include more than the costs of management and maintenance; their subtraction tends therefore unduly to depress our estimates of net income. The detailed valor of Fastolf's manor of Bentley, Yorks, for 1442-3 (Brit. Mus., Add. MS. 28207, fos. 20r-20v.) includes nothing among the reprises that could not be regarded as a necessary outgoing.

[43] FP 28. In its clear values it agrees closely but not exactly with FP 69 and therefore helps to confirm the latter's accuracy for 1445.

[44] FP 3. This appears to mention all the tenements then in Fastolf's occupation apart from his wife's inheritance.

[45] This and all other figures are to the nearest £. Apart from the Tiptoft lands Fastolf's property was distributed as follows: Norfolk (£491 p.a.), Suffolk (£152 p.a.), Dedham and Pentlow, Essex (£76 p.a.) and Southwark, Surrey (£102 p.a.).

[46] Brit. Mus., Add. Ch. 14597; *Paston Letts.*, ii. 4.

[47] It is a little difficult to disentangle the values of the inherited from the purchased tenements in Caister, but the possible error is small.

[48] Distributed between Yorks. (£137 p.a.), Wilts. (£60 p.a.), Gloucs. (£35 p.a.) and Somerset (£8 p.a.). These had been settled on Milicent Tiptoft and her first husband Stephen Scrope jointly and afterwards on their issue in 1390 (G. P. Scrope, *History of Castle Combe*, pp. 144-5). In spite of this they were re-settled by fine in 11 Hen. IV on Fastolf and Milicent jointly and afterwards on her issue (*ibid.*, pp. 169-70). Stephen and Robert Scrope, Milicent's sons by her first husband, confirmed their stepfather's estate for life in most of these manors on 19 July 1433 (*Cal. Close Rolls, Henry VI*, ii. 257).

nearly three-quarters of his total landed income on this side of the Channel—he had bought. They had cost him £13,855.

Of these purchases all but a few or roughly nine-tenths were made after 1420.[49] Since he was no more than an esquire when he sailed for Harfleur in 1415 and only obtained his first important command, that of king's lieutenant for Normandy, after the death of Henry V, it is hardly surprising that his gains were inconspicuous until he reached the age of forty.[50] But for the good fortune—doubtless assisted by good management—that enabled him to secure the hand of a lady twelve years his senior, of baronial family and with five times his landed wealth, the first half of his long life was noticeably devoid of success. The great prizes, retarded by his want of birth and connection, came to him in the last two decades of his active career as a soldier. A menial servant of princes since boyhood,[51] he got his chance as grand master of Bedford's household in 1422 and as a member of Henry VI's French council from then until 1439.[52] At 35 he was still only the duke of Clarence's esquire and 'household-man';[53] at 46 he had become a knight of the garter and a baron of France.[54] Then or soon after he began to rebuild his manor-house at Caister on a scale befitting his new dignity.[55]

Though he was able from time to time to visit England to confer

---

[49] Those mentioned in the 1420 will (FP 3) had cost him £1237 and in 1444-5 yielded £73 p.a.

[50] Worcester (*Itinerarium*, p. 343) is our authority for his birth in 1380 and not in 1378 as is often stated. He was retained as an esquire by the king, 18 June 1415 (*Fœdera*, ed. T. Rymer, ix. 270) and is so called as late as 5 July (Beighton 5); by 29 January 1416 he had been knighted (*Fœdera*, ix. 329-30). The most important charge committed to him by Henry V was the keeping of the *bastille* of St. Antoine, Paris, on 24 January 1421 [FP 69, m. 4; *Archaeologia*, xliv (1873), pp. 113-22]. According to Worcester (FP 69, m. 4) Bedford appointed him lieutenant for Normandy at Henry VI's death.

[51] He is said (*Dict. Nat. Biog.*, s.n., on the authority of Blomefield) to have been 'page to Thomas Mowbray, duke of Norfolk, before the duke's banishment, 13 Oct. 1398.' After his father's death in 1383, his mother married John Farwell, esquire in the household of Mowbray's grandmother, Margaret countess (afterwards duchess), of Norfolk (ob. 1399), and later 'master and governor' to John of Lancaster, the future Regent Bedford [Brit. Mus., Add. MS. 28207, fo. 18r (notes made by, but not in the handwriting of, Worcester; they are partly printed in Scrope, *op. cit.*, pp. 170-2)]. By 1401 Fastolf was an esquire in the retinue of John of Lancaster's brother Thomas, lieutenant of Ireland [*Letters and Papers illustrative of the Wars of the English in France*, ed. J. Stevenson (Rolls Ser.), vol. ii, pt. ii, 758-9].

[52] FP 69, m. 4   [53] Beighton 101 (after 5 July 1415)

[54] FP 69, mm. 4-5.

[55] It was already building up 1430-1 (FP 8, m. 5), so that Worcester's statement that it took thirty years need not be an exaggeration (*Paston Letts.*, iv. 235).

[56] His annual farms in 1433-4 cost him £96 (FP 9, m. 5), in 1435-6 only £5 (FP 14, m. 3).

with his ministers, it was upon these latter that the main
responsibility for buying land as a matter of course devolved. Each
of the surviving receiver-general's accounts has a section headed
'*Terra Empta*' followed by another devoted to '*Terra conducta*' of
land for which an annual farm was paid to the crown or some other
proprietor.[56] For the year 1433-4 land-purchase accounted for an
expenditure of some £1,222;[57] in the next year but one the total was
£889.[58] Little if anything was bought thereafter in East Anglia. It was
Southwark's turn: the acquisition of three tenements in the borough
for rather more than a thousand pounds between 1439 and 1446
provided Fastolf with the site for a residence near the capital.[59] The
period of steady expansion was brought to a close in 1450 when he
paid £200 for the Boar's Head inn with which his name will always
be associated.[60] The 1430's seem likewise to have been the time of
greatest building activity. An inventory compiled in 1448, listing the
contents of various rooms at Caister, shows that the castle was by
then nearing completion.[61] According to the great valor already
cited, it had cost its owner '£6,046 *plus*',[62] while another £1,100 had
been laid out on his new town-house beside the Thames.[63] Hellesdon,
Cotton, Norwich, Dedham and Yarmouth in turn received the
attention of the builders;[64] and a new south choir-aisle at the abbey
of St. Benet of Hulme was, as we learn from Worcester, constructed
and furnished at Fastolf's charges.[65] Altogether his recorded
expenditure on works as opposed to current estate-repairs had
reached £9,495 some time before his death, bringing the amount
spent on land and works together to the considerable total of
£23,350.

This figure leaves out of account anything that he may have owned
in France. Yet at the date of his return home he was still drawing well
over a quarter of his landed income from properties in Normandy

---

[57] FP 9, m. 5   [58] FP 14, m. 3.

[59] Donley's for £319 on 1 December 1439 (Southwark 2); the Buck's Head for £162
on 20 April 1440 (Southwark 60); and Horseydown for £547 on 9 November 1446
(Southwark 36).

[60] On 1 October 1450 after a good deal of negotiation (Southwark 170). The £1,227
Fastolf spent on land in Southwark not only gave him the site for a house but also an
annual return of £102 (FP 69, m. 3).

[61] FP 43. It has additional entries in Worcester's handwriting made in 1454-5.

[62] FP 69, m. 1. This justifies Worcester's statement after John Paston's death in 1466
that it had cost £6000 (*Paston Letts.*, iv. 235).

[63] FP 69, m. 3.

[64] Hellesdon £670 (*ibid.*, m. 2), Cotton £418 (*ibid.*, m. 3), Norwich £246 (*ibid.*, m. 2),
Dedham £200 (*ibid.*, m. 3), Yarmouth £200 (*ibid.*, m. 2).

[65] FP 84. It cost £616.   [66] FP 69, mm. 5-7.

and Maine.[66] Their clear annual value at Michaelmas 1445 was given as £401 sterling, which, added to that of the English etates, made a total income of £1,463 a year. The majority of his French lordships Fastolf had acquired by grant from Henry V and the duke of Bedford;[67] some had been ceded in lieu of money owing;[68] and some he had bought for himself. The valor lists some ten castles, fifteen *manoirs* and an inn at Rouen. But by 1439 he had already bitter reason to doubt the soundness of investing too heavily in the permanence of the English conquest and was beginning to sell out. A peasants' rising in 1435 had reduced the annual value of his holdings in the Pays de Caux from £200 to £8 sterling, while his barony of Cilly, reckoned to be worth a thousand marks a year in time of peace, only yielded a fifth of that amount in 1444-5. Already before this latter date he had alienated at a low price French lands which had been bringing him in £85 *per annum*;[69] and he may have sold more thereafter, though nothing like all he owned when the surrender of Maine and the fall of Normandy deprived him of what was left. The events of 1449-50 involved Fastolf and others like him in heavy and sudden financial loss. No wonder that the dispossessed wanted Suffolk's blood! Over the fifteen years since the death of his patron Bedford Fastolf had seen the income from his French lands dwindle from an annual total of more than £675 sterling to nothing at all. He had been the duke of York's councillor since 7 May 1441, though that by itself was no sure guide to his political attachments.[70] Henry VI's French marriage and its disturbing effects in the *Pays de Conquête* touched his interests where they were more exposed. It is therefore not surprising that in the manoeuvres of the factions at the time of Suffolk's impeachment in 1450 he like a good many of

---

67 The most valuable of these was the barony of Cilly-Guillaume granted him by Bedford to maintain his state as banneret (*ibid.*, m. 6).

68 In particular lands worth 1,560 saluts (390 marks) p.a. granted 2 January 1433 as compensation for the loss of the ransom of Guillaume Remon captain of Pacy whom he had taken prisoner in 1423 and agreed to release for 20,000 saluts (5000 marks). The grant is registered in Paris, Arch. Nat., Reg. JJ 175, no. cciii, fos. lxvir.-lxviir. (I owe this reference to Dr J. R. L. Highfield.) See also *Paston Letts.*, iii. 58 and 64-5.

69 He obtained £847 for them, i.e. ten years' purchase.

70 York's patent granting his 'beloved councillor' an annuity of £20 is Brit. Mus., Add. Ch. 14598. But Fastolf 'fuit ad diuersa tempora de principali concilio diuersorum principum, videlicet Humfridi ducis Gloucestrie, Thome Beauford ducis Excestrie fratris regis Henrici quarti, Ricardi ducis Eboraci, Johannis ducis de Somerset, Johannis ducis de Norfolk et Thome ducis Clarencie necnon armiger electus inter alios pro corpore incliti regis Henrici v^ti' (FP 69, m. 5). It would be rash to prophesy on the basis of this list which side this hireling councillor would take in the Wars of the Roses.

Bedford's lieutenants—Oldhall and Ogard in the lead[71]—found his way into the Yorkist camp.[72] These mercenary captains had grown rich by their own exertions only to find themselves impoverished by the treachery and incompetence of those about the king. Without the traditional loyalties of men with an inherited stake in the country they were freer to pick their side. The fact that many of their gains had been safely harvested did not reconcile them to the cutting-off of all further supplies; they wanted more and welcomed in York a man who might give it them and who in any case shared their wrongs. We may sympathise with their aspirations while remembering that for a quarter of a century at least they had helped each other to suck France dry. If Fastolf for one had incurred serious losses, we know what value he placed upon the lands and buildings he retained.

About the contents of his French and English houses, the furnishings, plate, jewels and clothes, it is, alas, impossible to attain an equal precision. Some idea of what was at Caister in 1448 can be derived from the inventory of that year, an imperfect copy which was assigned by Gairdner to 1459;[73] but its omission to value the articles listed greatly reduces its utility for our purpose. All the same, it provides unmistakable evidence that Fastolf, like most other members of the fifteenth-century nobility, maintained a high degree of outward state. The cloths of arras and tapestry-work it briefly describes must alone have been worth a good many hundreds of pounds; there were over forty of them and we are told that a pair of them had cost Fastolf more than £220.[74] What he kept at Southwark and in his other manor-places is nowhere recorded; nor what, if anything, he had left behind in France. But a list of bullion and plate

[71] The fullest list of Bedford's household and retinue is in Lambeth MS. 506, fos. 8r.-11r. (with Worcester's additions). A modern translation, from which much is omitted, was printed in *Wars of the English in France*, ii. 433-8. Compare the witnesses to York's charter to the Franciscans of Babwell, Bury St. Edmunds, 28 February 1447 (*Cal. Pat. Rolls, 1446-1452*, p. 231). For Oldhall, see C. E. Johnston, 'Sir William Oldhall', *Eng. Hist. Rev.* xxv (1910), 715-22. There are full, but not wholly accurate, biographies of him and Ogard in J. C. Wedgwood, *History of Parliament, Biographies*, 1439-1509, s.n.

[72] Fastolf stood pledge for a loan of £3000 borrowed by York from Cardinal Beaufort's executors sometime before 18 December 1452 (*Paston Letts.*, 280-1; iv. 233).

[73] FP 43, a parchment-covered book of thirty-two paper leaves, fifteen of which are blank. The inventory is on fos. 2v.-15r. and is dated 'the laste day of October the xxvij yere of kyng Henr' the sixte.' On fos. 17r.-19v. are additions made between November 1454 and July 1455. The most important omission from Gairdner's version (*Paston Letts.*, iii. 174-89) is the list of books 'in the stewe hous' (fo. 11r.) printed in *Hist. MSS. Com. 8th Rept.*, p. 268a.

in the hands of a party among his executors at his death provides us with a few hard figures.[75] There was, for example, £2,643 10s. 0d. in cash, most of it on deposit at the abbey of St. Benet of Hulme. Allowing 2s. 10d. an ounce troy for silver and 40s. an ounce for gold, the bare value of the metal from which the plate was fashioned amounted to £2,456.[76] The descriptions prove that much of it was elaborate in workmanship, gilt, enamelled, pounced, gadrooned and decorated with figures and heraldic beasts.[77] It had been accumulated over a long period.[78]

No complete inventory of Fastolf's jewels has been preserved. But several are mentioned and a few described in some detail in his executor's papers.[79] The most important was a spear-pointed diamond set in 'a very rich collar [*monile*] called in English "a White Rose".'[80] This, it was said, had been bought by Richard, duke of York, for 4000 marks and given to Fastolf partly in repayment of a loan, partly as recompense for his 'great labours and vexations' when the donor was the king's lieutenant in France.[81] As far as I know, this is the most valuable jewel outside the royal treasure of which there is record in fifteenth-century England. It is pleasant to think of Fastolf on some great occasion wearing round his neck a collar that had cost as much as his nine Suffolk manors. Of his more everyday jewellery, 'a crosse wyth a cheyn & of the holye crosse thereynne that Sir John Fastolf dyd were dayly aboute hys nek', priced at £200, formed part of Sir William Yelverton's share of the

---

[74] FP 84: 'a riche cloth of arras of ymagery work of Justice adminystryng wᵗ another cloth of arras conteyngyng euery of the seid clothez about xvj yerdis long & v yerdis in brede whiche that cost mor þan ccxxli, sterlingiz'. Arras was included in the goods sold to the bishop of Ely for over £400 after Fastolf's death (FP 91, m. 1). A rough list of stuff in John Paston's hands at Caister in 1461 or 1462 (FP 77) includes arras and tapestry-work of little value.

[75] *Paston Letts.*, ii. 166–74.

[76] Made up of 15,628½ oz. silver and 121 oz. gold. The prices of the two metals are given by Worcester (*Paston Letts.*, iii. 232 from FP 87).

[77] Some of the pieces are described in fuller terms by Worcester in FP 79. The use of the word 'goderoned' is nearly 300 years earlier than the first quotation in the *Oxford English Dictionary*, s.v. FP 78 consists of three other partial inventories of Fastolf's plate.

[78] For £271 spent on silver plate in 1433, see above, p. 180.

[79] Especially in FP 79.

[80] *Paston Letts.*, ii. 281-1 and iii. 233. It is called 'sperpoynted' in FP 79.

[81] The duke's debt was for a loan of £466 13s. 4d.; 'et pro aliis justis causis' £266 – 13 – 4. This accounts for the valuation (*Paston Letts.*, iii. 233) at £733 6s. 8d., i.e. the amount it had cost Fastolf. Besides the White Rose, the duke gave him 'a nowche of gold in facion of a ragged staf, with ij ymages of man and woman garnysshed with a ruby, a diamande and a greet peerle' worth 500 marks and 'a floure of gold' worth £40 (*ibid.*, ii. 280; FP 79).

spoils along with 'a boke clepyt *Josephus*' and 'a grete Bible *cum historia scolastica* yn Frensh.'[82] The 'White Rose' was appropriated by John Paston.

There are two possible explanations of this scale of magnificence: the need to save and the urge to display. Were Fastolf and his contemporaries nervous hoarders afraid to venture their money in a sagging market or lordly spendthrifts squandering their war-profits on things of complaisance? There can be little doubt which is the correct answer to that question. The fortune of arms had brought these men enormous wealth and the impulse behind their expenditure on such articles as jewellery, plate and furniture—as on the palaces they built to house them—was a passion for conspicuous waste. Compared with the outlay of such aristocratic captains as Richard Beauchamp and Ralph Cromwell, Fastolf's buildings and their contents were for all their splendour as modest as his rank.

That prompts a further question: was all the capital that he sank in the purchase of manors intended by contrast to yield a good return? Or was it too, in whole or in part, but another form of expenditure on display? If a man was anxious to make a wise disposition of his fortune, land had at least one clear advantage. From the negligence or dishonesty of executors there was no sure refuge, but land was less easily misappropriated than cash. It did not evaporate as movables could during the nonage of the heir; it was better protected in the courts; whether its financial yield was high or low, it was altogether safer. But such arguments could scarcely appeal to a childless septuagenarian who had no great love for his kin and who, at any rate six months before his death, intended his feoffees to realise the greater part of his estate for the fulfilment of his will. It is more likely that he was influenced by the belief that land enjoyed another advantage; it was still the basis of all effective lordship; its possession bestowed social consequence and power over other men; the world could not afford to do without it—until the hour of death. But regarded merely as an investment its attractions were doubtful.

This can easily be demonstrated in Fastolf's own case. From a capital outlay of £13,855 he derived an estimated net income of £775 after the deduction of all local reprises, or rather less than 6 per cent. Now in that period the market-value of a rent-charge was taken as a rule to be twenty times its annual income.[83] Land, that is to say, free from all ordinary encumbrances and expenses of management, was reckoned to be worth twenty years' purchase.[84] That was the

[82] FP 70.

assumption upon which executors and feoffees normally worked.[85] Fastolf could therefore claim to rank as a careful buyer. Though he had paid as little as eleven, and as much as thirty, years' purchase for individual manors, his average worked out at $17\frac{4}{5}$.

But this was deceptive. In the first place it took no account of the expenses of administration at the centre which the running of a large, even if fairly compact, estate involved. His papers abound with evidence that Fastolf was plagued by the difficulty of collecting arrears of rent, that he employed a considerable number of 'riding servants', surveyors and auditors and that he was often driven to invoke the law on his dilatory, careless and, as he was apt to believe, dishonest ministers.[86] His determination not to be fleeced earned him a bad name among them: 'cruell and vengible he hath byn euer and for the most parte w^toute pite and mercy.'[87] This oft-quoted judgement on their master's character, by one servant writing to another, does not stand alone.[88] On Fastolf the cares of a landowner pressed heavily; they did not improve his temper. In his younger days he had not been without a measure of that *largesse* which the age expected in a knight.[89] It was suspicion and the impotence of the very old that made him harsh; but not always unjustly so, as the vultures

---

[83] Thus the only rent Fastolf himself bought, one of 25 marks p.a. payable by the prior of Hickling, cost him 500 marks (FP 69, m. 2). Unfortunately for him the vendor's title was disputable, there being enough doubt whether he held it to himself, heirs and assigns or only to himself and his heirs to encourage the prior to refuse Fastolf payment since he was only an assign. The purchase, which was made in 1428, was followed by a series of law-suits between 1445 and 1455 involving the purchaser in heavy legal expenses (FP 29 and 33; Hickling 59-157, *passim*).

[84] The earliest use of this phrase known to me is in a deed of sale of 10 November 1517 (*Cat. of Ancient Deeds*, v, no. A 12210): 'after xx yeers perchas accordyng to the trew and clere value of the said maner.' But the practice was much older.

[85] It is, for example, that of Ralph Lord Cromwell's executors when they valued some of his manors for sale, 30 November 1466 (Miscellanea 355). On 22 August 1454 Thomas Ingledew gave £400 to Magdalen College to buy lands of the value of £20 yearly (Miscellanea 436); and on 16 October 1461 he gave a further sum of £482 to purchase lands worth £24 yearly (Magd. Coll., Register A, fos. 31v.-33r.). But compare the promise in the verses quoted below, p. 193.

[86] A letter of 12 May 1448 (FP 26) shows him very incensed with John Rafman until recently his 'collector of monies' at Yarmouth and now 'hese prisoner'. The 1446 valor (FP 28) contains long lists of arrears of rent due, while FP 62(*c.* 1459) provides a mass of evidence for the legal proceedings by which Fastolf tried to bring his ministers to account.

[87] *Paston Letts.*, iii. 89.

[88] Apart from the well-known examples (*ibid.*, *passim*), there are the complaints of his former receiver-general Nicholas Bocking and of Bocking's son John, who was also in his service, to his executor, Bishop Wainfleet (FP 98). A neighbour in Southwark once told Fastolf to his face that he was afraid to have the law on him because he was sure that the old knight with his great riches 'wolde haue cruelly vexed hym' (FP 39).

gathered about his death-bed.[90]

Nor were the costs and vexations of supervision his only troubles. A worse one had its origins in the chief hazard of the fifteenth-century land market: the prevalence of defective title. The main reasons for this were admirably summarised in a piece of contemporary doggerel, attributed in two manuscripts rather improbably to Sir John Fortescue.[91] This offered advice to those in Fastolf's predicament:

> Jhesu as thou art heuen kyng
> Sende vs grace to haue knowyng.
> Who wille be warre in p^{r}chasyng
> Considre the poyntes here folowyng:
> First see that the lande be clere
> In title of the seller;
> And that it standen in noo daungier
> Of noo wommans dower;
> Se whether the tenure be bonde or free;
> And see relesse of euery feoffee;
> Se that þe seller be of age;
> And that it lye in noo morgage;
> Se whether a taille therof be foun[d]
> And whether it be in statuyt bond;
> Considre what seruice longeth þerto;
> And what rente therof out most go;
> And if it moeve of a wedded womman
> Thenke cuer de baron[92] thanne;
> And if ye may in ony wise
> Make your charter of warantise
> To your heirs and assignes also
> Thus shall a wise p^{r}chaser doo.
> In xv yere if ye wise be
> Ye shalle ayein your money see.[93]

---

[89] See, for example, his letter to Henry Inglose and John Berney [*Paston Letts.*, ii. 50; the date of this letter seems to be 1435 or earlier, since Inglose, called an esquire, was knighted by 29 November 1435 (*Cal. Close Rolls, Henry VI*, iii. 9-10)]. When John Rafman was in trouble, Fastolf hoped 'y^t he wold brynk to mynde y^t I payed for hese fynaunce and raunsom c marc and qu[itted him] ought of prison in Fraunce where alle the maysteres and frendz that ever he hadde wold nought a don it [for it was] nought the gyse ner costom of men of armes to acquite everye prisoner y^t is take, as I reporte me; and ma[ny] frendly dedes I dede for hym at the reuerens of God' (FP 26).

To carry out this advice prolonged and often vain record-searching was necessary. There were some pitfalls even the wariest might overlook, such as a conveyance imperfectly executed or an age-old entail long forgotten or deliberately concealed. Fear of a defective title was, I believe, the source of that interest in manorial descents that English antiquaries showed from the first. The complications of the land law were a powerful incitement to historical research. Fastolf's, though he employed an expert, was not always carried far enough.[94]

Entails broken but not shattered were more than once his undoing. At various times he bought property in three East Anglian villages: Titchwell, Beighton and Bradwell. His original outlay on the three together came to about £1,230, while their clear annual value at Michaelmas 1445 proved to be just over £77;[95] he had thus obtained them at almost exactly sixteen years' purchase. Defending his very questionable title in the courts for ten years with more success than the merits of his case justified added £1,085 in legal expenses and bribery to the price.[96] This rose in consequence from sixteen years'

[90] Two of Worcester's letters, though obscurely worded (*Paston Letts.*, iii. 115-19) seem to hint that Fastolf's affairs were in considerable disorder, partly owing to the slackness of his officials, partly to his own senile optimism. And John Paston and Thomas Howes frankly told him so (*ibid.*, iii. 129).

[91] Bodleian Lib., MS. Lat. misc. c. 66, fo. 101 v. (early 16th cent.), where the poem is headed: 'Fortescu'; *ibid.*, MS. Rawlinson B. 252, fo. 1r. (early 17th cent.) has the heading; 'Breue quoddam utile secundum Fortescu' [printed by Thomas lord Clermont, *Sir John Fortescue, Knight: His Life, Works and Family History* (1869), i. 543-4].

[92] i.e. covert-baron.

[93] The various manuscripts of this poem differ considerably in date and form. That printed here is from Brit. Mus., Royal MS. 17 B xlvii, fo. 59r. Most of the contents of this volume can be dated 1452-6. 'xv yere' appears in the last line but one of the version in Brit. Mus., Lansdowne MS. 762, fo. 2v, and of that in Brit. Mus., Lansdowne MS. 470, fo. 298r. (printed in the *Catalogue of Lansdowne MSS.*, pt. ii, p. 130); both appear to have been written about 1500. The former has a verse not found elsewhere:

'& so þᵗ the seller that therof seased be
Stonde not owtelawed in maner degre'.

The early sixteenth-century text in Bodl. Lib., MS. Douce 54, fo. 64r., printed with a number of mistakes in *Secular Lyrics of the XIVth and XVth Centuries*, ed. R. H. Robbins, pp. 70-1, has 'xiiii yeare.' Another, also early sixteenth century, in Balliol MS. 354, fo. 100v. [printed in *Songs, Carols and other Miscellaneous Poems*, ed. R. Dyboski (Early Eng. Text Soc.), pp. 137-138] has 'xv yere', while Lambeth MS. 306, of much the same date, fo. 203r. [printed in *Political Religious and Love Poems*, ed. F. J. Furnivall (Early Eng. Text Soc.), p. 44, and in *Three Fifteenth-century Chronicles*, ed. J. Gairdner (Camden Soc.), p. xxvi] has 'tenne yere', as has Bodl. Lib., MS. Ashmole 61 (late 15th cent.), fo 21v. The number of years seems to have nothing to do with date; some manuscripts were merely more hopeful than others; all appear to have been excessively hopeful, but the dangers they advised against were very real.

purchase to very nearly thirty. On several other manors such expensive mistakes were repeated.[97] Fastolf might have been excused for preferring a nice, quiet 5 *per cent.* on capital invested in the city to the profits of landowning as he knew them. His reason for acting as he did is hinted at in a letter from one of his servants, that same Henry Windsor whose remark on his cruelty has already been quoted. The letter describes a conversation Windsor had had as late as 1458 with Worcester in London. The latter, he wrote, 'seid that he wold be as glad and as feyn of a good boke of Frensh or of poetre as my maistre Fastolf wold be to purchace a faire manoir; and thereby I vnderstand he list not to be commynd w[t] in such matiers.'[98] Windsor was probably right; Fastolf over manors was like Worcester over books: he list not to be communed withal in such matters. Both were the victims of collector's mania, if the master's was the commoner form. It was as well as Fastolf could afford to indulge his wasteful passion. He aimed less at profit than at augmenting his land and fame. In spite of the extravagances into which this led him the old man did not cut up too badly—though his executors cut him up very differently from the way he had intended.

Not that he was insensible to profit. He did all that bullying and rack-renting could do to raise the yield of his estates; and he sought other means to increase revenue. One of these merits a brief reference. Fastolf was the grandson of a shipowner, while his father, though an esquire in Edward III's household, did not wholly sever his connection with the trade of Yarmouth on which many members of their family had thriven.[99] The possession of great wealth, an assured place in landed society and membership of the order of the Garter did not prevent Sir John from engaging in commerce on his own account. By a proclamation of 1443 six vessels belonging to him—two plates, a cogship, a farcost and a couple of balingers —were exempted during his life from the attentions of the royal

[94] The Fastolf Papers contain much evidence that Worcester was regularly set by his master to investigate pedigrees and manorial descents. On one occasion he had a colleague, 'Sir Andrew', perhaps Sir Andrew Ogard, whom 'it lykyd . . . to enserche the cronicles & pedegreys conveyng the fourme & ordre of such descentes as longeth to that matier whych I suppose he hath bokes redy & I shall seke vppon my partie' [Fastolf to ? a member of the duke of York's household, 1443 (FP 40)].

[95] FP 69, mm. 2 and 3.

[96] FP 42 is a long roll entitled 'Custus et expense in lege pro Bradwell, Beyton et Tychewell' from Michaelmas 1448 to Michaelmas 1458.

[97] The case of the Hickling rent has already been mentioned, above, p. 192. That of the manor of Caldecott in Fritton, Suffolk, occupies a good many of the Caldecott deeds and also FP 56; the Southwark deeds show similar trouble there.

[98] *Paston Letts.*, iii. 132.

purveyors; they were, according to the patent, being used by him for the carriage of his building-materials and household gear by water.[100] An account of his Yarmouth receiver, nominally for the autumn and winter of 1444-5 but containing references to the activities of several years, seems to prove that he owned a larger fleet than that mentioned in the king's letters and one that was by no means exclusively occupied on his domestic errands.[101] Although the references to voyages are only incidental, a little can be gathered about cargoes and ports of call. Now and then Fastolf's ships were chartered by other merchants for periods of a year or less, but for the most part his servants seem to have traded in them or collected freightage from others to their lord's advantage. As a rule they plied to and fro between Yarmouth and London, but there were visits to Newcastle, Boston and most of the havens on the east coast from the Wash to the Thames; on one occasion a cargo of fish was loaded at Cley in north Norfolk and carried for sale to France. Other evidence among his letters and papers suggests that Fastolf ventured considerable quantities of grain, malt, wool, cloth and bricks;[102] only the scale of his commercial activity eludes us. Yet there is no doubt that he was quite a substantial grazier; in 1446, for example, his East Anglian manors carried some 7800 sheep.[103] Local variations in the price of corn sometimes offered him the chance of a profitable gamble: according to Nicholas Bocking, his receiver-general at the time, 'in the dere yeris' in the late 1430's when there was a dearth he made a clear profit of £300 by buying grain in Norfolk and selling it at Colchester, Manningtree and elsewhere in Essex.[104] It is a pity that this side of his economic activities is so thinly documented.

Whatever made Fastolf spend his money how he did, it was not from any lordly indifference to material advantage. Evidently land had for him immaterial attractions: it brought him vexation but

---

99 The Fastolfs of Yarmouth were a prolific family and their kinships are not always clear. The will of Sir John's father, John Fastolf, son of Alexander and brother of Hugh, dated 28 September and proved 25 October 1383, is in District Probate Registry, Norwich, Reg. Harsyk, fos. 5v.-6r. He was in 1363 the earl of Warwick's esquire (*Cal. Papal Registers, Petitions*, i. 454) and received an annuity of £20 for life as Edward III's esquire on 28 January 1374 (*Cal. Patent Rolls, 1370-1374*, p. 405). On 7 March 1380 the brothers Hugh and John entered into recognisances to pay the king 600 marks if it were later proved that the goods in a captured ship of Barcelona were not enemy goods (*Cal. Close Rolls, 1377-1381*, pp. 362 and 492-3). Their father Alexander, several times bailiff of Yarmouth, disappears from the court-rolls of the borough after 1343 when he was accused with others of robbery (*Cal. Patent Rolls, 1343-1345*, pp. 166, 168 and 385). He was dead by 1363 at latest (Yarmouth court-roll 37-8 Edw. III, Placita, roll 3v.).

prestige—and the sheer joy of ownership. He was no narrow skinflint but a knight whose tastes had been formed amid the splendour of courts. If the princes he served were great warriors, they were also civilized, bookish and art-loving. So was he. If we are ever tempted to write him and his fellow-mercenaries off as no more than hard-faced business-men who had done well out of the war, it is only necessary to recall the artist whom Dr. Otto Pächt has named 'the Master of Sir John Fastolf', the varied literature in the stew-house at Caister and those two authors, Stephen Scrope and William Worcester, who Englished the works of Christine de Pisan and of Tully for their lord's solace in old age. But there is no need to quarrel with the statement that he had done well out of the war. With the facts of his gains before us Leyland's phrase about the '*spolia Gallorum*' has put on substance.

---

[100] *Fœdera*, xi. 44-5.

[101] FP 26. This is unfortunately not a detailed trading account. John Rafman the accountant was 'receptor denariorum' and 'custos diuersorum bonorum dicti Johannis Fastolf infra mesuagium suum nuper Deyngaynes in Jernemuth.' He refers frequently to a book 'de reparacione nauium' which is no longer among the Fastolf Papers. The account mentions 14 ships, but some of them are referred to by name and others by type and there may be a slight overlap. In 1446 (FP 28) there were said to be eight of the lord's ships at Yarmouth at the date of the valor.

[102] For grain and wool, see below. On 7 January 1451 he wrote to his servants in Norfolk from London: 'I merveyle greetly that ye sende not the greet ship w^t malt as I am wont to have', and five days later: 'I praye yow . . . that ye wold sende me heder my ship called the Blythe w^t malt as ye have ben a customed by fore tyme as my trust is in yow' (Brit. Mus., Add. MS. 39848, nos. 14 and 15). See also *Paston Letts*., ii. 213 and 252; FP 51 (account-roll of Christopher Hanson, collector of rents, farms and foreign moneys, 21 April 1454-25 December 1456) and FP 62 (roll of debts c. 1459).

[103] FP 28.   [104] FP 98.

X. WILLIAM WORCESTER:
A PRELIMINARY SURVEY

IN the history of English scholarship the middle years of the fifteenth century are commonly represented as an interval of slack water when the tide hesitated on the turn between the old learning and the new. Scholastic disputation, damped down by the fear of heresy, had sunk, we are often told, to a lifeless routine, while the first rare native disciples of Italian humanism were still weakly struggling to free themselves from the contaminating influence of a barbarised Latinity. In spite of much new educational endowment and some well-intentioned patronage, true learning languished.

This picture of stagnation may not be wholly false, but it is incomplete and it exaggerates. Even if we are compelled to admit that Netter was the last English schoolman with anything faintly resembling a European public and that there was no humanist worth the name before the days—at least—of Grocyn and Linacre, it is nevertheless impossible to deny all intellectual movement to the half-century that could boast such a varied collection of writers as Lyndwood, Gascoigne, Peacock, Fortescue, and Littleton. Yet what was perhaps its most striking achievement had nothing to do with the work of either schoolmen or lawyers, was quite as novel as humanism and could with reason claim a greater ultimate significance. This was the foundation and rapid development, along lines much the same as they have been pursued since, of antiquarian and topographical studies in England. It is usual to divide the credit for this more or less equally between John Rous the chaplain of Warwick and William Worcester alias Botoner of Bristol and Norfolk, gentleman. Were it necessary to award priority to one the choice would seem to be strongly in Worcester's favour. Although they were not widely separated in age, he was, if not the older man, at least the earlier resident at Oxford and by a great deal the earlier author. Born in 1415, he was already an undergraduate in Easter term 1432;[1] the first surviving manuscript from his pen, a series of astronomical tables, dates from 1437-8;[2] and by May 1449 he had begun to form antiquarian collections.[3] The evidence for Rous is markedly later,[4] but it contains nothing to suggest that his

---

[1] *Itineraria Symonis Simeonis et Willelmi de Worcestre*, ed. J. Nasmith, p. 178, A critical edition of this text is badly needed.

[2] Bodleian Library, MS. Laud Misc. 674. On fo. 61 is the date 10 July 1437.

[3] Norwich Public Library, MS. 7197 (for the nature and contents of this manuscript see pp. 219-21, below), fos. 297-9ᵛ.

enthusiasm for antiquities was derived from Worcester's example. While the latter is known to have journeyed two or three times through Warwickshire[5] and was on friendly terms with an esquire whom he describes as receiver-general to the great Richard Beauchamp,[6] there is no evidence for believing that either of these pioneers was aware of the other's existence. Should it be that they were products of the same school or tradition, we have lost track of their masters. Like as their accomplishments were, we are forced at present to regard them as independent explorers of this new world of scholarship.

Rous has left us few details of his source and methods of inquiry. Most of what he wrote and collected had disappeared before the seventeenth century. Altogether he is the more shadowy figure. Though it is true that only a handful of Worcester's writings has been preserved, those we have are much more informative. They reveal how long and widely he searched, how inquisitive he was, how varied the material that struck him as deserving of record. It was his normal practice not only to mention his authority for a statement but also the date and place at which he learnt it. He habitually annotated the margins of his books. As a result it would be easy to list many scores of individuals and corporations who were induced to put their reminiscences, their libraries, and their archives at his service. His character and tastes are clearly discernible in his familiar letters; from the correspondence of other members of his circle we know what he looked like—'oculis luscus et denigrato colore in facie fuscus' are the unflattering words of the disagreeable Brackley[7]—and how his friends and enemies regarded him. When so

---

4 The supposed date of his birth (*c.* 1411) rests on slight evidence. Since, as he himself tells us (*Historia regum Angliae*, ed. T. Hearne, pp. 5 and 120), he was at Oxford with John Tiptoft, born 1427 and occupying rooms at University College 1440-3 (G. E. C., *Complete Peerage*, ed. G. H. White, vol. xii, pt. 1, p. 749; R. J. Mitchell, *John Tiptoft*, pp. 13-14), and John Seymour who was proctor in 1453 (J. Le Neve, *Fasti Ecclesiae Anglicanae*, ed. T. D. Hardy, iii. 483) and held a canonry at Windsor from 1471 to 1502 (*ibid.*, pp. 388 and 390), he is more likely to have been born about 1425. Most of his known works appear to date from the 1470's and 1480's.

5 For two occasions see below, pp. 207-8. A third occurred in July and August 1460 when he went from London to Bristol via Coventry and Gloucestershire (Magdalen College, Oxford, Fastolf Paper 72, m. 5. This is a roll of accounts drawn up by Worcester for presentation to Sir John Fastolf's other executors).

6 The esquire, whose name was Brewster, not only told him about Earl Richard's building operations but allowed him to take extracts from chronicles in his possession (*Itineraria*, pp. 336-7, 338, and 349-54). Worcester met him at St. Benet's Holm in November 1479. The name of John Brewster, *valettus*, appears on the retinue-roll of Warwick as Captain of Calais, *c.* 1419 (B.M. Cotton Roll xiii. 7, m. 3). I have seen no evidence that he was ever the earl's receiver-general.

much can be known it is unfortunate that he should have been so haphazardly and often so ignorantly judged. He may have been uncritical and inaccurate;[8] but that is not a verdict passed on all the available evidence. It is the aim of this paper to call attention to some that has been overlooked and to scrutinise the familiar anew.

What could be more appropriate than that the first Englishman to deserve the name of antiquary should have been an amateur, landed enough for his widow to dignify him with the rank of gentleman![9] Worcester's status needs to be taken into account in assessing the quality of his performance, just as the latter can tell us much of interest about the educational attainments and intellectual resources of his class. He may have belonged to the fringes of the gentry, townsman's son though he was, but he made his living as a member of that large and highly trained profession whose duty it was to manage the estates and households of the great. He was a layman and, it seems, a layman from choice. This did not entirely suit his master, since menials in orders were cheaper to provide for—at the Church's expense.[10] Worcester was, in the long run, to pay heavily for his inability to accept a benefice. Unlike some other married clerks, he does not appear to have been a spoiled priest, one whose loss of vocation had led to matrimony. When in old age he sought to place a boy, who may have been one of his sons, at Lincoln's Inn, he recalled how sheltered had been his own upbringing:

> he hath cost me [he wrote] moch gode and labour and now he ys vppon hys makyng by vertues gouernance or vndoyng to the contrarye, and yn especyalle to be not conuersant ne neere among wommen as I was kept froo her company xxx yer or ony such were of my councelle, I thank God of yt.[11]

It hardly sounds as if his decision to marry was precipitate.

There was nothing exceptional about his unwillingness to enter the Church. Many who did the work of clerks, whether in the king's service like Hoccleve or in the households of the nobility like Worcester, were not in orders. In the fifteenth century such a career

---

7 *The Paston Letters*, 1422-1509, ed. J. Gairdner, 1904, iii. 229.

8 R. J. Mitchell, *John Free*, pp. 12-13. The example used to substantiate this judgement is derived from a misreading of *Itineraria*, pp. 185 and 275.

9 *Paston Letters*, vi. 51.

10 'My maister . . . seyd me yerstenday he wysshed me to hafe be a preest so I had be disposed to hafe gofe me a lyvyng by reson of a benefice' (*ibid*. ii. 334). The tone of the letter is not serious.

11 *Ibid*. v. 314.

as Sir Reynold Bray's, though it was abnormally successful, was not uncommon. This rise of the gentleman bureaucrat was one of the most significant results of the growth of lay literacy. Thus a succession of married Leventhorpes began to manage the affairs of the Duchy of Lancaster in the lifetime of John of Gaunt.[12] Thomas Tropenell, the builder of Great Chalfield, was receiver-general to Robert, second Lord Hungerford;[13] John Heaton, esquire, of Newton Blossomville served Humphrey, duke of Buckingham in the same office.[14] Among Worcester's immediate colleagues in Sir John Fastolf's central administration there were, in addition to a group of councillors learned in the law, several laymen holding places of responsibility.[15] One of them, Nicholas Bocking, receiver-general and esquire, put his knowledge of Norfolk families at Worcester's disposal;[16] his son John was brought up to serve, and to think himself badly served by, the same master.[17] These lesser gentry, expert in accountancy and estate-management, as well as the lawyers and beneficed clergy with whom they worked, helped to form the society in which our antiquary's official life was spent.

His was no sinecure. From 1438 when at the age of twenty-three he had already attached himself to Fastolf's service, until his employer's death on 6 November 1459, he was occupied with a great deal of estate, legal, and other business.[18] Probably he never held any regular office; he was sometimes called 'secretary' but more often merely 'servant.'[19] It was for long one of his chief duties to act as his master's personal attendant and amanuensis. His was the hand that wrote the only example of the knight's correspondence surviving from the period 1436–49, a letter dated at London on 21 October

[12] R. Somerville, *Duchy of Lancaster*, i, index s.n.

[13] His accounts for the years ending Michaelmas 1451 and Michaelmas 1454 survive (P.R.O., Ministers' Accounts, S.C. 6/971/10 and 12). *The Tropenell Cartulary*, ed. J. S. Davies, Wilts. Archaeol. and Nat. Hist. Soc., records his steady progress as a landowner.

[14] Appointed by patent on 21 April 1437 and still accounting as late as Michaelmas 1451 (S.C. 6/1304/4). From the fact that he served the duke's widow in a like capacity (*ibid*. 1117/11), it is probable that he remained in office until Buckingham's death in 1460. Both he and Tropenell were members of the House of Commons.

[15] e.g. Walter Shipdam, Geoffrey Sparling, Christopher Hanson, and William Barker, all of whom appear frequently in the *Paston Letters*.

[16] Norwich Pub. Lib. MS. 7197, fos. 305ᵛ – 6 and 309.

[17] Magd. Coll. Oxon, Fastolf Paper 98.

[18] He was possibly already Fastolf's surveyor at Castle Combe 27 Oct. 1436 (B.M. Add. MS. 28208, fo. 10). By 25 Oct. 1438 he was engaged in making astronomical tables specifically for Fastolf's use (Bodl. Lib. MS. Laud Misc. 674, fos. 81 and 99ᵛ – 100).

[19] Once he calls himself 'secretarius' (see below, p. 210).

1447.[20] How much earlier he undertook these secretarial functions we do not know; he continued to perform them to the end of Fastolf's life.[21] They were by no means all he did. One of his first recorded employments took him to Normandy to collect evidence for a lawsuit arising out of the death of Fastolf's nephew, Sir Robert Harling, at the siege of St. Denis in 1435; this cannot have occurred much later than 1440.[22] In the autumn of 1441 or the spring of 1442 he was busy assisting Sir John to rebut a charge, laid before the king and his peers by the aggrieved Lord Talbot, of conduct unbecoming a knight of the Garter at the battle of Patay (1429).[23] Soon afterwards he spent three terms—or something like nine months—in Normandy trying to straighten out the confusion in which the Regent Bedford had left his affairs.[24] He must have got to know the remains of the English lands in northern France fairly well.[25]

Fastolf came home from the wars not long after his fifty-ninth birthday in 1439 and spent most of his time at Southwark until he moved down to Caister in Norfolk late in 1458.[26] Worcester, except when he was absent on one of his many official missions or was permitted to combine his turn of duty as surveyor of Castle Combe with a visit to his home at Bristol, seems to have been throughout in regular attendance on his master.[27] His services were highly valued if, by his reckoning, ill-rewarded. After Sir John's death he was prepared to assert that he had spent ten years continuously night and day about his person, ministering to his growing bodily needs.[28] Not content to double the parts of doctor and man of business he wrote

[20] Magd. Coll. Oxon., Hickling 130 (abstracted *Paston Letters*, ii, 80).

[21] He wrote the last known (B.M. Add. MS. 39848, no. 49, abstracted *ibid*. iii. 142).

[22] Fastolf Paper 72, m. 9 Harling's will was proved 12 Dec. 1435 (Norwich District Probate Registry, Reg. Surflete, fo. 187ᵛ).

[23] Fastolf Paper 72, m. 8 (20 Henry VI). The presence of Stephen Wilton and Thomas Beckington confines the date to before 5 Nov. 1441 or between 2 Apr. and 5 June 1442 [*Proceedings and Ordinances of the Privy Council*, ed N. H. Nicolas, v. 169; L. Mirot and E. Déprez, *Les Ambassades anglaises, 1327-1450*, 85; *Official Correspondence of Thomas Bekynton*, ed. G. Williams (R.S.), ii. 177].

[24] Fastolf Paper 72, m. 7. Bedford's affairs were a source of trouble to his executors until Fastolf, the last of them, was dead (*Paston Letters*, iii. 69, 73, and 76).

[25] He was captured by the French at Dieppe and only escaped by bribing some seamen (Fastolf Papers 72, m. 7).

[26] There is a gap in his correspondence, 1452-4, following a deed transferring all his property real and movable to trustees in contemplation of a 'viage' (Fastolf Paper, 47; 19 Aug. 1452). Nothing more is known about this venture.

[27] His memoranda as surveyor show how often he was at Castle Combe (B.M. Add. MS. 28208).

[28] Fastolf Paper 72, m. 7. The details of Fastolf's last illness with its 158 days of 'hectic fever' are noted by Worcester (B.M. MS. Sloane 4, fo. 38ᵛ).

to keep his difficult invalid amused. As the irascible old knight sank under the weight of his years, the responsibilities of his secretary increased. Worcester refers to them in his letters with wry humour, but it is evident that the neglect of the property and the rivalries of his fellow servants caused him deepening anxiety.[29]

But Fastolf's death did not bring him freedom. The belief that, having declined all other service, he withdrew to the peace of his study at either Bristol, London, or Norwich, save for occasional antiquarian tours from his domestic base, arises from a misunderstanding.[30] For years after 1459 he led a harassed life trying in the face of interested obstruction and political uncertainty to carry out what he believed to be his late master's intentions as well as to secure for himself his deserved and promised reward. This involved him not only in constant vexation but many journeys as he traced and listed the dead man's goods, settled with his creditors, realised what he was owed, defended his lands against rival claimants, quarrelled and came to terms with the other executors, lobbied the powerful and risked his own savings in costly and futile litigation.[31] Until these efforts were frustrated by a verdict for their opponents, he and Mr Justice Yelverton fought the claims of the Pastons through repeated sessions of the court of audience of Archbishop Bourchier 'to thende of v produccions of lx witnesse producid of bothe partiez to the vttermost of the spirituell lawe.'[32] They even took the case on appeal to the Roman Curia,

the whiche plee so duryng by the space of ix yere and more, as hit is of record to showe, the whiche cost, the labour and ridyng of vij m[l] myle & more w[t] the circumstaunce, amountid more than vij[c] marke sterlingis paide by the seid Worcester beside the costis of his partie aduersary.[33]

29 *Paston Letters*, iii. 66-69, 71-72, 104-6 and 115-18.

30 G. P. Scrope (*History of Castle Combe*, pp. 197-8) favours Bristol; so does Miss Mitchell (*John Free*, p. 13). C. L. Kingsford (*English Historical Literature in the Fifteenth Century*, p. 162) prefers ten or twelve years' residence in London from 1458 onwards, followed by settlement at Pokethorp by Norwich.

31 Fastolf Papers 62-73, 76-92, 95-97, and 101. One of these (89) is printed in *Paston Letters*, iv, 284-6, and part of another (87), *ibid.*, pp. 231-6. Many are in Worcester's own hand.

32 Fastolf Paper 84 (a petition addressed by Worcester to Bishop Goldwell of Norwich, *c.* 1477). The evidence of witnesses in the case is summarised in *Paston Letters*, iv, 101-4, 154, 181-5, and 236-45. Bodl. Lib. MS. Top. Norfolk *c.* 4 (formerly Phillips MS. 9309) contains other examinations of witnesses. I am indebted to Dr. J. R. L. Highfield for telling me its present whereabouts and to Mr P. S. Lewis for lending me his transcript of it. Probate was granted by Bourchier to John Paston and Thomas Howes on 26 Aug. 1467 (Magd. Coll. Oxon., Chartae Regiae et Chartae Concessae 50.8.ii).

The result was that in the spring of 1470 he was forced to stop moving about and to economise by settling at Cambridge.

> The costys & chargys [he told the Bishop of Winchester] that I hafe born thys x yere day yn London & yn rydynges when I awayted vppon the infynyte processe of the decysyng of my maister Fastolf testamentys yn the Court of Audience that I am so yndebted and so vnpurveyed of goode to lyven that I may not ryde ne contynew yn London but am fayn to wyth-drawe me for my pore solasse to Cambrygge, that ys but a day jorney from my pore frendes, and to eschew gretter costys to abyde there I may be purveyed of a competent lyveng for me & such as I am constreyned to kepe & fynde.[34]

What had made this abandonment of the fight tolerable to him was Bourchier's decision on 13 February 1470 to remit the sole administration of Fastolf's estate to William Wainfleet, Bishop of Winchester.[35] If this appreciably lightened Worcester's burden, for another four years at least his co-operation was required and grudgingly given.[36] The compact which Wainfleet made with him on 7 December 1472 relieved his poverty and enabled him to profit from his obstinate refusal to compromise.[37] By 4 February 1474 he acknowledged that the bishop had paid him all he was owed.[38]

This should have been the moment of his release. His age was fifty-nine and thirty-seven years, if not more, had been consumed in doing Fastolf's work for small return. But a letter he wrote to Wainfleet from London on 21 August 1474 makes it clear that the recovery of Fastolf's manors in East Anglia was then still engaging his attention. His willingness to assist the bishop had involved him in fresh misfortunes and he appealed for help. He told of his arrest for debt, the seizure of his lands in Norfolk and Essex, his flight on release to London while his wife remained in prison and all the other hurts he had suffered at the hands of one Robinson of Norwich and his maintainers.[39] As late as 1477 he had not abandoned his efforts

---

[33] Fastolf Paper 84.

[34] Magd. Coll. Oxon., Titchwell 199 (17 May 1470), abstracted *Paston Letters*, v. 72.

[35] Fastolf Paper 93. A passage in *Paston Letters*, v, no. 742, omitted by the editor, contains Sir John Paston's account of this development. It should be dated *c.* 20 Feb. 1470 since it was answered on 1 Mar. (*ibid.*, pp. 66-68).

[36] Fastolf Paper 96 and Magd. Coll. Oxon., Titchwell 120.

[37] Magd. Coll. Oxon., Norfolk and Suffolk 75.

[38] Fastolf Paper 101.

[39] Magd. Coll. Oxon., Guton 290. It appears from Fastolf Paper 91 that John Robinson and William Barker were suspected by Worcester of having carried off from Thomas Howes's rectory at Blofield several boxes of Fastolf's evidences.

on his old master's behalf against the dilatoriness of the monks of St. Benet's Holm, where Fastolf was buried.[40] To that year belongs the last document to connect him actively with the settlement of Sir John's affairs.[41] It may not have been a coincidence that it was in 1478 that he was free to set out for St. Michael's Mount on no other errand than his own pleasure.[42] The 'infinite process' had reached its end. But if Worcester's troubles were over, so shortly also was his life. The last dated entry in his notes comes from 1482.[43] He died that year or slightly later, leaving a little real estate in various countries.[44]

One point should now be clear: Worcester was for a large part of his time a busy man and most of his business was not scholarship. Books and travel in search of antiquities were the refreshment of his few leisure hours. Nor did he give his time only to Fastolf; he was highly regarded and used by other members of the Caister circle. A lawyer's bill of 1460 records the expenditure of a shilling 'for wyn at Plomers hous dyuers tymes to harken of W. W. conceytes'; though we know that he amused his fellows, it was for his practical resourcefulness rather than his wit that this payment was thought necessary.[45] As a result, in addition to all his other chores during the restless 1460's, he was called upon to administer single-handed the goods of an intestate colleague, Christopher Hanson,[46] and the testament of his wife's uncle, Thomas Howes.[47] This latter charge alone caused him much time-consuming drudgery and provoked the quarrel that led to his imprisonment.[48] It was from preoccupations like these that he escaped to measure buildings and to read in libraries.

Not that his official career was all loss. If not too prolonged, the experience gained as a great landowner's 'riding-servant' offered an antiquary valuable training. Worcester's views on building-costs and estate finance are those of an expert. It was fortunate, too, that his work entailed a great deal of travel about the country—and outside it—with opportunities of contact with men of divers kinds and

---

[40] Fastolf Paper 84.   [41] Magd. Coll. Oxon., Southwark 12 (21 Feb. 1476/7).

[42] *Itineraria*, pp. 89-99, 116, and 142-60.

[43] MS. Sloane 4, fo. 50. I know of nothing else later than the autumn of 1480 (*Itineraria*, 275).

[44] The traditional date is 1482, based presumably on the fact that it was his son who dedicated Lambeth MS. 506 to Richard III (below, p. 213).

[45] Fastolf Paper 71, m. 1. Elsewhere in this account, 'conceit' clearly means a plan or scheme. But the meaning 'fancy' was already known before the end of the fifteenth century (*New English Dictionary*, Oxford, s.v.).

[46] *Ob.* 17 July 1462 (*Paston Letters*, iv. 49 and 50).

[47] *Ob.* 4 Feb. 1468/9 (Fastolf Paper 90).   [48] *Ibid.* 84 and 91.

nationalities picked up and cross-questioned on the road. The extent of Worcester's knowledge of England has often been grossly underestimated. Long before 'his principal antiquarian adventure' to Cornwall in 1478 he had frequently been in the saddle for days on end as he journeyed through the shires.[49] Only the more important of these expeditions can be touched on here.

Apart from the constant comings and goings every year between London and Fastolf's many properties in Essex and East Anglia[50] and the regular visits to Castle Combe and Bristol, Worcester was sent on a number of more extended tours, the object of which was the application of his historical studies to the current problems of a great estate: he put his knowledge of genealogy, heraldry, and the laws governing the descent of land to his master's profit. He was Fastolf's professional record-searcher and tracer of pedigrees. Thus in May 1449 he rode out from London to various places in Somerset 'ad inquirendum pro vera genealogia dominorum de Lovell & improbandum genealogiam vxoris Edwardi Hull militis.'[51] Not long afterwards a similar purpose took him to Castle Ashby, Northamptonshire, to Kent, Warwickshire, and Devon, in an attempt to find evidence to disprove the Duke of Suffolk's claim to Fastolf's manor of Drayton.[52] Another journey into Kent was undertaken to test the pedigree of the Cliffords of Bobbing and their title to a rent-charge in Hickling which Fastolf had somewhat rashly bought.[53] But the longest of these recorded missions belongs to 1457, the year in which Sir John made a new feoffment of his lands and thereby enlarged the scope of John Paston's expectations. Worcester's duty was to obtain releases from the old feoffees. This carried him first from London to Sudeley Castle and the home of Lord Beauchamp of Powick at Boddington near Cheltenham in Gloucester, thence to Henry VI's court at Coventry, and finally via London north to York.[54] Not only did the antiquary thus see a good many regions in the exercise of his calling, but it was a part of his

---

[49] The phrase is taken from T. D. Kendrick's admirable account of Rous and Worcester in *British Antiquity*, p. 30.

[50] Fastolf Paper 72, m. 8: 'ad partes diuersas & longinquas.' Two rolls of legal expenses [*ibid*. 42 (1448-57) and 51 (1454-7)] confirm Worcester's claim.

[51] *Ibid*. 42, m. 2, and 72, m. 8. These may refer to two different journeys on the same business. Worcester's sketch-pedigree of the Lovells and other notes survive in Magd. Coll. Oxon., Lovell Papers.

[52] Fastolf Paper 72, m. 8. See also *Paston Letters*, iv. 280-1.

[53] Fastolf Paper 29. The date of these notes is between 30 Nov. 1448, the ninth birthday of Alexander Clifford (Bodl. Lib., MS. Dodsworth 71, fos. 13ᵛ – 14), and the spring of 1450, twelve years after William Clifford's death (*C.F.R.* xvii. 2).

business to observe and accurately record the evidence of the past. It should be obvious that Fastolf's secretary was not useless to the compiler of the *Antiquitates Anglie*—though it does not follow that the *Decline and Fall* might have been better, or more rapidly produced, had Gibbon spent his whole life in the Hampshire militia. The blame for whatever of Worcester's remained unfinished lies, in part at least, at the door of the man who worked him hard and denied him the means to retire early.

At all events he provided him with congenial company and access to books. Fastolf, whatever his origins—and they were at worst courtly—had himself lived a servant in households where a taste for literature was keenly valued. John, Duke of Bedford, whose major-domo he was, may have had less advanced views than his brother Gloucester, but he was interested enough in the appearance of learning to buy the French royal library of 843 books, collected at enormous cost by the Valois, at a conqueror's knock-down price of about £300 sterling.[55] Of Fastolf's own books a few titles are known;[56] one of considerable beauty survives.[57] Among his dependants there were, apart from Worcester, as many as six authors.[58] There was nothing unfashionable about his desire to play the provincial Maecenas. The Lancastrian nobility widely imitated—and nowhere more than in East Anglia[59]—the literary patronage which its royal house had exercised since John of Gaunt's bereavement inspired the *Book of the Duchesse*.[60] The only trouble was that old Sir John's close-fistedness prevented him from giving money for value; 'and so I endure', joked Worcester, 'inter egenos vt

---

[54] Fastolf Paper 72, m. 7. *Paston Letters*, iii. 68, suggests another journey to Yorkshire rather earlier to oversee Fastolf's manors of Bentley and Wighton-on-the-Wolds. *Ibid.*, 132, shows him working up the history of the main line of the de la Poles of Hull and Wingfield in 1458 (*Collectanea Topographica et Genealogica*, ii. 175-6 confirms this date for Henry Bourchier's death).

[55] *Inventaire de la Bibliothèque du Roi Charles VI*, ed. L. Douët d'Arcq.

[56] Those in French in the stew-house at Caister are listed in Fastolf Paper 43, fo. 10, printed *Hist. MSS. Com., 8th Rept.*, App., p. 268. Fastolf Paper 70 mentions 'a boke clepyt *Josephus*' as well as 'a grete Bible *cum historia scolastica* yn frensh'.

[57] See below, p. 218.

[58] For Friar Brackley's Book of Arms see the *Ancestor*, x. 87-97; and for the others, Stephen Scrope, Peter Basset, Christopher Hanson, Luke Nantron, and John Bussard, see below, pp. 210-12 and 218.

[59] S. Moore, 'Patrons of Letters in Norfolk and Suffolk, *c.* 1450' in *Pubs. of Modern Languages Assoc. of America*, xxvii (1912), pp. 188-207, and xxviii (1913), pp. 79-105.

[60] That duchess's father had himself written a devotional treatise of no little subtlety and distinction: *Le Livre de Seyntz Medicines*, ed. J. Arnould, Anglo-Norman Text Society no. 2.

seruus ad aratrum' and continued to allow himself to be hard-driven.

It is time to observe him at his recreations. Now that that is what they are understood to be, their number is remarkable, their lack of finish easily explained. In no capacity is he better known and more poorly thought of than as a chronicler. It would indeed be difficult to rate his historical gifts as anything but mediocre on the strength of the *Annales* which have passed as his for more than two centuries. Hearne asserted that he had printed them from Worcester's autograph in Arundel MS. 48 at the College of Arms;[61] a Victorian editor claimed the same for himself, though in fact he merely reprinted Hearne's text—without some of the footnotes that might have put a reader on his guard against the ascription.[62] The doubt implanted by a careful scrutiny of the original edition should have been reinforced by a hint in the *Catalogue of the Arundel Manuscripts* that the 'autograph' was in at least three different hands.[63] As it happens this was a cautious understatement. Worcester's sole contribution to what has been fairly called a 'somewhat bald and uninteresting' narrative amounts to no more than fifty words;[64] and these have nothing to do with the various scraps of chronicles in which Hearne embedded them.[65] The *Annales* are a small part of the contents of the volume; many, but not all, of the rest undoubtedly passed through Worcester's hands, for some, unlike the *Annales*, have headings, corrections, and additions from his pen, and a few he wrote throughout.[66] This explains if it does not excuse Hearne's rash assumption. One would incline to believe that he worked from some other scholar's transcript, but this is ruled out both by his footnotes and by his private journal.[67] It is all too clear

61 'Ex autographo' (*Liber Niger Scaccarii*, ed. T. Hearne, 2nd edn., ii. 424).

62 'Ex autographo' (*Letters and Papers illustrative of the Wars of the English in France*, ed. J. Stevenson (R.S.), vol. ii, pt. ii, p. 743). Stevenson reproduces Hearne's misstatements about the manuscript. Thus Hearne writes (p. 435): 'Hic folium unum excissum esse ex ejusd. vestigiis deprehendo', while Stevenson remarks (p. 749, n. 2): 'Here a leaf has been cut out'; in fact the break occurs in the middle of fo. 123. Hearne usually notes where he has rearranged entries to get them into correct chronological order (e.g. pp. 462, n. 1 and 473, n. 1); Stevenson silently follows his lead in every case.

63 By W. H. Black, privately printed 1829 (but not scarce), p. 78 and note.

64 The just appraisal is C. L. Kingsford's (*English Hist. Lit.*, p. 164). Kingsford noticed how little original material the *Annales* contained and was on the point of suspecting Worcester's share in its composition, but he did not look at the manuscript.

65 *Liber Niger*, 452, the two paragraphs each beginning 'Memoranda . . .' under 1405. These come from an isolated group of jottings by Worcester on fo. 218ᵛ.

66 Those printed by Hearne (pp. 522-41) were probably not there in Worcester's time. Stevenson's selection, on the other hand, comes entirely from Worcester's papers.

67 *Remarks and Collections of Thomas Hearne*, ed. H. E. Salter, Oxford Hist. Soc. ix. 232-2, 347 and 356-7, and x. 389.

that he fabricated the *Annales* from a number of separate items in a miscellaneous collection which had acquired most of the narratives he and Stevenson printed after it had ceased to be Worcester's. The interesting stretch from November 1459 to May 1463, including all the autobiographical entries, was contributed by a writer at work in 1491.[68] Although Worcester may have gazed at Lord Scales's naked corpse on 25 July 1460, he did not tell us so.[69] Wise after the event, we now perceive that the only touches characteristic of him are in the two brief paragraphs he did actually pen.

The nearest he is known to have gone to composing a chronicle of the traditional sort is no easier to evaluate, though for different reasons. This is in French, except for Worcester's later additions, and occupies fos. xxxj-lxvj (contemporary foliation) of College of Arms MS. M. 9.[70] Its contents have been admirably described by Miss B. J. H. Rowe, but she did not succeed in deciphering the whole of Worcester's title, which runs as follows:[71]

> Iste liber de actibus armorum conquestus regni Francie, ducatus Normannie, ducatus Alenconie, ducatus Andegavie et Cenomanie cum alijs pluribus comitatibus compilatus fuit ad nobilem virum Iohannem Fastolf baronem de Cylleguillem (in anno Christi m^liiij^clix, 1459, anno quo dictus Iohannes Fastolf obijt) per Petrum Basset armigerum Anglice nacionis exercentem arma in Francia sub (victoriose principe) rege Henrico v^{to} (& Christoforum Hanson de patria almayn quondam cum Thoma Beaufort duce Excestrie ac Luket Nantron natus de Parys vnus de clericis dicti Iohannis Fastolf & per diligenciam Willelmi Wircestre secretarij predicti Iohannis Fastolf) et sub Iohanne duce Bedfordie regente regni Francie necnon aliorum principum locumtenencium sub rege Henrico vj^{to}, in toto per spacium xxxv annorum.

---

68 The short section for 1491 is in his hand (fo. 206); so too is the note added (fo. 42) to the list of emperors (fos. 39-42), once Worcester's (see his hand on fo. 40), to the effect that Frederick III was still living in 1491. It was, of course, for this writer and not for Worcester that Bishop Alcock of Ely (1486-1500) borrowed William Ferriby's chronicle from Prior Nicholas of Lynn (fo. 126^v; Hearne, p. 464). This upsets the argument about Ferriby and Worcester tentatively put forward in M. V., Clarke, *Fourteenth Century Studies*, ed. L. S. Sutherland and M. McKisack, p. 84-86.

69 He was in London on that day (Fastolf Paper 72, m. 4). The date is given in Scales's inquisition *post mortem* (cited by G. E. C., *Complete Peerage*, xi. 507).

70 I am indebted to Mr Anthony Wagner and his staff for access to this manuscript as well as Arundel 48 and to the chapter of the college for its permission to have them sent to the British Museum's photographic section on my behalf. The transfer was much assisted by the good offices of Mr G. R. C. Davis of the Museum's Department of MSS.

71 The words in brackets (. . .) are Worcester's own interlineations. See Miss Rowe's article in *E.H.R.* xli (1926), pp. 504-13. Worcester's peculiar Latin has been printed here and elsewhere without correction.

Though Peter Basset had served under Fastolf's command in Maine and Anjou, there is no trace of him among the archives of the knight's English administration. But both Hanson and Nantron were actively employed by Fastolf until his death.[72] Worcester, as we have already seen, administered the dead Hanson's goods; he also recorded the day on which Nantron died.[73] That leaves the problem: how do three men 'compile' a chronicle 'by the diligence of' a fourth? Did he reduce to order the materials they provided? He was later to revise and add to the finished text. Since the language chosen was Nantron's own and he was a clerk, it seems likely that he was responsible for the actual composition. But when on another occasion Worcester defined his share in a joint enterprise, he did not exaggerate. He claimed to have 'correctid and examyned' a translation and to have 'perrafed' it 'for more opyn and redye vnderstanding';[74] that, as his copy shows, was precisely what he did.[75] It would be unsafe to assume from his modest phrase that his part in the making of 'Basset's Chronicle' was of no account. His diligence contributed something of value, though we do not know what.

This 'plain soldierly' account of the French war was closely connected with one of Worcester's most memorable literary projects, the *Acta domini Johannis Fastolf*, the recorded *incipit* to which suggests that the part dealing with the first half of its subject's career was either never finished or soon lost.[76] Now nothing remains of this unusual attempt to write the life of an English soldier of fortune. But a few of the raw materials have been preserved and we catch more than one glimpse of the biographer as he set about his task. From an old waiting-woman who had lived in household with Fastolf's mother he gathered stories of long-dead kinsmen and an indication of the means by which the future captain achieved his start in life.[77]

---

[72] Miss Rowe has dealt fully with Basset and Hanson (*ibid.*, pp. 506-8). Fastolf Paper 51 is a roll of Hanson's accounts as collector of Fastolf's rents, farms and foreign moneys from Easter 1454 to 25 Mar. 1457. For Luke or Luket Nantron see *Paston Letters*, iii. 110, 131, and 305; iv. 235.

[73] *Itineraria*, p. 369 (4 Oct. 1471).

[74] This was the *Dicts and Sayings of the Philosphers* translated by Stephen Scrope from the French of Christine de Pisan and ed. C. F. Bühler, E.E.T.S., O.S. no. 211. For Worcester's claim see p. 292.

[75] *Ibid.*, frontispiece and *passim*. His corrected copy is now Emmanuel College, Cambridge, MS. I. 2. 10. The colophon to Cambridge University Library, MS. Gg. I. 34. 2 records the date of his final revision as Mar. 1473 ('the yere of Crist m¹iiij^c lxxii endyng').

[76] The *incipit* (or possibly *secundo folio*) was: 'Anno Christi MCCCCXXI et anno regni' (T. Tanner, *Bibliotheca Britannico-Hibernica sive de Scriptoribus*, p. 115).

His indebtedness to one of Fastolf's own servants may have been even greater. In 1460 John Bussard was poverty-stricken, broken in health, and very much in need of Worcester's charity.[78] In return he made himself useful to his benefactor. Bussard, wrote John Davy to John Paston,

> seyth the last tyme that he wrot onto William Wusseter it was beffor myssomer [1460], and thanne he wrot a cronekyl of Jerewsalem and the jornes that my mayster dede whyl he was in Fraunce, that God on his sowle have mercy! And he seyth that this drow more than xx whazereys off paper.[79]

It is unfortunately not clear from this whether Bussard was an informant or merely a scribe. But it looks as if the composition of the *Acta* was well advanced within a year of Fastolf's death. For another decade or more Worcester retained possession of many of his late master's military and diplomatic papers as well as some of the archives of his English estates.[80] Among these was a roll on which the secretary himself set down all the offices Fastolf held while overseas from 1412, when he became lieutenant-constable of Bordeaux, to the end of his active service in 1439 as governor of the Channel Islands. Here he is credited with the idea of founding a university at Caen; the names of the magnates he served as councillor are listed; and so too are the French castles and lordships which he won and lost.[81] To judge from this the *Acta*, however much they may have been moralized in the telling, were based on a sure foundation of fact. The use of Latin may even have served to keep them terse.

What Worcester's idea of a finished work in English was like can be gathered from the *Boke of Noblesse*. But first it is necessary to establish that that is his. As Sir George Warner long ago pointed out,[82] the clue to his authorship is to be found in his son's preface to Lambeth MS. 506, a collection of documents illustrating Bedford's

---

[77] B.M. Add. MS. 28206, fo. 19ᵛ: '—[blank] Marcij anno 38° regis Henrici secundum relacionem vxoris Thome Swayne.' There follow the notes about Fastolf's antecedents printed by G. P. Scrope, *Castle Combe*, p. 170 n. These are not, as there stated, in Worcester's autograph, but that they were copied from his memoranda is indicated by an entry in Fastolf Paper 72, m. I: 'Item die lune—[blank] die Marcij [1460, 38 Hen. VI] datum in elemosina relicta Thome Swayne non habenti denarium in bursa pro eo quod fuit quondam ancilla matris domini Johannis Fastolf—xij d.'

[78] Fastolf Paper 72, m. 2.

[79] *Paston Letters*, iii. 253-4. 'Whazereys' are presumably quires.

[80] Magd. Coll. Oxon., Norfolk and Suffolk 75; *The Boke of Noblesse*, ed. J. G. Nichols, Roxburghe Club, p. 68. He handed over what are now the Fastolf Papers in and after 1472 to Bishop Wainfleet.

regency of France.[83] This was originally addressed to Richard III, but the dedication was clumsily altered later to substitute 'Edwarde' for 'Richarde' and the word 'fourth' was put in the margin against the text's 'thred.'[84] The reader who made these corrections, if he had overlooked other difficulties, had at least noticed one that was real; for after a few paragraphs there is an unexpected reference to 'the queneys moder, dame Jaques, ducesse of Bedforde',[85] while the talk of an impending English invasion of France seems to fit the events of 1475 as it does not those of Richard III's watchful defensive.[86] But a more thorough revision would be needed to smooth out all the inconsistencies that still remain. If Edward IV was the intended recipient, then who was his 'most nobille brodyr and predecessoure'?[87] Finally the mention of 'the lordes of Fraunce of your partie obidience' seems out of place when addressed to either Edward IV or Richard III; the latest king for whom it had any aptness was Henry VI.[88] To explain this confusion we can only assume that Worcester the younger cobbled a preface originally composed by his father for presentation to Henry VI and afterwards altered by him—but not quite enough—to suit the circumstances of 1475. It is difficult to account for it in any other way.

This still leaves one further statement in need of elucidation, namely that in which the son speaks of his father as having 'compiled this boke . . . after his symple conyng after the seyng of the masters of philosophie, as Renatus Vegesius in his *Boke of Batayles*, also Julius Frontinus in his *Boke of Knightly Laboures* callid in Greke *Stratagematon* [and] a new auctoure callid the *Tree of Batayles*',[89] for the book this introduces contains absolutely nothing to fit this description. Here are no masters of philosophy and no chivalrous deeds, only financial statements, diplomatic and military instructions, lists of garrisons and retinues. It is true that these are also referred to in the dedication, but for Worcester's use of Vegetius, Frontinus, and Christine de Pisan's *Faits d'Armes et de Chevalerie*, oddly miscalled by him the 'Tree of Battles',[90] we must

[81] Fastolf Paper 69, mm. 4-7.

[82] S. Scrope, *Epistle of Othea to Hector*, ed. G. F. Warner, Roxburghe Club, pp. xliii-xlvii.

[83] Printed from fos. 2-6ᵛ by Stevenson, *op. cit.*, pp. 521-9.

[84] *Ibid*. 521.   [85] *Ibid*. 524.   [86] *Ibid*. 521-2.

[87] *Ibid*. 521.   [88] *Ibid*. 523   [89] *Ibid*. 522   .

[90] Christine de Pisan in her book made considerable use of *L'Arbre des Batailles* by Honoré Bonet (*The Book of Fayttes of Armes and of Chyualrye*, ed. A. T. P. Byles, E.E.T.S., pp. xlvi-li and 298-9; *The Tree of Battles of Honoré Bonet*, trans. G. W. Coopland, pp. 22-25). This seems to have confused Worcester.

look, as Warner directed us, to the *Boke of Noblesse*. Here the correspondence is exact.

In the form in which it has come down to us, the *Boke* resembles the preface to Lambeth 506 in that it bears traces of two successive but imperfect attempts at revision. Of these the second is the more easily detected since, unlike the rest of the manuscript, it is in Worcester's own hand.[91] Apart from some minor corrections, it involved the addition of a few long passages founded mostly on its author's recollection of Fastolf's table-talk. It was not a lengthy undertaking and there is little doubt when it was done. For in one place Worcester mentions his presentation of Fastolf's official copy of the Duke of Bedford's disciplinary ordinances of 10 December 1423 to Edward IV at London on 29 May 1475,[92] while he added the colophon 'under correccion' on the following 15 June.[93]

But there are also unmistakable signs that the manuscript which Worcester thus hurriedly revised was itself a more thorough-going revision made to suit the change of dynasty in 1461. The kinships mentioned are right for Edward IV: Richard of York is called 'youre father', Henry V and his brothers are 'cosyns germayns of youre kynne', while Henry VI is merely 'your antecessoure.'[94] On the other hand it is surprising to find Charles VII of France spoken of as 'youre grete adversarie.'[95] Then a whole series of statements read as if they had been written when the disasters that befell the English between 1449 and 1451 were still were recent and painful events.[96] Nor does the enthusiastic reference to Henry VI's French coronation, followed by a paragraph in which the king is invoked to clothe himself 'in armoure of defence ayenst youre ennemies' to recover Normandy, seem quite the most obvious or tactful way to appeal to the legitimist Edward Plantagenet.[97]

Once more it seems necessary to conclude that a book originally planned to induce Henry VI to imitate his father's policy was remodelled to attract Yorkist patronage on the eve of the war's renewal. The notice that it was Edward IV's purpose to invade France given to the parliament of October 1472 provides the obvious

---

[91] The manuscript is Brit. Mus., Royal B. xxii. The editor did not indicate that both the title and colophon were in what he calls 'the second hand', afterwards rightly identified as Worcester's by G. F. Warner (*Epistle*, p. xliv).

[92] *Boke of Noblesse*, p. 31. For Bedford's ordinances and Fastolf's commission to enforce them, see two articles by Miss B. J. H. Rowe, *E.H.R.* xlvi (1931), pp. 201-6 and 573.

[93] *Boke of Noblesse*, p. 85   [94] *Ibid.*, pp. 41, 44, and 3.

[95] *Ibid.*, p. 3   [96] *Ibid.*, pp. 5, 17, 28-29, 48, and 73.

[97] *Boke of Noblesse*, pp. 19-20.

terminus a quo for the *Boke's* first revision, at the end of which it was written out afresh by a professional scribe.[98] Then in June 1475 the newly copied manuscript received Worcester's last-minute additions before being offered to the king.[99] This impression, based on the internal evidence alone, of a treatise begun soon after 1451 and twice altered in the 1470's is strengthened, as is also the probability of Worcester's undivided authorship at every stage, by the contents of three of his notebooks now in the British Museum.[100] It is, for example, clear from one that in November and December 1453 he was making extracts from a French compendium of the histories of Orosius, Lucan, and Suetonius and from the *Quadrilogus* of Alain Chartier.[101] This not only accords well with the date at which the first draft of the *Boke* seems to have been executed, but disposes of the only serious objection to his authorship of it, namely the ill-founded belief that until 1458 he was ignorant of French.[102] These three notebooks show him at various times before 1472 digesting a number of the other 'authorities' with which the *Boke* is so liberally bespattered.[103] His reading, though it could not be described as narrowly purposeful, was a good deal less aimless than it at times appears. The special interests to which it was keyed were disconnected and numerous but not in the least ill defined. His collections prove how close one of them was to the subject-matter of the *Boke of Noblesse*. For many years, particularly between 1469 and 1472 in the libraries of Cambridge and London, he came upon and noted down examples from antiquity and recent history alike which supported its argument.[104]

[98] *Rotuli Parliamentorum*, vi. 6.

[99] Stevenson, *op. cit.*, p. 52, provides evidence that it was in fact offered.

[100] B.M., Cotton. MS. Julius F. vii, Royal MS. 13. C. i, and Sloane MS. 4.

[101] B.M., Royal MS. 13. C. i, fos. 135-46.

[102] S. Scrope, *Epistle*, pp. xlv-xlvi. This is based on a too literal interpretation of Henry Windsor's jibe (*Paston Letters*, iii. 132; 27 Aug. 1458). Warner is followed by C. F. Bühler, *Dicts and Sayings*, p. xlii, n. 2.

[103] Only a few coincidences can be noted here. The fifth book of the *Civitas Dei* is quoted in the *Boke*, p. 57; notes from it will be found on fo. 57 of Sloane 4. The *Communiloquium* of John of Wales on the virtues of a republic is cited, *Boke*, p. 57; the same passage is extracted on fos. 141-2^v of MS. Julius F. vii. Other obvious parallels will be found for the works of Tully, Ovid, and Boece.

[104] B.M. Arundel MS. 48 contains a copy of the 'Chronique de Normandie', 1414-22 (printed in *Henrici Quinti Regis Angliae Gesta*, ed. B. Williams, Eng. Hist. Soc., pp. 167-208). In Royal MS. 13 C. i are not only Worcester's notes on Roman history, but also book vii of Higden's *Polychronicon* and the so-called 'Giles's Chronicle', 1377-1455 (printed from 1399 as *Cronicon Angliae Incerti Scriptoris* by J. A. Giles). By 1459 Worcester could draw on 'Basset's Chronicle' as well as other books in Fastolf's library, among them a Livy and a Vegetius.

Lambeth 506 can now also be seen for what it is. On more than one occasion the younger Worcester speaks of it as 'this codycelle' or 'this litille codicelle.'[105] A codicil is a supplement and the use of the word becomes intelligible if the Lambeth volume—an octavo to the *Boke's* quarto—is regarded as a pendant to the other, containing its *pièces justificatives*. These, it seems, were intended to illustrate the way Normandy and the other provinces of English France were administered under the great Regent and to serve as guides in turn for Henry VI and Edward IV. They were copied in a number of different hands, mostly French, from the originals which Fastolf had accumulated during his years in Bedford's service; and they were provided with explanatory headings by Worcester himself. The existence of the originals is mentioned in the *Boke* itself;[106] from them its author chose one to hand personally to Edward IV as the king was about to cross to France in 1475. When he compiled war-history, Worcester set an example of full and accurate documentation. It was lost on his nineteenth-century editor, who made no distinction between the records themselves and their glosses.[107]

It has been less the intention of this paper to assess the quality of Worcester's *oeuvre* than to isolate what belongs to it from what does not. To have established that it should include the *Boke of Noblesse* but not the *Annales* is perhaps enough. Yet although students of literature may be right in thinking little of the *Boke*, it is no less clear that historians have neglected a work which, judged merely as a source, deserves a place beside Fortescue's *Governance of England*. Its author's point of view was very different from Fortescue's—for he blamed the peace rather than the war for the country's troubles—but his subject-matter was to some extent the same and his book, like the *Governance* and that other mid-fifteenth-century pamphlet, the *Libel of English Policy*, was meant to influence men's actions. It is a piece of vernacular polemic, the arguments in which need to be considered in any attempt to assess the effects of the Hundred Years War upon English society. This, we can surmise, is how it looked to the defeated captains and their hangers-on stranded by the loss of Normandy; here is one contribution to the debate that

---

[105] Stevenson, *op. cit.*, pp. 523, 527, and 529.　　　　　[106] *Ibid.*, p. 68
[107] These last are in Worcester's own hand. Stevenson usually prints them as if they were part of the documents, omits some of the contents altogether and in the case of one of its most important items (fos. 8-11 of Lambeth MS. 506) prefers to print a bad late translation without mentioning the existence of the fuller and more accurate original (*op. cit.*, pp. 433-8).

ended in civil war. It would be absurd to claim that the pamphleteering of either Fortescue or Worcester was of such an order as to appeal to the historian of ideas. But it is possible to think that the secretary was more perspicacious than the judge and had a better historical sense. They were, it happens, well acquainted.[108]

The *Boke of Noblesse* emphasises one other fact about Worcester's scholarship: that he read the classics as he studied modern authors, to use what they taught him. He was less interested in their manner than in their content. The ancients possessed knowledge he was anxious to learn; it never occurred to him to alter his Latin prose in imitation of theirs. This is what lovers of humanism find it impossible to forgive in him. He came into contact with the greatest stylists of old Rome, he made pages of extracts from Ovid, Cicero, and Seneca—and wrote nothing to show that he was touched by their beauties. He left it to others to ape these models; he stuck to the argument. When he commissioned a poetic lament for the death of Milicent Fastolf,[109] he was content with a piece of traditional Latinity, utterly barbarous and quite 'unaffected by modern values.'[110] His attitude was so obstinately 'medieval' that he went to the classics only for wisdom. This was what he wanted to share and to display; so he decorated even his business letters with this kind of moralising:

A very frende at nede experience will schewe be deede, as wele as be autorite of Aristotle in the *Etiques* that he made of moralite, also by the famous Reamayn Tullius in his litill booke *De Amicicia*; thangyng you for olde contynued frendschip stidffastely grounded . . .[111]

He evidently found the precepts of authority helpful.

With the *Boke of Noblesse* must be considered three other writings that have been associated with it, all translations from the French. Of the two English renderings of works by Christine de Pisan, the

---

108 Fortescue was given a bribe by Fastolf at Worcester's hands: 'Item datum in regardo cuidam Capitali Justiciarij domini Regis per Willelmum Wyrcestre seruientem Johannis Fastolf militis . . . vnam robam panni auri de crymson velwet vt dictus Judex esset plus ffauorabilis in judicio suo prefato Thome Howys quando jmprisonatus fuit in le kyngysbynche—vj li. xiij s. iiij d.' (Fastolf Paper 42, m. 4). In other entries in the account Fortescue's identity is not disguised. For Fortescue on the incorruptibility of English judges see his *De Laudibus Legum Anglie*, ed. S. B. Chrimes, p. 128 and n.
109 These *Laudes Milicente Scrope* (Fastolf's wife, who died 25 Aug. 1446) were formerly in the Phillipps Library; I have failed to trace their present whereabouts. A copy given by Sir Thomas Phillipps in 1852 to G. P. Scrope is in my possession.
110 R. Weiss, *Humanism in England during the Fifteenth Century*, p. 178.
111 *Paston Letters*, iii. 205.

Epistle of Othea to Hector and the *Dicts and Sayings of the Philosophers*, little more needs to be said. In the case of the *Dicts*, Worcester is known to have 'corrected' Scrope's translation in March 1473, because he said as much.[112] The *Epistle of Othea* which Scrope translated from an existing original written and illuminated for Fastolf in 1450[113] survives in two slightly different states, one with a long prose dedication to Fastolf, the translator's stepfather,[114] the other with some dedicatory verses to Humphrey, Duke of Buckingham.[115] There is nothing to connect Worcester with either and no manuscript has yet been found with additions identifiable as his. To make him the reviser and then 'on the basis of analogy' to give Scrope a hand, if not the chief part, in the composition of the *Boke of Noblesse* is justified by neither evidence nor logic.[116] If Worcester revised one of Scrope's books it does not follow that all books he revised, still less all the books he claims to have written, must really have been by Scrope.

That applies equally in the case of *Tullius of Olde Age*, the third of this group of English translations from the French. When Worcester himself states without qualification that what he gave Bishop Wainfleet on 10 August 1473 was 'librum Tullii *de Senectute* per me translatum in anglicis',[117] it will take more than analogy to prove him a liar. But whether it was his version that Caxton printed in 1481 as from the pen of John Tiptoft, Earl of Worcester (1427-70), is not so clear, though there are several circumstances that make it probable.[118] It was, Caxton tells us, composed at Fastolf's 'ordinance', and even if it did not strike the printer as odd that a knight could command the services of an earl it must so strike us. The terms in which the proem speaks of Fastolf are similar to those used elsewhere by his secretary and would come better from him

112 The date is 1473 and not 1472 as Mr. Bühler asserts (*Dicts*, pp. xli-xlii). That is the meaning of the phrase 'the monyth of Marche the yere of Crist m¹iiii꜀ lxxii endyng' (*ibid.* 292).

113 Bodl. Lib., MS. Laud Misc. 570. It was recognised as such by Miss Kathleen Chesney [*Medium Aevum*, i (1932), pp. 35-41].

114 Longleat MS. 253, that printed by G. F. Warner.

115 St. John's College, Cambridge, MS. 208. By 24 May 1487 it had passed into the possession of the Bramshott family (M. R. James, *Descriptive Catalogue of the MSS. of St. John's College, Cambridge*, pp. 238-40). The duke had been killed at Northampton, 10 July 1460.

116 *Dicts*, pp. xl, n. 1 and xliii.   117 *Itineraria*, p. 368.

118 Some allowance has to be made for Caxton's own revision. For his account of this see *The Prologues and Epilogues of William Caxton*, ed. W. J. B. Crotch, E.E.T.S. 44, where the proem is conveniently reprinted.

119 *Ibid.*, pp. 41-42.

than from Tiptoft;[119] and there are in places obvious parallels between the wording of the translation and that of Worcester's known works.[120] *Tullius of Olde Age* seems to be his rather than the earl's; and that may be true of its companion *Tullius of Friendship* also.[121]

Apart from a lost medical compilation mentioned by himself and a few titles of books to which no definite contents can be assigned,[122] we are now left with Worcester's two specifically antiquarian works, the *Antiquitates Anglie* in three books and the *De Agri Norfolcensis familiis antiquis*. For the first of these an *incipit* (or *secundo folio*) is known, so that the likelihood of its having once existed is great. The other is said to have belonged to the Elizabethan mathematician and book-collector, Thomas Allen (1542-1632). Allen undoubtedly possessed one of Worcester's notebooks which still contains his signature.[123] As not even the more careless reader could mistake it for an account of the landowners of Norfolk—it begins with Vergil and Ovid—Allen must have owned at least two of the antiquary's works, including what seems to have been an early example of that most English of scholarly undertakings, a county history. There is other evidence of the survival of this manuscript into the seventeenth century. For among the collections of Sir Henry Spelman which passed from Cox Macro to Hudson Gurney were some extracts made from it by the author of the *Icenia*, possibly just after Thomas Allen's death.[124] These include an interesting list of lords, knights and gentlemen of East Anglia—for *Norfolcensis* is a misleading description—who died without male issue between 1327 and 1461,

---

[120] Some of these are printed together by C. F. Bühler, *Dicts*, pp. xliii-xlv. The passage from the *Dicts* on p. xlv is largely an insertion, not in the original French nor in Scrope's translation, by Worcester's hand.

[121] Printed by Caxton with the *of Olde Age*. The fact that this was translated from the Latin and not from a French version (R. J. Mitchell, *John Tiptoft*, p. 173) does nothing to weaken the ascription to Worcester. His notes from the *de Amicitia* and Cicero's other works in MS. Julius F. vii, fos. 74 et seq., show that he worked from the Latin text.

[122] T. Tanner, *Bibliotheca*, p. 115. The 'Tabula vltimi libri Petri de Crescencijs per W. Wyrcestre compilata' is mentioned on fo. iv of Magd. Coll. Oxon. MS. 65, Worcester's copy of Walter Burley's arrangement of the *Problemata* ascribed to Aristotle.

[123] T. Tanner, *op. cit.*, p. 115.

[124] Spelman's volume was at Keswick Hall, Norwich, until 1936 (*Hist. MSS. Com., 12th Rept.*, App., pt. ix, MSS. of J. H. Gurney, p. 152). with the help of Mr. Ronald Gurney and Messrs. Quaritch I was able to trace it to Norwich Public Library (MS. 7197). The City Librarian courteously allowed it to be deposited in Bodley for my use during Trinity Term 1955. The extracts from Worcester's text occupy fos. 297-9ᵛ and 304-21. On fo. 301 is a note made 22 July 1619, on fo. 336 another, 23 Oct. 1633. These give a rough indication of the date.

the names of ten Norfolk knights who received the Garter for their services in France under the Lancastrian kings, genealogies of such families as the Warennes, Cliftons, Calthorpes, Burneys and Pastons, and notes on churches and towns. Spelman's extracts are few, but they are sufficient to prove that the original from which he copied them had at least 188 folios—and we know that Worcester's crabbed hand got much into a page.[125] The disappearance of the original is one the historian of medieval East Anglia must find hard to bear. The manufacture of bogus pedigrees had scarcely begun in Worcester's day; nor had the Reformation and William Dowsing's men between them destroyed or mutilated the hundreds of tombs in abbeys, friaries, and parish churches with inscriptions that provided him with details of family history now difficult to trace.[126] His notes, free from the hopeful fabrications of Tudor and Stuart heralds, would have been invaluable.

To judge from these surviving fragments, the manuscript of Worcester's *Ancient Families of Norfolk* was more like his other notebooks than a finished and publishable work. It seems to have contained the same lists, the same chance order and the same careful acknowledgement of his obligations. It is just possible to believe that Spelman only had access to the rough materials which Worcester afterwards worked up into a book, but this is not the most economical of hypotheses. For the present it is safer to assume that, like many another antiquary, Worcester made collections he did not live to use. Nor is this provisional conclusion without its relevance to the vexed problem of the *Antiquitates Anglie*. James Nasmith was surely wise to doubt whether this, the largest of Worcester's recorded writings, was ever finished.[127] Yet it is hard to deny all reality to something that could be described by Bale as in three books. Is not the reasonable inference that the *Itinerary*, devoted largely to the field-work of the years 1477-80, was itself a part, perhaps the last part, of Worcester's general antiquarian collections, the survivors of which were preserved after his death in three volumes? The manuscript which Spelman used may well have been a second. If so, then we need only lament the loss of it and another since Bale's day. But it is equally possible that the East Anglian collection, made as far

---

[125] Spelman noted the foliation; he took material from only 19 of 376 pages, so there may well have been many more.

[126] The reformers could not even leave brasses alone. Sheriff Toftes at Norwich is said to have pulled off more than a hundred in the cathedral alone (F. Blomefield, *Topographical History of the County of Norfolk*, iii. 389).

[127] *Itineraria*, preface, p. 3 n.

as we know in the 1460's, was additional to the general series.[128] Though he was not always successful, Worcester evidently meant to keep his various projects separate by noting their materials on different slips of paper.[129]

In scaling down the amount of Worcester's output, both known and inferable, my purpose has not been to belittle his work. If all he had done was to fill a handful of notebooks, that would still be remarkable on more than one count, of which the least weighty perhaps is the value of their contents to us; yet that is great indeed. It is rather for what they reveal of the man, his accomplishments, his tastes, his methods, that they deserve the closest attention. His times are not known to have had so many like him that he can be airily dismissed as a mere antiquary, 'a dilettante without qualifications for scholarship.'[130] Scholarship is of many kinds, some more and some less humane. That the things Worcester did were being done at all is itself significant.

But in appraising these *reliquiae*, it is well to be clear about their nature. They were intended for one eye only, their writer's. To blame them because they display 'no literary skill' is to apply a false criterion.[131] Few of us would care to be judged posthumously by the evidence of our notebooks alone, least of all for our prose style. Worcester chose to keep his private memoranda in Latin, though he sometimes made use of French or English. In all three languages he wrote to record intelligibly what he had seen, read, measured, heard. It is not usual to demand elegance in other antiquaries; Worcester should be rated by the standards we apply to them. His notebooks are close-packed, repetitive, hard for the uninitiated to follow; so are many of theirs. As often happens when the mind is intent on the thing said rather than the saying of it, he achieved a rough prose fit to its purpose. It was not Ciceronian, but a bastard got by English on Latin—and none the less healthy for that. Accountant's Latin rather

---

[128] All Spelman's extracts are dated between 1462 and 1467 except one which belongs to 1449. But Bale does not mention a separate work on the Norfolk families.

[129] Worcester ordinarily used sheets of paper, roughly 12¼ × 8½ in., folded in two down the longer edge. These seem to have been kept loose. Tall narrow books made from them survive as B.M. Add. MS 28208 (Castle Combe), Julius F. vii (Latin classics, &c.), Sloane 4 (medical), and Corpus Christi College, Cambridge, MS. 210 (the *Itinerary*). There are some loose sheets among Magd. Coll. Oxon. muniments. Their general appearance can be gathered from T. D. Kendrick, *British Antiquity*, pl. v. Sometimes, where a passage dealing with one subject has been misplaced among notes for another, it is crossed out (e.g. Sloane 4, fo. 57), but by no means always.

[130] R. Weiss, *Humanism*, p. 178.

[131] J. Tait, *D.N.B.*, s.n. Worcester.

than the Latin of the cloister and the schools, it had still less in common with the language of the sedulous, backward-looking humanists. Utilitarian and serviceable, it has had the misfortune to be condemned on theories the very opposite of its own.

Judged as a seeker after knowledge, Worcester can be most easily faulted for eclecticism. His undisciplined curiosity, though not all-embracing, neglected little. His interest in heraldry was a good deal milder than Friar Brackley's, for he left us no roll or book of arms. But he consorted with heralds and fully understood how their science could establish a pedigree or identify a tomb. Astronomy was, it seems, his first love; a table of 1022 fixed stars, 'verified' by him to 1440 at the command of Sir John Fastolf, demonstrates what he could do in that line.[132] His deep and prolonged concern with medicine is amply attested by a mass of notes made in various years from 1459 to 1478. As usual, they were derived from many sources, from books, from doctors and barbers, and from the recorded 'experiences' of sufferers.[133] Sloane MS. 4 contains rich materials for a study of the theory and practice of healing in the reign of Edward IV. The names of several medical treatises that belonged to Worcester are known.[134] His travels gave him a taste for the geography and natural history of Britain. He was always listing its islands, its rivers, its distances, its roads and its bridges. He mentions the puffins on Scilly, the gannets, sea-mews, and cormorants elsewhere.[135] But his curiosity did not stop short with Britain, and when someone who had served Henry IV's daughter Philippa in Denmark told him about that country, he wrote it down.[136] He was in Bristol in September 1480 to hear the news that a ship belonging to one of his kinsmen had been driven into an Irish port after nine weeks out in the Atlantic looking for the island of Brazil; the skipper was, he notes, 'scientificus marinarius tocius Anglie.'[137] And once again his interest is traceable in his reading: he owned a copy of

---

[132] Bodl. Lib., MS. Laud Misc. 674, fos. 81-99ᵛ. They were 'verificate . . . secundum tabulas Alfonsi et erudicionem fratris Radulphi Hoby professoris theologie ac disciplinam librorum fratris Johannis Somour ordinis minorum videlicet vtrique eorum'. The acknowledgements are typical of Worcester.

[133] B.M., MS. Sloane 4, *passim*.

[134] New College, Oxford, MS. 162 contains a number of texts by Arnold de Villanova and others. As noted above, p. 219, Worcester had Burley's *Problemata* of Aristotle and another medical compilation.

[135] *Itineraria*, pp. 98, 111, and 154.

[136] *Ibid*. pp. 315-16.

[137] *Ibid.*, pp. 267-8 and J. A. Williamson, *The Voyages of the Cabots and the Discovery of North America*, pp. 18-19.

Cristoforo Buondelmonte's book on the isles of Greece and used a fact he found in it about Crete to annotate another of his manuscripts, Poggio's translation of the *Historical Library* of Diodorus Siculus.[138] His own attempt to learn Greek under the tuition of William Selling of Canterbury was not pursued far.[139] He was hopeful enough to buy a volume containing three plays each by Sophocles and Euripides together with some Hesiod, Pindar, and Theocritus, but for once there is no mark to show that he ever read any of it.[140] Of Hebrew he at least acquired the alphabet;[141] and he liked to know—and not to be too serious about—the British equivalents of English place-names.[142] Even if he did not invent the science of palaeography, he grasped, however dimly, the fact that a manuscript could be dated by its handwriting.[143]

Thanks to Nasmith's early publication of the *Itinerary*, the rough measure of Worcester as a traveller, ecclesiologist, and user of libraries has long been taken, though his manuscripts have still much to tell us about the range of his scholarship. His most remarkable piece of topographical field-work—the detailed account of the streets, churches, and houses of his native Bristol—has not yet found the editor it deserves. While Leland was for the most part content with a perfunctory reference to 'praty, thriving, up country touns', the author of the description of Bristol was a long-unrivalled pioneer. For that reason alone, it is unfair to dismiss the *Itinerary* as 'interesting if only as an anticipation of Leland's greater work.'[144] Worcester was as keen a student of churches and family history as the great antiquaries of the seventeenth century; but he was perhaps keener than most of them about baronial finance, how much one castle had cost to build, another to buy; what Ralph Cromwell's

---

138 Balliol College, Oxford, MS. 124, fo. 242ᵛ. This manuscript which Worcester acquired from the library of John Free (ob. 1465) also contains a *Cosmographia mundi* derived from the *Natural History* of the elder Pliny. Both it and the Diodorus bare considerable traces of Worcester's study.
139 Some Greek sentences dated 16 Aug. 1471 appear in Julius F. vii, fo. 123. See also *ibid.*, fos. 118 and 205.
140 Bodl. Lib. MS. Auct. F. 3. 25. This also was bought from Free's library.
141 B.M., Cotton, MS. Julius F. vii, fos. 121-2ᵛ. On 31 Aug. 1471 Worcester made some notes from a Hebrew psalter at Peterhouse, Cambridge.
142 *Ibid.*, fo. 64. Cf. *Paston Letters*, iii, 118-19.
143 Bodl. Lib., MS. Laud Misc. 674, fo. 29ᵛ: 'Explicit hec medicina scripta per W. Wyrcestre dictus Botoner de quadam valde antiqua manu veluti per centum annos preteritos scriptos et plus, hic intitulata die Martis—[blank] die Junij anno Christi 1463 in via de Pokethorp Norwico civitate prope scita est.' Note also Julius F. vii, fo. 113: 'habui copiam huius tabule de quodam antiquo libro in manu romanorum scripto veluti manus bullarum papalium.'

annual expenses were and how many men he had in household;[145] what Sir Andrew Ogard made out of the French war and how he spent it;[146] and the amount of Sir William Oldhall's outlay on Hunsdon House.[147] These were questions few scholars were to ask until the evidence for answering them had been destroyed. It was fortunate that Worcester rated contemporary history quite as highly as the remote past. We still depend for much of our knowledge of the Regent Bedford's household and finances on the collections he made which bibliophils like Parker and Allen came just in time to save. There may be yet another survival for which we should thank Worcester. The group of people with whom he lived was, as far as we know, the first to keep its private correspondence on a scale which neither untidiness or accident can explain. The *Paston Letters* themselves may be the indirect outcome of an antiquary's passion for the sources.

So, in the unquiet England of Lancaster and York, when the roads were often unsafe for the peaceful traveller, did a busy estate official employ his scanty leisure. That in itself may prevent us from exaggerating the dislocation caused by civil war. But it should also leave us in no doubt about the 'medieval' origins of English historical scholarship as it is followed still. However much it may have been influenced by humanism, it traces its direct ancestry back through generations of dry-as-dusts to a fifteenth-century amateur who remained obstinately 'unaffected by modern values' and had none too nice an ear.[148]

---

[144] *D.N.B.*, s.n. Worcester
[146] *Ibid.*, pp. 86-88.
[145] *Itineraria*, pp. 162-3
[148] *Ibid.*, pp. 88-89.

[148] In addition to the help already acknowledged in previous notes, I am indebted to my colleagues Messrs. C. G. Hardie, N. R. Ker, A. Gill and, above all, C. T. Onions for their willingness to assist me with their advice on many points.

XI. WILLIAM WORCESTER AND A PRESENT OF LAMPREYS

AMONG a number of schedules attached to one of the ministers' accounts for the manor of Oxenton in Gloucestershire, recently acquired by the Records Office of that country, is a letter from the author and antiquary William Worcester.[1] The manor, dependent upon that of Castle Combe in Wiltshire and part of the inheritance of Milicent Tiptoft, came into the possession of her second husband John Fastolf of Caister at their marriage on 13 January, 1409. It continued to be enjoyed by him, despite a settlement to the contrary, until his death on 6 November, 1459, when it passed to Stephen Scrope, Milicent's eldest son and heir by her first husband.[2]

Worcester's letter, which is in his unmistakable autograph, is merely dated 16 March, but it is clear from the account to which it is annexed that the year was 1456. Its writer had then been for about twenty years surveyor of Fastolf's lordship of Castle Combe and although busily employed about his master's affairs elsewhere he was from time to time able to visit his charge and to keep a watchful eye on the activities and inactivities of its resident ministers.[3] If Fastolf derived great benefit from this part of his wife's inheritance, it was thanks in large measure to Worcester's vigilance.[4] More than one volume of genealogical notes, summaries of accounts, extracts from court-rolls and other memoranda bear witness to the industry with

---

[1] The Oxenton accounts formed part of the muniments of the Southern estate belonging to the Law family [Edward Law, 2nd Lord Ellenborough, governor-general of India 1841-44, was created viscount Southam of Southam, co. Gloucester, and earl of Ellenborough in 1844. He died at Southam in 1871 (G.E.C. *Complete Peerage*, V, ed. V. Gibbs and H. A. Doubleday, 52-3). There is a monument to him on the wall of the north aisle of Oxenton church]. They came to the Records Office through the British Records Association. I am grateful to my friend Mr Alec Gaydon for bringing the existence of these documents to my notice and for other help. I must also thank the Records Officer, Mr Irvine E. Gray, for allowing me to examine them before repair and for providing me with a photostat of the letter printed below.

[2] G. Poulett Scrope *History of the Manor and Ancient Barony of Castle Combe* pp. 169-287. The settlement of Milicent's inheritance by fine in Trinity term 14 Richard II is described on pp. 144-5.

[3] Apart from a number of knights' fees, by that time nearly worthless, the lordship of Castle Combe consisted in the fifteenth century of the manors of Castle Combe, Oxenton and Bathampton Wylye and the advowson of Castle Combe. For some account of Worcester's other employments in Fastolf's last years (see above, pp. 199-224, or above Chapter X).

which the surveyor carried out his duties.[5] The view of account to which his letter was sewn is in his hand as is also one of the four other schedules.[6] Thomas Wattys, reeve of Oxenton, was the accountant; the view was that for the year beginning at Michaelmas 1455.[7]

Worcester wrote as follows:[8]

Welbelovyd frendys, I grete yow well and lete yow wete that I have spoke wyth my lord bysshop of Worcestre[9] chauncellor that the processe and cause that the aumoner of Towkysbury hath ayenst yow myght be contynewed tille Mydsomer or Myghellmasse next commyng; so that yn the mene tyme the materes that ye be troubled for may be examyned and determyned here in London by indyfferent lerned men chosen by agreement of the aumoner and of my lord ys councell.[10] And my seyd lord ys chauncellor seyth he wolle comyn wyth the aumoner and meove hym to do soo. And by thys wey it shall be leest cost and trouble cesed. But ye most doo sende a remembraunce yn wrytyng to London of all all [sic] your ryght and the customs of the contree deuly approuued. My lord[11] myght trouble the abbot of Tewkysbury more than the aumoner wenyth yff he would. More ouer I have remembred my lord to geve a chesyple to your chyrch because ye be febly purveyed, and trust for certeyn ye shall have one. And ye shuld hafe had a coope also safe for the trouble that your parson makyth ayenst yow. And y have a cloth of sylk redye delyvered me for yow and shall put it to makyng. And ye, Thomas Wattes, that ye sende to Castelcombe xij goode lampreys poudred at the price of xxd. the pece. And they[12] of Castlecombe[12]

---

[4] The importance of Castle Combe in the knight's economy is brought out by E. Carus Wilson 'Evidence of Industrial Growth on some Fifteenth-century Manors', *Economic History Review*, 2nd series XII 190-205.

[5] B.M. Add MS. 28208 is Worcester's main Castle Combe notebook. Other memoranda will be found in Add. MS. 28212. Those in Add. MS. 28206, though not in his hand and perhaps copied at a slightly later date, can be shown to have been derived from lost notes made by him.

[6] See below, p. 230 n. 30.

[7] Although once called bailiff by Worcester (see p 230 n. 30) he is described as *prepositus* at the head of his account.

[8] The punctuation and capitals are mine, and I have extended all obvious abbreviations.

[9] MS.: 'Worcestr.' There is no sign of the possessive though the next sentence in the letter makes it clear that one is understood.

[10] This may refer to the bishop of Worcester's counsel but it seems more probable that Fastolf's is intended.

[11] Here and hereafter 'my lord' is certainly Fastolf.

[12-12] Interlineations in Worcester's own hand.

shall send hem to London. And foryete not a couple gode lampreys for my labour yn recuveryng the vij li. that ye had allmoste lost of my lordys monney—for ye know well the baylly had spend it awey—and let my lampreys com with the othyr lampreys. And yff the propters[13] of your chyrch sende me mo lampreys[12] for me and my felowys[12] y shall the better thynk uppon your vestment. Recommaund me to maister Moreyn and let hym see thys lettre. God kepe yow. Wryt at London the xvj day of March.

By William Worcestre.

[Endorsed:] To Herry Hallwey off Castelcombe to do sende thys lettre to Oxondon by Thomas Hakburn.[14]

It will be seen that the letter's address is somewhat vague. The intended recipients may have been Fastolf's servants at Oxenton or they and his tenants there. It is clear that Thomas Wattys was one of Worcester's worshipful friends and almost equally certain that Master Moreyn was not.[15] Apart from them the only official in the manor whose name is known to us was its steward William Nottingham.[16] Henry Hallwey, whose duty it was to forward the letter, was the eldest son of Richard and Agnes Hallwey, well-to-do customary tenants in Castle Combe.[17] He became bailiff there in succession to John Laurens, who is mentioned in Worcester's letter,

13 The word is clearly: *propters*. It has been suggested to me that Worcester meant to write *prepositus*, meaning the church reeve or warden. But this interpretation involves not only a slip of the pen but also the use of a Latin word in an English sentence where reeve would have been more natural. Although no example so early has been recorded, I am inclined to think that Worcester had in mind some such word as proprietor, impropriator or appropriator and was referring ironically to the monastic patron of Oxenton. It is worth noticing that on his brass in Eastbourne Church, Sussex, Mr John King, treasurer of Chichester Cathedral and therefore rector of Eastbourne (ob. 10 January 1445/6), is described as 'istius ecclesie proprietarius' (C.E.D. Davidson-Houston 'Sussex Monumental Brasses' *Sussex Archaeological Collections* lxxvi (1936) 161). Parishioners would undoubtedly fit the sense best in the absence of irony.

14 The letter which is on paper has been sealed. The marks of folding, the slits for the thread and traces of wax remain.

15 Wattys's account records the payments of 13*s*. 4*d*. 'in feodo Willelmi Moreyn de consilio domini existente auditore [*sic*] ibidem [i.e. at Oxenton] ac superuidendo dictum manerium.' Wattys was also allowed 2*s*. 'pro custibus & expensis Willelmi Wyrcestre morandi cum Willelmo Morrun apud Tewkysbury super scripturam compotis & apud Oxondon per ij noctes.' The view, drafted and much corrected by Worcester, is holed and stained by damp. But I am reasonably certain that my transcripts from it here and below are accurate.

16 Wattys paid him his annual fee of 26*s*. 8*d*.

17 The Hallweys are frequently mentioned in G. Poulett Scrope *op. cit.* pp. 207-49. For Richard Hallwey's will (he died 1454) a villein's will proved apparently in his lord's court, see *ibid.* pp. 210-11.

between 15 March and 26 August that year.[18] The messenger, Thomas Hakeborn, also of Castle Combe, describes himself elsewhere as Fastolf's 'pore tenaunt and a seruaunt at all tymys.'[19]

Worcester deals with four topics, three of which require—and by good fortune can for once be given—some elucidation from other sources. Only the matter of the powdered lampreys speaks for itself.[20] It adds a new and vivid, if hardly unexpected, touch to the self-portrait of their author which his many surviving notebooks and correspondence have provided for us. But the dispute with Tewkesbury abbey, the embellishment of Oxenton church and the recovery of £7 of Fastolf's money are referred to without the writer's feeling any need to mention details with which he knew the recipients of his letter were already familiar. We lack their advantage.

The first and most important of these was 'the process and cause' that the almoner of the nearby abbey of Tewkesbury was said to have brought against the men of Oxenton. The parish church was a chapel of which the abbot and convent were the proprietors and the curate who served it was appointed and paid by the monks.[21] The abbey also held a manor in the village. This and the tithe payable by all the inhabitants were assigned to the almoner's obedience.[22] It appears that Fastolf's tenants, actively supported by their lord, were disputing the amount of tithe demanded of them.[23] Proceedings had therefore been taken against them by the almoner in the court of the bishop of Worcester their diocesan, at that time John Carpenter.[24] The decision to press for its reference to the arbitration of 'indifferent learned men' chosen by both parties would seem to indicate that the defendants and their legal advisers were none too sure of success *in curia spiritualitatis* or elsewhere. On the other hand Carpenter's chancellor, Mr William Vance, with whom Worcester

---

[18] Magdalen College, Oxford, Fastolf Paper 51 ['Onus Cristofori Hanson collectoris reddituum, firmarum & denariorum forincecorum Johannis Fastolf militis', Easter (21 April) 1454—Christmas 1456] mm. 3 and 5.

[19] G. Poulett Scrope *op. cit.* pp. 212 and 243. The quotation is from a letter from Hakeborn to Fastolf (Magd. Coll. Oxf., Lovell Paper 18). Hakeborn was the common mediaeval spelling of Hagbourne, co. Berks.　　[20] Powdered = salted or cured.

[21] *Valor Ecclesiasticus* (Record Com.) II 443 and 483; W. Dugdale *Monasticon Anglicanum* ed. J. Cary, H. Ellis and B. Bandinel II 84-5.　　[22] *Valor Eccles.* II 483.

[23] See the following entry in Wattys's account: 'Et eidem computanti viij s. pro expensis & custubus trium viagiorum de Oxendon vsque Londoniam ad loquendum cum concilio domini [i.e. Fastolf] super defensione placiti abbatis & elemosinarij de Tewkysburye prosequendo tenentes domini in curia spiritualitatis jniuriose pro certis decimis illiciter petitis.'

[24] Bishop 1444-76. For him see A. B. Emden *A Biographical Register of the University of Oxford to A.D.* 1500 I 360-1.

discussed the case in London, evidently struck him as favouring an arbitrated settlement.[25] But in the last resort more reliance was placed in the comfortable knowledge that Fastolf 'might trouble the abbot of Tewkesbury more than the almoner weaneth if he would.'[26] The outcome of the dispute is not recorded nor 'the customs of the country' regarding the payment of tithe.[27]

When Worcester told his correspondents that he had reminded their master to give a chasuble to Oxenton church and added that 'ye should have had a cope also save for the trouble that your parson maketh against you', it is not obvious why the parishioners were to suffer for their priest's hostility. Perhaps the dispute had already cost Fastolf too much money. But it is interesting to find a distant landlord going to some expense to adorn a building in which he can have had no intimate concern and which he can have visited rarely. Wattys's account provides further evidence of his employer's benevolent interest in this remote church and the fortunes of its worshippers. The reeve was allowed half a mark 'of the lord's grace and alms' to help the men of Oxenton to buy a cross of copper gilt and an alabaster table carved with the figures of the Baptist, to whom the church was dedicated, and the 'Salutation'.[28] If they were 'feebly purveyed' before, something was being done to assist them to remedy their condition.

There remains the matter of the £7 of 'my lord's money' in danger of being lost by Wattys's negligence and recovered by Worcester's intervention. The bailiff of Castle Combe who 'had spent it away' was John Laurens, as a partly illegible entry in the reeve's account

---

[25] Vance, archdeacon of Worcester since 19 October 1452 (Worcestershire Record Office, Register of John Carpenter, fo. 104) was appointed the bishop's chancellor on 7 January 1454 (*ibid.* fo. 124). He was still in office on 7 May 1460 (*ibid.* fo. 154). Since he is omitted from Dr. Emden's *Register*, it seems likely that he was a Cambridge graduate.

[26] The identity of the abbot seems doubtful. On 14 August 1450 it was John Abingdon (Reg. Carpenter fo. 87); on 2 May 1460 it was John——(blank; *ibid.* fo. 154); on 2 July 1462 it was John Gales (*ibid.* fo. 172v). The theory that John Abingdon and John Gales were identical (*V.C.H. Gloucestershire* II 65 n, 11) is supported by the absence from Carpenter's register of any confirmation of Gale's election. The confirmation of that of his successor John Strensham, 12 October 1468, is on fo. 230. I have failed to discover the name of the almoner.

[27] Neither Carpenter's register, which is noticeably well-kept, nor that of the metropolitan (*Registrum Thome Bourgchier Cantuariensis Archiepiscopi, A.D. 1454-1486* ed. F. R. H. du Boulay, C. & Y.S.) records the process.

[28] 'Er allocantur eidem [i.e. Wattys] vjs. viij d. de gracia & elemosina domini ad auxiliandum tenentes domini super empcione crucis cupri deaurati et tabule sculpte de alablastro de inhonore sancti Johannis Baptiste et salutacionis [*sic*] beate Marie pro ecclesia parochiali sancti Johannis Baptiste in Oxendon.'

makes clear. Wattys and Worcester went together to Castle Combe to 'prove' that the money had been delivered to Laurens, a fact he denied. Their expedition was successful.[29] The replacement of the unreliable bailiff by Henry Hallwey followed, probably as a result. This journey by the surveyor and reeve must have taken place during the visit paid by Worcester to Oxenton in the last week of February 1456.[30] It was on his return to London immediately after that he wrote the letter Wattys preserved. His meeting with William Moryn at Tewkesbury for the writing up of the account may just possibly have occurred then also, but some time after Michaelmas would seem more appropriate.[31] If so it was his second journey into the west country that year.[32] What this group of documents brings out clearly is that his surveyorship was very far from being a sinecure. Even when senility caused Sir John Fastolf to lean more and more heavily on his secretary, when Dame Milicent's Yorkshire lands were thought to be falling prey to unscrupulous neighbours and negligent ministers, and Queen Margaret was preparing to overthrow the duke of York, Worcester crossed England and back at least once in his ungrateful master's service.[33] If he welcomed the chance it gave him to escape from Fastolf's querulousness and to revisit the friends and haunts of his youth, he did not scamp his tasks.

[29] 'Et eidem [i.e. Wattys] ij s. super expensis dicti computantis vsque Castelcombe eundis cum Willelmo Wyrcestre ad probandum deliberacionem vij li. de argento domini Johanni Laurens nuper balliuo de Castelcombe liberatorum ad portandum domino eo quod dictus Johannes Laurens negauit dictum receptum.' Christopher Hanson's account (see above, p. 228, n. 18) records the receipt 'de Johanne Laurens balliuo de Castelcombe per manus Galfridi Ewer xv die Marcij anno xxxiiij^{to} Regis [Hen. VI, i.e. 1456], vnde iiij li.per manus Galfridi Ewer & lx s. per manus Henrici Hallwey—vij li.' (m. 3).

[30] A schedule written by Worcester and attached to Wattys's account fixes the date: 'Exspenditur per W. Worcestre diebus dominica & lune jn secunda septimana xl ^{me} [22 and 23 February 1456] cum Thoma Wattes balliuo [*sic*] de Oxondon equitando cum argento domini vsque Castelcombe cum tribus equis—xxd.' The account itself states that this was 'tempore superuisionis manerij' and that Worcester examined the account with the auditor. Hanson, in his account (m. 3) records the receipt of £17 from Wattys on 7 March 1456. At the foot of Wattys's account is this: 'Inde allocantur eidem [i.e. Wattys] xls. quos liberauit Willelmo Worcestre seruienti domini super compotum.'

[31] For this meeting see above p. 227, n. 15. The passages quoted in the last footnote may indicate that it took place at the view in February.

[32] There are very few letters from Worcester that can be surely dated to 1456, but in one that was almost certainly written on 27 January that year he looks forward to visiting the 'west country' soon (*The Paston Letters* ed. J. Gairdner (1904) III 72) and on 12 February he was being sent from Caister to London by Fastolf (*ibid*. III 76).

[33] For evidence of anxiety about the condition of the manor of Bentley at this time see *ibid*. III 72. 90-1 and 129.

THE broken sequence of battles, murders, executions, and armed clashes between neighbours which we have chosen to miscall the Wars of the Roses has long made the second half of the fifteenth century in England repulsive to all but the strongest-stomached. Had it not been for the early discovery of some two or three collections of private letters, the whole period might have fallen with some show of justice under the reproach of utter inhumanity. As it is, the homely details preserved in the familiar correspondence of Pastons, Stonors, and their like may have been allowed to excuse too much. For they have suggested the consoling but possibly mistaken notion that while great lords were busy exterminating one another, lesser men, though enduring much at the hands of their betters, stood to some extent outside and below the conflict so that, unlike their betters, they were able to survive. And what is more deserved to survive, however humble their merits, because at least they were not monsters.

It might have been otherwise had we the private letters of but one ducal, comital, or even mere baronial family, what its members wrote to one another and to their friends. The magnates certainly sent and received letters in vast quantities, as their accounts prove. They may have been too wary to open their hearts often on paper where matters of state were at issue, but there were many other subjects on which circumspection was unnecessary. The letters which passed between Richard Nevill, Earl of Warwick, and his countess during their frequent separations are unlikely to have been less revealing than the correspondence of John and Margaret Paston. The mere accident of preservation has thus helped to establish and maintain the belief that the suicidal rancours which engulfed the old royal house, the ancient nobility, and such others from feed-men to misguided commons as allowed themselves to be drawn in, left the mass of the people indifferent to their senseless quarrels, and impatient only for the coming of a strong ruler who would see justice done on all lawbreakers. The participation of the non-noble in the Wars of the Roses, save as hirelings, conscripts, or dupes is rarely allowed for, despite a strange partiality for chroniclers' estimates of the size of armies.

At the same time the motives and aims of the baronial contestants for want of their intimate letters have been so simplified and generalized that, soaked though they clearly were in innocent and guilty blood, they nevertheless remain bloodlessly unreal to us. Sir John Fastolf in his querulous old age is almost as living a figure today as

Shakespeare's fat knight; not so Richard Plantagenet, Fastolf's last of
many masters, who only speaks to the historian in his political mani-
festoes. The thoughts of Margaret of Anjou are less easy to read than
those of Margaret Mautby. A mere handful of private letters enables
us to feel that we know Thomas Mull and Thomas Betson as we do
not have a chance of knowing Thomas Percy or Thomas Nevill or
Thomas Grey. The features of the principal actors are so obliterated
by what Horace Walpole lovingly called 'the true rust of the Barons'
wars' that it is hardly possible to distinguish one from another. Instead
of individual barons we are in danger of seeing only the representative
baron; and since the average man must be a dead man he can tell us no
tales. Yet though at this distance the members of the nobility are apt to
look alike they differed widely for all their common stock of
traditions, tastes, and prejudices, in native intelligence, practical
experience, and ability to learn from their own and other people's
mistakes. The thirteenth Vere earl of Oxford is no more likely to have
resembled the ninth Fitzalan earl of Arundel than did the fifth
Primrose earl of Rosebery the ninth Cecil earl (and third marquess) of
Salisbury. To lump the former pair and their contemporaries together
as feudal reactionaries or even as kites and crows without trying to
understand why each behaved as he did is to make a doubtful virtue
out of what has not yet been proved a necessity.[1] Badly served as we
may be by both chroniclers and public records, differences can be
traced. There can be little room for particulars in such a discourse as
this, but the diversities of its members must never be forgotten in
generalizations about the class.

The drying-up about 1450 of many familiar sources is only half the
problem. It was accompanied by the virtual disappearance within a
decade of another type of evidence, hitherto not much used by
scholars, which would have been of particular value for the troubled
years of civil war. In the first half of the century the financial and
other records accumulated by landed families, both great and small,

---

[1] The reference to a belief in 'feudal reactionaries' may seem to flog a dead horse.
But the horse was still alive eleven days after this lecture was read. Dr. J. H. Plumb,
reviewing Dr. Neville Williams's life of Thomas 4th duke of Norfolk (1538-72),
described the Howards as 'feudal dinosaurs, doomed to distinction.' Were it not clear
from the context (*The Sunday Times*, 8 Mar. 1964) that the last word was misprinted,
this might be taken for wit. Less than a century before the 4th duke's birth the
Howards were middling Suffolk gentry. Before the unforeseen consequences of an
earlier marriage raised them to ducal wealth they entered the peerage as servants of
Edward IV, in that resembling the Tudor 'nobility of service.' Again, unlike dinosaurs
they evolved and survived only slightly behind the times into our own day. It is vain to
flog a dead horse, vainer to flog a dead dinosaur.

give promise of increasing abundance. Then for no apparent reason scarcity sets in. It is not obvious why the muniments of the Nevill earls of Salisbury and Warwick are less well preserved than those of their Montagu and Beauchamp forebears. Nor is it easy to understand why those of Richard duke of York failed to pass, reasonably intact, into the safe-keeping of the crown after 1461. Perhaps they did and perished later. Their few scattered remains leave us in no doubt of their capacity to lighten our darkness. It seems that most of them are now past praying for. Yet without them and their like only a superficial narrative of the war is possible; and without a narrative any analysis we attempt must be limited also.

In the 1450's not all these lamps had been extinguished. From York's few accounts and those of two branches of the widely ramified Stafford family we are allowed to catch a few glimpses of the political manoeuvring and warlike preparation which led up to the first clash at St. Albans. The *Paston Letters* have long familiarised us with York's efforts to influence the choice of members of parliament for East Anglia immediately after his return from Ireland in the late summer of 1450.[2] An account belonging to one of his receivers shows that the same policy was actively pursued elsewhere. At or soon after Michaelmas the duke's auditor was dispatched to solicit the good offices of

---

[2] *Paston Letters*, ed. J. Gairdner (Library edn., 1904), vol. ii, pp. 184-5;

[3] 'Et in expensis dicti auditoris equitantis de loco suo in comitatu Oxon' vsque Milton & Haryngworth in comitatu North' ad loquendum cum domino la Souche & Henrico Greene necnon vsque locum Johannis Vaux & deinde vsque Mynster Lovell in comitatu Oxon' pro colloquio habendo cum Willelmo domino de Lovell mandato domini pro suis amiciciis habendis in ellecione militum comitatus in eisdem comitatibus hoc anno' (British Museum, Egerton Roll 8783, m. 3: account of the duke's receiver, cos. Somerset and Dorset, for the year ending Michaelmas 1450). The previous entries refer to the audit at the end of the year. The auditor was Thomas Willoughby of Wardington, Oxon. (*Calendar of Close Rolls, 1447-54*, p. 431). He was receiver cos. Wilts. and Glos. on 24 June 1432 (B.M. Eg. Roll 8774) and had become auditor by 10 Jan. 1439 (Westminster Abbey Muniment 12168, m. 1 dorse). He was still auditor in 1452-3 (B.M. Eg. Roll 8784, m. 2), by which time he had become treasurer of the duke's household (*ibid.*, m. 3 and 8365 dorse). On 3 December 1453 he was appointed king's escheator cos. Northants and Rutland (*Calendar of Fine Rolls*, vol. xix, p. 74). On 21 Feb. 1455 the hundred of Fawsley, Northants, was farmed by him for ten years (*ibid.*, p. 121). There is as far as I know no other evidence that either William lord Zouche (*c.* 1402-1462) or William lord Lovel (1397-1455) was a supporter of the Duke of York. Lovel's son and heir was with Henry VI at Ludford in 1459 (*Calendar of Patent Rolls, 1452-1461*, pp. 534-5). Henry Green is presumably he of Drayton, Northants, grandson of Richard II's servant and described in 1450 as the king's esquire (*Rotuli Parliamentorum*, vol. v, p. 195*b*). I can find no John Vaux *c.* 1450, apart from a townsman of Leicester (*Cal. Close Rolls, 1447-54*, p. 422). It seems probable that William Vaux of Harrowden, sheriff of Northants. 1449-50 (*History of Parliament, 1439-1509, Biographies*, ed. J. Wedgwood, p. 904), is intended. He too had no obvious ties with York.

lords Zouche and Lovel, of Henry Green and John Vaux for the election of knights of the shire in the counties of Northampton and Oxford.[3] To judge from the names of those returned these efforts were at most only half successful.[4] Nevertheless York had every reason to be pleased with the support given him by the commons when parliament met.[5] What robbed him of victory was rather the size and number of the armed retinues ranged against him.[6]

Already in the spring of that year, well before Cade's men had appeared at Blackheath, the outlook seemed to Humphrey duke of Buckingham so threatening that he caused some seventy-odd yeomen to be brought by the officials of his Stafford circuit to 'await upon'

---

[4] None of the four shire-knights was a certain supporter of York in 1450. Sir Robert Harcourt of Stanton Harcourt, Oxon., and Ellenhall, Staffs., may have been one by 1459 (*Rot. Parl.*, vol. v, p. 368*b*). Thomas Mulsho of Newton and Geddington, Northants, was a near kinsman of Sir Edmund Mulsho, York's councillor, but I can find no evidence connecting Thomas with the duke or his service. Edmund Reade of Boarstall, Bucks., and Checkendon, Oxon., was a lawyer and was described in 1447 as a king's servant (*Cal. Pat. Rolls, 1446-1452*, p. 81). Thomas Seyton of Maidwell, Northants, had no known affinity and seems to have been of little importance.

[5] His undoubted dependents in the commons were (i) the speaker Sir William Oldhall, his chamberlain since at least 1444 (J. S. Roskell, 'Sir William Oldhall, Speaker in the Parliament of 1450-1', *Nottingham Mediaeval Studies.*, vol. v (1961), pp. 97-98); (ii) Sir John Barre, and (iii) Sir Walter Devereux, each of whom was in receipt of an annuity of £20 from the duke in 1442-3 (Public Record Office, S.C. 11/818, m. 7); and (iv) Sir Edmund Mulsho to whom the duke had granted lands at Thaxted, Essex, for life by 1447-8 (Westmin. Abbey Muniment 12165, m. 9 dorse). All these witnessed York's charter to the friars of Babwell, dated Bury St. Edmunds 28 Feb. 1447 (*Cat. Pat. Rolls, 1446-1452*, p. 231). To them can be added (v) William Browning, senior, of Melbury Sampford, Dorset, who had been the duke's receiver for Somerset and Dorset since at least 1436-7 (B.M. Eg. Rolls 8781 and 8783-5) and surveyor there for life from 27 May 1449 (*ibid.*, 8783-4). He was still receiver at the duke's attainder and was continued in office by Henry VI (*Cal. Pat. Rolls, 1452-1461*, p. 592). On the strength of this last entry Wedgwood (*op. cit.*, p. 125) chooses to describe him as 'obviously a good Lancastrian.' His effigy in Melbury Sampford church wears the collar of suns and roses with the lion of March as pendant (*Royal Commission on Historical Monuments, West Dorset*, p. 162 and pl. 23). Later Yorkists whose attitude in 1450 cannot be presumed were Walter Blount, Thomas Frowick, Sir John Melton junior, Sir Thomas Parr, Sir William Peachey, Robert Poynings (though from his connexion with Cade he may at least be counted as against the court) and John Russell of Lydiard Millicent. The lawyers William Burley, Richard Forster, Thomas Palmer, and Thomas Young raise special problems which are discussed below, pp. 251-2; here it may be noted that Burley was not only retained as legal counsel by the duke but was chief steward of York's lordships of Denbigh and Montgomery by 1442-3 (P.R.O., S.C. 11/818). It seems likely that York may have had some ten or twelve servants in the commons on whose support he could rely. That other lords were electioneering is proved by the letter sent by the Duke of Exeter to the Earl of Devon for his interest in the return of Hugh Payne as M.P. for Exeter (Wedgwood, *op. cit., Register,* p. 162, n. 4, *ex inf.* Miss M. McKisack from Exeter Receivers Accounts; M. McKisack, *Parliamentary Representation of the English Boroughs during the Middle Ages,* p. 61 and n.).

their lord in the capital during May and June.[7] For the next six years his knights, esquires, and gentlemen were from time to time ordered to come to him defensibly arrayed or warned to be ready to march at short notice.[8] For this reason he was not taken quite by surprise when York and his friends at last decided to fight on 22 May 1455. Ninety men from Kent and Surrey alone were later rewarded for 'beyng w^t my lord at Seynt Albons';[9] and there are traces that his ministers elsewhere were equally busy. Whether all arrived on the field in time is less certain. The duke's namesake and very distant cousin, Humphrey Stafford esquire of Grafton, almost certainly did, since he set out

[6] The Duke of Buckingham was later paid £400 for joining Henry VI at Kenilworth and Coventry 'with a strong guard' in Sept. 1450 (*Issues of the Exchequer*, ed. F. Devon, p. 478). See the remarks in *Historical Collections of a Citizen of London*, ed. J. Gairdner (Camden Soc.), p. 195.

[7] Staffordshire Record Office, D 641/1/2/20, m. 3 (declaration of account of Roger Draycote, Stafford receiver, for the year ending Michaelmas, 1450). There were seventy-four yeomen accompanied by Humphrey Cotes (former receiver), William Mytton, and Draycote. The costs amounted to £17. 10s.

[8] Only a few examples can be quoted here. Draycote's account for the year ending Michaelmas, 1451 (Staffs. R.O., D 641/1/2/57) mentions letters sent to Sir John Burgh of Wattlesborough, Sir Nicholas Longford of Longford, and thirteen named esquires, the summoning of sixty yeomen to meet the duke at Atherstone 'versus Thomam Mallery militem', of 'divers' yeomen to be 'in presencia domini apud Leyc' essentis ibidem cum Rege' and of 'omnes valectos de retinencia domini in comitatibus Staff' & Cest' ad essendum paratos super premunicionem trium dierum' (m. 7 dorse). The accounts for 1452–3 and 1454–5 (D 641/1/2/58–59) contain similar entries. Finally, in Draycote's declaration of account for 1455–6 (D 641/1/2/22) there is this: 'And in diuerse foren expencez necessaries be þe seid receyuour done þis yere uppon diuerse messangerez þat were sent be my lordes commaundment frome Staff' vnto diuerse knyghtez and sqwyers for to come to my lord to Staff' for diuerse causez with other necessarie expenses—39/3' (m. 4). The Earl of Stafford, the duke's heir, can be seen taking an active part in his father's concerns.

[9] Staffs. R.O. D 641/1/2/22, m. 7 dorse (William Hexstall, receiver Kent and Surrey). They were paid 6s. 8d. a head. On m. 7 is also the following entry: 'And in the wages of diuerse yomen and gromes of my lordes with þe wages of þe pages of diuerse gentilmen and yomen of my lordes beyng at liuery at Tonbr', Hadele, Yeldyng and Penshurst at diuerse tymes withynne the tyme of þis accompt—£35–14–0¼.' Entries in other accounts show that the duke's officers and grooms were keeping large numbers of horses at or near Tonbridge during the early 1450's. Though the duke's household was usually at Maxstoke or Writtle, Tonbridge and Stafford seem to have been the headquarters of his retinue.

[10] B.M. Add. MS. 74174 (account of John More, receiver, and steward of the household of Humphrey Stafford, esq., 11 Nov. 1454–10 Nov. 1455), m. 3: payments 'ad manus proprias domini' include £6. 13s. 4d. 'in crastino ascencionis domini ipso tunc equitanti versus Seint Albon'. John Lyghthert was paid 4d. 'eunti versus Hales [= Halesowen) & alibi pro seruientibus mouendis ad equitandum cum domino versus Seint Albon'.

from Worcestershire on 16 May with a small band of servants for the same rendezvous.[10] He had close ties with the leaders of both armies;[11] to judge from other entries in his accounts it seems likely that he too fought on the losing side.[12]

Of York's success in mobilising his retinue then and thereafter much less is known, though one small group of documents preserved at Longleat helps to fill out the story of his last critical months. He had returned once again from Ireland in September 1460, now for the first time openly resolved to seize the crown for himself. As we learn from Wheathampstead and can infer from the deadlock in parliament that followed his arrival at Westminster, York's decision was as unexpected as it was unwelcome, even by his principal allies. That it was acceptable to at least some of his obscurer followers is proved by the terms on which they agreed to help him. In the indenture, sealed by the parties at Gloucester on 2 October, Simon Milburn, a Hereford-shire esquire, was

> belast and wᵗholdyn for terme of his lyf wᵗ and toward the said Duc and his son Edward Erl of Marche, promitting & binding hym by the faythe of his body & by this present endentures to do trew, diligent & faithfull seruice vn to the said Duc & Erle and wᵗ thaym for to be ayenst all erthly criatures of what estate, condicion or preeminence so euer thay be.'[13]

There was no longer any question of saving Milburn's ligeance to King Henry. And to emphasize the point both the indenture and the patent

[11] For these see below, p. 251. On 24 May 1455 Ralph lord Sudeley's servant was rewarded for bringing Stafford 'j togam de liberata dicti domini'. In 1448–9 Stafford had accompanied the Earl of Warwick riding towards Abergavenny (B.M. Add. MS. 74169). The Countess of Warwick stayed at Grafton on 5 and 6 Sept. 1454, her visit costing her host £4. 12s. 3d. (B.M. Add. MS. 74172, m. 2).

[12] B.M. Add. MS. 47174, m. 3: 'Et solutum seruientibus Ducis Somerc' deferentibus le Chariot &c.—33/4; et solutum alio garcioni eiusdem ducis deferenti equos &c.—3/4.' On the other hand there was another visit from the Countess of Warwick that year, costing £4. 10s. (ibid.). But since her husband seems to have decided not to fee Stafford and the Earl of Wiltshire was still paying him an annuity of 20 marks (B.M. Add. MS. 47173, m. 1) the balance of evidence favours the conclusion in the text.

[13] The muniments of the Marquess of Bath, Longleat 10494 (the seal of Simon Milburn is missing). Longleat 10493, now badly shrunk and partly illegible, is the counterpart, sealed with York's signet. There are two similar indentures (Longleat 10491 and 10492) of the same date and with the same terms retaining Thomas Holcot and Henry Hackleton. The annual fee for all three retainers was 10 marks from the issues of York's lordships, co. Herefs. My thanks are due to Lord Bath and to Miss D. Coates, librarian of Longleat, for welcoming my many visits to the muniment-room there.

accompanying it are dated, not by the regnal year in conformity with the normal practice of York's chancery, but by the year of grace, A.D. 1460.[14] By comparison with the stout Earl of Warwick and his prudent father, Simon Milburn may have been a political innocent. On this occasion his gamble proved a sound one.[15] It was not long before a defeated Warwick was persuaded by events to follow his example.

These scrappy survivals reinforce the impression we derive from our sources that, for all the military preparedness, the repeated calls to arms, the sporadic outbreaks of violence in the provinces, and the frequent likelihood of a major clash, the onset of real warfare was agonizingly slow, because desired by no one. It is impossible to believe that York's course had been charted beforehand or that he—or indeed any one else among the nobility—was spoiling for a fight. Even the theory that he had before 1455 grasped the importance of Calais for the balance of power in England may well read too much back from later events.[16] For ten long years of crisis, apart from one morning of uninhibited action at St. Albans, he had been beset by doubts and hesitations, if not by scruples of conscience. In spite of these he had more than once overestimated the strength of his name and cause, and failed to assess correctly the temper of his fellow magnates. For much of the time he seems to have hoped that his objectives (and these surely changed with events) could be secured by political action backed by the mere show of force and assisted by electoral management in the shires. The news of the less-hesitant Warwick's victory at North-

[14] The patent (Longleat 10495) has a fine example of the duke's seal, France and England quarterly with a label of three points each charged with a lily. There is another original patent of York's at Longleat (Devereux Papers, box 1, no. 6) appointing Walter Devereux, esq., steward of Radnor and many other Welsh lordships. It has the same seal and is dated Usk, 7 Apr. 30 Henry VI (1452). On the patent rolls of Edward IV's first year there are copies of eighteen of his father's letters patent ranging between 26 Mar., 1434 and 14 Nov. 1460. All but three (*Cal. Pat. Rolls, 1461-1467*, pp. 60, 94, and 96) are dated by Henry VI's regnal years [*ibid.*, pp. 14, 15, 22, 44, 46, 51, 53, 57, 81, 82, 89, 97 (2), 121, and 146]; these three are dated Chester 13 Sept. 1460, Gloucester 2 Oct. 1460, and London 1 Nov. 1460; by 4 Nov. 1460 he had reverted to 39 Hen. VI and called himself 'true heir to the kingdom' (*ibid.*, p. 14). This suggests that even at Chester on 13 Sept. York had renounced his allegiance to Henry VI. He had used the year of grace in dating letters addressed to his receiver-general in France (B.M. Add. Chs. 8031-2 and 26043, &c.).

[15] Simon Milburn of Tillington, co. Herefs. was made escheator in that county, 7 Nov. 1459 (*Cal. Fine Rolls*, vol. xix, p. 252). He became sheriff there on 5 Nov. 1463 (*ibid.*, *1461-1471*, p. 122). He must be distinguished from a namesake who died in 1464 with lands in cos. Hants., Wilts., Berks., and Somerset (*ibid.*, p. 126). Thomas Holcot was also a Herefordshire landowner (*ibid.*, p. 176). Henry Hackleton has eluded me.

[16] For an able development of the thesis here rejected see G. L. Harriss, 'The Struggle for Calais: an aspect of the rivalry between Lancaster and York', *Eng. Hist. Rev.*, vol. lxxv (1960), pp. 30-53.

ampton at length inspired him to go all out for the crown. But even that was a miscalculation, since others, including the indispensable Nevills, were still unwilling to depose a *de facto* king and only consented to disinherit Edward Prince of Wales to resolve a deepening crisis.

The bearing of these events upon the question of the cause or causes of the war should be obvious. To adapt Clausewitz's famous definition, civil war was the continuation of politics by other means. As is not unusual in politics, it was a conflict between ins and outs. Henry VI's advisers were blamed not only for the collapse of English hopes in France and for the incompetence and partiality of their rule at home, but for the exclusion of the lords of the king's blood and other 'true' servants from his counsels. How far the anger they excited was from being confined to the magnates and their liveried hangers-on the pamphlet literature inspired by Cade's rebellion is there to show.[17]

Had the war any other origins? The 'family settlement' of Edward III? Is it suggested that a king could reasonably have made no provision commensurate with their birth for his younger sons? Or merely that Edward ought not to have had any? Having them, he treated them as his ancestors had treated theirs. It is too often forgotten that both Edward IV and Henry VII did their poor best to found and endow cadet lines of their own blood. In losing its chance of another King Arthur England was also deprived of the prospect of Henry Tudor, Duke of York, and whatever male issue he succeeded in begetting in that private station. Historians of the sixteenth century would be well advised to bear in mind that Arthur's childless death at Ludlow may alone have robbed them of the spectacle of an over-mighty subject much closer to the throne than Edward of Buckingham.

Responsibility for the civil war has long been laid at the door of Sir John Fortescue's greatest bugbear. But in fact only an undermighty ruler had anything to fear from overmighty subjects; and if he were

---

[17] This widespread and popular clamour is best summed up in the second clause of the bill circulated by the common of Kent in 1450: 'his trewe Comyns' desired of Henry VI 'þat he woll voyde all the false progeny and afynyte of the Duke of Southefolke, the whiche ben opynly knowyn traitours, and they to be ponysshed affter custome and lawe of the lond. And to take abowte hym a nobill persone, þe trewe blode of þe Reame, þat is to sey the hye and myghty prince þe Duke of Yorke, late exiled from our soueraigne lordes presens of the false traitour Duke of Southefolke and his affinite, and take to yow þe myghty prince the Duke of Excetter, Duke of Bokyngham, Duke of Northefolke, Erlys and barons of this londe' (C. L. Kingsford, *English Historical Literature in the Fifteenth Century*, pp. 360–1).

undermighty his personal lack of fitness was the cause, not the weakness of his office and its resources. Henry VI's head was too small for his father's crown, but it was long before anyone was prepared to dispute his right to it. In the mid-fifteenth century many of the nobility were descended from the third Edward, more still from the first. That in itself was not a source of danger to the king—unless he was himself totally unsuited to his task. Only then did the question of the succession arise. If Edward III must be blamed it would be more sensible to point to his failure to settle the crown when Lionel of Clarence's death without male offspring made it possible that the house of Anjou, though not extinct, might be displaced by a Mortimer. After all in similar circumstances Edward I had settled the crown in 1290, placing his daughter's descendants before his brother.[18] In 1368 Edward III might well have preferred John of Gaunt to the great-grandson of his father's murderer, all the more so because during the fourteenth century the heir male had been gaining ground upon the heir general.[19] But whichever way he might have decided it, such a settlement would have been a flimsy barricade against a resolute usurper. The dynastic issue was a side issue and so remained until it was embraced by the theologians of legitimacy a century or more after Lancaster and York had died out. Edward IV had to make himself a king *de facto* first; his questionable, though convenient, *ius* would not do it for him.

The want of precipitancy shown by the combatants makes it difficult to argue that the very existence of armed bands of retainers caused the war. These had often been present during parliaments and councils without coming to blows. Since they were the centuries-old means by which English society was organized for war—and, as the terms of their indentures regularly specified, for peace also—it would have been odd if the main burden of the fighting had not been borne by them. Surely it is more desirable to remark how well the lords were able to enforce discipline in their retinues. And before we place the blame instead upon a demoralized, unpaid, and mutinous soldiery fleeing from Normandy and Guyenne—such men certainly existed— we need to have some measure of their contribution. It was most obvious in 1450. Like the inmates of sanctuaries and prisons they

[18] *Foedera* etc., ed. T. Rymer, Rec. Com. edn., vol. i, pt. ii, p. 742.
[19] The entailing of their inheritances on their male issue by Richard earl of Arundel (1347-54 (*Cal. Pat. Rolls, 1345-1348*, pp. 328-9; *ibid.*, *1354-1358*, p. 131)) and by Thomas earl of Warwick (1344-69 (*ibid.*, *1343-1345*, pp. 251-2 and 517-18; *ibid.*, *1354-1358*, p. 416; *ibid.*, *1361-1364*, pp. 48 and 105; *ibid.*, *1369-1374*, p. 108)) suggests what their sovereign's attitude might have been.

may have been promising recruits—in subordinate positions. They went to swell the turbulent commons. When from time to time they are mentioned in the private accounts of contemporaries, it is to receive, along with the prisoners in Newgate and the Fleet, charity rather than weapons and a fee.[20] Veterans of Henry V's army, many of them were old in years as well as in experience. There is an alternative possibility: that the magnates themselves, deprived of the profits of war which had compensated them for falling rents, sought to escape threatened ruin in the lottery of civil war. Though superficially attractive, this too must be discarded. The men readiest to take up arms, York, Salisbury, and Warwick on one side, Somerset, Buckingham, and Wiltshire on the other, were without exception richer than their fathers. Their ministers' accounts could show mounting arrears and unpaid debts, but the signs of a reckless indifference to consequences are wanting. They had still too much to lose. Lord Cromwell, whom Warwick held to have been 'begynner of all þᵗ journey at Seynt Albonez', had accumulated an immense fortune in lands and goods since the first decade of the reign.[21] He was a supporter, though a cautious one, of York. It was not poverty that made him and his like desperate but the political situation. The war was fought because the nobility was unable to rescue the kingdom from the consequences of Henry VI's inanity by any other means. It does not follow that they liked the task.

So far I have been speaking about the first of the wars. The plural may perhaps be taken to stand for three: the first beginning in 1450 but only reaching the boil in 1460 and 1461 to cool off by 1464, the second lasting from Edward IV's marriage to its climax at Barnet and Tewkesbury, and the third from Edward IV's death to the final terminus at Stoke. The causes of the last two were not very different

[20] As Sir John Fastolf's executor William Worcester early in 1460 gave a mark to John Lawney esquire because he was Fastolf's kinsman '& eciam fuit cum domino in guerris Francis pluribus annis non habens vnde viuere', and a few months later 16*d*. to John Chambre gentleman, 'quondam soldarius cum domino in Frauncia & valde pauper postea' (Magdalen College, Oxford, muniments, Fastolf Paper 72, mm. 1 and 3).

[21] In 1429-30 the clear annual value of his and his wife's lands was estimated to be £1,020 (*Hist. MSS. Com. Report on the MSS. of Lord De L'Isle and Dudley*, vol. i, pp. 207-8. There are a few mistakes in the calendar but the total is correct). Towards the end of his life (he died 4 Jan. 1456) the clear value had risen to £2,263 (P.R.O., S.C. 11/822, m. 10). Unfortunately the head of the roll is wanting and the date is uncertain. For observations on the landed income of Lord Cromwell see T. B. Pugh and C. D. Ross, 'The English Baronage and the Income Tax of 1436', *Bull. Inst. Hist. Research*, vol. xxvi (1953), pp. 6-7). About January 1465 Cromwell's executors valued his cash and goods, including jewels and vestments given to Tattershall College during his life (£2,666. 13*s*. 4*d*.), at £21,456 (Magd. Coll., Oxford, muniments, Misc. 357).

from those of the first. Only a most thorough-going determinist would maintain that in no conceivable circumstances could Warwick have served Edward of York as loyally as (say) Buckingham served Henry of Lancaster. It just happened that for simple and quite understandable reasons he did not. Whose fault that was is a much more involved and possibly, given our sources, insoluble problem. Similarly no one but a member of the invincible brotherhood of the White Boar (our latter-day Baconians) could fail to agree that the secure position of the Yorkist house in 1483 was destroyed, even if for the best of reasons, by Richard of Gloucester and those who helped him to his nephew's throne. In talking of causes it is necessary to avoid the temptations of profundity. It was after all, as Henry VII's reign bears witness, at a superficial level that all cures were found. Neither the structure of English society nor of its administration was radically altered between 1450 and 1500. If there were the makings of a revolutionary situation in the year of Suffolk's murder and Cade's capture of London no revolution followed. Their grievances involved the commons in the struggle but they were unable to affect its outcome. Whatever divided the opposing armies it did not arise from differences of class. Those village Hampdens, the Robins of Redesdale and Holderness, were as gently born as Hampden himself.

Nor can the belligerents be given any definite geographical limits. These were neither wars between north and south nor between the lowland south-east and the dark corners of the north and west. The sides had no frontiers to defend, no large home-grounds where they could only be challenged in force.[22] Except at the Tower in 1460 and in the northern marches between 1461 and 1464 when Margaret's troops had a base in Scotland, there were few sieges: Denbigh, Thorpe Waterville, Harlech, Caister, St. Michael's Mount.[23] The great private castles

---

[22] That is in England and Wales. York's hold on Ireland and Warwick's on Calais in 1459-60 were exceptional. The invasions of 1470, 1471, and 1485 show that a foreign port could serve the same purpose as well.

[23] Caister's siege was scarcely an incident in the wars. And it is doubtful whether Thorpe Waterville, the duke of Exeter's castle in the Nene valley between Thrapston and Oundle, deserves its place in the list. On 1 Apr. 1461 Sir John Wenlock (who had been given authority to suppress Lancastrians in the area on 16 Jan. (*Cal. Pat. Rolls, 1452-1461*, p. 657)) was commissioned to summon the gentry of cos. Northants, Beds., Bucks., Cambs., and Hunts. to assist him to besiege it (*ibid.*, *1461-1467*, p. 28). Since he was at Towton on 29 Mar. (J. S. Roskell, 'John Lord Wenlock of Someries', *Pubs. of Beds. Rec. Soc.*, vol. xxxviii (1958), p. 37) and Thorpe Waterville was reported on 4 Apr. to have surrendered (*Paston Letts.*, vol. iii, p. 267) it looks as if the threat was enough to reduce the garrison to terms (but see Roskell, *op. cit.*, p. 37, n. 89 for evidence of Wenlock's having been there, presumably before he went north with the Yorkist army). Another castle briefly held in 1461 was Buckenham, Norfolk (*Cal. Pat. Rolls, 1461-1467*, pp. 67, 83, and 135).

on which the higher nobility had spent so much since the beginning of the fourteenth century were scarcely ever held against an enemy.[24] Nor were those of the king. Though the walled towns might shut their gates against an approaching army they were not put to the test of assault. The 'wars' consisted of short sharp engagements in the field with intervals of inactivity as well as the longer periods of peace following the victory of one side. Sometimes the advancing or retreating armies behaved as if they were in a foreign country, but their indulgence in plunder and destruction did not interfere to any marked degree with the normal pursuits of everyday life.[25] The accounts submitted to Fastolf's executors by William Worcester cover in some detail the months between Warwick's landing in June 1460 and Towton, the longest stretch of intense military activity and disorder in all the wars. Five major battles and the passage of armies to and from them did not seriously interrupt the winding-up of Fastolf's estate. This took Worcester several times from Norwich to London; he also went on his own account to Coventry and Bristol.[26] Only once did he put off a journey. That was in February 1461 'because there were so many soldiers on the road to the battle joined at St. Albans that no one could safely go and return.'[27] However, conditions were not so bad that he was unable to send his servant Adam instead.[28] Otherwise the civil war takes its place beside the floods of November 1460 as a temporary obstacle to the conduct of business.[29] When there were soldiers about it was only prudent to lock up your title-deeds; Worcester twice took precautions to ensure that those at Southwark came through the

[24] The contrary is implied but without evidence in *The History of the King's Works*, ed. H. M. Colvin, vol. i, p. 240.

[25] Margaret's moss-troopers provide the best-known cause of devastation, but the habits of the Hundred Years War were not quickly forgotten. As late as 1471 the Londoners ransomed prisoners taken in Kent 'like Frenchmen' (*Chronicles of London*, ed C. L. Kingsford, p. 185).

[26] Magd. Coll., Oxford, Fastolf Paper 72 shows Worcester in London 9 May-6 June, then via Cambridge and Bury St. Edmunds to Norwich. On 19 June he left Norwich and arrived in London on the 21st, remaining there until 28 July. Between 28 July and 11 August he went via Buckingham, Coventry, and Withybridge (in Boddington, Glos., where Lord Beauchamp of Powick lived) to Bristol. He was back in London 11 Aug.-2 Sept. He reached Norwich on 4 Sept. and remained in East Anglia until 24 Nov. Between 24 and 27 Nov. he went to London. On 3 Jan. 1461 he returned to Norwich, arriving on the 5th.

[27] *Ibid.*, m. 5: 'pro eo quod fuerunt tunc euntes tot numeri soldariorum per viam ad bellum commissum apud Sanctum Albanum quod nemo potuit secure ire neque redire.'   [28] *Ibid.*

[29] *Ibid.* (24 Nov. 1460), 'tempore inundacionis magnarum aquarum per viam.' For these floods compare *Registrum Abbatiae Johannis Whethamstede*, ed. H. T. Riley (Rolls Ser.), vol. i, pp. 384-5.

danger-periods unharmed, namely before the battles of Northampton and Towton.[30]

For the combatants the chances of survival were less good, but here again a tendency to exaggeration must be resisted. If blood-feuds did arise they were rare. It was natural that the young heirs of York's victims at the first battle of St. Albans should have been moved by the desire to avenge a father's death.[31] The evidence that such feelings markedly affected their behaviour is slight. Lord Clifford's cry when he struck Rutland down at Wakefield is of course always quoted as if it epitomized the spirit of the civil war: 'By God's blood, thy father slew mine and so will I do thee and all thy kin.' As evidence it stands alone and comes to us from no earlier source than Hall's chronicle, where it is followed by a statement that can easily be disproved.[32] Against it can be set the perhaps equally apocryphal story of Clifford's son, the 'Shepherd Lord', who dreamt so little of revenge that he waited tending his sheep for better times. In 1472 the king, who was Rutland's brother, instead of taking his life threw him a pardon.[33]

It would be idle to deny that the casualties in the field, at least among those of noble and gentle birth, were numerous. They were bound to be when all captured in arms against either of the rival kings were liable to summary execution by the law of England as well as that of Padua.[34] Surrender therefore had its perils. But escapes often occurred and clemency, although not to be relied upon, was far from uncommon. Sometimes an enemy spared was a friend gained, but not so invariably as to encourage the most easy-going or humane to take

[30] Magd. Coll., Oxford, Fastolf Paper 72, m. 5: 'in custubus & exspensis factis cum amicis meis custodientibus evidencias manerij domini in Southwork pro eorum salua custodia tempore advenientis soldariorum London' ad bellum de Northampton cum rege Henrico ac ad bellum commissum Ferybrygg in comitatu Ebor' mense Marcij die ramis palmarum.' It was as late as 9 July 1461 that Margaret Paston warned her husband: 'item, at the reverence of God, be ware howe ye ryd or go, for nowgty and evyll desposyd felacheps. I am put en fere dayly for myn abydyng here' (*Paston Letters*, vol. iii, p. 288).

[31] *An English Chronicle*, ed. J. S. Davies (Camden Soc.), p. 77.

[32] Edward Hall, *Chronicle*, ed. H. Ellis, p. 251. Queen Margaret, according to Hall, was 'not lying far from the field' of battle. She was in fact in Scotland.

[33] *Cal. Pat. Rolls, 1467-1477*, p. 327.

[34] The figures for the descendants of Edward III in the male line (Lancaster, York, and Beaufort) are 7 killed and 5 executed or murdered. For peers and the heirs of peers (excluding the royal houses) the figures seem to be, including the doubtful cases of the Earl of Kent in 1463 and John Ratcliffe in 1461, 31 killed and 20 executed. As might be expected, the worst years were 1460-1 (13 peers killed and 6 executed and 2 princes killed) and 1469-71 (10 peers killed and 7 executed; 3 princes killed and 1 murdered). For the jurisdiction of the court of chivalry in later-medieval England see M. H. Keen, 'Treason trials under the Law of Arms', *Trans. R. Hist. Soc.*, 5th ser., vol. xii (1962), pp. 85-103.

risks. A few saved their skins by a timely desertion; others hung back long enough to make sure that it was the victors they joined. The savagery of one or two 'butchers' must be admitted and it is almost certain that some private scores were settled either out of court by violence or in by judicial murder.[35] If Margaret associated her seven-year-old son with the executions that followed the second battle of St. Albans, her anxiety to teach him too soon the way of his world may forfeit our sympathy; as it evidently did that of some of her con-temporaries.[36] But the sentences then passed on Bonville and Kyriel had been legally incurred. As the evidence stands it is not Worcester, who however much he may have enjoyed the task was only obeying orders, but Warwick who has the worst record.[37] It was typical of Edward IV that his practice touched all extremes. To judge from the results its want of consistency was not due to superior insight.[38]

Given the penalties of failure and the absence, save for the kings and the few pretenders to kingship, of a cause worth dying for, it is easy to see why opportunism rather than loyalty prevailed among those with most to lose, the heads of the great landed families. They risked not only their lives but the rank, fortunes, and prospects of their issue. No doubt some, either from blind stupidity or blind devotion, took no thought for such morrows. Their chances of survival diminished with time and so, therefore, did they. But even the intelligent had no means of knowing who would be king at the close of the struggle or when that would be; they could not be sure from day to day. Between Northampton and Towton victories and disasters succeeded one another so rapidly that it was impossible to foresee

[35] e.g. Humphrey Stafford of Southwick's alleged responsibility for Henry Courtenay's execution in 1469 (*Warkworth's Chronicle*, ed. J. O. Halliwell (Camden Soc.), p. 6) and the killing of Sir William Lucy after the battle of Northampton by John Stafford's servants (*Collections of a Citizen of London*, p. 207; *Letters and Papers . . . of the Wars of the English in France*, ed. J. Stevenson (Rolls ser.), vol. ii, pt. ii, p. 773).

[36] Margaret's unpopularity made them credulous of any slander at her expense, but this story is too well attested to be discounted (*ibid.*, p. 776; *Coll. Citizen of London*, p. 212; *Three Fifteenth-Century Chrons.*, ed. J. Gairdner (Camden Soc.), p. 76).

[37] The execution of Pembroke, Rivers, and others after Edgcote had, as Ramsay rightly observes (*Lancaster and York*, vol. ii, p. 343), no 'legal justification', since they were not in arms against the king Warwick then acknowledged. The beheading of Osbern Mundford and his two companions in 1460 at Calais, of which Warwick was captain, is an early example of such lawlessness.

[38] Political necessity did not justify the execution of Owen Tudor. The impaling of Worcester's victims at Southampton in 1470, we have contemporary evidence (*Warkworth*, p. 9), was unsuccessful as a piece of 'frightfulness' intended to deter others. The treatment of Henry duke of Somerset and that of the Veres suggest that Edward wobbled between the two possible policies of severity and appeasement.

what would be the outcome. Nevertheless it was difficult for any members of the class, however constitutionally wary, to hold aloof. Their position involved them. To opt out meant the sacrifice of their inherited responsibilities as patrons of a territorial clientèle, the local expression of their lordly status. Even so a surprising number preferred to lie low. Their absenteeism was as marked on the battle-fields as it was in parliament. For those too ambitious to sit still the best hope lay in trying to foresee and lend their support betimes to the next *fait accompli*. The perils of the game were obvious and tempted them to hedge their bets. Without luck chances were thin.

Yet among those who did manage to survive were a few who could be described as die-hards from choice. Jasper Tudor remained loyal throughout to his half-brother and then to his nephew. He had a long wait for his reward.[39] By 1464 impenitent Lancastrians were either dead or in exile. The failure of the readeption added to the dead and to the penitent; the exiles were fewer. Faithful Yorkists, if not killed, benefited for most of the time and were therefore more numerous. Richard III's treatment of Edward V even helped some of them to finish up on the winning side at Bosworth, though the sincerity of their professions in favour of Henry Tudor may be open to doubt. William Hastings, had he lived, would scarcely have quarrelled with his son's decision to offer loyal service to the new dynasty. Whatever they may have been by preference most reconciled themselves to the inevitable when it had become so. At every stage the majority of the survivors were trimmers either by conviction or necessity. Lord Rivers spoke for them when in 1461 he came to tender obedience to Edward of York on the ground that his former master's cause was 'irretrievably lost.'[40] A willingness to accept the *de facto* king was on the increase for the next quarter of a century, but it was already potent on the morrow of Towton. Many of the 'Yorkist' lords in the 1461 parliament had been 'Lancastrians' in that of 1459.[41] If the labels are to mean anything they need to be exactly dated. Outward conformity may have covered

---

[39] John earl of Oxford's acceptance of a Yorkist king before 1468 and his betrayal of some of his Lancastrian fellow conspirators in that year make it impossible to regard him as an unwavering supporter of Henry VI (*Plumpton Correspondence*, ed. T. Stapleton (Camden Soc.), pp. 18-20; J. S. Roskell 'Sir Thomas Tresham, Knight', *Northamptonshire Past and Present*, vol. ii (1959), p. 320). He may also have joined Warwick in July 1469 well before the latter had decided to drop Clarence in favour of the readeption (John Stone, *Chronicle*, ed. W. G. Searle (Cambridge Antiq. Soc.), pp. 109-11). See also p. 246, n. 43.

[40] *Cal. State Papers Milan*, ed. A. B. Hinds, vol. i, p. 102.

[41] A calculation is hindered by uncertainty about the attendance of those summoned at these, as at other, parliaments (J. S. Roskell, 'The Problem of the Attendance of the

strong attachments to temporarily lost causes; then they are hidden also from us. It is unlikely that every treasonable correspondence with the enemy was inspired by a calculation of what was likely to happen next, though we cannot be sure. The spies and informers who brought exposure, ruin, and death to those whose treason had not yet arrived at overt acts were not concerned with the motives of their victims. It may be safe to deduce that in 1495 William Stanley was engaged, like John Churchill in the 1690s, in an unnecessary piece of reinsurance.[42] On the other hand the Veres in 1462 could equally well have been moved by their attachment out of season to a fading cause.[43]

For those in doubt the higher clergy set an example, albeit one hard for a layman to follow, of passive obedience. As professional non-combatants they escaped the worst consequences of being on the losing side. Though they were busy, if ineffective, peacemakers there is little excuse for regarding most of the bishops as neutrals aloof from the rivalries which divided others. Until it came to blows they had taken their share in the debates that ended in war.[44] Some were the close kinsmen of the men who fought. Others had risen in their service and were deep in their counsels. Yet only a Nevill or a Stillington showed too much partisan zeal to be acceptable to a victorious opponent. The long-lived and respected Bourchier and Wainfleet, whatever their ties and secret preferences—and they are unlikely to have been wholly secret—accommodated themselves to every change.[45] If for this they are to be dismissed as unheroic time-servers it is as well to remember that their lay colleagues and successive masters were more charitable. It was, after all, a problem with which these too were familiar. With reason they were less vindictive towards churchmen

Lords in Medieval Parliaments', *Bull. Inst. Hist. Research*, vol. xxix (1956), pp. 153-204). But of the thirty-seven known to have been present at least once between 28 Nov. and 11 Dec. 1461 (*Fame Fragment of the 1461 Lords' Journal*, ed. W. H. Durham Jr., Yale Hist. Pubs. (1935), pp. 3-25. 'A New Fragment of the Lords' Journal of 1461', ed. R. Virgoe, *Bull. Inst. Hist. Res.*, vol. xxxii (1959), pp. 86-87, unfortunately adds no new names) 9 were new since 1459. In 1459 Warwick and Clinton were among those attainted and Worcester was in Italy; all were present in 1461. Of the remaining 25, 11 took the oath to maintain the house of Lancaster in parliament at Coventry on 11 Dec. 1459 (*Rot. Parl.*, vol. v, pp. 351-2) and at least 3 more (Oxford, Rivers, and Lovel) were then Lancastrians.

[42] W. A. J. Archbold, 'Sir William Stanley and Perkin Warbeck', *Eng. Hist. Rev.*, vol. xiv (1899), pp. 529-34.

[43] C. L. Scofield, 'The Early Life of John de Vere, thirteenth Earl of Oxford', *Eng. Hist. Rev.*, vol. xxix (1914), pp. 228-45, and the same author's *Life and Reign of Edward IV*, vol. i, pp. 230-4. The various chronicle accounts of these incidents are difficult to assess and reconcile.

[44] For example, both archbishops and sixteen bishops took the Coventry oath to maintain the Lancastrian dynasty (*Rot. Parl.*, vol. v, p. 351).

than their ancestors had been less than a century before. There were no martyrs like Richard Scrope.

While individuals in the main conformed, with or without reservations, until the next turn of the wheel, the families of the dead found the transition all the easier. That the widow and son of the murdered Suffolk should, by 1460, have found temporary safety in the Yorkist camp may appear odd to those who believe that fifteenth-century England resembled the Verona of the Capulets. It was a precaution others followed. To speak of a Yorkist or a Lancastrian family, apart from the royal houses themselves, is almost impossible when successive generations changed sides with so much freedom.[46] Not that families themselves were often split, in the words which eloquent but careless chroniclers borrowed from the Gospels, 'brother against brother, son against father, kin against kin.'[47] Clarence's disloyalty, which may have helped to inspire the belief, was exceptional. Stepbrothers, like the Mountfords of Coleshill, rival claimants to their father's lands, might easily fall out and take opposite sides. Apart from such special cases the ties of blood proved strong, though they did not hold beyond fairly narrow limits. Remote consanguinity and connexion by marriage could mean little or much. But it was only a fratricidal war in a metaphorical sense.

Chroniclers may also have led historians to overstate the extent to which local disputes between families played a part in bringing about the general conflict. The central government's failure to compose the quarrels of Nevill and Percy, Courtenay and Bonville, in their early

[45] The archbishop's half-brother, Humphrey duke of Buckingham, seems to have shown him respect and affection (see a copy of the duke's letter to him, written not earlier than December 1457 (Stafford, William Salt Lib., D 1721/1/1, fol. 346^v; C. A. J. Armstrong, 'Politics and the Battle of St. Albans, 1455', *Bull. Inst. Hist. Res.*, vol. xxxiii (1960), p. 69, n. 8), but the Bourchiers were cautious supporters of York, whose sister the eldest brother Henry had married, in and after 1455, cautious supporters of Henry VI in 1459 and open supporters of York after Warwick's landing in 1460 (*ibid.*, p. 21; *Rot. Parl.*, vol. v, pp. 351-2; *Cal. S.P. Milan*, vol. i, p. 38). Though Buckingham and Henry Bourchier fought on opposite sides at Northampton there is no evidence that they were personal enemies. The youngest of the Bourchier brothers John had been granted an annuity of 40 marks for life by his half-brother on 4 Mar. 1443, and was still being paid it as late as 1456-7 (Staffs. R.O. D 641/1/2/18, m. 6; /21, m. 7; /23, m. 6; P.R.O., S.C. 6/1305/4, m. 5; Longleat 6410, m. 2 dorse). He and Henry Bourchier were hunting in Kent and Surrey for the duke's larder in 1445-6 (Staffs. R.O., D 641/1/2/233 (2)). By 1449-50 Henry Bourchier was a member of York's council (B.M., Eg. Roll 8364).

[46] The Staffords of Stafford provide an excellent case in point, the Beaumonts the one notable exception.

[47] It seems to be derived from Matthew x. 21 and Mark xiii. 12. To the examples cited by C. A. J. Armstrong (*op. cit.*, p. 31, n. 2) may be added the Croyland chronicler (*Rerum Anglicarum Scriptores*, vol. i, ed. W. Fulman, 1684, p. 529).

stages was evidence of its collapsing authority. On the other hand, the civil war did not grow out of them; rather they grew out of the paralysis at the centre induced by the struggle of Somerset and York for control. There is a want of proportion in describing the encounters at Stamford Bridge and Clist Heath as battles. Such clashes had in any case occurred often enough before without leading to civil war. It was a function of government to pacify the contestants and impose a solution.[48] Thanks to the practice of entailing land, inheritances disputed between heirs male and heirs general were becoming commoner in the Lancastrian period. Of the major examples which threatened the peace after 1422, Fitzalan against Mowbray, Lovel against Hungerford, Berkeley against Beauchamp, and—a variant on the usual theme—Nevill against Nevill, all were equitably settled by the efforts of Henry VI's council and courts.[49] Only one of them burst forth afresh, after the civil war had started, to contribute its mite at Nibley Green to the disturbances of the war period. It has still to be demonstrated that they did much to influence the alignment of Lancastrians and Yorkists.

A lord already hesitant about committing himself had another reason for holding back: the doubt whether the members of his affinity would respond to his call. He could punish them for their disobedience if his gamble came off but that was not always sufficient to compel attendance.[50] For the gentry shared the baronial dislike of lost causes and desperate ventures. Hence Wedgwood's failure to classify the knights of the shire by their allegiances. They turned their coats as often and with the same chequered success as their betters. Since many of them were wise or greedy enough to have more coats than one to turn, they may well have been more dexterous

[48] To cite two earlier examples: (i) the disorders caused by the Courtenays in Devon in the early 1390s and at the beginning of Henry IV's reign (*Select Cases before the King's Council, 1243-1482,* ed. I. S. Leadam and J. F. Baldwin (Selden Soc.), pp. ci-ciii and 77-81; J. F. Baldwin, *The King's Council,* p. 490; *Rot. Parl.,* vol. iii, pp. 302, 488-90, and 493b); (ii) the feud between Ferrers of Chartley and Erdswick of Sandon 1413-14 (*ibid.,* vol. iv, pp. 32-33).

[49] Following the deaths of Thomas earl of Arundel (1415), Hugh lord Burnell (1420), Thomas lord Berkeley (1417), and Ralph earl of Westmorland (1425). The last case differs from the others in that the earl wished to deprive the heir in tail in favour of his male issue by his second wife. None of these complicated disputes has been adequately described and since only one played any part in the Wars of the Roses the details may be omitted here. For the Berkeley-Beauchamp and Berkeley-Talbot troubles see J. Smyth, *The Lives of the Berkeleys,* ed. J. Maclean (Bristol and Gloucs. Archaeol. Soc.), vol. ii, pp. 41 et seq., J. H. Cooke, 'The Great Berkeley Law Suit', *Trans. Bristol and Gloucs. Arch. Soc.,* vol. iii (1879), pp. 305-24, and C. D. Ross, 'The Household Accounts of Elizabeth Berkeley, Countess of Warwick, 1420-1', *ibid.,* vol. 70 (1951), pp. 81-105.

than the lords at changing them to suit the demands of survival, though the casualties in battle and on the scaffold show how many were unlucky or misguided.[50] To command their exclusive service against all men save the king—which king being left conveniently vague—was beyond the reach of all but the greatest and best-placed lords in England. The indentures of William lord Hasting's retinue, in that they mostly date from the period after 1471, when Edward IV was secure and his chamberlain high in the royal favour, may give a false impression on this point.[52] The success with which Hastings had called out his friends to join the Yorkist army as it advanced into the midlands from Ravenspur had left the king deeply in his debt.[53] Even before the flight from England he had enjoyed great influence. But it is significant that that shrewd trimmer Henry lord Grey of Codnor (who had been with Queen Margaret at St. Albans in 1461 and lived it down) in his indenture of 30 May 1464 excepts his duty to the Duke of Clarence and Sir Thomas Burgh in addition to his ligeance;[54] and this his disciple Sir Thomas Stathom two years later made a like reservation in his favour.[55] We remember that when the axe suddenly ended Hasting's life in June 1483 it was soon reported that 'all þe lord Chamberleyne mene be come my lordys of Bokynghame menne.'[56] It was, in Friar Brackley's immortal phrase, 'a coysy

50 In 1455 Sir William Skipwith refused to follow York to St. Albans, and on the advice of Sir John Nevill, Sir James Pickering, and Thomas Colt was expelled from his stewardship of the manors of Hatfield and Conisbrough, from the chief forestership and parkership there, the constableship of Conisbrough, the keepership of Hatfield warren and annuities of £40, all granted to him for life by the duke (*Cal. Pat. Rolls, 1452-1461*, pp. 552-3). He got them back temporarily from Henry VI during the Coventry parliament of 1459.

51 So too do the lists of those attainted in 1459 (*Rot. Parl.*, vol. v, pp. 348-50) and 1461 (*ibid.*, pp. 476-83).

52 W. H. Dunham Jr., 'Lord Hastings' Indentured Retainers 1461-1483', *Trans. Connecticut Acad. of Arts and Sciences*, vol. xxxix (1955), pp. 1-175. All but 6 of the 67 retainers belong to the years 1474-83.

53 *Arrivall of Edward IV*, ed. J. Bruce (Camden Soc.), pp. 8-9: 'At Leycestar came to the Kynge ryght-a-fayre felawshipe of folks . . . suche as were veryly to be trustyd. . . . And, in substaunce, they were suche as were towards the Lorde Hastings, the Kyngs Chambarlayne, and, for that entent above sayd, came to hym, stiryd by his messages sent unto them, and by his servaunts, frinds, and lovars, suche as were in the contrie.'

54 Dunham, p. 133. For Grey's presence at St. Albans *ex parte Henrici sexti* see *Letters and Papers . . . Wars of the English in France*, vol. ii, pt. ii, p. 776.

55 Dunham, p. 124. For 'disciple' as a synonym for client see *Paston Letters*, vol. iii, p. 47.

56 *The Sonor Letters and Papers, 1290-1483*, ed. C. L. Kingsford (Camden Soc.), vol. ii, p. 161. It was an exaggeration. Some like William Catesby had climbed into Richard III's service by betraying Hastings (*The English Works of Sir Thomas More*, ed. W. E. Campbell, p. 53).

werd';[57] or, as another of the Pastons' correspondents remarked, '*Circumspecte agatis*, and be war of lordis promysses.'[58] It is to be doubted whether gentlemen's promises were any less fragile. At the first sign that a lord's power was tottering his 'well-willers' were quick to look elsewhere.[59] Even when it was firm they were not averse from contracting other ties when it suited them.

A letter from one of Hastings's esquires to the Bishop of Winchester, dated 27 June 1481, well illustrates the Lord Chamberlain's inability to command a servant's undivided adherence:

Pleasith it your lordship to wit that on Saturday in the vigil of seint John Baptist sir Robert Markh[a]m knyght with other diuerse seruauntes of the lorde Lovell come to Briggeford and ther made an entre in the title of the said lorde Lovell in the manoir that ye haue ther;[60] and caused the tenauntes to retourne and made officers therof. And if I had hade afor that tyme interest ther as your officer by your writing I shulde haue put theym oute of possession agayn or this tyme. Bot as it is now, considering he is a lorde, I may not soo deale. Neuertheles if ye muste nedist juperde in the lawe with hym I shall be w[t] you to the vttermast that I can or may. I trust to God to make you bigge ynough to trye with hym within the shire w[t] help of such other as ye shall easely haue the goode willes of, soo that my lorde Chaumbreleyn take not the contrarie parte. And what seruice I can doo shall be readye to your lordship at all tymes. With the grace of Jhesu whom I beseche to preserue your goode lordship with good liff and long. Scribiled at Notingh[a]m the xxvij daye of Juyn.

By youre seruaunt Gervas Clyfton.[61]

It is hardly surprising to find that Clifton came to no harm in 1483, served Richard III, and made his peace with Henry VII.[62]

The ties binding another and even more useful retainer, Sir James

---

57 *Paston Letters*, vol. iii, p. 196 (1459-60).

58 *Ibid.*, vol. ii, p. 159 (James Gresham, perhaps 1450).

59 e.g. Edmund Paston's report on the men of Norfolk's attitude when Suffolk's 'rule' there was thought to be in jeopardy: 'I fele by him he wold forsake his master and gette him a newh yf he wyste he schuld rewle; and so wene I meche of all the contre is so disposyd' (*ibid.*, vol. ii, p. 80).

60 Wainfleet had acquired a manor in East Bridgford, Notts., which had come to Ralph lord Cromwell by his marriage with Margaret Deincourt. After Cromwell's death without issue it passed into the possession of his niece, Joan Stanhope, who died childless on 12 Mar. 1481 (*Hist. MSS. Com., De L'Isle and Dudley MSS.*, vol. i, p. 227). Thereupon, despite a quitclaim of 1 July 1468 (*Cal. Close Rolls, 1468-1476*, p. 25) by Alice lady Sudeley through whom he claimed, Francis lord Lovel as the other coheir of Deincourt entered as described in this letter. Wainfleet's title derived from Ralph Cromwell's feoffees, but it was entailed on the heirs of William Deincourt (ob. 1364) and Lord Lovel's claim was just (Magd. Coll., Oxford, East Bridgford 11 and 21).

Strangways, to the Nevills, though close and for a time profitable to both parties, were as conditional. In the indenture of 1 October 1446 in which he was retained for life by the Earl of Salisbury, he saved not only his ligeance but also his obligations to 'yᵉ high and myghty princesse Katerin duchesse of Norffolk, yᵉ reverend fadre in God Robert bisshop of Duresme'—all Nevills so far—'and yᵉ kynne and alies of yᵉ said James at and within the thirde degree of mariage.'[63] This was a commodious escape-route. Sir James avoided the fate of his Nevill connexions, having taken advantage of their prosperity, to die a natural death in 1480.[64]

The giving and receiving of fees had by the middle years of the century become so indiscriminate that their effectiveness may be doubted. For example, in 1449 Sir Humphrey Stafford of Grafton, killed at Sevenoaks a year later, received forty marks from the Duke of Buckingham, twenty marks each from the Duchess of Warwick and the Earl of Wiltshire, ten marks from Sir Andrew Ogard, and smaller sums from four ecclesiastical lords.[65] By 1451 his young heir had already collected ten marks a year each from the Earl of Wiltshire and Lord Beauchamp of Powick, forty shillings from Lord Sudeley, six other fees from neighbouring prelates, and the promise or at least the hope of two more from the Earl of Warwick and the Bishop of Worcester.[66] Lawyers naturally attracted such patronage. In 1435

[61] Endorsed: 'To my Lorde of Wynchestre' (Magd. Coll., Oxford, East Bridgford 33). Only the signature and the three words preceding it are holograph. The writer's uncle and namesake, who was executed after Tewkesbury, had been the husband of Ralph Cromwell's other niece, Maud Stanhope (G.E.C., *Complete Peerage*, vol. xii, pt. ii, ed. A. B. White and R. S. Lea, p. 666; Wedgwood, *op. cit.*, *Biographies*, pp. 194-6).

[62] *Cal. Pat. Rolls, 1476-1485*, pp. 439-40 and 475; *Testamenta Eboracensia* (Surtees Soc.), vol. iv, pp. 64-71.

[63] Fitzwilliam muniments, Milton, Northants, no. 2051. I have not seen the original and take my quotation from a typescript catalogue formerly in the Northants Record Office at Lamport Hall.

[64] J. S. Roskell, 'Sir James Strangeways of West Harlsey and Whorlton', *Yorks Arch. Journal*, vol. xxxix (1958), pp. 455-82.

[65] B.M., Add. MS. 74168, m. 2. The total of £70. 13s. 4d. p.a. was made up by £4 from the Abbot of Evesham, 53s. 4d. from the Bishop of Worcester, and 40s. each from the Prior of Worcester and the Abbot of Pershore.

[66] *Ibid.*, Add. MS. 74171, m. 2. The names of the Earl of Warwick and Bishop of Worcester appear on the list of fees with the sums left blank. Later accounts (*ibid.*, Add. MSS. 74173-4) show that in 1453-4 and 1454-5 the earl and the bishop have disappeared. Since Wiltshire and Sudeley remain it is reasonable to suppose that they influenced Stafford's actions in May 1455. The ecclesiastics paying fees in 1451 were the Abbots of Pershore (£4), Evesham (£4), Halesowen (26s. 8d.), and Bordesley (20s.) and the Priors of Studley (53s. 4d.) and Worcester (40s.). By 1453-4 they seem to have fallen to Evesham, Halesowen, and Studley.

Edmund Brudenell of Chalfont, when still at the beginning of a successful career, drew small annual retaining fees from seventeen clients ranging from the Countess of Cambridge and the Abbot of Westminster to the gentry of Buckinghamshire and their ladies.[67] The men of law were an influential element in the commons and in the shires, but their profession did not allow them to keep both feet planted firmly in one camp. William Tresham's last journey in 1450 seems to need no other explanation; his death does not prove that he was much of a Yorkist.[68] Thomas Young, on the strength of his petition of 1451, has generally been regarded as a wholehearted one.[69] Yet on 27 October 1446 he had been retained by Humphrey of Buckingham as a councillor learned in the law receiving his fee of forty shillings during pleasure;[70] and, despite his petition of 1451 and the imprisonment it earned him, the ducal pleasure continued to be shown to him until at least 1457-8.[71] Nor does Young's later career as a judge give much excuse for labelling him a political zealot.[72] It is hardly surprising that Wedgwood found it necessary to add the category of lawyer to those of Lancastrian and Yorkist.

The truth is that the lawyers were not the only ambidexters. The relationship between a paymaster and his feed-men was both complex and delicate. For one thing, he was not always their superior in rank and political influence. By offering fees, often in the guise of sinecure stewardships, all kinds of landowners hoped to attract the favour and protection of those in power. Thus during the first year of Edward IV's reign Anne duchess of Buckingham, the widow of the slain Lancastrian leader (though herself a Nevill), had engaged herself to pay annuities for life to William lord Hastings, John lord Wenlock, and Sir Thomas Burgh, pillars of the new Yorkist regime.[73] The very number of such sinecures collected by influential courtiers makes it evident that although the grant of an annual fee for life conferred some kind of obligation upon the recipient it cannot have been felt by either party to tie his hands.[74] Those who made the grant obviously

---

[67] Westm. Abb. Muniment 6036, m. 6. The total only reached £15. 6s. 8d. p.a. The largest fee was 40s. from the dean and chapter of Windsor. Maud (Clifford) Countess of Cambridge was York's step-mother.

[68] J. S. Roskell, 'William Tresham of Sywell', *Northants Past and Present*, vol. ii (1957), pp. 201-3.

[69] J. Wedgwood, *op. cit.*, *Biogs.*, pp. 981-2.

[70] Staffs. R.O., D 641/1/2/175, roll 8.

[71] *Ibid.*, D 641/1/2/176, roll 8 and /179.

[72] He was dismissed from his office as Justice C.P. by Edward IV in 1471 for the support which he had given to the readeption but in 1475 he was appointed Justice K.B. (Wedgwood, *u.s.*).

nursed expectations. They also feared to be isolated and at a disadvantage at times when 'it semythe that the worlde is alle qwaveryng.'[75] As the *Paston Letters* more than once emphasise, friendship was as desirable as lordship *'quia ibi pendet tota lex et phophete.'*[76] A feeling of insecurity prompted the search for both patrons and clients.

Though wealth and inherited position could do much, successful patronage was an art to the mastery of which the lord had to bring a number of obvious but by no means universal qualities: a cool judgement, some insight into other men's springs of action, some firmness of purpose, an affability however rough and a reputation for success. His councillors might supply some of his deficiencies but not all. John lord Strange of Knockin, to judge from his letter to Sir William Stonor, was too blustering;[77] John the last Mowbray duke of Norfolk was both obstinate and weak-willed;[78] neither did much to influence events. Nothing did more to destroy a flourishing connexion than an obvious want of political sense. So, despite his great past achievements, was Warwick ruined in 1471. We see it happening in the

---

[73] P.R.O., S.C. 6/1117/11, m. 6. Hastings was granted 20 marks p.a. for life on 25 Nov. 1461 as constable of Oakham castle and her steward co. Rutland; Wenlock was granted the same amount on 20 Feb. 1462 as her steward cos. Hunts., Beds., and Bucks.; Burgh, late esquire of the body, was granted 40 marks p.a. for life as surveyor of all her lands in England and Wales on 1 Apr. 1461. The first two are specifically allowed to perform their duties by deputy.

[74] W. Dugdale long ago called attention William Hastings's windfall of fees after Edward IV's accession (*Baronage of England*, vol. i, p. 580).

[75] As it was to Sir John Paston in 1477 (*Paston Letters*, vol. v, p. 270).

[76] *Ibid.*, vol. ii, p. 180. See also *ibid.*, p. 179: 'Ze have both lordshep and frendshep in your countre'; obviously both were necessary.

[77] *Stonor Letters*, vol. ii, p. 70: 'as for my graunt of a fee I wold ye thowght yf ye do me servyce, as the wrytinge is, I woll dele more largly with yow, but I woll not be ovirmastred with none of my feed men; notwithstanding, at this tyme I have done for yow of my voluntary send yow xls. . . . Yf ye dele as ye owght I wolbe your goode lorde, and eke I dare better displese yow than ye me.'

[78] He started with great advantages and in 1465 Margaret Paston had a high opinion of his worship: 'It ys thoght here that yf my Lord of Norfolk wolld take uppon hym for you . . . that then all the contray wyll a wayte uppon hym and serve your entent; for the pepyll lovyth and dredyth hym more then any other lord except the King and my Lord of Warwyk' (*Paston Letters*, vol. iv, p. 207). Edward IV on the other hand in 1469 thought the duke a puppet in the hands of his councillor Sir William Brandon (*ibid.*, vol. v, p. 31). But when my lord was angry and 'the tempest aros' neither my lady nor his whole council could manage him in 1472, though lord Hastings was expected to 'meve' him (*ibid.*, pp. 150-1).

[79] *Hist. MSS. Com., Rutland MSS.*, vol. i, pp. 2-6 and frontispiece. Warwick's description of him comes from the earl's warrant to Thomas Throckmorton, his receiver in Glamorgan, dated 22 Nov. 1469 to pay him £30 (Throckmorton muniments, Coughton Court, Warwicks., no. 177. I have to thank the late Dowager Lady Throckmorton for permission to see these).

bunch of letters he and Clarence addressed to Sir Henry Vernon of Haddon during the crisis before Barnet. 'Henry I pray you ffayle not now as ever I may do ffor yow' wrote Warwick in his own hand to the man he imagined to be his 'right trusty and welbeloued Harry Vernan esquier' just when Harry, after waiting carefully on events, was about to slip off with his other lord, Clarence, into the opposite camp.[79] No obligation could deprive the esquire of the ability to judge the political prospects for himself and come to the correct decision.

Whether the common people, either in town or country, possessed the same degree of flexibility and discrimination may be doubted. Whatever they were they cannot be described as indifferent. It was the Thames watermen who lynched Lord Scales in 1460 when he was spared at the capitulation of the Tower.[80] It was the men of Northampton whose hostility to Henry duke of Somerset undid the good effects of Edward IV's magnanimous or politic willingness to be reconciled.[81] And, according to one reliable source, the Earl of Salisbury's death after Wakefield was not due to the implacability of the Lancastrian commanders but to the resentment felt by the countrymen thereabouts against a local magnate.[82] On the other hand, the success with which Edward IV persuaded the citizens of York in 1471 that he had returned to claim only his duchy indicated that they were also gullible; possibly they were only pretending to be.[83] With little to lose and grievances that were real enough, the commons were easily incited to rebellion by magnates they admired. Warwick for long possessed the dangerous ability to draw the simple after him and used it with effect.[84] So did others: Robin of Redesdale, Robin of Holderness, Sir Robert Welles, the Bastard of Fauconberg, and Richard of Gloucester.[85] It is understandable that Edward IV grew tired of

[80] *Three Fifteenth-century Chrons.*, p. 169; *Wars of the English*, vol. ii, pt. ii, p. 773; *Coll. Citizen of London*, p. 211 ('But the lordys were fulle sory of hys dethe).'

[81] 'The comyns a rosse uppon that fals traytur thee Duke of Somersett and wolde have slayne hym with yn the kyngys palys' (*ibid.*, p. 221).

[82] 'But the commune peple of the cuntre, whyche loued hym nat, tooke hym owte of the castelle [Pontefract] by violence and smote of his hed' (*Eng. Chron.*, ed. J. S. Davies, p. 107). The lords had proposed to ransom him. A bastard brother of the Duke of Exeter is said to have done the killing (*Wars of the English*, vol. ii; pt. ii, p. 775).

[83] *Arrivall*, pp. 4-6. One has to suppose that Henry of Lancaster's employment of that ruse in 1399 had been completely forgotten in Yorkshire. The *Arrivall*, though an admirable account of the king's return, is a piece of 'official history.'

[84] The policy of killing the gentry and nobility and sparing the commons which he initiated at the battle of Northampton (*Eng. Chron.*, p. 96) must have reinforced the popularity he had earned at sea in 1458-9.

[85] Bishop Lyhert in 1455 was said to have 'so flattered the lay pepill as he hath redyn a bought his visitacion that he hath thers herts' (*Paston Letters*, vol. iii, p. 46).

sparing the commons. With them the policy of clemency failed.[86]

On the degree of participation of the various classes a survey of the imperfect evidence prompts some very tentative conclusions. The first is that the commons may well have been the most genuinely committed. Their discontents were not readily assuaged by the substitution of one dynasty for another. Inevitably they were disposed to regard whoever was in power as responsible for the evils they suffered. Some of them could usually be relied upon to join in any attempt to turn out the existing government, Henry VI's in 1460-1, Edward IV's in 1469-70. In 1471 they had not had time to forget the shortcomings of Yorkist rule or to realize those of the Lancastrian readeption. Their welcome for Edward when he came back from Flanders was notably unenthusiastic, as even the Yorkist author of the *Arrivall* does not conceal. In Kent their hostility was manifest even after Barnet. Much the same feeling was astir in 1484 and helped to isolate Richard when Henry Tudor landed. Nevertheless the battles were not won by the commons. Their influence on the course of the wars was largely negative.[87]

Discontent at the lack of governance was not confined to them. It permeated all classes and for the same reasons. If it moved the gentry, the well-to-do citizens and the nobility to less spontaneous, more calculated actions, that was natural to men who of necessity and by political training were apt to reckon the consequences. With much more hesitation than Cade had shown, the Yorkist lords steeled themselves in the early 1450s to perform the nobility's traditional duty, that of ridding the king and kingdom of unworthy and rapacious favourites. The first battle of St. Albans was not followed, as Radcot Bridge had been, by an easy political triumph, though in the long run the outcome was similar. Civil war bred civil war. At no time in the Middle Ages had a baronial attempt to compel the king to reform his ways and those of his servants had more than a temporary success. What was needed was a new king. But he, whether his predecessor's heir or a usurper, had to restore and reimpose the crown's shaken authority. A change of dynasty made this task all the harder. Edward of York had not been king long before it became doubtful whether he

---

[86] C. L. Scofield, *Edward IV*, vol. i, p. 580 (at Barnet 1471). But as recently as 1470 he had used 'plentyvously his mercy in saving of the livez of his poure and wreched commons' ('Chron. of Rebellion in Lincolnshire', ed. J. G. Nichols (*Camden Misc. I*,) p. 10).

[87] Gregory's vivid account of the second battle of St. Albans makes it clear that he had a low opinion of the military value of the commons: 'The substance that gate that fylde were howseholde men and feyd men' (*Coll. Citizen of London*, p. 212).

was the man to give nervous politicians the stability they desired. Until he did their support would be withheld. The real blame for each of the successive Wars of the Roses, it seems to me, lay in the failures of Henry VI, Edward IV (until after 1471), and Richard III to establish any presumption that order, justice, and the rights of property would be maintained. It inevitably took Henry VII some time, as it had both Henry IV and Edward IV, to reassure those who did not possess the advantage of our knowledge. There must have been several occasions before—and even after—1509 when doubts still seemed justified. The loyalty of the propertied classes, that is to say, was engaged more by the hope of effective rule than by attachment to a particular ruler or dynasty. Meanwhile they had, if possible, to exist.

Their prominence made this most difficult for the higher nobility. The best service that the Percy earl of Northumberland could do Edward IV in 1471 was to sit still and persuade his 'fellowship' to do likewise: 'and so it may be reasonably judged that this was a notable good service, and politiquely done, by th'Erle.'[88] His gentlemen, we are told, were less politique than he and could not have been trusted to follow him to fight in the Yorkist cause; his wisdom saved them as well as Edward IV. It is impossible to maintain the thesis that the knightly and the gentle were less involved than the nobility towards whose ranks they aspired. Though by the mid-fifteenth century 'lords' formed a recognizable caste—as Gervase Clifton's letter bore witness[89] —there is no reason for treating the substantial landowners of knightly family who fought in every battle as the deluded tools or faithful liegemen of those who commanded them. Like Sir Henry Vernon they

---

[88] *Arrivall*, pp. 6-7. The whole passage deserves to be carefully pondered. Of another earl—the Oxford who was executed in 1462—it could be said: 'if it kepe faire weder he wold not tarye, and if it reygned he wold not spare' (*Paston Letters*, vol. ii, p. 111).

[89] The distinction between a 'lord' and a 'master' (and therefore between 'good lordship' and 'good mastership') is frequently made in the *Paston Letters*. For 'good mastership' or '-hood' see vol. ii, p. 314 and vol. iii, pp. 4 and 287. There is a particularly good example of it in a letter from Lord Scales to Sir John Fastolf omitted in Gairdner's abstract (vol. ii, p. 82): 'wherfore hertyly j pray you to shewe youre goode maistershippe vnto my seid seruant.' This lord clearly recognized Fastolf's lower status. In 1454 Thomas Dennis is defamed 'of settyng up billes agayn lordis' (vol. ii, p. 317). In 1455 Henry Windsor was 'loth to write any thing of any lord' (vol. iii, p. 45) and John Paston was 'not usid to meddel with lordes maters meche forther than me nedith' (*ibid.*, p. 46). Ten years later John Paston asks his wife to 'let my Lord of Norwich wete that it is not profitabe ner the comen well of gentilmen that any jentilman shuld be compellid be an entre of a lord to shew his evidens or tytill to his lond, ner I wil not begine that example ne thralldam of gentilmen ner of other; it is god a lord take sad cowncell or he begyne any sech mater' (vol. iv, pp. 165-6). Sir John Paston protests in 1472, 'I was never yitt Lordys sworyn man, yit have I doone goode servyce and nott leffte any at hys most neede ner for feer' (vol. v, p. 163).

freely chose their part; and as often chose wrongly and paid for it beside their lordly patrons. Though the casualty lists preserved by chroniclers are often inaccurate and, save for the lords, incomplete, they leave us in no doubt that the gentry mourned their full share of the dead. Often we are told no more than 'many knights and esquires.'[90] By contrast few townsmen outside London put themselves in peril of their lives.[91]

Finally, one impression still needs to be corrected: if any generalisation about the Wars of the Roses is sure of wide agreement it is that they resulted in the extermination of most of the 'old nobility'; and none is more demonstrably false.[92] As we have noticed, a large number of peers were executed or killed in battle; and so were their sons and brothers. It is again true that during the war period some great houses failed in the direct male line. The danger lies in putting these two statements together as cause and effect. It is also a mistake to assume that either statement is peculiarly applicable to the last half of the fifteenth century. There had been civil wars in England as well as prolonged foreign wars before 1450. Noble families had ended in an heiress or heiresses earlier and were to do so later. If those listed in the *Complete Peerage* are taken as the sample, it will be discovered that failure in the direct male line happened on the average to some quarter of them every twenty-five years throughout the fourteenth and fifteenth centuries; and that the third and fourth quarters of the fifteenth century did not exceed the average.[93] Further it will be found that this high extinction-rate was in every period at least as much the result of natural causes as of premature and violent deaths. Infant mortality, especially in the case of males, and the inter-marriage of infertile stocks each contributed something to the wastage.

In at least four cases where the Wars of the Roses might seem responsible, they merely hastened an inevitable process: the stock was already withered. Thus when Warwick fell at Barnet his countess was forty-six and lived for another twenty-one years. Their children were daughters of marriageable age. War or no war, the earl's chances of

---

[90] e.g. *Wars of the English*, vol. ii, pt. ii, pp. 775, 776, 778, and 780; *Coll. Citizen of London*, pp. 210-12 and 217.

[91] Nicholas Faunt and his fellow citizens of Canterbury and others from the Cinque Ports who had supported the Bastard of Fauconberg in 1471 provide the obvious exceptions (C. L. Scofield, *Edward IV*, vol. ii, pp. 1-2).

[92] Doubts had been voiced nearly a century ago by T. L. Kington Oliphant, 'Was the old English Aristocracy destroyed by the Wars of the Roses?', *Trans. R. Hist. Soc.*, vol. i (1872), pp. 351-6, but they do not seem to have been heeded.

[93] G.E.C., *Complete Peerage*, 2nd edn., ed. V. Gibbs and others.

surviving male issue were hardly good.[94] Warwick's uncle, William Nevill, Earl of Kent, left a wife aged fifty-seven at his death in 1463. To have outlived her in order to marry again he would have had to survive to over eighty.[95] His only sons were bastards. Lord Wenlock was seventy and more, and childless when he was killed at Tewkesbury.[96] Lord Scales, born in the late 1390s and murdered in 1460, had an only daughter of at least twenty-four. He is believed to have had one legitimate son who had already died unmarried and a child.

If these are added to the total of peers who died in their beds without heirs male, the residue is scarcely impressive. Apart from the royal house, which was utterly destroyed by 1499 in all its branches, Lancaster, Beaufort, and Plantagenet, the only ancient families to be extinguished were those of Courtenay and Lovel. But it needed only one war casualty—a case of 'missing, presumed dead'—to end the main line of the house of Lovel, natural causes doing most of the work of destruction.[97] And collateral heirs male were able to prolong the Courtenay's tenure of the earldom of Devon well into the sixteenth century.[98] Otherwise the extinctions for which the wars must be held

[94] *Ibid.*, vol. xii, pt. ii, pp. 385-93. No other children are known to have been born. If any had been they must have died in infancy.

[95] *Ibid.*, vol. v, pp. 281-7. He left three grown-up daughters.

[96] *Ibid.*, vol. xi, pp. 504-7; and see above, p. 241, n. 23.

[97] Francis viscount Lovel ('our dogge') was never seen again after Stoke (1487). His grandfather William lord Lovel had left 4 sons at his death from illness 13 June 1455 (*ibid.*, vol. viii, pp. 221-5; *Lincoln Diocese Documents*, ed. A. Clark (Early Eng. Test Soc., orig. series, no. 149), pp. 70-87). When William's grandson, Henry Lovel, Lord Morley, died childless in 1489 six Lovel males had died in their beds since 1450 as against one (probably) violent death.

[98] *Complete Peerage*, vol. iv, pp. 327-32. And however absurd the 'revival' in 1831 of the earldom created in 1553 may have been, the modern earls of Devon are at least the heirs male of Hugh Courtenay whom Edward III declared to be earl in 1335 (although Hugh's earldom was of course one in fee, the entailing of much of the inheritance on the heirs male during the fourteenth century (G. A. Holmes, *Estates of the Higher Nobility in XIV century England*, pp. 32-35, 44, and 47-48) would almost certainly have secured the descent of the comital dignity, but for the attainders, to the heirs male in the fifteenth and sixteenth centuries).

[99] Rutland is excluded from this calculation because of his royal blood. That leaves Bonville, Hoo, Lisle (Talbot), Richmount Grey, and Wiltshire (but not Ormond).

[100] They were exclusively responsible for the failure of the male lines of Norfolk (Mowbray), Grey of Codnor, Greystoke, Strange of Knockin, Sudeley, and Vessy. From 1493 to *c*. 1510 the heir general of Scrope of Masham kept out the heir male; her succession was not facilitated by deaths caused by war. War may have *assisted* to a greater or lesser degree in the cases of Montagu, Pembroke (Herbert), Rivers, Worcester, and Egremont, all recent creations. The Holland dukedom of Exeter is in a class by itself. The duke was separated (and ultimately divorced) from his wife for political as well as personal reasons, after one child, a girl, had been produced. His death was described as accidental though by drowning, but the existence of a state of war may have prevented him from getting sons before he died.

answerable were of peers of recent creation and minor importance.[99] Infertility and disease were far more potent enemies.[100]

Wars kill; they also demoralize. Civil wars are usually the more lethal and the more demoralizing. It is possible that what has given rise to the belief that the old nobility was no longer there after 1487 is that its members had become more self-effacing, less sure of their mission to coerce incompetent or high-handed rulers, in all but a few misguided instances congenitally wary, convinced of the benefits of passive obedience. On and off for more than a generation there had been much bloodshed, treachery, and abrupt reversals of fortune. The suspected presence of spies everywhere added to the general sense of insecurity;[101] and so had the failure of those traditional bonds which were meant to give some permanence to the relationship between a man and his lord.[102] The married calm of the medieval policy was rent. Disloyalty could all too often be seen to pay. Astrology flourished as a guide to political decision, and necromancy also since it promised to

[101] The use of spies during the later Middle Ages has been little explored. The large households and the indiscriminate hospitality practised in them must have made espionage easy to arrange. Henry V's knowledge of Oldcastle's plot in Jan. 1414 may have been derived in part from voluntary informers, but Thomas Burton 'the king's spy' (*explorator*) afterwards received £5 reward (*Issues*, ed. Devon, p. 333). John Stodeley's newsletter of 19 Jan. 1454 (with its list of those who had 'espied and gadred' his material) may exaggerate but shows the seriousness of the problem and the fears it aroused: 'The Duke of Somerset hathe espies goyng in every Lordes hous of this land; some gone as freres, som as shipmen taken on the sea, and som in other wise; whiche reporte unto hym all that their kun see or here touchyng the seid Duke. And therfore make gode wacche, and beware of suche espies' (*Paston Letters*, vol. ii, p. 299). It is clear that Warwick had agents in London and Sandwich early in 1460 rallying supporters and watching their opponents. The Duke of Exeter's servant, John Tithesley, was active on the other side and brought Roger Nevill and others to summary execution (Scofield, *Edward IV*, vol. i, p. 55; *Wars of the English*, vol. ii, pt. ii, p. 772; *Three 15th-Cen. Chrons.*, p. 73). Other examples come from 1471. In April Edward IV was able to keep the Lancastrian army's movements under observation 'by meane of espies and by them he had knowledge from tyme to tyme of theyr purposes' (*Arrivall*, p. 24). On 15 Sept. Sir John Paston wrote to his brother John to find out what the Duke of Norfolk was doing in Caister castle 'and have a spye resortyng in and owt, so maye ye know the secretys among them' (*Paston Letters*, vol. v, p. 110). When the chronicle says that 'God sent the kynge hym selfe knowleche' of the Vere conspiracy in 1462 one suspects the existence of a human agent (*Three 15th-Cen. Chrons.*, p. 78).

[102] We learn without surprise that in 1450 'the kyng nor his lordes durst not trust their own housold menys' (*Chrons. of London*, p. 159). In 1520-1 Edward duke of Buckingham's 'fumes & displeasurs' were reported to Wolsey by a disgruntled poor relation who thought himself wronged by the duke (Charles Knyvett) and two of the duke's clerical servants (Robert Gilbert his chancellor and Thomas Delacourt his chaplain) who had been fellows of Magdalen College, Oxford, in the cardinal's time there (P.R.O., S.P. 1/22, fol. 57; B.M., Cotton Titus B 1, fols. 179-82; *Letters and Papers, Henry VIII*, vol. iii, pt. i, pp. cviii-cxlvii and pp. 490-51; A. B. Emden, *Biographical Register of Univ. of Oxford to A.D. 1500*, pp. 557-8 and 767).

influence events.[103] Prisoners were trapped into admissions of guilt and even tortured to betray others.[104] Heroism could only be achieved by those who met death stoically beneath the executioner's axe—as John Tiptoft did in 1470 and Edward of Buckingham in 1521.

It is an attractive theory. My main doubt is whether so obvious a lesson had still to be learnt in 1450. The magnates had surely been grounded in all its rudiments between 1386 and 1415. The long prelude to the outbreak of hostilities in 1455 is more intelligible when one bears in mind that York was Cambridge's son, and Thomas of Woodstock the grandfather of Humphrey duke of Buckingham and the Bourchiers. Even so the Wars of the Roses had hammered the lesson well home. To those in any danger of forgetting it under the first two Tudors it was soon recalled by the practical consequences of the least false step. Most of their fellows needed no such warning. In the words attributed to Edward duke of Buckingham, 'it would do well enough if the noblemen durst break their minds together, but some of them mistrusteth and feareth to break their minds to other, and that marreth all.'[105] This was not the spirit of 1297 or 1311. Most men, including the descendants of the great Anglo-Norman families, preferred almost anything to another civil war. So violently had their fathers untuned the string that the discord could still be heard well into the sixteenth century. There is an early echo of it in the testament of John, the third lord Mountjoy, written within six weeks of Bosworth. In it he begs his sons 'to leve rightwisley and never to take the state of baron upon them if they may leye it from them, nor to desire to be grete about princes, for it is daungeros.'[106] Though the letter of the

---

103 References in the sources to astrological and other predictions are common, e.g. to Stacy and the death of William first duke of Suffolk (*Paston Letters*, vol. ii, p. 147), to Dr. Grene and 'the grettest bataill that was sith the bataill of Shrewisbury' (*ibid.*, vol. iii, p. 48) and to 'Hogan the prophet' sent to the Tower because 'he wolde fayne speke with the Kyng [Edward IV], but the Kynge seythe he shall not avaunt that evyr he spake with hym' (*ibid.*, vol. v, p. 181); and see C. A. J. Armstrong, 'An Italian Astrologer at the Court of Henry VII,' *Italian Renaissance Studies*, ed. E. F. Jacob, pp. 433-54. The Carthusian Nicholas Hopkins of Hinton contributed towards the downfall of Edward duke of Buckingham by prophesying the greatness of his issue (*Letters and Papers, Henry VIII*, vol. iii, pt. i, pp. 491-5). The black arts as political weapons came into prominence with the trials of two royal ladies of the Lancastrian house, Joan of Brittany and Eleanor duchess of Gloucester (A. R. Myers, 'The Captivity of a Royal Witch', *Bull. John Rylands Lib.*, vols. xxiv (1940), pp. 263-84; and vol. xxvi (1941-2), pp. 82-100; K. H. Vickers, *Humphrey Duke of Gloucester*, pp. 270-9).

104 As in the examinations of Cornelius and Hawkins in 1468 (Scofield, *Edward IV*, vol. i, pp. 454-5).

105 *Letters and Papers, Henry VIII*, vol. iii, pt. i, p. cxxx.

106 *Complete Peerage*, vol. ix, p. 338, n. (f).

injunction went unheeded, this was the chastened, indeed craven, mood in which those who had served Edward IV and lived through the events of 1483-5 greeted yet another new dynasty.

APPENDIX

TABLE A

ANALYSIS OF THE RETURNS OF THE COMMISSIONERS, 1412[1]

Dorset landowners with lands in Dorset, Devon, Hampshire, Somerset and Wiltshire assessed at £100 p.a. and more[2]

No.	Name of landowner	Annual value in pounds sterling of lands in Dorset and adjacent counties						Family[3] total
		Dorset	Devon	Hants	Somerset	Wilts[5]	Total	
1.a.	Thomas, earl of Salisbury[4]	60	—	235	90	120[5]	505	929
b.	Maud, countess of Salisbury[6]	—	100	—	—	—	100	
c.	Elizabeth, countess of Salisbury[7]	23	—	—	301	—	324	
2.	Edward, duke of York[8]	11	—	261	116[9]	231[10]	618	618
3.a.	Edward, earl of Devon[11]	60	400	—	40	—	500	600
b.	Sir Edward Courtenay[12]	—	—	40	60	—	100	
4.	Queen Joan[13]	67	—	281	40[14]	158	546	546
5.	Sir Humphrey Stafford[15]	237	—	?16	155	12	405+	405+
6.a.	William, Lord Botreaux[17]	20	—	27	168	28	243	355
b.	Elizabeth, Lady Botreaux[18]	—	40	—	72	—	112	
7.	Sir John Tiptoft[19]	51	—	—	232	50	333	333
8.a.	Sir Thomas Brooke[20]	20	40	—	189	20	269	313
b.	Thomas Brooke junior[21]	44	—	—	—	—	44	
9.	Duchy of Lancaster[22]	200	—	85	—	—	285	285
10.	Sir Hugh Mortimer[23]	110[24]	—	3	84[25]	80	277	277
11.a.	William Stourton[26]	64	—	20	40	70	194	275
b.	John Stourton[27]	4	—	—	67	—	81	
12.a.	John, Lord Lovel[28]	—	10	—	—	—	20	275
b.	Maud, Lady Lovel[29]	20	—	—	—	145	165	
c.	Robert Lovel[30]	50	40	—	—	—	90	
13.	Margaret, countess of Somerset[31]	15[32]	—	12	200	—	267	267
14.	Sir John Arundel, styled Lord Mautravers[33]	149	—	—	60	48	257	257

263

1 See above, p. 14.

2 In addition to the other sources mentioned in the notes, use has been made of the *Dictionary of National Biography* (those whose lives are noticed therein are marked by asterisks) and both editions of G.L.C.'s *Complete Peerage*.

3 'Family' is here taken to include only its head, his sons and brothers and the widows of his ancestors enjoying dower lands.

4 *4th earl (1388-1428) (*Register of Henry Chichele*, ed. E. F. Jacob, ii. 390-400 and 664-5).

5 £20 p.a. from issues of the county included.

6 Widow of John*, 3rd earl (1350?-1400), and mother of last-named. *Ob.* 1424 (*Cal. Fine Rolls*, xv, 52).

7 Widow of William*, 2nd earl (1328-97), and aunt by marriage of the 4th earl; daughter and co-heir of John, Lord Mohun* (1320-75). Her assessment includes that of her Mohun lands to which the Montagu earls were not heirs. *Ob.* 1415 (*Chichele Reg.*, ii. 14-18 and 664; *Cal. Inq. post mortem*, iv. 27 and 33).

8 *2nd Duke (1373?-1415) (*Chichele Reg.*, ii. 63-6 and 670-1).

9 During the minority of William Bonville the younger.

10 £66 13s. 4d. p.a. from issues of the county included.

11 3rd earl (1357?-1419) (*Chichele Reg.*, ii. 178 and 649).

12 Son and heir of last-named. *Ob. s.p.* 1418.

13 *Second wife of Henry IV (1370?-1437).

14 During the minority of John Daubeny.

15 See above, p. 14

16 He is said in his Dorset return (*Feudal Aids*, vi. 428) to have lands in Hampshire, but these were not assessed by the commissioners for that county.

17 (1389-1462).

18 Widow of William, Lord Botreaux (1367?-1395) and mother of last-named. *Ob.* 1433 (*Cal. Fine Rolls*, xvi. 104).

19 See above, p. 15

20 See above, p. 15.

21 See above, p. 15.

22 In the king's hands since 1399.

23 M.P. for Gloucestershire, September 1397. *Ob.* 1416 (*Chichele Reg.*, ii. 86-7 and 666).

24 Including £40 p.a. during minority of Alice Seymour.

25 Including £60 p.a. during minority of Alice Seymour.

26 M.P. for Somerset, 1401, 1402 and January 1404; for Wiltshire, 1407; and for Dorset, 1410 and May 1413. Speaker, May 1413. *Ob.* 1413. (*Cal. Fine Rolls*, xiv. 30; *Cal. Inq. post mortem*, iv. 5). His son and heir, Sir John, afterwards 1st Lord Stourton (1403-62), was M.P. for Wiltshire, December 1421; for Dorset, 1423; and for Wiltshire, 1425 and 1432.

27 Brother of last-named. M.P. for Somerset, 1419, 1420, December 1421, 1423-4, 1426, 1429-30 and 1435. *Ob.* 1439 (*Cal. Fine Rolls*, xvii. 52; *Cal. Inq. post mortem*, iv. 186).

28 (c1375-1414).

29 Widow of John, Lord Lovel (c. 1342-1408) and mother of last-named. *Ob.* 1423.

30 Brother of 12a. M.P. for Dorset, May 1421 and 1422. *Ob.* 1428.

31 Widow of John, earl of Somerset* (1373?-1410), whose son and heir, Henry (1401-18), was a minor. She had already married, 1411, Thomas of Lancaster* (1389-1421), the king's second son. *Ob.* 1439.

32 During the minority of her son Henry.

33 (1385-1421). Cousin and heir male of Thomas, earl of Arundel* (1381-1415). Never summoned to the house of lords, though his son and heir, John* (1408-35), afterwards was. (*Chichele Reg.*, ii. 322, 381-2, 541-4 and 637-8).

TABLE A—*continued*

No.	Name of landowner	Dorset	Devon	Somerset	Hants	Wilts	Total	Family total
				Annual value in pounds sterling of lands in Dorset and adjacent counties				
15.	Henry prince of Wales[1]	140[1]	100	—	—	—	240	240
16.	Sir Maurice Russell[2]	122	—	40	40	—	202	202
17.	John Chidiok[3]	118	—	40	—	43	201	201
18.a.	Henry Popham[4]	8	—	—	60	90	158	191
b.	Sir John Popham[5]	—	—	—	20	13	33	
19.a.	John Lisle[6]	—	—	—	86	40	126	188
b.	Elizabeth, Lady Lisle[7]	35	—	—	27	—	61	
20.	Robert More[8]	108	—	—	20	60	188	188
21.	Robert, Lord Poynings[9]	60	—	123	—	—	183	183
22.	John Roger(s)[10]	56	—	100	27	—	183	183
23.	John Kirkby[11]	76[12]	—	—	33	53	162	162
24.	Mr. Richard Courtenay[13]	40	100	21	—	—	161	161
25.	Edward, Lord Cherleton[14] of Powys	125[15]	—	—	20	—	145	145
26.	Sir Ivo Fitzwaryn[16]	86	—	44	—	13	143	143
27.	Sir William Cheyne[17]	20	20	44	—	52	136	136
28.	John Kaynes[18]	60	20	40	10	—	130	130
29.	William Filoll[19]	124	—	—	—	—	124	124
30.a.	Robert Derby[20]	40	—	—	—	—	40	104
b.	Anice, Lady Derby[21]	43	—	21	—	—	64	
31.	Walter Beauchamp[22]	10	—	—	—	90	100	100
32.	Sir John Moigne[23]	50	?[24]	—	5	—	55 +	55 +

[1] During the minority of Edmund, earl of March.

[2] M.P. for Gloucestershire, 1402 and January 1404. *Ob.* 1404 (*Cal. Fine Rolls*, xiv. 143).

[3] Son and heir of Sir John Chidiok (M.P. for Dorset, 1369). M.P. for Dorset, November 1414. (*Ob.* 1415 (*Ibid.*, xiv. 104). He had married Eleanor, daughter and co-heir of Sir Ivo Fitzwaryn (*see below*, no. 26) and had succeeded to the latter's estate just before his own death (*Ibid.*, xiv. 89). His son and heir, Sir John, was M.P. for Dorset, 1433.

4 Son and heir of Sir John Popham (M.P. for Hampshire, 1352). M.P. for Hampshire, February 1383, 1385, February 1388, September 1388, November 1390, 1394 and October 1404. *Ob.* 1418 (*Chichele Reg.*, ii. 137-9 and 671). His son and heir, Sir Stephen Popham (*ob.* 1444) was M.P. for Hampshire, 1420, 1423-4, 1425, 1431, 1442 (*Hist. of Parl., Biogs.*, p. 693). Sir Philip Popham (*ob.* 1397), M.P. for Hampshire, 1369, 1371, 1372, 1378 and November 1384, was a kinsman, possibly his father's younger brother.

5 Younger brother of last-named. M.P. for Hampshire, January 1397, 1402, January 1404 and 1407. *Ob. c.* 1415. His son and heir (and ultimately heir to Henry Popham's entailed lands), Sir John Popham* (*ob.* 1463), was M.P. for Hampshire, 1439-40 and 1449-50 (speaker-elect). (*Hist. of Parl. Biogs.*, pp. 692-3).

6 Son and heir of Sir John Lisle (M.P. for Hampshire, 1401 and January 1404. *Ob.* 1408). M.P. for Hampshire, 1417 and 1422. *Ob.* 1429 (*Cal. Fine Rolls*, xv. 236; *Cal. Inq. post mortem*, iv. 121). His son, Sir John Lisle (*ob.* 1471) was M.P. for Hampshire in 1433 and February 1449 (*Hist. of Parl. Biogs.*, 546).

7 Widow of Sir John Lisle and mother of last-named. *Ob.* 1435 (*Cal. Fine Rolls*, xvi. 216; *Cal. Inq. post mortem*, iv. 158).

8 M.P. for Dorset, 1417. *Ob. c.* 1426 (*Cal. Inq. post mortem*, iv. 101).

10 M.P. for Bridport, 1395, 1410 and May 1413; for Dorset, December 1421. *Ob.* 1441 (*Chichele Reg.*, ii. 589 and 674).

11 M.P. for Hampshire, 1420. *Ob.* 1424 (*Cal. Fine Rolls*, xv. 51).

12 £5 6s. 8d. during minority of Thomas, son of Thomas West, included.

13 *Son and heir of Sir Philip Courtenay of Powderham, (M.P. for Devon, February 1383, 1386, February 1388, January 1390, 1393, 1395, 1399 and 1401. *Ob.* 1406). Chancellor of the university of Oxford, 1407-12; bishop of Norwich, 1413-15. *Ob.* 1415. His nephew and heir, Sir Philip Courtenay, was M.P. for Devon, 1427 and 1455. *Ob.* 1463 (*Hist. of Parl., Biogs.*, pp. 229-30).

14 *(c. 1371-1421).

15 During the minority of his stepson, Edmund, earl of March* (1391-1425). His first wife, Eleanor, dowager countess of March, *Ob.* 1405.

15 M.P. for Dorset, 1378; for Devon, February 1383; for Somerset, 1397-8; for Dorset, 1406 and 1407. *Ob.* 1414 (*Chichele Reg.*, ii. 18-22, 32 and 653; *Cal. Inq. post mortem*, iv. 9).

17 M.P. for Dorset, 1402. *Ob.* 1420 (*Cal. Fine Rolls*, xiv. 334-5; *Cal. Inq. post mortem*, iv. 48).

18 *Ob.* 1419 or 1420 (*Cal. Fine Rolls*, xiv. 275; *Cal. Inq. post mortem*, iv. 44).

19 M.P. for Dorset, April 1414. *Ob.* 1415. His son, John Filoll (*ob.* 1467), was M.P. for Dorset, 1437, 1442, 1447, 1449-50, 1450-1, 1455-6 and 1467 (*Hist. of Parl., Biogs.*, pp. 325-6).

20 *Ob.* 1421 (*Cal. Fine Rolls*, xiv. 377; *Cal. Inq. post mortem*, iv. 60). Son of Sir Stephen Derby (M.P. for Dorset, 1372, 1379), January 1380, November 1380, 1381-2, May 1382, October 1383, February 1383, October 1382, February 1383, April 1384, 1385 and 1386; for Somerset, January 1390; and for Dorset, November 1390 and 1394).

21 Widow of Sir Stephen Derby and mother of Robert. *Ob.* 1420 (*Cal. Fine Rolls*, xiv. 331; *Cal. Inq. post mortem*, iv. 51).

22 *M.P. for Wiltshire, March 1416, speaker.

23 M.P. for Dorset, September 1388, 1393 and January 1397. *Ob.* 1429 (*Cal. Fine Rolls*, xv. 236; *Cal. Inq. post mortem*, iv. 125).

24 He is said in his Dorset return (*Feudal Aids*, vi. 425) to have lands in Devon, but these are omitted from the returns for that county.

TABLE B

Sussex landowners with lands in Sussex, Hampshire, Kent and Surrey assessed at £100 p.a. and more

No.	Name of landowner	Annual value in pounds sterling of lands in Sussex and adjacent counties				Total	Family total
		Sussex	Hants	Kent	Surrey		
1.a.	Thomas, earl of Arundel[1]	546[2]	4	35	60	645	745
b.	Margaret, Lady Lenthale[3]	100[4]	8	—	—	100	
2.	Sir John Pelham[5]	497[6]	—	—	—	505	505
3.a.	Thomas, Lord St. John[7]	60	70	149	—	279	303
b.	Thomas Poynings[8]	20	4	—	—	24	
4.	Nicholas Carew[9]	80	9	45	80	214	214
5.	Richard, Lord Grey of Codnor[10]	100[11]	12	83	—	195	195
6.	John Norbury[12]	120	—	66	—	186	186
7.	John Bohun[13]	151[14]	2	—	—	153	153
8.	Thomas, Lord Camoys[15]	100	30	—	20	150	150
9.	Alice, countess of Kent[16]	8[17]	10[18]	110	20	148	148
10.	Robert, Lord Poynings[19]	144	—	—	—	144	144
11.	Sir Thomas Skelton[20]	30	107	—	—	137	137
12.a.	William Kyriell[21]	—	—	109	—	109	129
b.	Elizabeth, Lady Kyriell[22]	20	—	—	—	20	
13.	Sir John Arundel, styled Lord Mautravers[23]	70	—	35	20	125	125
14.	Prince Thomas[24]	100	—	—	20	120	120
15.	Thomas, Lord de la Warr[25]	100	—	—	—	100	100
16.	Joan, Lady Dallingridge[26]	100	—	—	—	100	100

1 *5th earl (1381-1415) (*Chichele Reg.*, ii. 71-8 and 652).

2 £56 of this from lands held by feoffees 'ad usum domini comitis Arundellie'.

3 3rd sister of last-named and ultimately his co-heir, wife of Sir Rowland Lenthale.

4 'Ex assignacione predicti comitis [Arundellie]'.

5 See above p. 15.

6 £138 of this from manors of the Earl Marshal in Pelham's keeping by royal grant during the earl's minority, which did not end until 1413: £53 in addition by reason of the minority of John St. Clair; and a further £148 for which he had to pay annuities of that value to others. For a 'rent-roll' of Pelham's estates and offices, 1403, see Collins's *Peerage of England*, ed. Sir E. Brydges, 1812, v, 494-5.

7 (c. 1357-1429) (*Chichele Reg.*, ii. 387-90, 432 and 672).

8 Son of last named.

9 Son of Nicholas (keeper of the privy seal, 1371-7; M.P. for Surrey, 1360 and October 1377. *Ob.* 1390 (T. F. Tout, *Chapters in the Administr. History of Medieval England*, v. 44-5; *Cal. Fine Rolls*, x. 329 and 359; *Cal. Inq. post mortem*, iii. 124 and 131). M.P. for Surrey, 1394, 1395, January 1397, 1397-8 and 1417. *Ob.* 1432 (*Cal. Fine Rolls*. xvi. 102). His son, Nicholas (1405?-58), was M.P. for Surrey, 1439-40.

10 *(c. 1371-1418). The Sussex returns have *Thomas*, Lord Grey of Codnor. This must be an error.

11 The manor of Rotherfield, formerly Lord Despenser's, Lord Grey's 'ex concessione domini regis', he paying Joan, widow of Sir John Dallingridge (see no. 16 below), £40 p.a.

12 M.P. for Hertfordshire, 1391. In Henry IV's service as earl of Derby. Treasurer of England, 1399-1401. Alive 27 March 1414 (*Cal. Close Rolls, Henry V*, i. 179), but seems to have died soon afterwards. (J. H. Wylie, *History of England under Henry the Fourth*, i. 28 and iii. 43, n. 10).

13 *Ob.* 1432 or 33 (*Ca*. *Fine Rolls*, xvi. 103; *Cal. Inq. post mortem*, iv. 140).

14 £41 'de iure uxoris'.

15 *(c. 1360-1421).

16 Widow of Thomas*, 2nd earl (c. 1350-97). *Ob.* 1416). There were two other dowager countesses living, Joan, widow of Thomas, 3rd earl* (c. 1371-1400, *s.p.*) and Lucia, widow of Edmund*, 4th earl (1382?-1408), *s.p.l.*, when the lands of the family were divided between co-heiresses).

17 Annuity paid by Richard Prat from manor of Iden to 'the countess of Kent'; probably the Countess Alice.

18 During the minority of the sons and heir of William Audley.

19 *(1380-1446).

20 M.P. for Cambridgeshire, January 1397; for Hampshire, 1399 and 1406. *Ob.?*

21 Son of Sir Nicholas Kyriell. *Ob.* 1413 (*Cal. Fine Rolls*, xiv. 2, *Cal. Inq. post mortem*, iv. 2). His son, Sir Thomas Kyriell (c. 1399-1461), was M.P. for Kent, 1455-6 and 1460-1 (*Cal. Fine Rolls*, xiv. 328-9; *Hist. of Parl., Biogs.*, pp. 521-2).

22 Widow of Sir Nicholas Kyriell and mother of last-named. *Ob.* 1419 (*Cal. Fine Rolls*, xiv. 274).

23 See above, p. 265, n. 33.

24 *The King's second son (1389-1421) (*Chichele Reg.*, ii. 293-6 and 647).

25 (c. 1346-1427).

26 Widow of Sir John Dallingridge (M.P. for Sussex, 1402, October 1404, 1406 and 1407. *Ob.* 1408 (*Cal. Fine Rolls*, xiii. 122; *Cal. Inq. post mortem*, iii. 321), whose father, Sir Edward Dallingridge, was the builder of Bodiam Castle, councillor to Richard II and M.P. for Sussex, 1379, January 1380, November 1380, 1381-2, May 1382, April 1384 (*Cal. Close Rolls, Richard II*, ii. 453; the *Returns* have 'Edmund'), November 1384, 1385, 1386 and February 1388).

INDEX

Adam of Usk, 64, 110

Agincourt, battle of (1415), 65, 109, 141, 147, 148n., 157, 175

Aldermaston (Berks.), 116

Alençon, duke of, 179n.

Allen, Thomas, 219, 224

Allington, William, 87n.

Amersham, Walter, 52n.

Ampthill (Beds.), 175

Anstey, Richard, xix

Arthur, prince of Wales, 238

Arundel, Richard, earl of, 27, 135, 232

Arundel, Thomas, archbp. of Canterbury, 105

Arundell, John, of Bideford, 97-8

Arundell, Sir John, and family, 16, 17n.

Ashridge (Herts.), Bonhommes, house of, 135

Atkyns, Sir Robert, 49n.

Audley, James, 33, 34

Audley, Nicholas, lord, 33; his wife, 34n.

Aylmer, John, bp. of London, 43

Bacon, Sir Edmund, 97n.

Bacon, Sir Francis, 75

Bagot, Sir William, 18, 36

Bagpuize, family, 50, 51

Baker, Dr. John, 116-7, 121

Baldwin, Sir William, xiii 35

Bale, John, 220

Bannockburn, battle of (1314), 53

Bardi, bankers, 57n.

Barnet, battle of (1470), 240, 254, 255, 257

Barton, Henry, merchant, 127

Basle, Council of, 132

Basset, Peter, 208, 210, 211, 212n.

Bastard Feudalism, ix, x, xvi, 1-21, 23-43; and indentures, 26-8; and lordship, 17-18; its name, 23-4; and parliament, 24-43; and politics, 36-7, 41; and service, 29-30, 32, 36-40; and Wars of

Roses, xxiii, xxiv, 251-2; see tenure

Bean, J. M. W., x-xi

Beauchamp, earls of Warwick, Richard (†1439), xi, xiii, xv, xviii, 155, 175, 191, 199-200; Thomas (†1401), 27, 30n; family, 248

Beauchamp, of Powick, lord, 207, 251

Beauchamp, Sir William, 37

Beaufort, earls/dukes of Somerset: Edmund, formerly Marquis of Dorset (†1455), 133n., 134; Henry (†1464), 240, 248, 254, 259n.; John (†1444), 119, 120, 133n.; John, 'bastard of Somerset', 134, 188n.; Margaret, lady, 120, 133n.

Beaufort, Henry, bp. of Winchester and Lincoln, Cardinal of England (†1447), his Bohemian journey, 109; his character, 111-3, 121; his council, 116; his death; 114-37 *passim*; his family, 134; his daughter, Joan, 134; his father, 120; his gifts to Henry VI, 130-1; and Henry V, 79-113 *passim*; his jewels, 122-6; legate *a latere*, 80-2; his loans to Henry V and Henry VI, 58, 68-9, 71-8, 110-12, 121-4; his pardon, 130; his pilgrimage, 86-87, 89, 92-3, 95, 104-5; his soul, 135-6; his tomb, 136; his wealth, 132-4; his will, 114-37 *passim*

Beaugé, battle of (1421), 110-1, 147

Beckington, Thomas, bp. of Bath and Wells, 117

Bedford, John, duke of (†1435), 34, 37, 72n., 116n., 129, 148, 161-4, 168, 175, 179n., 186, 188-90, 203, 208, 210, 215-7; Jacques, duchess of, 213; benevolences, 61, 64

Ber(e)ford, family, 32; Sir Baldwin, 27n.
Berkeley (Gloucs.), 47
Berkeley, family, 48, 52n.; Maurice, 48-9; Robert, 24n.; Thomas, 49, 54n.
Berkerolles, Lawrence, 97-8
Berney, John, 7-9, 193n.
Berwick (Northumb.), 51n.
Betson, Thomas, 232
Beverley (Yorks.), 62n., 109
Bigod, Roger, earl of Norfolk, xiv
Blackheath (Kent), 234
Blackman, John, 132
Blackstone, Sir William, 69
Blount, Sir Thomas, 67
Boar's Head, Inn (Southwark), 165-6, 168, 170-1, 187
Bocking, Nicholas, 196, 202; and his son, John, 192n.
Bohun, family, 33n., 46, 93n.; Humphrey, earl of Hereford, 39
Bonville, Sir William, 12n.; family, xxv, 16, 244, 247, 258n.
Bordeaux, 140, 178, 212
Bosworth, battle of (1485), 260
Boteler, Sir Ralph, 176; family, 32
Bourchier, Henry, lord (†1483), 247n.; Thomas, archbp. of Canterbury, 204-5, 246; William, 33n.; family, 260
Bowes, Sir William, 176
Bracciolini, Poggio, 86-7, 105n., 108-9, 223
Brackley, Friar, 200, 222, 249
Brandon, Sir William, 19-20, 253
Braunch, family, 50n.
Bray, Sir Reginald (Reynold), xxn., 202
Breton, Sir William, 179-81
Bringhurst (Leics.), 118
Bristol, 203-4, 207, 222-3
Brittany, 101, 141, 147; Joan of, 260n.
Brixton, hundred of, 165
Brooke, Sir Thomas, 15; his family, 15, 97-8
Brothers-in-arms, 151-74 *passim*
Brudenell, Edmund, 252

Bruges (Belgium), 143n.
Buckingham, dukes of, *see* Stafford
Buondelmonte, Christofero, 223
Burgh, Elizabeth, lady of Clare, xii
Burgh, Sir Thomas, 249, 253
Burghersh, Maud, wife of Thomas Chaucer, 97-8; her father, Sir John, and family, 97-8
Burgundy, John the Fearless, duke of (†1419), 88; his murder, 104
Burley, William, 16
Burton, John, clerk, 129
Burwash, Bartholomew, 39
Bury St. Edmunds (Suff.), 5
Bushy, Sir John, 18
Bussard, John, 208n., 212
Buzançais (Fr.), 147

Cade, Jack, his rebellion (1450), 4, 234, 238, 241, 255
Caen (Fr.), 134, 212
Caister (Caistor), castle (Norf.), 41, 176-7, 182, 185-7, 190n., 197, 203, 206, 208n., 230n., 241, 259n.
Calais (Fr.), 59n., 87, 89, 95, 111, 140-1, 237
Calthorp, William, 5n.
Calverley, Hugh, 33
Cam, Helen, x, 2
Cambridge, 205, 215, 223n.; King's College, 131, 135
Cambridge, Richard, earl of (†1415), 260; countess of, 252
Canterbury, Christ Church, 135; St. Augustine's, 135
Carlisle, 51n.
Carpenter, John, bp. of Worcester, 226, 228
Castle Ashby (Northants.), 207
Castle Combe (Wilts.), 163, 203, 207, 225-30
Castillon, battle of (1453), 147
Catesby, William, 249n.
Catherine of Valois, queen of Henry V, 90; her coronation, 107
Catterick, John, bp. of Coventry and Lichfield, 84-5, 86n.
Cavendish, 70n., 182, 184
Caxton, William, 218, 219n.
Cecil, Robert, xxn.

Chamberlain, Sir Roger, 6; Sir
William, 5, 8
Chandos, John, 33
Channel Islands, 178, 212
Charles VI, of France, 90
Charles VII, of France, 156, 161
Charterhouses, 144
Chartier, Alain, 215
Chaucer, Geoffrey, 90, 97; his wife,
Philippa (Roet), 97; his *Book of
the Duchesse*, 208
Chaucer, Thomas, 12, 80, 89, 90,
91, 95-107 *passim*; his family, 97;
his daughter, Alice, marchioness
of Suffolk, 97n., 135; and
Geoffrey Chaucer, 90, 97; his
possessions, 99-100
Chaundler, Thomas, humanist, 117
Cheddar, family, 97-8
Cherbourg (Fr.), 167n., 169n.
Chester, Ranulf, earl of, 46n.
chevances (chevisances), 65, 66, 75-7
Chichele, Henry, archbp. of
Canterbury, 78n., 79, 80n., 81-8
Chiltern Hundreds, honour of, 99
Chirk, castle and lordship, 133-4
Cicero (Tully), 197, 217-9
Clapham (Surrey), 168-9
Clarence, dukes of: George
(†1478), 247, 249, 254; Lionel
(†1368), 239; Thomas (†1421),
88, 110, 147, 186, 188n.;
his wife, Margaret, xiii
Clifford, family, 207, 243
Clifton, Gervase, 32n., 250, 256;
Sir Robert, 32
Clist Heath, battle of, 248
Clyf, William, 182n.
Cobham (Surrey), 144
Coburley, Thomas, 163-5, 169-71
Compostela, St. James (Santiago)
of, 87, 89, 92-3, 95, 104-5
Compton, Ashden or West
Compton in, 51, 53
Constance, Council of, 81, 83, 85,
86n., 87n., 105, 113
Convocation, 143
Corfe (Dorset), 133
Cotford, John, 170
Council, King's, 62, 69, 74n., 125

Courtenay, earls of Devon, xvii,
xxv; Edward, xii, xv; family,
247, 258
Coventry, 207
Crécy, battle of (1346), 140, 148
Cressy, Sir John, 30n.
Cromwell, Ralph, lord, 73, 124n.,
191, 192n., 223, 240, 250; his
wife, Margaret (Deincourt), 124n.
Croyland, *Chronicle (Anonymus
Croylandensis)*, 118-21; abbey,
121
Curia, 83-5, 104-5, 124, 204
Curzon, John, 67
Cynllaith Owain (Wales), 133

Dagworth, Sir Thomas, 28, 33
Dale, Sir Thomas, 38
Damme, John, 5
Damory, family, 35n.
Danvers, Sir Charles and Sir
Henry, 43n.
Darley, abbot of, 67
Davy, John, 212
De la Beche, family, 53n.
De la Mare, Sir Peter, 4, 12,
15n., 20
De la Pole, earls/dukes of Suffolk,
xvii; Michael, earl of Suffolk
(†1389), 39, 72n.; William, earl,
marquis, 49, 75, 207, 238, 241,
260n.; duke of Suffolk (†1450),
4, 6, 10-11; his wife, Alice
(Chaucer), 98n., 135
De la Pole, Sir William, 58-9, 73
De Vere, earls of Oxford; John
(†1462), 5, 9, 10, 232, 244n.,
245n., 246, 255n., 259n.; Robert,
64
de mutuo faciendo, 62-3, 66, 68
Dedham (Essex), 162
Deincourt, family, 124n., 250n.
Denia, count of, 152
Dennis, Thomas, 7
Despenser, Henry, bp. of Norwich,
40; Hugh, 55n.; Thomas, lord,
34-5
Dipres, family, 32
Drayton (Norfolk), manor of 207
Dreux (Fr.), 88

Droitwich (Worcs.), 159
Dudley, Edmund, xxvi
Dudley, John, lord, 35n.
Dunham, W. H. jr., x, xi
Dunwich (Suffolk), 5
Dyke, Hugh, merchant, 59n., 71n.

Edinburgh, 50, 52
Edward I, xi, xxiv, 1, 24-5, 42,
    45-6, 48, 51-2, 147, 239
Edward II, 1, 45, 49n.
Edward III, xxiv, 1, 12, 23, 25,
    40-1, 90; and bankers, 57n.,
    58-9, 79; and war, 140-3, 146,
    152, 155, 175, 195; and Wars
    of the Roses, 238-40
Edward IV, formerly earl of March,
    xvii, 6, 10, 19, 29-30, 53n., 64,
    79, 147, 170, 213, 216, 222,
    232n., 238-45, 249, 252-6, 261
Edward V, 241, 245
Edward VI, 42
Edward, the Black Prince, 27, 39,
    140; his companions, 40
Edwards, J. G., xvi
Egremont, dukes of, 258
Ellis, Richard, 70n., 183
Erpingham, family, 39
Estfield (Eastfield), family, 59n.,
    71n., 130, 181
Eton College, 131, 135
Eu, count of, 40
Ewelme (Oxon.), 91n., 95-6, 97n.,
    98, 102, 144
Exeter, dukes of, see Holland
Exchequer, 60, 63, 66, 68, 71, 73-6,
    123-4, 128

Falkirk (Scotland), 46, 52
Farleigh (Somerset), 175-6
Fastolf, Sir John, 41, 70-1, 148,
    157n., 161-4, 167, 231, 240, 242,
    256n.; and Castle Combe, 225-30;
    his death, 203-4; his estates,
    185-7, 191, 194, in London,
    164-6, 168, 170-1, in Normandy,
    187-8; his family, 183n., 196n.;
    his wife, Milicent (Scrope, née
    Tiptoft), 185, 217, 225, his
    goods, 189; his jewels, 190; his

profits of war, 175-97 passim;
    his ships, 195-6; and William
    Worcester, 199-224 passim
Fastolf, John of Olton, 70n., 183
Fauconberge, lord, 35; 'bastard of',
    254
Felton, 40
Ferriby, William, 210n.
Feudalism, ix, x, 23-6, 29, 31-2, 42;
    feudal host, 25
FitzAlan family, 248 see Arundel
FitzRalph, Robert, 39-40
FitzWalter, William, 170
Flanders, 141, 145, 255
Fleming, Richard, bp. of Lincoln,
    94, 107
Florence (Italy), 84
Fokeram, William, 50n.
forced loans, 60-1, 66
Fortescue, Sir John, 193, 199; his
    Governance of England, 23,
    73-5, 78, 133, 216-7, 238
Fotheringhay (Northants.), 144
Fougères (Fr.), 142, 147, 167
Fowcher, Matthew, 169
Foxholes, John, 122n.
Frampton Mansell (Gloucs.), 47
France, 139-49
Frontinus, Julius, 213
Froissart, Jehan, 35, 40n.

Galbraith, V. H., 19
Gascoigne, Thomas, 96, 199
Gascony, 141, 147, 153
Gaugi, Roger de, 152
Gaunt, John of, duke of Lancaster
    (†1399), x-xii, xxii, 3, 19, 20,
    27-8, 32, 37-40, 72-3; his
    chancery, 27-9; and Thomas
    Chaucer, 97; and finance, 75, 77;
    and France, 147, 202, 208, 239;
    household, 27-9; his first wife,
    Blanche, 208; his third wife,
    Katherine (Swynford), 97
Gerberge, Sir Thomas, 30n.
Ghent (Belgium), 72n.
Gibbon, Edward, 208
Giffard, John, 55n.; Osbert, 51n.
Gildesborough, John, 15n.
Glendower, Owen, 41, 147, 160n.

Gloucester, earls/dukes of:
Humphrey, duke of (†1447), 69,
71, 83-6, 88, 103, 106n., 115,
122, 124, 126-30, 133-4, 178n.,
188n., 208; his *Complaint*, 79,
83, 115; as Protector, 122, 128n.;
Robert, earl of, 46n.; Thomas,
of Woodstock, duke of (†1397),
260; Eleanor, duchess of, 260n.
see Richard III
Glyn Dyfrdwy (Wales), 133
Gough, Matthew, 153
Gower, Thomas, 153, 167n.,
169
Gray, H. L., 13
Green, Sir Henry, 18, 36, 233n.,
234
Grenville, Sir John, 98
Gresham, James, 5n.
Gresley, Sir Thomas, 67
Grey, Henry, lord, of Codnor, 5, 7,
8, 249; Thomas, 232
Grey, of Ruthin, lords, 41
Greystoke, lord, 258n.
Grocyn, William, 199
Guyenne (France), 41, 67, 76, 142,
239
Gwyllim, John, 164

Hakeborn, Thomas, 228
Hall, Edward, chronicler, 71, 115-7,
243
Hallwey, family, 227; Henry, 227,
230
Hampton, John, escheator, 53n.
Hampton Court (Herefs.), 175
Hanham, family, 97-8
Hanson, Christopher, 202n., 206,
208n., 210-11, 230
Harcourt, Sir Richard, 10, 11n.;
Sir Robert, 234n.
Harfleur (Fr.), 141, 160, 163, 178,
186; church of St. Martin,
151, 155, 174
Harling, Sir Robert, 203
Harrington, Sir Nicholas, 16, 17n.
Hastings, William, lord (†1483), xi,
28, 31, 39, 53n., 245, 252; his
grandfather, Richard, 39; his
retainers, xvii, 249

Hawley, Robert, 152
Hearne, Thomas, 209-10
Heaton, John, 202
Henry II, x
Henry III, 24
Henry IV (Bolingbroke), formerly
earl of Derby and duke of
Hereford and Lancaster, 1, 2n.,
13nn., 15, 31, 35-6, 62n., 90, 100,
133n., 135, 256; his daughter,
Philippa, 222
Henry V (of Monmouth), 13n.,
15, 31, 33, 36, 41, 131, 135,
140-2, 146-7, 152-5, 160-1, 166,
175, 184, 186, 210, 240, 259n.;
his character, 79, 102, 113; his
death, 112, 122, 123; and Henry,
Cardinal Beaufort, 79-113
passim; his marriage, 89-90, 95-6;
and taxation, 64-6, 110
Henry VI (of Windsor), xxv, 9,
13n., 15, 42, 62, 70, 71, 74,
78, 83, 91, 112, 121-2, 126, 142n.,
143, 156, 161-2, 181-2, 207, 210,
213, 216, 236, 238, 240, 241,
248, 255, 256; his character,
122, 139; his coronation (in
France), 128-9; his son, Edward,
238, 244; and Henry, Cardinal
Beaufort, 131-2
Henry VII, xiii, 42, 62, 90, 118, 147,
238, 240, 245, 250, 256
Henry VIII, 79, 81, 115, 175,
238
Hereford, earls/dukes of,
see Bohun; Henry IV
Heron, family, 35n.
Herrings, battle of, 178
Heyworth, William, bp. of
Lichfield, formerly abbot of St.
Albans, 85
Hickling (Kent), 207
Hoccleve, John, 201
Howes, Thomas, 206
Holland, earls of Kent: Edmund
(†1408), 119; Thomas (†1400),
xiii, 35, 119; 135n.; his mother,
Alice, xiv, 35; his wife, Alice,
135n.
Holland, Sir Thomas, 40-1

Hopkins, Nicholas, 260n.
Holderness, Robin of, his rebellion,
  241, 254
Honfleur (Fr.), 164
Howard, Sir John, 6-8, 11
Huddington (Worcs.), 158; family,
  158-9
Hull, Sir Edward, 207
Hunt, William, 58
Hundred Years War, 33, 36, 40-1,
  62; brothers-in-arms, 149-74
  passim; Fastolf, Sir John, in,
  175-97, 217; finances of, 57-78
  passim; profit and loss in,
  146-9; size of armies in, 140-2;
  and taxation, 142-6
Hungerford, family, 15n., 16-17,
  32, 248; Sir Thomas, 39, 176;
  Sir Walter, 39, 176; his wife,
  Margaret (Botreaux), 41
Hunsdon (Herts.) 175, 176n., 224
Hussey, family, 35n.
Hyde, abbey, 135

indentures, 25, 26, 29, 33-8, 45-55
Ingledew, Thomas, 192n.
Inglose, Sir Henry, 170, 183n.,
  193n.
Ireland, 4, 153, 236
Isabel, queen of France, 88
Italy, 84-7

Jargeau, battle of, 147
Jenny, John, 5, 6, 9-11; William, 5
Jerusalem, 94, 105
Josephus, 191
justice, xix-xx

Kemp, John, bp. of Rochester, 107
Kennington (Surrey), 170
Kent, earls of: *see* Holland; Nevill
Kingsford, C. L., 64
Kingston, Bagpuize, 50
Kingston, Sir Nicholas (the elder),
  46-55 *passim*; his family, 49,
  50n., 51; his daughter, Hawise,
  49; his son, Sir Nicholas (the
  younger), 49; his wife, Margaret,
  50; Osbert, 52n.; Roger, 50-1
Kirtling, John, 179-81, 183

Knolly's Manor, Camberwell
  (Surrey), 165-6, 168, 169n., 170
Kynwolmerssh, William, 110
Kyriel, family, 40; Sir Thomas, 244

Lambeth (Surrey), 82, 85n., 110,
  168, 171
Lancaster, dukes of: Thomas, xi,
  xii; and John, 186n.; *see* Gaunt;
  Henry IV
land value, 191-2
Langley, Thomas, chancellor, 91
Lathom, Sir Thomas, 32
law: bribery, x; lawlessness, xix-xx;
  lawyers, xii, xiv, 3, 251-2;
  litigiousness, xx-xxi;
  punishment, xx
Leche, Sir Roger, 34
Laken, William, 170
Latimer, family, 35n.
Laurence, Thomas, 50n.
Laurens, John, 227, 229
Le Mans (Fr.), 162, 169n., 170
Le Strange, family, 40
Legh, Ralph, 171
Leicester, 66n.
Leventhorp(e), John, 78n., 202
Leyland, John, 175-6, 197
Libel of English Policy, 216
Limnour, 5
Linacre, Thomas, 199
Lingard, John, 71, 84
Lisle of Rougemont, lord, 35
Littleton, Sir Thomas, 199
livery, xxii-xxiii; Acts of, 1468 and
  1504, xxiii; and maintenance, 42,
  43n.
loans to crown, 57-78 *passim*;
  110-113; and usury, 69-78; *see*
  Beaufort, Henry; benevolence;
  chevance; plaisance; taxation
London, 4, 6, 8, 9, 60, 70-7, 78n.,
  80, 108-10, 196, 204-5, 215,
  226-7, 230, 257; and Cade, 241;
  Lincoln's Inn, 201; merchants of,
  127; port of, 123; St. Thomas
  Acon, church, 151, 173; Tower of
Lovel(l), family, 207, 248, 250n.,
  258; lords: Francis (†1487),
  258n.; John (†1408), 62n.; John

(†1465) 30; William (†1455), 233n.
Lumley, Marmaduke, bp. of
   Carlisle, 136
Luxembourg, Lewis of, 164, 179
Lydgate, John, 102
Lyndwood, William, 199
Lyons, Richard, merchant, 72, 77-8

Magna Carta, 24
Malden (Essex), 10
Mansell, Sir William, 46; his family,
   47-8; his wife, Margaret, 53; his
   lands, 47-51, 53; Philip, 53n.
Mautby, Margaret, 232
March, earls of: see Mortimer;
   Edward IV
Margaret of Anjou, queen of
   Henry VI, 135, 162, 230, 232,
   241, 243n., 244n., 249
Markham, Sir Robert, 250
Martin V, pope, 79-86, 103-4, 107,
   112
Maulay, Peter, 25, 33
Mautby, Margaret, 232
Mautravers, Sir John, 14
Meaux, abbot of, 146
Merke, Thomas, bp. of Carlisle, 106
Meulan (Fr.), 88
Meverell, Sir Sampson, xiv, 33-4;
   his family, 33-4
Milburn, Simon, 236
Mohun, Joan, lady, of Dunster,
   97-8
Moleyns, Adam, bp. of Chichester,
   156, 157n.
Moleyns, Robert, lord, 5, 41, 202;
   his mother, Margaret, 41
Moleyns, Sir William, 99n.
Molyneux, Nicholas, 151-74 passim;
   his family, 157-8; his son,
   William, 158
Monarchy: familia, x, xxv; its
   finances, 57-78 passim, 124, 125;
   forced loans and benevolences,
   60-66; Italian bankers, 57-8; and
   'Lancastrian Constitution', 3, 65,
   79; and landowners, xxi-ii; and
   legal system, xxii; and nobility,
   xxiv, xxv, 42, 79, 238-9, 255;
   personality of kings, 41, 79,

102, 113, 122, 139, 238-9; Tudors,
   xi, xviii, xxiii, xxv, xxvi, 42-3, 67;
   and Wars of the Roses, xxv,
   41-2, 238-9
Montague, earls of Salisbury:
   Thomas (†1428), 34, 154-6;
   William (†1397), 39-40
Montford, Sir John and family, 16
Moreyn, William, 227, 230
Mortimer, Edmund, earl of March,
   (†1425), 25, 33
Mortimer, Sir John, 125
Mountjoy, John, lord, 260
Mountsford, of Cole, family, 247
Mowbray, dukes of Norfolk: John
   (†1432), 153-4, 188; John
   (†1461), 5, 6, 10-11, 19-20, 250n.,
   251, 253, 256n., 258n., 259n.;
   his wife, Katherine, 5, 10, 18, 251
Mull, Thomas, 232
Mulsho, family, 234n.

Najera, battle of (1367), 152
Namier, L. B., 19
Nantron, Luke, 208n., 210-11
Naxos, duke of, 86
Neale, J. E., 1
Netter, Thomas, 199
Nevill, family, 248; Richard, earl
   of Salisbury (†1460), 233, 240,
   251, 254; Richard, earl of
   Warwick (†1471), 231, 233, 238,
   240-2, 242, 244, 245n., 246n.,
   247, 251, 253, 257, 259n.; his
   wife, 251, 257; William, earl of
   Kent (formerly lord Fauconberg)
   (†1463), 258
Newark (Leics.), 144
Newcastle-upon-Tyne, 46
Nibley Green, battle of, 248
Niccoli, Niccolo, 108
Normandy, 89-90, 94, 96, 101, 103,
   107-8, 140-9, 161, 167, 170, 186,
   188, 203, 211, 216, 239
Norfolk, dukes of, see Mowbray
Norfolk, families, of, 220
Northampton, battle of, 237-8, 243,
   244
Northampton, 254
Northumberland, earls/dukes of,

see Percy; Dudley
Norwell, William, 58n.
Norwich, 5, 7-10, 109, 183, 204-5;
   mayor of, 7
Nottingham, Thomas, earl of, 27
Nottingham, William, 227

Obizzi, John of, 82
Ogard, Sir Andrew, 177n., 189,
   195n., 224, 251
Oldcastle, Sir John, lord Cobham,
   15, 259n.
Oldhall, Sir William, 176, 189,
   224, 234n.
Orleans (Fr.), 156
Over Lypiatt and Tunley (Gloucs.),
   47
Ovid, 219
Owen, John, 154
Oxenton (Gloucs.), manor of,
   225-30
Oxford, earls of, *see* De Vere
Oxford, university: New College,
   117; Winchester College, 177, 120

Paris, 92, 140
Parkhouse, Thomas, 170
Parlement, of Paris, 92
Parliament, xvi, xvii, 1-21 *passim*,
   29, 32, 60, 65, 72, 77, 142, 234;
   Commons, xvi-xvii, xxii, 1-2, 12,
   16, 20, 60, 65-6, 72-3, 123-4,
   142-9, 234; Lords, xvi, 1-2, 12,
   17, 29; parliamentary elections,
   3-11, 14, 234; and taxation, 13,
   25, 123n., 124, 126n., 144-5
Paston letters, 4, 31, 75, 176, 224,
   231, 233, 250, 253, 256
Paston family, 204, 220; Edmund,
   19, 31; John, 4-11, 231, 243;
   his wife, Margaret, 7, 9; their
   sons, 9; Sir John, xiv, 9-11, 18,
   75-6, 177, 182n., 187n., 190n.,
   194n., 207, 212, 259; William,
   75-6
Patay, battle of (1429), 147, 203
Pavia, Council of, 105
Pecock, Reginald, bp. of
   Chichester, 19, 199

Pelham, Sir John, 15
Pembroke, earls of (Herbert), 258n.
Percy, earls of Northumberland;
   Henry (†1487), xiii, 232, 256;
   family, xv, xvii, xxin., xxvi,
   247
Perrour, Henry, 169
Peruzzi, bankers, 57n.
Peterborough, abbey, 118
Phillip, Matthew, 169
Pickering, Sir James, 12, 16n.
Pisan, Christine de, 197, 211n.,
   213, 217, 218
plaisance, 64
Plummer, Charles, 23, 68
Plumpton, letters, xxn.
Poitiers, battle of (1355), 140, 148
Polton, Thomas, bp. of
   Worcester (formerly bp. of
   Chichester and Hereford), 84-5
Pontorson (Fr.), 161n.
Port, William, 137
Postan, M. M., 41, 59, 70, 148;
   and Power, E., 59, 144
Poynings, Robert, lord (†1446), 125
Praemunire, Statute of, 129
Prestwich, J. O., x
Provisors, Statute of, 81, 103
Pryce, William, 7, 8
Pugh, T. B., xiii
Pusey (Berks.), 46, 55; family, 50n;
   Mansell's Court in, 50, 53
Pyall, John, 77n.

Radcot Bridge, battle of (1487),
   32, 255
Rafman, John, 192n., 193n., 197n.
Raleigh, family, 97-8
Ramsay, Sir James, 77, 109n.
Raynald, John, master-cook, 28n.
ransom, 26, 146-7, 151-2, 172-3, 175
Ravenspur (Yorks.), 249
Redesdale, Robin of, 241, 254
Redland, Bristol, 48-9, 53, 54n.
Remon, Guillaume, 188n.
Repyngdon, Philip, bp. of Lincoln,
   119n.
Resumption, 1st Act of (1450), 73
Rheims (Fr.), 140
Richard II, xiii, xv, xviii, 1, 3n.,

14-15, 18, 31-2, 35-6, 41, 97, 120, 135, 143, 153; his deposition, 61; his forced loans, 60, 61, 64, 75; his soul, 135

Richard III, formerly duke of Gloucester, xiii, 241, 243, 250, 254, 256

Richard the Redeles, 2

Richardson, H. G., 1-3, 12, 32n.

Rivers, Richard, earl (1469), 244n., 245, 258n.

Robinson, John, 205

Rogers, Thorold, 145, 146

Rome, 86, 105

Roos, Thomas, lord (†1455), 30n.; family, 32

Roses, Wars of the, xxiii-v, 28, 41-2, 45, 188n., 231-61 *passim*; its causes, xxiii-v, 41-2, 238-9; mortality of nobility in, 243, 257

Roskell, J. S., xvi-xvii

Rous, John, 199-200

Roussel, John, 179

Rousen (Fr.), 86, 109, 147, 160, 188

Russell, John, bp. of Lincoln, xvii, 118, 120

Rutland, Edmund, earl of (†1460), 163, 243, 258n.; *see* York

Rye, (Herts.) 175, 176

St. Albans, abbot of, 66; 236; *Chronicle* of, 60, 63

St. Albans, first battle of (1455), 5, 235, 237, 240, 243, 255; second battle of (1461), 242, 244, 247n., 249

St. Andrew's, diocese of, 106

St. Benet of Hulme, abbey, 190, 200n., 206

St. Michael's Mount (Cornwall), 206

St. Sauveur-le-Vicomte (Fr.), 147

Sak, John, 183, 184

Salisbury, 62n., 109

Salisbury, earls of, *see* Montagu

Sandwich (Kent), 107, 133n.

Scales, Thomas, lord (†1460), 18, 153, 169, 210, 254, 256n., 258

Scotland, 46, 51n., 52, 128

Scrope, of Masham, lords, 258n.

Scrope, Richard, archbp. of York (†1405), 247

Scrope, Stephen, 197, 208n., 211n., 218, 225; his wife, Milicent (Tiptoft), 185, 217, 225, 230; their sons, Robert and Stephen, 185n.

Seagrave, Sir John, xiv

Seine, river, 90

Selling, William, 227

Shakel, John, 152

Shakespeare, William, 71n., 115

Sheen (Surrey), Cathusian abbey, 144

Shipdam, Walter, 180, 202n.

Shrewsbury (Salop), 109

Shrewsbury, earls of, *see* Talbot

Sion (Middlesex), Bridgettine nunnery, 144

smuggling, xviii, 139-40

Somerset, dukes of, *see* Beaufort

Southampton (Hants.), 29n., 92, 122; customs of, 122-3

Southwark (Surrey), 164-6, 168, 170, 187, 189, 192n., 203, 242

Spain, 141

Spelman, Sir Henry, 219-20, 221n.

spies, 259n.

Spinola, Bartolomeo, 179, 180n., 184

Spofford, Thomas, abbot of St. Mary's, York, 86

Stafford, Anne, countess of, 33n.

Stafford, dukes of Buckingham: Edward (†1521), 238, 259n.; Henry (†1483), 249; Humphrey, formerly earl of Stafford (†1460), xi, 202, 218, 234-5, 240-1, 247n., 251-2, 260; Anne, his wife, 252

Stafford, family, x, xiii, 233; Sir Henry, 30; Sir Humphrey, the elder, 14; Sir Humphrey, the younger, 14; Humphrey, of Grafton, 235; William, 135n.

Stafford, John, bp. of Bath and Wells, later archbp. of Canterbury, 34, 126, 129, 247n.

Stamford Bridge, battle of, 248

Stanley, Sir John, his family, 16, 17n., 32
Stanley, William (†1495), 246
Stapleton, Sir Miles, 5, 11n.
Stapley, Philip; his daughter, Margaret, 33
Starkey, Thomas, xviii
Stathom, Sir Thomas, 249
Steel, A. B., 57, 59, 70, 74
Stephen, King, 46
Stillington, Robert, bp. of Bath and Wells, 246
Stockwell, manor of, 165, 168, 171
Stoke, battle of (1487), 240, 258n.
Stonor, Sir Ralph, 99n.; Sir William, xiii, 253; family, 231
Stourton, family, 16, appendix
Stradling, Sir Edward, 134; his wife, Joan, daughter of Henry, Cardinal Beaufort, 134; Sir John; his wife, Maud, 166n.
Strange, of Knockin, John, lord (†1449), xiii, 253, 258n.
Strang(e)ways, Sir James, 250-1
Streatlam (Durham), 175
Stubbs, William, 1-3, 58-9, 71; on Cardinal Beaufort, 120-1, 136; on 'The Lancastrian Construction', 3, 65, 79; on royal finances, 61, 66, 69, 79
Sturmy (Esturmy), Sir William, 12
Sudeley, castle (Gloucs.), 176, 206
Sudeley, lord, 251, 258n.
Suffolk, earls/dukes of, see De la Pole
Sutton, Hamon, 59n., 71n.
Swaffham (Norf.), 4
Swynford, Katherine, duchess of Lancaster (3rd wife of John of Gaunt), 97; her 1st husband, Sir Thomas, 97n.; her son, Sir Thomas, 111

Talbot, John, earl of Shrewsbury (formerly lord Talbot) (†1453), 67, 142, 149, 203; John (†1460), 258n.
taxation: assessment, 13; evasion, xx, 139-40; clerical, 143-4; customs, 143-6; in France, 146-8; maltote, 145-6; scutage, 25; subsidies, 13, 25, 65, 123n., 124, 142, 144; see benevolence, chevance, plaisance
tenure, feudal, ix, x, 23-5, 29, 31-2, 42; and bastard feudalism, 1-24, 24, 27-8, 32-4
Teramo, Simon of, 82
Tewkesbury (Gloucs.), abbey, 226-9
Tewkesbury, battle of (1471), 240, 258
Tideswell (Derby.), xiv, 33
Tiptoft, family, 17, 39; John, lord (†1443), 135n.; John, earl of Worcester (†1470), 200n., 218-9, 260; Sir John, 15, 100n.; Sir Pain, 15; Milicent, 185, 217, 225, 230
Tortworth (Gloucs.), 47-49, 53, 54n.
Touques (Fr.), 155
Tout, T. F., 2
Towton (Yorks.), battle of (1461), 41, 242-5
Treasurer, 74n., 76-7, 110, 124n., 125-7
Tresham, William, 252
Tropenall, Thomas, 202
Troyes (Fr.), 104; treaty, 90, 92, 111, 142
Trumpington, William, 70n., 183
Tuddenham, Sir Thomas, 6
Tudors, xi, xviii, xxiii, xxv-vi, 42-3, 67; Jasper, 245; Owen, 244n.
Tyrell, Sir John, 130n.
Sir Thomas, 16; his family, 17n.

Ulverston, Richard, 123
Upton, Nicholas, 40
Urswyk, Robert, 12n.
Usk, Adam of, 64, 110

Valence, Aymer de, earl of Pembroke, 49n., 52n.
Vance, William, 226, 228
Vaux, John, 233n., 234
Veel, Sir Robert, 49
Vegetius, Renatus, 213
Venice, 86, 107
Vere, see De Vere

Vergil, 219

Verneuil (Fr.), battle of (1430), 147, 148n., 153, 169n., 178, 179n.

Vernon, Sir Henry, 254, 256; Sir Richard, 67

Vessy, lords, 258n.

Victori, Giovanni, 84n.

Wakefield, battle of (1460), 243, 254

Waldegrave, Sir Thomas, 15n.

Walden, Robert, bp. of London, 106

Waller, Thomas, 159-60

Wallingford (Oxon.), 39; castle, 99

Walpole, Horace, 232

Walsingham, Thomas, merchant, 60-1, 63, 71n.

Waltham (Bishop's Waltham) (Hants.), 91, 95, 108

Warner, Sir George, 212, 214

Warenne, earls of, xv

Warwick, earls of: see Beauchamp; Nevill

Waterton, family, 39; Sir Hugh, 62n.

Wattys, Thomas, 226-7, 229-30

Waynflete, William of, bp. of Winchester, 136, 171, 192n., 205, 212n., 246, 250

Welles, John, lord (†1421), 38; Sir Robert, 254

Wells, John, merchant, 70-2, 162n., 179-84

Wenlock, John, lord, 241, 252, 258

West Deeping (Cambs.), 119

Westminster, 4, 12, 67, 68, 109, 236; abbey, 152; abbot of, 252

Whaplode, 120n.

Whittington, Richard, 75

Wilington, John, 54n.

William II, Rufus, xi

Willicotes, John, 34-5

Willoughby, Robert, lord, 125, 162

Wiltshire, earls of, 64, 240, 251, 258n.

Winchester, 119, 135; Hospital of

St. Cross, 136

Windsor, Henry, 195; William of, 13n., 46

Windsor, St. George's chapel, 144

Wingfield, Sir Robert

Winter (Wynter) John, 151-74 passim; his death, 163; his family, 158-60; his son, John, 168; his wife, Agnes, 171; his lands, 164-5; Roger, 158-9

Wolsey, Thomas, Cardinal, 79, 81, 115, 259n.

Wolvesey (Hants.), 117, 120

Woodstock, Thomas of, see Gloucester

Woodville, family, 30

wool staple, 58n., 59n., 77, 145-6

Wooton-under-Edge (Gloucs.), 48

Worcester, earls/dukes of, 244, 258n.; (see Tiptoft)

Worcester, William (alias Botoner), 148, 163n., 164, 166n., 170, 175, 177, 178, 182n., 195, 197, 199-230, passim, 240n., 242; his death, 206; his knowledge of the classics, 215, 217, 223; his literary works: Acta Johannis Fastolf, 178, 211, 212; Annales, 209-10, 216; Antiquitates Angliae, 208, 219; Boke of Noblesse, 212, 214, 216-18; De Agri Norfolcensis, 219-20; Itinerary, 176, 220, 222-3; his son, 213

Worsley, Richard, merchant, 72n.

Wycliffe, John, 75

Wylie, J. H., 33, 90

Yarmouth (Suffolk), 10, 195, 196

Yelverton, Sir William, 190, 204

York, Edmund, duke of (†1402), 27; Richard, duke of (†1460), xvii, xxv, 4-6, 30, 31, 162, 188-90, 230, 232-3, 235-40, 248, 260; his son, Edmund, earl of Rutland (†1460), 162, 243, 258n.

York, 53, 207, 254

Young, Thomas, 252

Zouche, William, lord, 233-4